Grade Aid

for

Boyd and Bee

Lifespan Development

Fourth Edition

prepared by

Karen P. Saenz
Houston Community College

PEARSON

Boston New York San Francisco
Mexico City Montreal Toronto London Madrid Munich Paris
Hong Kong Singapore Tokyo Cape Town Sydney

ISBN 0-205-46430-0

Printed in the United States of America

10 9 8 7 6 5 4 3 2 1   10 09 08 07 06 05

CONTENTS

Preface

What to Know About Studying Psychology

A Model for Critical Thinking

HELEN BEE'S STUDENT PROJECTS

A specific example may demonstrate how our thinking becomes more complex as we progress through the cognitive levels of Bloom's theory. A friend of yours states that someone you are about to meet is pretty aggressive. When you ask your friend how she knows this, she reports that she saw him yell at someone in the hall for absolutely no reason. Your job as a critical thinker is to take this piece of information and determine what to do with it. In order to accomplish this, you must take the information that you know and take it through the cognitive levels of Bloom's theory.

1. *Knowledge*: At this level, we have the statement by our friend that the individual is aggressive. We may also have some information about our friend including the following:
   - how accurate she has been about others in the past
   - whether "aggressive" is a label she uses a lot
   - whether it is unusual for her to categorize someone

2. *Comprehension*: At this level, we utilize the facts that we have to try and understand the implications of our knowledge. In this case, the only concrete facts we have is that the friend has labeled the other person as "aggressive." From this, we determine what we understand "aggressive" to mean.

3. *Application*: At the application level, we try to apply information to the current situation. In this case, our friend has suggested that the person we are about to meet is aggressive and she is using his "yelling at someone" as evidence for that label.

4. *Analysis*: From the application of facts to the current situation, we break the information down into meaningful units. In this scenario, we have a label of "aggressive" being placed on someone because he yelled at someone else. There are several questions that a critical thinker would ask him or herself in this situation. These questions include:
   - Is there a definite connection between "yelling" and being "aggressive"?
   - Are there any other possible explanations for why the individual yelled at someone else?
   - Does yelling at someone in one situation predict that the individual will behave "aggressively" in other situations?

   To the extent that I cannot answer these questions affirmatively, I should discard any assumptions based upon them.

5. *Synthesis*: Now that I have discarded any meaningless information, I put the meaningful pieces back together to draw my conclusions. In this case, I cannot critically utilize any of the information that I have been given. Thus, the only usable information I have going into the situation is that I am about to meet someone.

6. *Evaluation*: Once I have discarded meaningless information (or information that is based on opinion rather than fact), I am better suited to approach the situation in an unbiased fashion. I can objectively evaluate the person that I am meeting, make unbiased observations about his behavior, decide whether his behaviors are average given the situation in which I am observing him, and reach my own conclusions about his relative degree of aggressiveness.

What are the implications in this case if I had not done critical thinking before I approached the situation and met this new person? It is highly probable that I would have approached the individual assuming that he was going to be aggressive. From this, a few simple questions and their answers can reveal the potential impact of not engaging in critical thinking. These questions and answers are:

Q: How do we act toward individuals whom we assume are going to be aggressive?
A: We behave cold or even aggressive.

Q: How do others act toward us when we act cold or aggressive to them?
A: They tend to act aggressive or hostile.

PREFACE

The goal of this *Grade Aid* is to provide a user-friendly guide to the fourth edition of the *Lifespan Development* text. It is designed to help you focus your reading and study of the key elements of each chapter, with the ultimate goal of helping you learn the material and apply the concepts to your life as well as to your career.

Each chapter begins with a Chapter Summary, Learning Objectives, and Term Identification. Make flashcards using the terms as you go, using the definitions in the margin of the text for help. If you write the definitions in your own words, though, you will remember them better! The Guided Study Questions include the Learning Objective for each section, as well as specific questions about the material in the text. There is a Practice Test at the end of each section. Check your answers at the end of each chapter. The Critical Reflection Exercises provide you with an opportunity to apply what you have learned to real-life examples. The Comprehensive Practice Test at the end of the chapter serves as a preview of exam questions. A criss-cross puzzle gives you another opportunity to use the key terms. Most chapters include one or more Student Projects that your instructor may assign as part of a written assignment or even as extra credit. The chapter concludes with the answers to the Practice Tests and the puzzle.

Following the Preface are two sections for making the most of your psychology course. The first, What to Know about Studying Psychology, offers study suggestions to maximize your study time. The second, A Model for Critical Thinking, provides hints to help you apply the material in the course.

Lifespan Development may be one of the most useful courses you will ever take. It provides explanations and resources for your personal and workplace relationships, hints for rearing your children, and insight into the joys and concerns of your parents and grandparents. It may even help you learn more about yourself. Enjoy!

ACKNOWLEDGEMENTS

Unending thanks go to my family—both immediate and extended—for providing me with the lifespan perspective. In the time since I prepared the third edition, our son and his wife gave birth to our two grandchildren (currently ages eight weeks and three-and-a-half years), our daughter married and was widowed 16 months later, my husband and I celebrated 37 years of marriage, and my father-in-law died leaving my mother-in-law (age 90) alone. Among us, we've got the chapters covered! Each has patiently "rearranged the world" to allow me time to write. Thank you!

Karen P. Saenz
Houston Community College System—Southeast College
Houston, Texas

WHAT TO KNOW ABUT STUDYING PSYCHOLOGY

CLASS PREPARATION AND STUDY GUIDELINES

The study of psychology is not hard, but there is a lot of material to learn. Students are expected to keep up with all of the assigned reading. You should understand the material and be able to relate it to real human behavior. The information presented below is designed to help you learn the subject by providing the kinds of study hints you can employ successfully in any college class you take.

HOW MUCH TIME SHOULD I SPEND STUDYING PSYCHOLOGY?

To be successful, a good guideline for any college class of the amount of time you need to invest outside of class is two hours for each hour you spend in class. If you can make this commitment, you should encounter no serious problems in completing all assignments and preparing comfortably for tests. You should spend your time doing the following:

Read Ahead

The best starting place is the Course Schedule in your Syllabus. It will specify the material that needs to be covered in the sequence deemed most appropriate by your instructor. You should always maintain a disciplined reading schedule so that you can stay current with assigned readings; falling behind in your reading can be disastrous. You should read ahead all the material that will be covered in the next class. This reading will acquaint you with the Learning Objectives that will be covered in class. With this knowledge, you will be prepared to ask questions and discuss relevant topics.

Read Effectively

Create a comfortable reading environment for yourself. Avoid distractions and interruptions. Be alert and attentive. Don't rush yourself. These "little things" will increase your comprehension of the subject. Use your *Study Guide* as a guide for your reading. Keep a dictionary by your side to look up any unfamiliar words. From time to time, you may need to look back at a previous chapter to refresh your memory of the concepts. Remember, as in sports, music, dance, or other arts, learning takes time and effort; the more you put in, the more you will get out of the learning process.

SHOULD I ATTEND CLASS?

Studies indicate that students who attend their classes do better than students who do not attend. In class, you will not only cover important course-related information, but, additionally, announcements will be made, due dates assigned, and study suggestions offered. In college, you are largely responsible for your own learning. Your instructor is a facilitator. Use class time to ask questions, seek clarification, and participate in discussions. The more involved you are in your own learning, the more fruitful the activity will be, and the more you will learn.

WHAT SHOULD I DO DURING CLASS TIME?

There are several things you can do to improve your chances of being successful in your class. You are in control of all of them, so do the following things to maximize the benefits of being in class.

Be On Time

The start of class is an important time. Be prepared to take notes, participate, or take a test. Tardiness is disruptive to you and your classmates.

Take Good Notes

Good note taking keeps your mind focused on the subject being discussed. Attentiveness should lead to better comprehension. Note taking provides you with documentation about what the instructor feels is the most relevant, important, difficult, or interesting information about a subject. You should couple your notes with related text material for a comprehensive understanding of the subject. Use your notes to prepare for assignments and tests. Make sure your notes are legible, thorough, and organized.

Participate in Class Discussions

Whenever you have the opportunity to participate, do so! Show off what you have learned, but do it in a way that contributes to a positive learning environment for you and your classmates. Be involved in the learning process. Ask relevant questions. Offer insights. Give examples. Participation should be constructive and fun.

Get to Know Your Classmates

Together you can do several things that enhance learning. Every time you explain a concept to someone else, you increase your understanding of the material. You can share ideas and information. You can check each other to make sure you are learning the material. You can "bounce" ideas around. You can study together in advance of tests. If you miss a class, you'll know someone who will share notes with you or who can tell you about up-coming assignments or tests.

These suggestions are offered to assist you in making the most of your study of psychology, and indeed, of your college experience. You are exceptional because you chose to pursue higher learning. *Invest in yourself and you should be successful.*

A MODEL FOR CRITICAL THINKING

Several good resources exist on how to develop and practice critical thinking skills, so that critical thinking can be applied to specific issues and problems. Randolph Smith (1995) suggests the following seven characteristics of critical thinkers:

1. Critical thinkers are flexible—they can tolerate ambiguity and uncertainty.
2. Critical thinkers identify inherent biases and assumptions.
3. Critical thinkers maintain an air of skepticism.
4. Critical thinkers separate facts from opinions.
5. Critical thinkers don't oversimplify.
6. Critical thinkers use logical inference processes.
7. Critical thinkers examine available evidence before drawing conclusions.

Thinking and critical thinking differ in at least three important ways.

- Thinking involves basic information processing; critical thinking involves understanding that information in such a way that the information is useful and usable.
- Thinking is often based on emotion and supposition; critical thinking sets emotions aside and addresses a problem from the position of facts.
- Thinking is based on the information that is known; critical thinking requires more than what is already known because it may reveal that not enough is known. This revelation, of course, then requires that more facts be gathered.

Most individuals take their ability to think for granted. In this fashion, the development of critical thinking ability requires that the individual be taught to take a more controlled and systematic approach to one's thinking. Benjamin Bloom (1956) suggested that critical thinking requires going beyond a simple recitation of facts that most testing situations require. From this, Bloom suggested a progression of cognitive levels that individuals can be taught to use in their thinking. Bloom's taxonomy suggests that thinking and understanding are only truly accomplished when an individual takes information through six levels.

Bloom's Cognitive Objectives

Level	Skill	Description
1	Knowledge	Specific, isolate, factual information
2	Comprehension	Understanding of those facts
3	Application	Can generalize those facts to current and/or other situations
4	Analysis	Can break the problem down, recognize connections between sub-parts, analyze whether each sub-part is meaningful, and discard those that are deemed meaningless
5	Synthesis	Can reassemble meaningful parts into a more meaningful whole
6	Evaluation	Can look at the end product and critically evaluate and use that information to begin a continuous reassessment

Q: What do we, then, assume about that individual?
A: That he or she is aggressive.

In this cycle, the expectations we had about the person caused us to behave in ways that elicited, in return, behaviors from the other person that verified our original assumptions. It is just as likely, however, that he would not have behaved aggressively if we had not precipitated those behaviors through our own actions. The cycle that results because of the bias introduced into our behaviors due to our expectations is called a self-fulfilling prophecy. It is defined as a tendency for our expectations about others to be confirmed because we engage in behaviors that elicit from others the very behaviors that we expected. Our lack of critical thinking might have caused an unpleasant encounter that could have been prevented.

CHAPTER 1

BASIC CONCEPTS AND METHODS

BEFORE YOU READ . . . CHAPTER SUMMARY

The goal of scientists who study human development is to produce observations and explanations that can be applied to as wide an age range of human beings and contexts as possible. To accomplish this goal, they study both change and stability. Additionally, they study cultural expectations, make predictions about development and use scientific methods to test them, and hope their findings can be used to positively influence development in individuals.

An Introduction to Human Development

- The philosophical concepts of original sin, innate goodness, and the blank slate have influenced Western ideas about development.
- The concept of developmental stages comes, in part, from Darwin's evolutionary theory. G. Stanley Hall identified norms at which developmental milestones happen. Gesell focused on genetically programmed sequential patterns of change.
- Important changes occur during every period of development across the lifespan, and these changes must be understood in the cultures and contexts in which they occur.
- There are three broad categories, called domains of development, to classify the changes—physical, cognitive, and social.

Key Issues in the Study of Human Development

- Historically, developmentalists have looked at nature and nurture as an either-or controversy. Modern developmentalists understand that developmental change is a product of both genetics and the environment.
- A key issue in the study of human development is the continuity-discontinuity issue. The question is whether age-related change is primarily a matter of amount or degree (continuity) or it involves changes in type or kind (discontinuity).
- Universal changes are common to every individual in a species and are linked to specific ages.
- Group-specific changes are shared by all individuals who grow up together in a particular group. One of the most important groups to which we all belong is our culture.
- Individual differences are changes resulting from unique, unshared events.

Research Designs and Methods

- Developmental psychology uses the scientific method to achieve its goals: to describe, explain, predict, and influence human development from conception to death.
- There are three choices for studying age-related change: a cross-sectional design to study different groups of people of different ages; a longitudinal design to study the same people over a period of time; and a sequential design to combine cross-sectional and longitudinal designs in some fashion.
- Case studies are in-depth examinations of single individuals. The naturalistic observation method observes people in their normal environments. Correlational studies measure the relationship between variables. To test causal hypotheses, experimental designs in which subjects are assigned randomly to experimental or control groups are necessary.
- Cross-cultural research helps developmentalists identify specific variables that explain cultural differences.

▪ Ethical principles in human developmental research include the following: protection from harm, informed consent, confidentiality, knowledge of results, and protection from deception.

AS YOU READ . . . LEARNING OBJECTIVES

After completing Chapter 1, you should be able to:

1.1   Explain each of the philosophies that are important to the study of human development.
1.2   List the theorists and their theories that influence modern developmental psychology.
1.3   Summarize the advice of child-rearing experts over the years.
1.4   Explain the concept of the lifespan perspective.
1.5   List and describe the three domains of development.
1.6   Define the nature-nurture controversy, and describe the ways of looking at both types of influences.
1.7   Distinguish between continuity and discontinuity.
1.8   Give examples of universal developmental changes.
1.9   Describe how groups specific changes affect development.
1.10   Summarize the cohort effects of the Great Depression of the 1930s on children and adolescents.
1.11   List ways individual differences affect development.
1.12   List and describe the four goals of developmental psychology.
1.13   Summarize how variables might influence the impact an event has on a person's development.
1.14   Describe the three types of age-related research, and state the advantages and disadvantages of each.
1.15   Distinguish among the types of studies used to identify relationships between variables, and state the advantages and disadvantages of each.
1.16   Describe cross-cultural or cross-context designs.
1.17   Summarize the importance of thinking critically about research.
1.18   Identify five areas of ethical concern in human developmental research.

AS YOU READ . . . TERM IDENTIFICATION

Ageism (p. 10)
Atypical development (p. 12)
Case study (p. 16)
Cognitive domain (p. 6)
Cohort (p. 11)
Control group (p. 17)
Correlation (p. 17)
Critical period (p. 11)
Cross-sectional design (p. 13)
Dependent variable (p. 17)

Ethnography (p. 18)
Experiment (p. 17)
Experimental group (p. 17)
Human development (p. 3)
Independent variable (p. 17)
Lifespan perspective (p. 6)
Longitudinal design (p. 13)
Maturation (p. 4)
Naturalistic observation (p. 16)
Nature-nurture controversy (p. 7)

Norms (p. 4)
Physical development (p. 6)
Qualitative change (p. 9)
Quantitative change (p. 8)
Research ethics (p. 19)
Sensitive period (p. 12)
Sequential design (p. 13)
Social clock (p. 10)
Social domain (p. 6)

GUIDED STUDY QUESTIONS

IN INTRODUCTION TO HUMAN DEVELOPMENT

Philosophical Roots (pp. 3-4)

Objective 1.1: Explain each of the philosophies that are important to the study of human development.

1.   Define human development (p. 3)

2.   Compare how the philosophies of original sin, innate goodness, and the blank slate explain development.

Philosophy	Explanation of Development
Original Sin	
Innate Goodness	
Blank Slate	

Early Scientific Studies (p. 4)

Objective 1.2: List the theorists and their theories that influence modern developmental psychology.

3.   Define the following terms:
       a.   norms (p. 4)

       b.   maturation (p. 4)

4.   State the major contributions to developmental psychology by each of the following theorists:

Theorist	Contribution
Charles Darwin	
G. Stanley Hall	
Arnold Gesell	

Development in the Information Age: Child-Rearing Experts (p. 5)

Objective 1.3: Summarize the advice of child-rearing experts over the years.

5.   What is one consequence of the mass dissemination of information?

6.   Describe the views on child rearing and their impact on parenting of each of the following experts:

Theorists	View	Impact on Parenting
John Watson		
Dr. Benjamin Spock		
T. Berry Brazelton		

7.   How has the Internet impacted child rearing?

The Lifespan Perspective (pp. 4-6)

Objective 1.4: *Explain the concept of the lifespan perspective.*

8.   List two reasons why psychologists' views of adulthood have changed recently.

9.   How has developmental psychology become more interdisciplinary as interest in the entire lifespan has grown?

10.   Define the lifespan perspective (p. 6).

Domains of Development (p. 6)

Objective 1.5: *List and describe the three domains of development.*

11.   Define the following terms:
        a.   physical domain (p. 6)

        b.   cognitive domain (p. 6)

        c.   social domain (p. 6)

12.   Give an example of how the domains are interrelated.

AFTER YOU READ . . .PRACTICE TEST #1
THE SCIENTIFIC STUDY OF HUMAN DEVELOPMENT

Match the letter of the term in the right column with its description in the left column.

_____ 1.	The gradual unfolding of genetically programmed sequential patterns of change.	a. Blank slate
_____ 2.	Domain that focuses on the size, shape, and characteristics of the body.	b. Cognitive
_____ 3.	View that asserts that all human beings are naturally good and seek experiences that help them grow.	c. Charles Darwin
_____ 4.	The scientific study of age-related changes in behavior, thinking, emotion, and personality.	d. G. Stanley Hall
_____ 5.	Average ages at which developmental milestones are reached.	e Arnold Gessell
_____ 6.	The view that maintains that important changes occur during every period of development.	f. Human development
_____ 7.	Used "baby biographies" in the hope of finding evidence to support the theory of evolution.	g. Innate goodness
_____ 8.	The capacity for positive change in response to environmental demands.	h. Lifespan perspective
_____ 9.	Domain that emphasizes changes in thinking, memory, problem-solving, and other intellectual skills.	i. Maturation
_____ 10.	His research suggested the existence of a genetically programmed sequential pattern of change.	j. Norms

a. Blank slate
b. Cognitive
c. Charles Darwin
d. G. Stanley Hall
e Arnold Gessell
f. Human development
g. Innate goodness
h. Lifespan perspective
i. Maturation
j. Norms
k. Original sin
l. Physical
m. Plasticity
n. Social

(Check your answers to Practice Test #1 on p. 20.)

KEY ISSUES IN THE STUDY OF HUMAN DEVELOPMENT

Nature versus Nurture (pp. 7-8)

Objective 1.6: *Define the nature-nurture controversy, and describe the ways of looking at both types of influences.*

13.   Define nature-nurture controversy (p. 7).

14.   Give examples of each of the following:
      a.   inborn biases shared by virtually all children.

      b.   inborn biases that vary from one individual to another.

15.   List two key elements of the concept of internal models of experience.

16.   How do vulnerabilities and resiliences (protective factors) interact with a child's environment?

Continuity versus Discontinuity (pp. 8-9)

Objective 1.7: *Distinguish between continuity and discontinuity.*

17.   Define the following terms:
      a.   quantitative change (p. 8)

      b.   qualitative change (p. 9)

18.   Give examples to distinguish between continuity and discontinuity.

Universal Changes (pp. 9-10)

Objective 1.8: *Give examples of universal developmental changes.*

19.   List two ways universal changes happen, and give an example of each.

20.   Define the following terms:
      a.   social clock (p. 10)

      b.   ageism (p. 10

21.   Give examples of ageism.

Group Specific Changes (pp. 10-11)

Objective 1.9: *Describe how group specific changes affect development.*

22.   How does culture affect group-specific changes?

23.   Define cohort (p. 11).

Research Report: Children and Adolescents in the Great Depression: An Example of a Cohort Effect (p. 11)

Objective 1.10: Summarize the cohort effects of the Great Depression of the 1930s on children and adolescents.

24.   How did the Great Depression of the 1930s affect each of the following groups?
   a.   The teens (born in 1920):

   b.   The children (born in 1928):

Individual Differences (pp. 11-12)

Objective 1.11: List ways individual differences affect development.

25.   Give examples of individual differences as age-related changes.

26.   Distinguish among the following:
   a.   critical period (p. 11)

   b.   sensitive period (p. 12)

27.   Give examples of how off-time events can pose more difficulties for an individual than on-time events.

28.   List several synonyms for atypical development (p. 12). Give examples of atypical development.

AFTER YOU READ . . . PRACTICE TEST #2
KEY ISSUES IN THE STUDY OF HUMAN DEVELOPMENT

1.   **The term _____ encompasses the entire human lifespan rather than just childhood and adolescence.**
   a.   quantitative change
   b.   development
   c.   blank slate
   d.   plasticity

2.   **The basic notion that children are born with tendencies to respond in certain ways is called _____.**
   a.   nurture
   b.   age norms
   c.   inborn biases
   d.   atypical development

3.   **If you regularly hear criticism in other people's comments, we might infer that you will develop an internal model of experience. To which of the following basic assumptions is it most similar?**
   a.   "I usually do things wrong, and that is why others criticize me."
   b.   "I usually do things wrong, and people are cruel."
   c.   "Apparently others do not see things in the same way that I do."
   d.   "When I do things wrong, I can depend on others to help me."

4.   **By far the most negative outcomes for a child are the result of a _____.**
   a.   highly vulnerable child
   b.   poor or unsupportive environment
   c.   combination of high vulnerability and poor environment
   d.   combination of low vulnerability and unsupportive environment

5.   **A change in amount is called _____ change.**
   a.   a specific
   b.   atypical
   c.   a qualitative
   d.   a quantitative

6.   **The _____ issue concerns whether age-related changes are a matter of degree or changes in type or kind.**
   a.   nature-nurture
   b.   continuity-discontinuity
   c.   universal-specific
   d.   individual differences

7.   **The social clock, or a set of _____, defines a sequence of normal life experiences.**
   a.   vulnerabilities
   b.   inborn biases
   c.   age norms
   d.   internal models

8.   **The term _____ describes some system of meanings and customs, including values, attitudes, goals, laws, beliefs, moral guidelines, and physical artifacts.**
   a.   culture
   b.   cohort
   c.   critical period
   d.   inborn biases

9.   **The idea that there may be specific periods in development when an organism is especially sensitive to the presence (or absence) of some particular kind of experience is called _____.**
   a.   individual differences
   b.   a cohort
   c.   atypical development
   d.   the critical period

10.   **Atypical development is also known as each of the following EXCEPT:**
   a.   maladaptive behavior
   b.   normal development
   c.   psychopathology
   d.   abnormal behavior

(Check your answers to Practice Test #2 on p. 20.)

RESEARCH DESIGNS AND METHODS

Relating Goals to Methods (pp. 12-13)

Objective 1.12: List and describe the four goals of developmental psychology.

29.   List and define the four goals of human development.

Goal	Definition

30.   Why are theories important in studying developmental psychology?

No Easy Answers: It Depends . . . (p. 14)

Objective 1.13: Summarize how variables might influence the impact an event has on a person's development.

31.   List as many variables as possible that might affect an event (such as child abuse) in a child's life.

Studying Age-Related Changes (pp. 13-16)

Objective 1.14: Describe the three types of age-related research, and state the advantages and disadvantages of each.

32.   Define the following terms:
        a.   cross-sectional design (p. 13)

        b.   longitudinal design (p. 13)

        c.   sequential design (p. 13)

33.   Identify the advantages and disadvantages of each of the following designs:

Design	Advantages	Disadvantages
Cross-Sectional		
Longitudinal		
Sequential		

Identifying Relationships Between Variables (pp. 16-18)

Objective 1.15: Distinguish among the types of studies used to identify relationships between variables, and state the advantages and disadvantages of each.

34.   Define the following terms:
    a.   case studies (p. 16)

    b.   naturalistic observation method (p. 16)

    c.   correlation (p. 17)

    d.   experiment (p. 17)

    e.   experimental group (p. 17)

    f.   control group (p. 17)

    g.   independent variable (p. 17)

    h.   dependent variable (p. 17)

35.   State the advantages and disadvantages of each of the following research methods:

Method	Advantages	Disadvantages
Case Study		
Naturalistic Observation		
Correlational		
Experimental		

36.   How do researchers prevent possible observer bias?

37.   What do each of the following correlations indicate?
    a.   +1.00
    b.   -1.00
    c.   0.00

38.   Give an example of a relationship (such as the example of temperature and air conditioner use in the text) of each of the following:

Correlation	Example
Positive	
Negative	

39.   Why is random assignment to groups essential to an experiment?

40.   Suppose you want to see if children who watch violence on television are more aggressive than children who do not watch violent television. Identify the following parts of the experiment:
a.   Independent Variable:
b.   Dependent Variable:
c.   Experimental Group:
d.   Control Group:

41.   Why are quasi-experiments used instead of fully controlled experiments?

Cross-Cultural Research (pp. 18-19)

Objective 1.16: Describe cross-cultural or cross-context designs.
42.   Define ethnography (p. 18).

43.   Describe two ways investigators may conduct cross-cultural research.

44.   List two reasons why cross-cultural research is important to developmental psychology.

The Real World: Thinking Critically about Research (p. 20)

Objective 1.17: Summarize the importance of thinking critically about research.
45.   Explain why it is important to think critically about research.

Research Ethics (p. 19)

Objective 1.18: Identify five areas of ethical concern in human developmental research.
46.   Define research ethics (p. 19).

47.   Describe each of the following ethical standards:

Standard	Description
Protection from Harm	
Informed Consent	
Confidentiality	
Knowledge of Results	
Deception	

AFTER YOU READ . . . PRACTICE TEST #3
RESEARCH METHODS AND DESIGNS

Match the letter of the term in the right column with its description in the left column.

_____ 1.	A detailed description of a single culture or context.	a. Case studies
		b. Correlation
_____ 2.	A research design in which groups of different ages are compared.	c. Cross-sectional
		d. Describe
_____ 3.	Sets of statements that propose general principles of development.	e. Ethnography
		f. Experiment
_____ 4.	The goal of human development that involves telling why a particular event occurs.	g. Explain
		h. Hypothesis
_____ 5.	A research design in which people in a single group are studied at different times in their lives.	i. Influence
		j. Longitudinal
_____ 6.	The process of studying people in their normal environments.	k. Naturalistic observation
		l. Observer bias
_____ 7.	A difficulty of research that is overcome by using "blind" observers who do not know what the research is about.	m. Practice Effects
		n. Predict
_____ 8.	A relationship between two variables that can be expressed as a number ranging form +1.00 to –1.00.	o. Quasi-experiment
		p. Sequential
_____ 9.	In depth examination of a single individual.	q. Theory
_____ 10.	The goal of human development that simply states what happens.	

(Check your answers to Practice Test #3 on p. 20.)

AFTER YOU READ . . .CRITICAL REFLECTION EXERCISES

Critical Evaluation of Research

1. You are reading the newspaper, and you read a story about a product called Melatonic. It is described as a derivative of a natural brain chemical and is touted to "make you feel better, help you sleep, and increase your sex drive." The article goes on to cite the research evidence supporting these claims. According to the article:
    - white mice given 500 mg doses, slept 40% longer than mice not given the tonic.
    - subjects given a free 30 day trial sample of the tonic reported "feeling invigorated, having fewer troubles falling asleep, and having sex once each week during the trial period."

    Write out answers to the following questions and cite the reasons you have for each of your answers:
    a. What are the facts as they are presented?
    b. What are the implications if these facts are true?
    c. How have those facts been applied to the current research?
    d. When you analyze the information to determine what is verifiable, and discard what is meaningless, what facts are left?
    e. What questions do you have about the information that would need to be answered to make the original information more meaningful? (For example, "Is a 500 mg dosage a lot for a white mouse?").
    f. Now that you have only the meaningful pieces, what conclusions can you draw about the effects of Melatonic?
    g. What kind of a study could you develop to test the claims made in the article about Melatonic? Make sure that your study includes methods for testing (rather than assuming) that the claims are accurate.

2. You are a teacher, and a colleague of yours tells you that Rachel (a second grader) is a victim of child abuse. When you ask how she has reached this conclusion about Rachel she states, "She has all of the classic symptoms:
    - she can't sit still,
    - she is performing below her ability,
    - she has trouble making friends,
    - she has difficulty concentrating, and
    - she only partially completes her assignments."

    Write out answers to the following questions and cite the reasons you have for each of your answers.
    a. What evidence is the teacher citing for her conclusion that Rachel is an abuse victim?
    b. Can you verify that this evidence is accurate? How might you verify this?
    c. What other information would you need to gather (or what other questions do you think would need to be answered) in order for you to determine if this teacher's conclusion is accurate?
    d. Describe how this teacher's conclusion, if invalid, could actually lead to a self-fulfilling prophecy as outlined earlier in this chapter.
    e. Based on the facts that you have, what conclusions can be drawn about Rachel?
    f. What other alternative explanations can you think of (besides abuse) that might explain Rachel's behaviors?

AFTER YOU READ . . .COMPREHENSIVE PRACTICE TEST
MULTIPLE CHOICE QUESTIONS

1. The scientific study of age-related changes in behavior, thinking, emotion, and personality is termed _____.
    a. ageism
    b. maturation
    c. cohort effect
    d. human developmental

2. The philosophy which teaches that all humans are born with a selfish nature becaues of the sin of Adam and Eve in the Garden of Eden is called _____.
    a. morality
    b. the blank slate
    c. original sin
    d. innate goodness

3. The term used to describe the average age at which milestones happen is _____.
    a. norms
    b. baby biographies
    c. case studies
    d. cohort effect

4. Genetically programmed sequential patterns of change are termed _____.
    a. growth
    b. maturation
    c. learning
    d. development

5. The perspective that maintains that important changes occur during every part of development is called the _____.
    a. cognitive-developmental perspective
    b. central timing perspective
    c. psychosocial perspective
    d. lifespan perspective

6. The behavior of an individual _____.
    a. is completely fixed by his or her genetic inheritance
    b. will be entirely consistent over a person's lifespan
    c. will always be a joint product of the genetic pattern and the environment
    d. is based on his or her socioeconomic status

7. Thomas is forced to retire at age 70, even though he is physically and mentally healthy and does his job well. This is an example of _____.
    a. age norms
    b. ageism
    c. the social clock
    d. culture

13

8. The term used by social scientists to describe groups of individuals born within some fairly narrow band of years who share the same historical experiences at the same times in their lives _____.
    a. is a cohort
    b. are age mates
    c. represents time banding
    d. illustrates the co-existence phenomena

9. The idea that experiences occurring at the expected times for an individual's culture or cohort will pose fewer difficulties for an individual than experiences occurring at unexpected times is called _____.
    a. the critical period
    b. the historical period
    c. the sensitive period
    d. on-time and off-time events

10. Each of the following is one of the domains of development EXCEPT:
    a. social
    b. cohort
    c. physical
    d. cognitive

11. In the cross-sectional method, _____.
    a. the same group of subjects is repeatedly given the same test over a twenty-year period
    b. surveys are administered to samples of people from around the country
    c. groups of subjects of different ages are observed
    d. the behaviors of subjects in a laboratory environment is compared with their behaviors in their natural setting

12 Nicole studies parents and their children by watching them interact at the zoo. This is an example of the _____.
    a. naturalistic observation method
    b. case study method
    c. experimental method
    d. correlational method

13. As the temperature climbs, so does the number of air conditioners in use. This is an example of _____.
    a. a positive correlation
    b. a negative correlation
    c. no correlation
    d. a hypothesis

14. An experiment is testing the effects of observed violence on children's behavior. One group of children views a violent cartoon. A second group views a humorous non-violent cartoon. A third group is not exposed to any cartoon. The amount of violence observed is the _____.
    a. independent variable
    b. dependent variable
    c. comparison group
    d. observational group

15. **Which of the following ethical standards for research involves the right to a written summary of a study's results?**
    a. knowledge of results
    b. deception
    c. informed consent
    d. confidentiality

TRUE-FALSE QUESTIONS

Indicate whether each of the following statements is true or false.

_____ 1. The doctrine of original sin teaches that all human beings are naturally good and seek out experiences that help them grow.

_____ 2. The capacity for positive change, or plasticity, in response to environmental demands is possible throughout the entire lifespan.

_____ 3. The social domain includes variables that are associated with the relationship of an individual to others.

_____ 4. The ecological approach emphasizes the context in which the child is growing.

_____ 5. A qualitative change involves the continuity side of the continuity-discontinuity debate.

_____ 6. In each culture, the social clock defines a sequence of normal life experiences.

_____ 7. The four goals of research in human development are to describe, to explain, to predict, and to influence.

_____ 8. Cross-cultural research is important in identifying universal changes.

ESSAY QUESTIONS

1. Choose a typical event from human development, and give examples of how the three domains interact. Events could include starting school, going to college, getting married, having a baby, experiencing menopause, retiring, etc.

2. Describe how inborn biases, internal models of experience, and the ecological approach are aspects of the nature-nurture controversy.

3. Describe how cross-cultural research is important to the study of human development.

(Check your answers to the comprehensive Practice Test on p. 20.)

15

WHEN YOU HAVE FINISHED . . . PUZZLE IT OUT

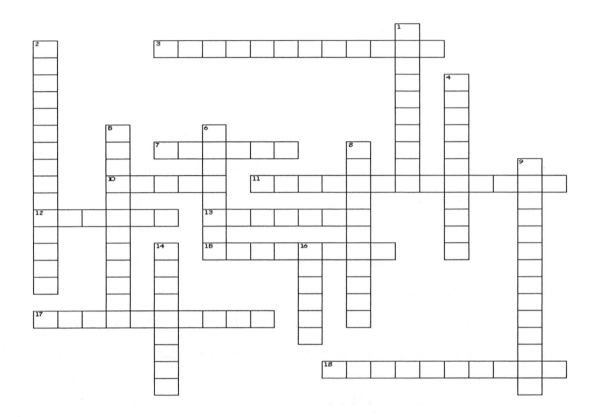

Across

3. A single group of people are studied at different times
7. Individuals who share the same historical experiences
10. Average ages at which developmental milestones are reached
11. Debate about relative contributions of heredity and environment
12. A prejudicial view of older adults
13. Some system of meanings and customs
15. Important changes occur in every period of development
17. A study that tests a causal hypothesis
18. Combines cross-sectional and longitudinal

Down

1. Genetically programmed sequential patterns of change
2. Researchers must not reveal the identities of participants
4. A detailed description of a single culture or context
5. Change in amount
6. Changes in the size, shape, and characteristics of the body
8. Relationship between two variables expressed as +1.00 to -1.00
9. Groups of different ages are compared
14. Changes in thinking, memory, problem-solving
16. Changes in variables associated with the relationship to others

Created by Puzzlemaker at DiscoverySchool.com

(Check your answers on p. 20.)

WHEN YOU HAVE FINISHED . . . RESEARCH PROJECT

Student Project 1: A First Observation of a Child:
An Example of a Narrative Report

There are several purposes in suggesting this project. First, if you have had relatively little contact with young children, you may need to spend some time simply observing a child to make other sections of the book more meaningful. Second, it is important for you to begin to get some sense of the difficulties involved in observing and studying children. Later projects involve other types of observation, but it is helpful to start with the least structured (but perhaps the most difficult) form, namely a narrative report in which the observer attempts to write down everything a child does or says for about one hour.

Step 1: Locate a child between 18 months and 6 years of age; age 2, 3, or 4 would be best.

Step 2: Obtain permission from the child's parents for observation, using whatever form and procedure are specified by your instructor. When you speak to the parents, be sure to tell them that the purpose of your observation is for a course assignment, and that you will not be testing the child in any way but merely want to observe a normal child in his or her normal situation.

Step 3: Arrange a time when you can observe the child in his or her "natural habitat" for about one hour. If the child is in a nursery school, it is acceptable to observe him or her there as long as you get permission from the teachers. If not, the observation should be done in the home or in some situation familiar to the child. You must not baby-sit during the observation. You must be free to be in the background and cannot be responsible for the child during the observation.

Step 4: When the time for the observation arrives, place yourself in as unobtrusive a place as possible. Take a small stool with you if you can, so that you can move around as the child moves. If you are in the child's home, he or she will probably ask what you are doing. Say that you are doing something for school and that you will be writing things down for a while. Do not invite any kind of contact with the child; do not meet the child's eye; do not smile; and do not talk except when the child talks directly, in which case you should say that you are busy and will play a little later.

Step 5: For one hour, try to write down everything the child does. Write down the child's speech word-for-word. If the child is talking to someone else, write down the other person's replies, too, if you can. Describe the child's movements. Throughout, keep your description as free of evaluation and words of intent as you can. Do not write "Sarah went into the kitchen to get a cookie." You don't know why she went. What you saw was that she stopped what she had been doing, got up, and walked into the kitchen. There you see her getting a cookie. Describe the behavior that way, rather than making assumptions about what is happening in the child's head. Avoid words like "tries," "angrily," "pleaded," "wanted," and the like. Describe only what you see and hear.

Step 6: When you have completed the observation, reread what you wrote and consider the following questions:
- Did you manage to keep all description of intent out of your record?
- Were you able to remain objective?
- Since you obviously could not write down everything that the child did, think about what you left out.
- Did you find that you paid more attention to some aspects of behavior than others, such as listening to language rather than noting physical movements?
- What would such a bias do to the kind of information you could obtain from your narrative?
- Would it be possible for you or some other person doing the rating to obtain systematic information about the child from your record, such as a measure of the child's level of activity or a score reflecting the number of times the child asked for attention?
- What changes in this method of observation would you have to introduce to obtain other sorts of information?
- What do you think were the effects of your presence on the child?

WHEN YOU HAVE FINISHED . . . RESEARCH PROJECT

Student Project 2: Naturalistic Observation of a Nursing Home Resident

Follow the same procedure as in Project 1, except instead of observing a young child, observe an elderly adult in a nursing home. Permission will be required from the nursing home, and from the individual to be observed, following whatever procedure your instructor specifies.

Arrange to spend at least an hour in the nursing home. Inquire about the daily schedule and choose a time when the residents are likely to be together in some kind of recreational activity, or at least when not isolated in their individual rooms. Place yourself as inconspicuously as possible by the side of the room, and observe your selected subject for one hour. As with the observation of the child, attempt to write down everything your subject does for that hour. When you are finished, ask yourself the same questions as in Project 1.

WHEN YOU HAVE FINISHED . . . AT HOME PROJECT

Student Project 3: Analysis of Research Presented in Popular Sources

Find at least eight separate mentions of research on children, adolescents, or adults in newspapers and magazines, and analyze each one. For each item, describe the research design that appears to have been used.
- Is that design appropriate for the question being asked?
- Are there any flaws you can detect?
- Does the report in the magazine or newspaper give you enough detail to decide whether the research was any good?
- What other information would you want to have to decide on the quality of the research?

Some sources you might try for suitable articles are as follows:

1. The *New York Times* has a section on science every Tuesday which includes articles about behavior and development fairly regularly. The *Times* also has a column on personal health every Wednesday that often covers relevant material, as well as a column on children's behavior or on parenting every Thursday.

2. *Time* and *Newsweek* have sections on behavior that may be relevant.

3. Most so-called "women's magazines" (*Ladies Home Journal*, *Redbook*, *Family Circle*, etc.) have columns on child-rearing or children's development.

CHAPTER 1 ANSWER KEY

Practice Test #1 The Scientific Study of Human Development

1. i   2. l   3. g   4. f   5. j   6. h   7. c   8. m   9. b   10. e

Practice Test #2 Key Issues in the Study of Human Development

1. b   2. c   3. a   4. c   5. d   6. b   7. c   8. a   9. d   10. b

Practice Test #3 Research Methods and Designs

1. e   2. c   3. q   4. g   5. j   6. k   7. l   8. b   9. a   10. d

Comprehensive Practice Test

Multiple Choice Questions

1. d   2. c   3. a   4. b   5. d   6. c   7. b   8. a   9. d   10. b
11. c   12. a   13. a   14. a   15. a

True-False Questions

1. F   2. T   3. T   4. T   5. F   6. T   7. T   8. T

Essay Questions

1. ▪ Answers should include aspects of all three domains for the event.

2. ▪ Answers should include how each of the three (inborn biases, internal models of experience, and the ecological approach) relate to nature versus nurture.

3. ▪ Cross-cultural research is helpful in identifying universal changes and in producing findings that can be used to improve people's lives. Answers should include reference to both functions.

Puzzle It Out

Across	Down
3. Longitudinal	1. Maturation
7. Cohort	2. Confidentiality
10. Norms	4. Ethnography
11. NatureNurture	5. Quantitative
12. Ageism	6. Physical
13. Culture	8. Correlation
15. Lifespan	9. CrossSectional
17. Experiment	14. Cognitive
18. Sequential	16. Social

CHAPTER 2

THEORIES OF DEVELOPMENT

BEFORE YOU READ . . . CHAPTER SUMMARY

Three "families" of theories have significantly influenced the study of development. Current trends in research focus on other areas of study. The comparison of theories is based on three assumptions about theories and evaluated by criteria for usefulness.

Psychoanalytic Theories

- Freud's emphasis is on the importance of both conscious and unconscious processes. The personality is composed of the id, the ego, and the superego that influence our motives. He proposed five psychosexual stages, and he believed that each of the first three stages potentially impact our development.
- Erikson's theory stated that social forces are more important than unconscious drives as motives for development. He proposes eight stages of personality development across the lifespan, each of which involves resolving a crisis.
- Psychoanalytic theories provide useful concepts, such as the unconscious, that contribute to our understanding of development. They are, however, difficult to test.

Learning Theories

- Classical conditioning is learning through the association of unrelated stimuli so that we respond in a similar manner. It helps explain the acquisition of emotional responses, such as fear.
- Operant conditioning involves learning based on the consequences of our actions. Reinforcement happens when a behavior is repeated because of the consequences that followed it. When a behavior stops because of a consequence, punishment has occurred.
- The social-learning variation of learning theory focuses more on the cognitive elements of learning, such as modeling.
- Learning theories provide useful explanations of how behaviors are acquired, but they fall short of a truly comprehensive picture of human development.

Cognitive Theories

- Piaget's focus is on the development of logical thinking across four stages in childhood and adolescence.
- Information-processing theory uses the computer as a model to explain intellectual processes such as memory and problem-solving.
- Research confirms the sequence of skill development that Piaget proposed, but it suggests that young children are more capable than he believed. Information-processing theory helps to clarify some of the cognitive processes underlying Piaget's findings as well as our understanding of memory.

Current Trends

- Biological theories, such as nativism, ethology, sociobiology, and behavior genetics have gained popularity as developmentalists seek to better understand the role of physiological processes in development.
- Vygotsky's socio-cultural theory is important in developmentalists' attempts to explain how culture impacts development.

- Bronfenbrenner's ecological theory helps developmentalists categorize environmental factors and their impact on individuals.
- Eclecticism is the use of multiple theoretical perspectives to explain and study human development.

Comparing Theories

- Theories vary on three basic assumptions: Are individuals active or passive in their own development? How do nature and nurture interact to produce development? Does development happen continuously or in stages?
- Useful theories provide hypotheses to test their validity, are heuristically valuable, provide practical solutions to problems, and explain the facts of development.

AS YOU READ . . . LEARNING OBJECTIVES

After reading the chapter, you should be able to:

2.1   Describe Freud's theory of psychosexual development.
2.2   Summarize the dilemma surrounding the issue of repressed memories.
2.3   Describe Erikson's theory and explain the focus of four of the eight stages.
2.4   Evaluate the psychoanalytic theory.
2.5   Explain the process of classical conditioning.
2.6   Explain the process of operant conditioning.
2.7   Provide real-life examples of the principles of learning.
2.8   Give examples of observational learning, or modeling.
2.9   Critique the learning theories.
2.10   Describe the basic concepts of Piaget's theory.
2.11   Explain the basic concepts of information-processing theory.
2.12   Critique the cognitive theories.
2.13   Describe Piaget's research methods.
2.14   Compare the biological theories of development.
2.15   Describe Vygotsky's socio-cultural theory.
2.16   Describe Bronfenbrenner's ecological theory.
2.17   Define eclecticism and explain its importance.
2.18   Distinguish between the three assumptions about development.
2.19   List the criteria for the usefulness of a theory.

AS YOU READ . . . TERM IDENTIFICATION

Accommodation (p. 34)
Assimilation (p. 34)
Behavior genetics (p. 39)
Behaviorism (p. 29)
Classical conditioning (p. 29)
Cognitive theories (p. 33)
Defense mechanisms (p. 24)
Eclecticism (p. 42)
Ecological theory (p. 41)
Ego (p. 24)
Equilibrium (p. 34)

Ethology (p. 39)
Extinction (p. 30)
Id (p. 24)
Information-processing theory (p. 35)
Learning theories (p. 29)
Libido (p. 24)
Nativism (p. 38)
Neo-Piagetian theory (p. 36)
Observational learning, or modeling (p. 31)
Operant conditioning (p. 30)

Psychoanalytic theories (p. 24)
Psychosexual stages (p. 24)
Psychosocial stages (p. 26)
Punishment (p. 30)
Reinforcement (p. 30)
Scheme (p. 34)
Shaping (p. 31)
Sociobiology (p. 39)
Socio-cultural theory (p. 40)
Superego (p. 24)

AS YOU READ . . . GUIDED STUDY QUESTIONS

PSYCHOANALYTIC THEORIES

Freud's Psychosexual Theory (pp. 24-26)

Objective 2.1: Describe Freud's theory of psychosexual development.

1. Define the following terms:
    a. psychoanalytic theory (p. 24)

    b. libido (p. 24)

    c. id (p. 24)

    d. ego (p. 24)

    e. superego (p. 24)

    f. defense mechanisms (p. 24)

    g. psychosexual stages (p. 24)

2. List the three parts of personality, and describe the function of each.

Structure	*Function*

3. What would the three parts of Freud's theory "say" to you about your desire for your favorite cheesecake? Choose one of the following for each of the examples listed:

	Id	*Ego*	*Superego*

    _____ a.   "Don't even think about eating cheesecake. You know it has too much fat, too much sugar, and too much cholesterol. Besides, if you eat it all you'll get sick to your stomach. Forget it and go get a carrot stick!"

    _____ b.   "Go for it—and put whipped cream and a cherry on top! Just bring me the whole thing."

    _____ c.   "How about a small piece? If I eat some now, then I will just have a small salad for supper and I'll do extra exercises tomorrow."

4.   List, in order, Freud's five psychosexual stages, and summarize each by completing the following table.

Name of Stage	Age	Focus of Libido	Developmental Task	Characteristics of Fixation in Adulthood
1.				
2.				
3.				
4.				
5.				

5.   Describe the Oedipus complex for boys and the Electra complex for girls.

6.   Explain the process of identification.

No Easy Answers: The Repressed Memory Controversy (p. 25)

Objective 2.2: Summarize the dilemma surrounding the issue of repressed memories.

7.   Explain how the defense mechanisms of repression and denial may cause distress in the personality.

8.   Write a support statement for each side of the controversy surrounding repressed memories.

Therapists should try to uncover repressed memories.	Therapists should not try to uncover repressed memories.

Erikson's Psychosocial Theory (pp. 26-28)

Objective 2.3: Describe Erikson's theory and explain the focus of four of the eight stages.

9.   Define psychosocial theory (p. 26).

10.   According to Erikson, how does a person develop a healthy personality?

11.   List, in order, Erikson's eight psychosocial stages, and complete the following table.

	Stage	*Age*	*Positive Characteristics Gained and Typical Activities*
1.			
2.			
3.			
4.			
5.			
6.			
7.			
8.			

12.   Describe the parents' behavior that might result in an infant learning trust, and describe the parents' behavior that might result in an infant learning mistrust.

13.   What must an adolescent do to achieve identity?

14.   Why did Erikson believe that identity must be established before intimacy?

15.   List several ways a middle-aged adult could achieve generativity.

Evaluation of Psychoanalytic Theories (pp. 28-29)

Objective 2.4: Evaluate the psychoanalytic theory.

16.   List five strengths of psychoanalytic theory.

17.   What is the greatest weakness of psychoanalytic theory?

AFTER YOU READ . . . PRACTICE TEST #1
PSYCHOANALYTIC THEORIES

1.   **The _____ is the instinctual drive for physical pleasure.**
   a.   libido
   b.   conscious
   c.   ego
   d.   superego

2.   **The _____ is responsible for keeping the three components of personality in balance.**
   a.   libido
   b.   id
   c.   superego
   d.   ego

3.   **The psychosexual stage in which a girl experiences the Electra complex is _____ .**
   a.   oral
   b.   anal
   c.   phallic
   d.   genital

4.   **In Freud's view, a defense mechanism called _____ is used to overcome the Oedipus complex.**
   a.   regression
   b.   identification
   c.   denial
   d.   suppression

5.   **According to Erikson's theory, a healthy personality is built on the formation of _____.**
   a.   self-awareness
   b.   autonomy
   c.   initiative
   d.   trust

6.   **According to Erikson's theory, if an individual does not make a successful transition through adolescence, he or she develops _____.**
   a.   an inferiority complex
   b.   role confusion
   c.   a sense of isolation
   d.   a sense of personal guilt

7. **In order for the young adult to realize a successful outcome in Erikson's sixth stage, she or he must learn to establish a sense of _____.**
    a. identity
    b. intimacy
    c. initiative
    d. industry

8. **Psychoanalytic theories highlight the importance of _____.**
    a. genetically determined survival behaviors
    b. mental aspects of development such as logic and memory
    c. the child's earliest relationship with caregivers, and suggest that the child's needs change with age
    d. development in terms of behavior changes caused by environmental influences

(Check your answers to Practice Test #1 on p. 43.)

LEARNING THEORIES

Pavlov's Classical Conditioning (pp. 29-30)

Objective 2.5: Explain the process of classical conditioning.

18. Define the following terms:
    a. behaviorism (p. 29)

    b. learning theories (p. 29)

    c. classical conditioning (p. 29)

19. In classical conditioning, the conditioned response is always very similar to the unconditined response. Why?

20. A child learns to associate a teddy bear with a loud noise that scares him. Match the classical conditioning term to its appropriate action.

    1. _____ fear (of teddy bear)
    2. _____ fear (of loud noise)
    3. _____ loud noise
    4. _____ teddy bear

    a. unconditional stimulus
    b. unconditional response
    c. conditional stimulus
    d. conditional response

21. How is classical conditioning relevant to the study of development?

Skinner's Operant Conditioning (pp. 30-31)

Objective 2.6: Explain the process of operant conditioning.

22.   Define the following terms:
        a.   operant conditioning (p. 30)

        b.   reinforcement (p. 30)

        c.   punishment (p. 30)

        d.   extinction (p. 30)

        e.   shaping (p. 30)

23.   You want your daughter to clean her room. Label the following operant conditioning term that matches the action.

Positive Reinforcement	*Negative Reinforcement*	*Punishment*

_____ 1.   If she cleans her room, she doesn't have to do the dishes.

_____ 2.   If she cleans her room, she can go to the movies.

_____ 3.   If she does not clean her room, she cannot watch TV.

24.   Describe how you can use extinction to stop your son's whining.

25.   Your task is to teach a tiger to jump through a small, flaming hoop. Arrange in the correct order the following steps in shaping the behavior.

        _____ 1.   a. Jump from one platform to another through a small hoop.
                               b. Sit on a platform.
        _____ 2.   c. Jump from one platform to another through a large hoop.
                               d. Jump from one platform to another through a large flaming hoop.
        _____ 3.   e. Jump from one platform to another through a small flaming hoop.
                               f. Jump from one platform to another.
        _____ 4.

        _____ 5.

        _____ 6.

The Real World: Learning Principles in Everyday Life (p. 32)

Objective 2.7: Provide real-life examples of the principles of learning.

26.   You're at the cereal aisle of the grocery store. In the same aisle is a mom with a preschool child in the shopping cart. The child wants an expensive, sugary cereal, and the mom says no. The child has a temper tantrum, and everyone in the aisle turns to see what happened. The mom gives in and puts the cereal in the basket, and the child stops screaming.

      a.   Who received positive reinforcement? How?

      b.   Who received negative reinforcement? How?

      c.   How could extinction be used in this scenario?

Bandura's Social-Learning Theory (pp. 31-32)

Objective 2.8: Give examples of observational learning, or modeling.

27.   Define observational learning, or modeling (p. 31).

28.   List the four factors that determine whether or not an observer will learn from watching someone else.

Evaluation of Learning Theories (pp. 32-33)

Objective 2.9: Critique the learning theories.

29.   Give an example of each of the following implications of the learning theories.

Implication	*Example*
Learning theories can explain both consistency and change in behavior.	
Learning theories tend to be optimistic about the possibility of change.	
Learning theories give an accurate picture of the way many behaviors are learned.	

30.   Why are learning theories not considered to be developmental theories?

AFTER YOU READ . . . PRACTICE TEST #2
LEARNING THEORIES

1.　**Conditioned response is to unconditioned response as _____.**
　　a.　unlearned is to learned
　　b.　nature is to nurture
　　c.　learned is to unlearned
　　d.　learned is to forgotten

2.　**All of the following are examples of an unconditioned response EXCEPT:**
　　a.　Tony's eyes tear up when he is peeling an onion.
　　b.　John's pupils dilate in response to a bright light.
　　c.　Rich wipes his dirty hands off on his pants before he grabs the mail off the table.
　　d.　Mike pulls his hand back quickly after touching a hot stove.

3.　**In operant conditioning, the response comes _____.**
　　a.　before the consequence
　　b.　after the consequence
　　c.　during the consequence
　　d.　between the consequence and the unconditioned stimulus

4.　**You take aspirin for your headache. This is an example of which of the following?**
　　a.　positive reinforcement
　　b.　negative reinforcement
　　c.　punishment
　　d.　extinction

5.　**The gradual elimination of a behavior through repeated nonreinforcement is called _____.**
　　a.　shaping
　　b.　punishment
　　c.　reinforcement
　　d.　extinction

6.　**All of the following are factors that determines whether or not an observer will learn from watching someone else EXCEPT:**
　　a.　what she pays attention to
　　b.　what she is physically able to copy
　　c.　what she read in her textbook
　　d.　what she is motivated to imitate

7.　**Each of the following is a strength of learning theories EXCEPT:**
　　a.　They are not really developmental theories.
　　b.　They tend to be optimistic about the possibility of changing behavior.
　　c.　They can explain both consistence and change in behavior.
　　d.　They give an accurate picture of the way many behaviors are learned.

(Check your answers to Practice Test #2 on p. 43.)

COGNITIVE THEORIES

Piaget's Cognitive-Developmental Theory (pp. 33-35)

Objective 2.10: Describe the basic concepts of Piaget's theory.

31.   Define the following terms:

      a.   cognitive theories (p.)33

      b.   scheme (p. 34)

      c.   assimilation (p. 34)

      d.   accommodation (p. 34)

      e.   equilibrium (p. 34)

32.   Your present scheme for drive-in windows at fast-food restaurants includes the following:
- Order from a menu at the speaker box.
- Drive to the first window and pay.
- Drive to another window and pick up your food.

You stop at the drive-in window of a new fast-food restaurant and discover that the window to pay and pick up your food is on the passenger side of the car, not the driver's side. According to Piaget, what process is involved in changing the scheme based on the new information?

33.   List, in order, the four stages of Piaget's theory, and complete the following table.

	Stage	*Age*	*Description*
1.			
2.			
3.			
4.			

Information-Processing Theory (pp. 35-56)

Objective 2.11: Explain the basic concepts of information-processing theory.

34.   Define the following terms:
        a.   information-processing theory (p. 35)

        b.   neo-Piagetian theory (p. 36)

35.   Did you listen to music on the radio this morning while you were getting ready for school or work? If so, do you remember all the songs you heard? Probably not, even though you might have sung along with several of them. Which ones do you remember? Why don't we remember everything that enters our sensory memory?

Evaluation of Cognitive Theories (p. 37)

Objective 2.12: Critique the cognitive theories.

36.   List three contributions of Piaget's theory.

37.   In what area was Piaget sometimes wrong?

38.   How has information-processing theory helped clarify some of the cognitive processes underlying Piaget's findings?

39.   What are the criticisms of information-processing theory?

Research Report: Piaget's Clever Research (p. 38)

Objective 2.13: Describe Piaget's research methods.

40.   Give examples of how Piaget's method of study tested children's understanding of the concepts of conservation and multiple categories.

AFTER YOU READ ... PRACTICE TEST #3
COGNITIVE THEORIES

1.   **The group of theories known as _____ emphasizes mental aspects of development such as logic and memory.**
        a.   learning theories
        b.   cognitive theories
        c.   biological theories
        d.   useful theories

2.   **A _____ is an internal and cognitive structure that provides an individual with a process to follow in a specific circumstance.**
        a.   model
        b.   stage
        c.   reflex
        d.   scheme

3.   **_____ is the process of balancing assimilation and accommodation to create schemes that fit the environment.**
        a.   Behavior
        b.   Equilibrium
        c.   Cognition
        d.   Learning

4.   **According to Piaget, in the _____ stage, children acquire symbolic schemes, such as language and fantasy.**
        a.   sensorimotor
        b.   preoperational
        c.   concrete operational
        d.   formal operational

5.   **According to Piaget, in the _____ stage, adolescents learn to think logically about abstract ideas and hypothetical situations.**
        a.   sensorimotor
        b.   preoperational
        c.   concrete operational
        d.   formal operational

6.   **Another name for short-term memory is _____.**
        a.   sensory memory
        b.   episodic memory
        c.   long-term memory
        d.   working memory

7.   **_____ is unlimited in capacity.**
        a.   short-term memory
        b.   long-term memory
        c.   working memory
        d.   sensory memory

(Check your answers to Practice Test # 3 on p. 43.)

CURRENT TRENDS

Biological Theories (pp. 38-40)

Objective 2.14: Compare the biological theories of development.

41.   Define the following terms:
        a.   nativism (p. 38)

        b.   ethology (p. 39)

        c.   sociobiology (p. 39)

        d.   behavior genetics (p. 39)

42.   The text states that, "Some biological theories explain universal changes while others address individual differences." Which biological theories fit in the universal category? Which fit in the individual category? What evidence is there to support this statement?

43.   What are the criticisms of each theory?

Vygotsky's Socio-Cultural Theory (p. 40)

Objective 2.15: Describe Vygotsky's socio-cultural theory.

44.   Define socio-cultural theory (p. 40).

45.   How does the role of the teacher differ in the Vygotskian classroom from the Piagetian classroom?

Bronfenbrenner's Ecological Theory (pp. 41-42)

Objective 2.16: Describe Bronfenbrenner's ecological theory.

46.   Define ecological theory (p. 41).

47.   Give examples of each of the contexts in Bronfenbrenner's theory.

Context	*Example*
Macrosystem	
Exosystem	

Context	Example
Microsystem (and Mesosystem)	
Biological	

Eclecticism (p. 42)

Objective 2.17: Define eclecticism, and explain its importance.

48.   Define eclecticism (p. 42).

49.   Give examples of how the interdisciplinary nature of today's developmental science may contribute to eclecticism.

AFTER YOU READ . . . PRACTICE TEST #4
CURRENT THEORIES

Match the letter of the term in the right column with its description in the left column.

_____ 1.   The study of society using the methods and concepts of biology; an approach that emphasizes genes that aid group survival.

_____ 2.   The socioeconomic context that includes the institutions of the culture that affect children's development indirectly.

_____ 3.   The view that humans possess unique genetic traits that will be manifested in all members of the species, regardless of differences in the environments

_____ 4.   Tasks that are too hard for the child to do alone but that she can manage with guidance.

_____ 5.   The child's genetic make-up and developmental range that affect development.

_____ 6.   Vygotsky's view that complex forms of thinking have their origins in social interactions rather than in an individual's private explorations.

_____ 7.   The use of multiple theoretical perspectives to explain and study human development.

_____ 8.   Emphasized genetically determined survival behaviors presumed to have evolved through natural selection.

a. Behavioral genetics
b. Biological context
c. Ecological
d. Eclecticism
e. Ethology
f. Exosystem
g. Macrosystem
h. Mesosystem
i. Microsystem
j. Nativism
k. Scaffolding
l. Sociobiology
m. Socio-cultural
n. Zone of proximal development

(Check your answers to Practice Test #4 on p. 43.)

COMPARING THEORIES

Assumptions About Development (pp. 43-44)

Objective 2.18: Distinguish between the three assumptions about development.

50.   State at least one theory that views development as each of the following:

Active	
Passive	
Nature	
Nurture	
Continuity	
Discontinuity	

Usefulness (p. 44)

Objective 2.19: List the criteria for the usefulness of a theory.

51.   State at least one theory that fits each criteria of usefulness.

Testability of Theory	
Heuristic Value	
Practical Value	
Explains Facts	

AFTER YOU READ . . . PRACTICE TEST #5
COMPARING THEORIES

Indicate whether each of the following statements is true or false.

_____ 1.   Developmentalists don't think of theories in terms of right or wrong, but, instead, compare theories on the basis of their assumptions and how useful they are in promoting understanding of development.

_____ 2.   Theories that claim a person's actions on the environment are the most important determinants of development are on the passive side.

_____ 3.   All developmental theories, while admitting that both nature and nurture are involved in development, make assumptions about their relative importance.

_____ 4.   Stage theories emphasize a stable, continuous process.

_____ 5.   A theory's assumptions shape the way it is applied in the real world.

_____ 6.   One way to evaluate usefulness is to assess a theory's ability to generate predictions that can be tested using scientific methods.

_____ 7.   A theory's heuristic value is the degree to which it stimulates thinking and research.

_____ 8.   A theory may be deemed to have heuristic value if it provides solutions to problems.

(Check your answers to Practice Test #5 on p. 43.)

AFTER YOU READ . . . CRITICAL REFLECTION EXERCISE

Match the letter of the theoretical perspective in the second column with its description in the first column.

_____ 1.   Behavior is associated with the consequences of our actions.

_____ 2.   Uses multiple theoretical perspectives to explain and study human development.

_____ 3.   Development occurs in a series of stages, based on the libido, through which the child moves in a fixed sequence.

_____ 4.   This theory explains the relationship between people and their environment, or contexts.

_____ 5.   Emotional responses, such as fear, are developed by associations.

_____ 6.   Complex forms of thinking have their origins in social interactions rather than in the child's private explorations.

_____ 7.   This theory proposes links between physiological processes and development.

_____ 8.   The goal of the theory is to explain how the mind manages information.

_____ 9.   Focus of the theory is on the development of logical thinking.

_____ 10. Learning can occur by watching others

a. Psychoanalytic (Freud)
b. Psychoanalytic (Erikson)
c. Classical Conditioning
d. Operant Conditioning
e. Bandura's Social-Learning
f. Piaget's Cognitive-Developmental
g. Information-Processing
h. Biological
i. Vygotsky's Socio-Cultural
j. Bronfenbrenner's Ecological
k. Eclecticism

(Check your answers to on p. 43.)

AFTER YOU READ . . . COMPREHENSIVE PRACTICE TEST
MULTIPLE CHOICE QUESTIONS

1. **Each of the following terms is used in Freud's theory of development EXCEPT:**
   a.   psychosocial stages
   b.   ego development
   c.   id integrity
   d.   psychosexual stages

2. **Erikson's theory differed from Freud's in that Erikson _____.**
   a.   emphasized instincts more heavily than Freud
   b.   believed that our urges are primarily destructive
   c.   believed that development continued throughout the lifespan
   d.   is considered more pessimistic than Freud

3. **Which of the following is a weakness of the psychoanalytic theories?**
   a.   They are hard to test and measure.
   b.   They provide helpful concepts, such as the unconscious, that are part of everyday language.
   c.   They invented psychotherapy.
   d.   They focus on the emotional quality of the child's earliest relationship with caregivers.

4. **Whenever the eye doctor puffs air in your eye, you blink. Now, before she puffs the air, she says "ready," puffs the air, and you blink. After doing this several times, you begin to blink as soon as she says "ready." In this example, what kind of learning has taken place?**
   a.   classical conditioning
   b.   sensitization
   c.   operant conditioning
   d.   habituation

5. **What is the conditioned stimulus in the previous question?**
   a.   blinking of the eye
   b.   saying the word "ready"
   c.   the puff of air
   d.   fear of the puff of air

6. **Which of the following is an example of shaping?**
   a.   paying your son for mowing the lawn
   b.   praising your son for his good grades
   c.   reinforcing each step of your son's behavior during toilet training
   d.   withholding allowance from your son when he talks back

7. **Bandura suggests that learning can take place without direct reinforcement. What is this type of learning called?**
   a.   positive reinforcement
   b.   modeling
   c.   instrumental conditioning
   d.   classical conditioning

8. **You learn how to drive a car with an automatic transmission, then you try to drive a car with standard transmission. The adjustment you make is an example of the process of:**
   a. equilibration
   b. assimilation
   c. accommodation
   d. hierarchical categorizing

9. **Chris is in elementary school and has learned to solve problems logically. Which of Piaget's stages best describes her level of cognitive development?**
   a. concrete operational
   b. sensorimotor
   c. preoperational
   d. formal operational

10. **Which of the following is the goal of information-processing theory?**
    a. to distinguish the relative impact of nature and nurture
    b. to trace the stages of how thinking develops
    c. to uncover the hidden meaning of dreams
    d. to explain how the mind manages information

11. **Which of these theories focuses on the study of the role of heredity in individual differences?**
    a. behavior genetics
    b. nativism
    c. psychoanalytic
    d. sociobiology

12. **Arrange the following contexts of Bronfenbrenner's Ecological Theory in the proper order, from the largest circle to the smallest.**
    a. macrosystem, exosystem, microsystem, biological context
    b. microsystem, biological context, macrosystem, exosystem
    c. biological context, exosystem, microsystem, macrosystem
    d. macrosystem, biological context, microsystem, exosystem

13. **Which of the following theories is most likely to be influenced by nature rather than nurture?**
    a. Freud's Psychosexual Theory
    b. Classical Conditioning
    c. Operant Conditioning
    d. Piaget's Cognitive Developmental Theory

14. **In which of the following theories is a person most likely to be a passive participant in her own environment?**
    a. Information-Processing Theory
    b. Social-Learning Theory
    c. Cognitive-Developmental Theory
    d. Classical Conditioning

15. **Each of the following is one of the criteria of usefulness listed in the text EXCEPT:**
    a. Does it stimulate thinking and research?
    b. Does it explain the basic facts of development?
    c. Does it explain a person's motivation for their behavior?
    d. Does it generate predictions that can be tested with scientific methods?

TRUE-FALSE QUESTIONS

Indicate whether each of the following statements is true or false.

_____ 1.   Defense mechanisms lessen the pain of anxiety, but they do not cure the problem.

_____ 2.   Erikson believed that children whose early care has been erratic or harsh may develop mistrust.

_____ 3.   In classical conditioning, the conditioned response is seldom similar to the unconditioned response.

_____ 4.   Positive reinforcement strengthens behavior, negative reinforcement weakens behavior, and punishment eliminates behavior altogether.

_____ 5.   Assimilation is the process of using schemes to make sense of experiences.

_____ 6.   The three components of human memory are sensory memory, short-term memory, and long-term memory.

_____ 7.   In Vygotsky's theory, scaffolding means developing a firm sense of self-identity.

_____ 8.   By adopting an eclectic approach, developmentalists' theories and studies may more closely match the behavior of real people in real situations.

ESSAY QUESTIONS

1.   Describe each of Freud's five stages of development, giving the ages, sources of conflict and possible solutions, with their accompanying impact on adult behavior.

2.   Explain the major differences between classic conditioning and operant conditioning.

3.   Provide an example of each of the following as they apply to Piaget's theory of cognitive development: schemes, assimilation, and accommodation.

(Check your answers to the Comprehensive Practice Test on pp. 43-44.)

WHEN YOU HAVE FINISHED . . . PUZZLE IT OUT

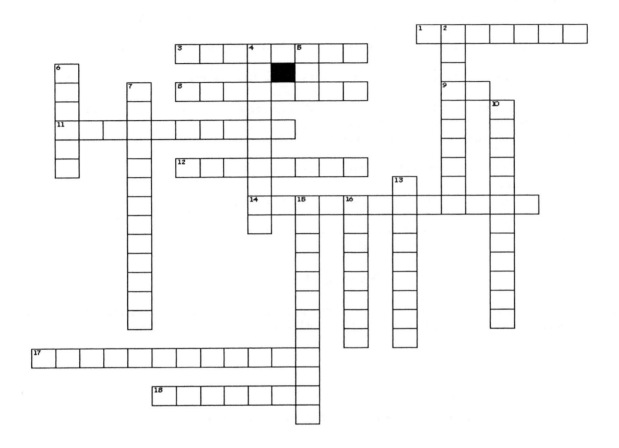

Across

1. Conditioning by learning consequences
3. Part of the personality that is the moral judge
8. Emphasizes genetically determined survival behaviors
9. Motivates the person to seek pleasure and avoid pain
11. Gradual elimination through repeated nonreinforcement
12. View that all humans posses unique genetic traits
14. Using a scheme to make sense of an event
17. Freud's stages
18. Reinforcement of intermediate steps

Down

2. Causes behavior to stop
4. Relationship between individuals and their environments
5. The thinking element of the personality
6. A procedure to use in a specific circumstance
7. Causes behavior to be repeated
10. Erikson's stages
13. Conditioning by learning from the association of stimuli
15. Emphasizes genes that aid group survival
16. Learning from seeing others reinforced

Created by Puzzlemaker at DiscoverySchool.com

(Check your answers on p. 44.)

CHAPTER 2 ANSWER KEY

Practice Test #1 Psychoanalytic Theories

1. a	2. d	3. c	4. b	5. d	6. b	7. b	8. c

Practice Test #2 Learning Theories

1. c	2. c	3. a	4. b	5. d	6. c	7. a

Practice Test #3 Cognitive Theories

1. b	2. d	3. b	4. b	5. d	6. d	7. b

Practice Test #4 Current Trends

1. l	2. f	3. j	4. n	5. b	6. m	7. d	8. e

Practice Test #5 Comparing Theories

1. T	2. F	3. T	4. F	5. T	6. T	7. T	8. F

Critical Reflection Exercise

1. d	2. k	3. a	4. j	5. c	6. i	7. h	8. g	9. f	10. e

Comprehensive Practice Test

Multiple Choice Questions

1. a	2. c	3. a	4. a	5. b	6. c	7. b	8. c	9. a	10. d
11. a	12. a	13. a	14. d	15. c					

True-False Questions

1. T	2. T	3. F	4. F	5. T	6. T	7. F	8. T

Essay Questions

1.
   - Stage 1, Oral Stage, birth to about 12 months. Conflict is weaning: too little or too much gratification. As an adult, may be either dependent, gullible, and overly optimistic or extremely pessimistic, sarcastic, hostile, and aggressive. Also tend to eat, drink, smoke, and talk too much.
   - Stage 2, Anal Stage, 1-3 years. Conflict is toilet training: If too harsh or too lenient the child will become fixated. As an adult, if anal retentive, they will be overly clean, neat, stingy, precise, and may become hoarders. If anal expulsive as an adult, will be sloppy, rebellious, hostile, and destructive.
   - Stage 3, Phallic Stage, 3-6 years. Conflict is resolving Oedipus or Electra complex. Child develop s a conscience and imprints on the same-sex parent so that they may achieve a healthy heterosexual relationship as an adult. As an adult, they will be vain, reckless, sexually dysfunctional, or sexually deviant.
   - Stage 4, Latency, 6-12 years. No conflict.
   - Stage 4, Genital, 12+ years. No conflict. Adults who have successfully integrated earlier stages should emerge with sincere interest in others and mature sexually.

2.
   - In classical conditioning an association is formed between two stimuli; in operant conditioning the association is established between a response and its consequences.
   - In classical conditioning the subject is generally passive and reacts to the environment; in operant conditioning, the subject is active and operates on some aspect of the environment.
   - The range of responses in classical conditioning is relative simple; responses involved in operant conditioning are simple to highly complex.

- The types of conditioned responses in classical conditioning are generally associated with emotions; operant responses are goal-oriented.
- Classically conditioned responses are reflexive; operant responses are voluntary.

3.
- Schemes: When you pick up a ball, you use your picking-up scheme. When you throw it to someone, you use your looking scheme, your aiming scheme, and your throwing scheme.
- Assimilation: When a baby grasps a toy, she is assimilating it to her grasping scheme.
- Accommodation: When a baby grasps a square toy for the first time, he will accommodate his grasping scheme; the next time he reaches for a square object, his hand will be more appropriately bent to grasp it.

Puzzle It Out

Across
1. Operant
3. Superego
8. Ethology
9. Id
11. Extinction
12. Nativism
14. Assimilation
17. Psychosexual
18. Shaping

Down
2. Punishment
4. Ecological
5. Ego
6. Scheme
7. Reinforcement
10. Psychosocial
13. Classical
15. Sociobiology
16. Modeling

CHAPTER 3

PRENATAL DEVELOPMENT AND BIRTH

BEFORE YOU READ . . . CHAPTER SUMMARY

Human development begins with the genes and chromosomes passed on to the new individual at the moment of conception and it is impacted by the prenatal environment. From conception to birth, prenatal development follows a truly amazing course that begins with a single cell and ends with a crying, but curious, newborn making his or her debut in the outside world.

Conception and Genetics

- The first step in the development of an individual human being happens at conception when a sperm fertilizes an ovum (egg cell). Fraternal twins come from two eggs that are fertilized by two separate sperm; identical twins result when a single fertilized ovum separates into two parts and each develops into a separate individual. Assisted reproductive techniques are available to couples who have trouble conceiving.
- At conception, the combination of genes from the father in the sperm and the mother in the ovum creates a unique genetic blueprint, the genotype, that characterizes the individual. The phenotype is comprised of an individual's actual characteristics. The simplest set of genetic rules is the dominant-recessive pattern in which a single dominant gene strongly influences phenotype.

Pregnancy and Prenatal Development

- Pregnancy is a physical condition in which a woman's body is nurturing a developing embryo or fetus. Prenatal development, or gestation, is the process that transforms a zygote into a newborn. Pregnancy is usually divided into trimesters, three periods of three months each. The three stages of prenatal development are defined by specific developmental milestones and are not of equal length.
- Because prenatal development is strongly influenced by maturational codes that are the same for both males and females, there are only a few sex differences in prenatal development.
- Prenatal behavior includes fetal responses to music and other stimuli. Fetal learning is the subject of research to determine what fetuses can learn and how the learning may affect later development.

Problems in Prenatal Development

- Many disorders appear to be transmitted through the operation of dominant and recessive genes. Autosomal disorders are caused by genes located on the autosomes; the genes that cause sex-linked disorders are found on the X chromosome.
- A variety of problems can be caused when a child has too many or too few chromosomes, a conditional referred to as chromosomal error or chromosomal anomaly.
- Deviations in prenatal development can result from exposure to teratogens, substances that cause damage to an embryo or fetus. The general rule is that each organ system is most vulnerable to harm at the time when it is developing most rapidly. Teratogens included maternal diseases, such as rubella and HIV, and drugs, such as nicotine and alcohol.
- The mother's diet, her age, and her mental and physical health can also adversely affect prenatal development.
- Medical tests, such as chorionic villus sampling and amniocentesis, are used to identify problems prenatally.

Birth and the Neonate

- Once gestation is complete, the fetus must be born into the world. In industrialized countries, especially in the United States, parents have several choices including birth attendants, whether or not to use drugs during delivery, and the location of the birth.
- Labor is typically divided into three stages. Stage 1 covers dilation and effacement, stage 2 is the delivery of the baby, and stage 3 is the delivery of the placenta and other material from the uterus.
- A baby is referred to as a neonate for the first month following birth. The health of the neonate is assessed with the Apgar scale at one minute and five minutes after birth. The Brazelton Neonatal Behavioral Assessment Scale is used to track a newborn's development over the first two weeks or so following birth.
- Classification of a neonate's weight is another important factor in assessment. All neonates below 2500 grams, about 5.5 pounds, are classified as low birth weight (LBW). Most LBW infants are preterm, born before the 38th week of gestation; infants that are small-for-date have completed 38 weeks or more of gestation but are still LBW.

AS YOU READ . . . LEARNING OBJECTIVES

After completing Chapter 3, you should be able to:

3.1   Explain the process of reproduction.
3.2   Summarize the results of research on twin studies.
3.3   Summarize the impact of genetics on inheritance.
3.4   Describe the mother's experience during the three trimesters of pregnancy.
3.5   Outline the milestones of the three stages of prenatal development.
3.6   List some of the sex differences in prenatal development.
3.7   Describe some of the research findings about the behaviors of fetuses.
3.8   Identify some common autosomal disorders and common sex-linked disorders that affect prenatal development.
3.9   Identify common trisomy errors and sex-chromosome anomalies that can affect prenatal development.
3.10   Summarize the effects of maternal diseases on the embryo or the fetus.
3.11   Identify drugs taken by the mother during pregnancy that can cause damage to the child, and describe the symptoms the child might exhibit.
3.12   List and describe other influences on prenatal development.
3.13   Summarize the dilemma associated with pregnant women who have epilepsy.
3.14   List various types of prenatal diagnostic tests to detect fetal abnormalities.
3.15   Summarize the choices about birth that may be available in Western countries.
3.16   List and describe what happens in each of the three stages of labor.
3.17   Summarize the research on infant-directed singing.
3.18   Distinguish between the two tools use to assess the health of infants.
3.19   Describe the risks associated with low birth weight in infants.
3.20   Summarize the pros and cons of the media attention given to multiple births.

AS YOU READ . . . TERM IDENTIFICATION

Amnion (p. 58)
Anoxia (p. 77)
Cephalocaudal pattern (p. 56)
Cesarean section (c-section) (p. 76)
Chromosomes (p. 49)
Deoxyribonucleic acid (DNA) (p. 49)
Dominant-recessive pattern (p. 51)
Embryonic stage (p. 58)
Fetal stage (p. 59)
Gametes (p. 49)

Genes (p. 49)
Genotype (p. 50)
Germinal stage (p. 58)
Glial stage (p. 59)
Gonads (p. 58)
Low birth weight (LBW) (p. 78)
Multi-factorial inheritance (p. 53)
Neonate (p. 78)
Neurons (p. 58)

Organogenesis (p. 59)
Phenotype (p. 50)
Placenta (p. 58)
Polygenic inheritance (p. 53)
Proximodistal pattern (p. 58)
Teratogens (p. 64)
Umbilical cord (p. 58)
Viability (p. 59)
Zygote (p. 49)

AS YOU READ . . . GUIDED STUDY QUESTIONS

CONCEPTION AND GENETICS

The Process of Conception (pp. 49-50)

Objective 3.1: Explain the process of reproduction.

1.   Trace the paths of the ovum and the sperm in the process of fertilization.

2.   Define the following terms:
        a.   chromosomes (p. 49)

        b.   gametes (p. 49)

        c.   zygote (p. 49)

        d.   deoxyribonucleic acid (DNA) (p. 49)

        e.   gene (p. 49)

3.   Explain how the sex of a zygote is determined.

4.   Distinguish between the following terms:
        a.   fraternal twins (dizygotic)

        b.   identical twins (monozygotic)

5.   Identical twins are always the same sex. Why?

6.   List two factors that underlie the association between multiple birth rate and maternal age.

Research Report: Twins in Genetic Research (p. 50)

Objective 3.2: Summarize the results of research on twin studies.

7.   What do twin studies tell us about the impact of environment on development?

Genotypes, Phenotypes, and Patterns of Inheritance (pp. 50-54)

Objective 3.3: Summarize the impact of genetics on inheritance.

8.   Define the following terms:

    a.   genotype (p. 50)

    b.   phenotype (p. 50)

    c.   dominant-recessive pattern of inheritance (p. 51)

9.   Distinguish between homozygous and heterozygous.

10.   Explain how a child's phenotype is influenced by the inheritance of a dominant gene. How does that differ from the inheritance of a recessive gene? Give examples.

11.   Explain the impact of expressivity on phenotypes. Give examples.

12.   Define polygenic inheritance (p. 53), and give examples of polygenic traits in which the dominant-recessive pattern is at work.

13.   What is genomic imprinting? Describe the different effects a defective gene on chromosome 15 will have if it is inherited from the mother or from the father.

14.   How does mitochondrial inheritance differ from other types of inheritance patterns?

15.   Define multi-factorial inheritance (p. 54).

16.   List five general principles proposed by Rutter that help explain how genes and the environment work together to produce variations in traits.

AFTER YOU READ . . . PRACTICE TEST #1
CONCEPTION AND GENETICS

1.   Conception typically takes place in the _____.

    a.   uterus
    b.   womb
    c.   fallopian tube
    d.   ovary

2. **Zygotes containing _____ develop into females.**
   a. DNA
   b. one X and one Y chromosome
   c. two X chromosomes
   d. 23 single chromosomes

3. **All of the following statements about multiple births are true EXCEPT:**
   a. Women who use fertility-enhancing drugs are more likely to have multiple births than a single birth.
   b. Over 75% of twins are monozygotic twins.
   c. Women over age 35 are more likely to conceive twins and other multiples.
   d. The annual number of multiple births has increased in the United States in the past 25 years.

4. **People who carry one dominant and one recessive gene are said to be _____.**
   a. homozygous
   b. dizygotic
   c. monozygotic
   d. heterozygous

5. **The degree to which any gene influences phenotypes varies from person to person. This is called _____.**
   a. expressivity
   b. dominance
   c. recessiveness
   d. co-dominant

6. **_____ is the pattern of inheritance in which many genes influence a trait.**
   a. mitochondrial inheritance
   b. co-dominance
   c. expressivity
   d. polygenic inheritance

7. **In _____, children inherit genes that are passed only from the mother to the child.**
   a. Angelman syndrome
   b. mitochondrial inheritance
   c. co-dominance
   d. multi-factorial inheritance

(Check your answers to Practice Test #1 on p. 67.)

PREGNANCY AND PRENATAL DEVELOPMENT

The Mother's Experience (pp. 54-56)

Objective 3.4: Describe the mother's experience during the three trimesters of pregnancy.

17. Distinguish between pregnancy and prenatal development.

18.   Summarize the events, discomforts, prenatal care needed, and serious problems frequently associated with each trimester of pregnancy.

Trimester Begins/Ends	Events	Discomforts	Prenatal Care	Serious Problems
First				
Second				
Third				

19.   Why is prenatal care during the first trimester critical to the prevention of birth defects?

Prenatal Development (pp. 56-60)

Objective 3.5: Outline the milestones of the three stages of prenatal development.

20.   Define the following terms:
    a.   cephalocaudal principle (p. 56)

    b.   proximodistal principle (p. 58)

    c.   germinal stage (p. 58)

    d.   placenta (p. 58)

    e.   umbilical cord (p. 58)

    f.   amnion (p. 58)

    g.   embryonic stage (p. 58)

    h.   neurons (p. 58)

    i.   gonads (p. 58)

    j.   organogenesis (p. 59)

k.   fetal stage (p. 59)

l.   glial cells (p. 59)

m.   viability (p. 59)

21.   Summarize the major events in each prenatal stage, and indicate when they occur.

Prenatal Stage Begins/Ends	*Major Events*
Germinal	
Embryonic	
Fetal	

Sex Differences (pp. 60-61)

Objective 3.6: List some of the sex differences in prenatal development.

22.   Why are there only a few sex differences in prenatal development?

23.   List some of the documented sex differences in prenatal development.

Prenatal Behavior (pp. 61-62)

Objective 3.7: Describe some of the research findings about the behaviors of fetuses.

24.   List some of the documented behaviors of fetuses.

AFTER YOU READ . . . PRACTICE TEST #2
PREGNANCY AND PRENATAL DEVELOPMENT

1.   **If a zygote implants in the fallopian tubes instead of the uterus, the condition is called _____.**
    a.   a spontaneous abortion
    b.   a miscarriage
    c.   morning sickness
    d.   an ectopic pregnancy

2.   **A type of diabetes that happens only during pregnancy is called _____ diabetes.**
    a.   gestational
    b.   vaginal
    c.   temporary
    d.   pregnancy

3.   **A sudden increase in blood pressure that can cause a pregnant woman to have a stroke is called _____.**
    a.   spontaneous abortion
    b.   toxemia of pregnancy
    c.   morning sickness
    d.   ectopic pregnancy

4.   **_____ is the term for the pattern of growth that proceeds from the head downward.**
    a.   Amniotic pattern
    b.   Blastocyst pattern
    c.   Proximodistal pattern
    d.   Cephalocaudal pattern

5.   **The brain and the spinal cord develop from the _____.**
    a.   gonads
    b.   glial cells
    c.   yolk sac
    d.   neural tube

6.   **The ability of the fetus to live outside the womb is called _____.**
    a.   organogenesis
    b.   viability
    c.   engagement
    d.   the cephalocaudal pattern

7.   **Which statement is TRUE about the behavior of fetuses?**
    a.   Newborns do not remember stimuli to which they were exposed prenatally.
    b.   Fetuses can distinguish between familiar and novel stimuli as early as the 20th week.
    c.   Prenatal behavior is stable in male fetuses but not in female fetuses.
    d.   Fetuses respond to sounds and vibrations with heart rate changes, head turns, and body movements.

(Check your answers to Practice Test #2 on p. 67.)

PROBLEMS IN PRENATAL DEVELOPMENT

Genetic Disorders (pp. 62-63)

Objective 3.8: *Identify some common autosomal disorders and common sex-linked disorders that affect prenatal development.*

25. Indicate whether each of the following disorders that is caused by the dominant-recessive pattern of inheritance is autosomal or sex-linked, and list the symptoms for the disorder:

Disease	*Autosomal or Sex-linked*	*Symptoms*
Fragile-X Syndrome		
Hemophilia		
Huntington's Disease		
Phenylketonuria (PKU)		
Red-Green Color Blindness		
Sickle-Cell Disease		
Sickle-Cell Trait		
Tay-Sachs Disease		

Chromosomal Errors (pp. 63-64)

Objective 3.9: *Identify common trisomy errors and sex-chromosome anomalies that can affect prenatal development.*

26. Indicate whether the likelihood of each of the following disorders is influenced by the mother's age, and list the symptoms for the disorder:

Disease	*Influenced by Mother's Age?*	*Symptoms*
Klinefelter's syndrome (XXY)		
Turner's syndrome (XO)		
Extra X Chromosome (XXX)		
Extra Y Chromosome (XYY)		

Teratogens: Maternal Diseases (pp. 64-66)

Objective 3.10: Summarize the effects of maternal diseases on the embryo or the fetus.

27.   Define teratogen (p. 64).

28.   Complete the following table.

Teratogen	When Most Vulnerable?	Symptoms
Cytomegalovirus		
Genital herpes		
Gonorrhea		
HIV		
Rubella		
Syphilis		

29.   The general rule is that each organ system is most vulnerable to harm when it is developing most rapidly Why does this make the first eight weeks of gestation the period of greatest risk for most teratogens?

Teratogens: Drugs (pp. 66-68)

Objective 3.11: Identify drugs taken by the mother during pregnancy that can cause damage to the child, and describe the symptoms the child might exhibit.

30.   List symptoms of each of the following teratogens:

Teratogen	Symptom
Cocaine	
Drinking Alcohol	
Marijuana and Heroin	
Smoking	

Other Maternal Influences on Prenatal Development (pp. 68-70)

Objective 3.12: List and describe other influences on prenatal development.

31.   Summarize the potential problems to the developing fetus if the mother's diet is inadequate in specific nutrients.

32.   Describe the problems if the mother has insufficient overall calories and protein.

33.   Why is the impact of maternal malnutrition greatest on the developing nervous system? (Hint: Consider the principles of development.)

34.   List several problems to the fetus which are associated with the mother's age (over 30 and young teens).

35.   List several problems that are associated with the mother's chronic illness (emotional and physical).

36.   List and describe 8 environmental hazards to prenatal development.

Hazard	Description

37.   The fetuses of severely distressed mothers tend to grow more slowly than others. What are some possible explanations?

No Easy Answers: Pregnancy, Epilepsy, and Anti-Convulsant Drugs (p. 71)

Objective 3.13: Summarize the dilemma associated with pregnant women who have epilepsy.

38.   What are the risks of untreated epilepsy? What are the risks of using anticonvulsant drugs during pregnancy?

Fetal Assessment and Treatment (pp. 71-72)

Objective 3.14: List various types of prenatal diagnostic tests to detect fetal abnormalities.

39.   List the assessment tests that can indicate chromosomal errors and many genetic disorders before birth.

AFTER YOU READ . . .PRACTICED TEST #3
PROBLEMS IN PRENATAL DEVELOPMENT

1.   **Each of the following is a sexually transmitted disease that may cause birth defects EXCEPT:**
    a.   rubella
    b.   syphilis
    c.   cytomegalovirus
    d   genital herpes

2.   **All of the following statement about smoking during pregnancy are true EXCEPT:**
    a.   Prenatal exposure to tobacco may have long-term effects on children's development.
    b.   There may be higher rates of learning problems and anti-social behavior among children whose mothers smoked during pregnancy.
    c.   Children of mothers who smoked during pregnancy are more likely than their schoolmates to be diagnosed with attention deficit hyperactivity disorder (ADHD).
    d.   Infants of mothers who smoke are on average half a pound heavier at birth than infants of nonsmoking mothers.

3.   **The most frequently used illegal drug the world over is _____.**
    a.   cocaine
    b.   heroin
    c.   marijuana
    d   "crack" cocaine

4.   **_____ is caused by inadequate amounts of folic acid during prenatal development.**
    a.   Brain stunting
    b.   Turner's syndrome
    c.   Spina bifida
    d   Cytomegalovirus

5.   **Each of the following may be an environmental hazard on prenatal development EXCEPT:**
    a.   mercury
    b.   lead
    c.   epilepsy
    d   parasite-bearing substances

6.   **_____ can be used to identify chromosomal errors and many genetic disorders prior to birth.**
    a.   Fetoscopy and amniocentesis
    b.   Chorionic villus sampling (CVS) and ultrasonography
    c.   Ultrasonography and fetoscopy
    d   Chorionic villus sampling (CVS) and amniocentesis

(Check your answers to Practice Test #3 on p. 67.)

BIRTH AND THE NEONATE

Birth Choices (pp. 72-74)

Objective 3.15: Summarize the choices about birth that may be available in Western countries.

40.   Distinguish between certified nurse-midwives and certified midwives.

41.   Distinguish among the following drugs that may be used during delivery by completing the following table.

Medication	Purpose
Analgesics	
Sedatives or Tranquilizers	
Anesthetics	

42.   Describe how natural childbirth, such as the Lamaze method, helps women avoid drugs during delivery.

43.   Describe four available options for the location of the birth.

The Physical Process of Birth (pp. 74-78)

Objective 3.16: List and describe what happens in each of the three stages of labor.

44.   List the length of each of the phases of stage 1 of labor, and the major events occurring in that phase.

Phase	Approximate Length of Stage	Major Events
Early		
Active		
Transition		

45.   List some complications of the process of birth.

46.   Define cesarean section (c-section) (p. 76), and list several situations that justify its use.

47.   Define anoxia (p. 77).

The Real World: Singing to Your Newborn (p. 77)

Objective 3.17: Summarize the research on infant-directed singing.

48.   List the two categories of infant-directed singing, and give examples of each.

49.   List the important contributions of infant-directed singing to babies' development in each of the following areas:
        a.   preterm infants

        b.   language development

        c.   attachment

Assessing the Neonate (p. 78)

Objective 3.18: Distinguish between the two tools use to assess the health of infants.

50.   Define neonate (p. 78).

51.   Distinguish between the following scales of assessment of the neonate:
        a.   Apgar Scale

        b.   Brazelton Neonatal Behavioral Assessment Scale

Low Birth Weight (pp. 78-80)

Objective 3.19: Describe the risks associated with low birth weight in infants.

52.   Define low birth weight (LBW) (p. 78).

53.   Distinguish between preterm neonates and small-for-date neonates.

54.   What are some factors that may impact a low-birth-weight neonate's chances of catching up to his normal peers within the first few years of life?

Development in the Information Age: The Youngest Celebrities (p. 79)

Objective 3.20: Summarize the pros and cons of the media attention given to multiple births.

55.   List some concerns health professionals may have about the media attention given to multiple births.

AFTER YOU READ . . . PRACTICE TEST #4
BIRTH AND THE NEONATE

Match the letter of the term in the right column with its description in the left column.

_____ 1. Often called the Lamaze method.

_____ 2. Another name for hyaline membrane disease.

_____ 3. An infant's feet or bottom are delivered first.

_____ 4. The delivery of the placenta.

_____ 5. Neonates born before the 38th week of gestation.

_____ 6. The flattening out of the cervix.

_____ 7. When used, is usually given later in labor to block pain.

_____ 8. The phase of labor during which the last two centimeters of the cervix are dilated.

_____ 9. Tracks a newborn's development over about the first two weeks following birth.

_____ 10. Oxygen deprivation to the fetus during delivery that can result in death or brain damage.

a. Active phase
b. Afterbirth
c. Analgesics
d. Anesthesia
e. Anoxia
f. Apgar Scale
g. Brazelton Neonatal Behavioral Assessment
h. Breech presentation
i. Dilation
j. Early phase
k. Effacement
l. Low birth weight
m. Natural childbirth
n. Preterm
o. Respiratory distress syndrome
p. Sedatives
q. Small-for-date neonates
r. Transition phase

(Check your answers to Practice Test #4 on p. 67.)

AFTER YOU READ . . .CRITICAL REFLECTION EXERCISES

Healthy Pregnancies

Imagine you have a friend who has just discovered that she is pregnant. She is taking a lifespan development course, and they are discussing all of the things that can "go wrong" during prenatal development. She is worried that the chances of her baby being born healthy are very slim. Utilizing information from this chapter, answer the following questions from your friend:

1.   What things can I do to minimize the risks to my developing baby? (Provide at least four examples for your friend.)

2.   What if my baby is born "low birth weight?" Is there anything I can do to minimize the long-term effects of this? (Provide at least three examples for your friend.)

3.   How much smoking or drinking can I do while pregnant? Is there a "critical period" during which the effects of these would be most harmful?

Genotype Versus Phenotype

Utilizing the information from the text, indicate if each statement illustrates "Genotype," "Phenotype," or the "Interaction" between genotype and the environment.

_____   1.   The observed characteristics of the person.

_____   2.   The genetic material received from the mother and father.

_____   3.   Observable sexual characteristics.

_____   4.   Developmental limits.

_____   5.   Developmental patterns within developmental limits.

_____   6.   Eye color.

_____   7.   Measured intelligence.

(Check your answers on o. 69.)

AFTER YOU READ . . . COMPREHENSIVE PRACTICE TEST
MULTIPLE CHOICE QUESTIONS

1. **Gametes contain _____.**
    a.   23 pairs of chromosomes
    b.   23 unpaired chromosomes
    c.   only autosomes
    d.   46 chromosomes

2. **An individual's particular set of observed characteristics is called _____.**
    a.   phenotype
    b.   a chromosome
    c.   a gamete
    d.   genotype

3. **Which statement is TRUE about recessive genes?**
    a.   They are not a part of one's genotype.
    b.   They can be passed on genetically.
    c.   They are related only to physical characteristics.
    d.   They are related to inherited diseases.

4. **Each of the following is one of the general principles proposed by Rutter about multi-factorial inheritance EXCEPT:**
    a.   People act on their environment so as to shape and select their experience.
    b.   The interplay between persons and their environments needs to be considered within an ecological framework.
    c.   People are passive recipients of environmental forces.
    d.   Individuals differ in their reactivity to the environment.

5. **Which of the following statements about pregnancy is TRUE?**
    a.   Pregnancy is a physical condition in which a woman's body is nurturing a developing embryo or fetus.
    b.   Pregnancy is the process that transforms a zygote into a newborn.
    c.   Pregnancy is divided into three stages that are defined by specific developmental milestones.
    d.   Pregnancy begins when ovulation occurs.

6. **The three stages of prenatal development, in order, are _____.**
    a.   germinal, embryonic, fetal
    b.   viability, organogenesis, germinal
    c.   embryonic, fetal, viability
    d.   embryonic, germinal, fetal

7. **Which statement most accurately represents the sex differences in prenatal development?**
    a.   There are numerous sex differences in prenatal development.
    b.   Female fetuses are more active than male fetuses.
    c.   There are only a few sex differences in prenatal development.
    d.   Male fetuses are more sensitive to external stimuli than female fetuses.

8. **Which statement correctly illustrates sex-linked transmission?**
    a.   A girl inherits hemophilia from the father.
    b.   A boy inherits hemophilia from the mother.
    c.   A girl inherits hemophilia from both parents.
    d.   A boy inherits hemophilia from both parents.

9. **An anomaly in which a girl receives only one X chromosome and no Y chromosome is called _____.**
    a.   Klinefelter's syndrome
    b.   Turner's syndrome
    c.   fragile-X syndrome
    d.   Tay-Sachs disease

10. **Which of the following diseases is most likely to cause damage to the embryo or fetus early in prenatal development?**
    a.   syphilis
    b.   gonorrhea
    c.   rubella
    d.   cytomegalovirus

11. **At what age does the risk for complications in pregnancy increase significantly?**
    a.   25
    b.   30
    c.   35
    d.   40

12. **Which of the following medications is sometimes used during the transition period or the second stage of labor to block pain?**
    a.   analgesic
    b.   sedative
    c.   anesthesia
    d.   tranquilizer

13. **During which stage of labor will the actual delivery take place?**
    a.   second
    b.   transition
    c.   third
    d.   first

14. **Which of the following is used immediately after birth to assess the neonate's health?**
    a.   Brazelton Neonatal Behavioral Assessment Scale
    b.   chorionic villus sampling
    c.   Apgar scale
    d.   alpha-fetoprotein sampling

15. **Which statement is TRUE about low-birth-weight babies?**
    a.   Low-birth-weight girls are more likely to show long-term effects than boys.
    b.   Low-birth-weight infants show markedly lower levels of responsiveness.
    c.   Most low-birth-weight babies never catch up to their normal peers.
    d.   Low-birth-weight is not related to the neonate's health.

TRUE-FALSE QUESTIONS

Indicate whether each of the following statements is true or false.

_____ 1.   Monozygotic twins will always be the same sex.

_____ 2.   The implications of genomic imprinting will be different if the defective gene is from the father or from the mother.

_____ 3.   The technical term for organ development is organogenesis.

_____ 4.   Most experts accept 23 weeks as the average age of viability.

_____ 5.   The most common trisomy is trisomy 21, or Down syndrome.

_____ 6.   Problems resulting from fetal alcohol syndrome seldom persist past infancy.

_____ 7.   Anoxia can result in death or brain damage.

_____ 8.   It is impossible for an infant to have completed 38 weeks or more of gestation and still be a low-birth-weight baby.

ESSAY QUESTIONS

1.   Explain why it is important for women to begin receiving prenatal care during the first trimester.

2.   List at least four different kinds of teratogens and describe the effect they may have on prenatal development.

3.   Describe and give examples of the problems caused when an infant is a low-birth-weight baby.

(Check your answers to the Comprehensive Practice Test on p. 67.)

WHEN YOU HAVE FINISHED . . . PUZZLE IT OUT

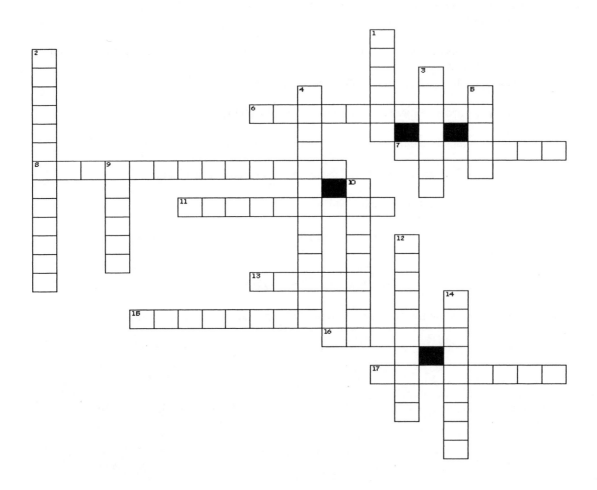

Across
6. Strings of genetic material
7. Cells that unite at conception
8. Process of organ development
11. Second stage of prenatal development
13. Third stage of prenatal development
15. First stage of prenatal development
16. Single cell created when sperm and ovum unite
17. The unique genetic blueprint of each individual

Down
1. Fluid-filled sac in which the fetus floats
2. Growth from the head downward
3. Term for a baby between birth and one month of age
4. Growth from the middle of the body outward
5. Pieces of genetic material that influence traits
9. Oxygen deprivation experienced by a fetus
10. Ability of the fetus to survive outside the womb
12. Substances that can cause birth defects
14. Observed characteristics of an individual

Created by Puzzlemaker at DiscoverySchool.com

(Check your answers on p. 68.)

WHEN YOU HAVE FINISHED . . . INVESTIGATIVE PROJECT

Student Project 4: Available Prenatal Services

Basic Questions to Answer

The purpose of the project is to discover what kinds of prenatal services are available to poor mothers in your area.

- What programs are available through the public health service, local hospitals, or other clinics?

- What funds are available to support those services from local, state, and federal sources?

- How many women take advantage of such services? Is there a waiting list? Is there any information available about the percentage of local women who receive no prenatal care at all, or receive such care only in the final trimester?

- Has there been any change in the availability of such services in your area in the past decade or two? (This may be difficult to determine, but it is worth a try.)

- What is the infant mortality rate for your state, and for your community? How does this compare to national statistics?

Sources

Some of the statistics may be available through the federal document center at the library. The annual volume, *Statistical Abstract of the United States*, normally has state-by-state figures on infant mortality; more detail may be available through data from the Centers for Disease Control. The December issue of the journal *Pediatrics* also has a summary paper each year. Most states have departments of vital statistics that may be helpful.

For local information, try the city, county, or state public health departments. The Yellow Pages of your local phone book is a good place to start. A visit to the offices of the local public health department is likely to be fruitful. You should of course explain that this is part of a class project, and that you wish to be able to report back to your class.

WHEN YOU HAVE FINISHED . . . INVESTIGATIVE PROJECT

Student Project 5: Investigation of Birth Options

Basic Questions to Answer

- How many of the four main choices of birth options (regular hospital, hospital-based birth center or birthing room, free-standing birthing center, or home delivery) are available in your area? When did non-hospital delivery become available in your area?

- How are the local births distributed among the options?

- What is the relative cost of each option?

- Who sponsors or runs each program? Are the deliveries in the birth center or at home done by midwives? Do midwives deliver babies at hospitals as well?

Sources of Information

The Yellow Pages may be your best first source. If that does not yield information, you might make inquiries of several local obstetricians' offices. You will then need to call hospitals, birthing centers, and midwives for further information, or visit each site to get a firsthand look, and to obtain brochures, etc. At all times you should represent yourself accurately as a student working on a project for a class on human development. Do not present yourself as a pregnant woman looking for a place to deliver. Remember always that your questions may be seen as an intrusion on the busy work days of your respondents, so be sensitive to the demands you are placing on them.

Reporting

Your instructor may want you to report back to the class on your findings, either orally or in writing. In any case, you should prepare a written report of what you did, to whom you talked, and what you found out.

CHAPTER 3 ANSWER KEY

Practice Test #1 Conception and Genetics

1. c   2. c   3. b   4. d   5. a   6. d   7. b

Practice Test #2 Pregnancy and Prenatal Development

1. d   2. a   3. b   4. d   5. d   6. b   7. d

Practice Test #3 Problems in Prenatal Development

1. a   2. d   3. c   4. c   5. c   6. d

Practice Test #4 Birth and the Neonate

1. m   2. o   3. h   4. b   5. n   6. k   7. d   8. r   9. g   10. e

Critical Reflection Exercise: Genotype Versus Phenotype

1. Phenotype   2. Genotype   3. Phenotype   4. Genotype   5. Interaction   6. Genotype   7. Interaction

Comprehensive Practice Test

Multiple Choice Questions

1. b   2. a   3. b   4. c   5. a   6. a   7. c   8. b   9. b   10. c
11. c   12. c   13. a   14. c   15. b

True-False Questions

1. T   2. T   3. T   4. F   5. T   6. F   7. T   8. F

Essay Questions

1.   ■ Identification of maternal conditions that may prevent birth defects.
   - Encouragement by doctors and nurses to abstain from drugs and alcohol early in prenatal development, when such behavior may prevent birth defects.
   - Protection of the woman's health by identification of potential problems, such as ectopic pregnancy.

2.   ■ Autosomal disorders: phenylketonuria (PKU), sickle-cell disease, sickle-cell trait, Tay-Sachs disease, Huntington's disease.
   - Sex-linked disorders: red-green color blindness, hemophilia, fragile-X syndrome.
   - Trimosies: trisomy 21 (Down syndrome).
   - Sex-chromosome anomalies: Klinefelter's syndrome, Turner's syndrome, XXX pattern, XYY pattern.
   - Maternal Disease: rubella, HIV/AIDS, syphilis, genital herpes, gonorrhea, cytomegalovirus.
   - Drugs: smoking tobacco, drinking alcohol (including fetal alcohol syndrome), marijuana, heroin, cocaine.
   - Other Maternal Influences: diet, age, chronic illness, environmental hazards, maternal emotions.

3.   ■ Retarded fetal growth.
   - Lower levels of responsiveness at birth and in the early months of life.
   - Respiratory distress syndrome (or hyaline membrane disease) and other breathing problems.

Puzzle It Out

Across	Down
6. Chromosome	1. Amnion
7. Gametes	2. Cephalocaudal
8. Organogenesis	3. Neonate
11. Embryonic	4. Proximodistal
13. Fetal	5. Genes
15. Germinal	9. Anoxia
16. Zygote	10. Viability
17. Genotype	12. Teratogens
	14. Phenotype

POLICY QUESTION I

SHOULD PREGNANT WOMEN WHO USE ILLICIT DRUGS BE PROSECUTED?

Learning Objective: Summarize the issues about prosecuting pregnant women who use drugs (pp. 82-83).

1.　Define the following terms:
   a.　delivering drugs to a minor
   b.　injury to a child

2.　Specify the issues involved in determining whether a fetus can be considered legally equivalent to a child.

3.　What fairness issues are involved in the controversy?

4.　What are the questions involved with determining the kind of evidence that is required?

5.　What problems are incurred if doctors are required to report drug use by their pregnant patients?

6.　Describe three alternatives to prosecution.

7.　Policies addressing drug use during pregnancy are different in every state. What are the relevant government and institutional policies in your area? Research could include answering the following questions:
   a.　Do hospitals in your area routinely test newborns for drug exposure? If so, how?

   b.　What do doctors in your area do when they suspect a baby's problems are caused by prenatal drug exposure?

   c.　Does your state require doctors to report pregnant women who use drugs to the police or state agency?

   d.　Are there drug rehabilitation programs specifically for pregnant women in your area?

   e.　Has your state prosecuted any women for using drugs while pregnant? What were the details of the case(s)?

   f.　Do you agree or disagree with the way this issue is addressed in your state and city? Why?

CHAPTER 4

PHYSICAL, SENSORY, AND PERCEPTUAL DEVELOPMENT IN INFANCY

BEFORE YOU READ . . . CHAPTER SUMMARY

During the first two years after birth, infants go from being relatively unskilled newborns to toddlers who can move about efficiently, formulate goals and plans, and use words. There are also many important variations across individuals and groups.

Physical Changes

- At birth, the midbrain and the medulla are the most fully developed structures of the brain. Changes in the nervous system in the first two years include dendrite and synaptic development, the "pruning" of synapses, and myelinization of the nerve fibers.
- Adaptive reflexes, such as sucking, help infants survive; primitive reflexes, such as the Moro or startle reflex and the Babinski reflex, disappear in about six months. Visual acuity is poor at birth but improves rapidly in the first year. Neonates move through five states of consciousness in a cycle that lasts about two hours.
- The acquisition of motor skills depends on brain development as well as substantial changes in other body systems, such as the bones, the muscles, the lungs, and the heart.
- Babies depend on the adults in their environments to help them stay healthy. They need the right foods in the right amounts, and they need medical care and immunizations. Sudden infant death syndrome (SIDS) is the most common cause of death in the first year.
- SIDS (sudden infant death syndrome) is a leading cause of death after the first month of life. The infant mortality rate in the United States is highest for African-American and Native-American babies. The relationship between poverty and infant mortality is complex.

Sensory Skills

- Visual acuity and visual tracking skills are relatively poor at birth, but develop rapidly in the first few months.
- Hearing skills, smell, taste, and touch are well developed at birth.

Perceptual Skills

- The nativism/empiricism controversy is a central issue in the study of perceptual development.
- Depth perception is present in at least rudimentary form by three months. The "looking" strategies of newborns seem to be focused on locating objects; after about two months, their focus changes to identifying objects.
- Babies appear to attend to and discriminate among speech contrasts present in all possible languages. Babies also attend to and discriminate among different patterns of sounds, such as melodies or speech inflections.
- Intersensory integration increases dramatically by about five months, whereas cross-modal (intermodal) transfer is probably inborn.

71

AS YOU READ . . . LEARNING OBJECTIVES

After completing Chapter 4, you should be able to:

4.1 Summarize the typical daily routine of a six-month-old baby and a nine-month-old baby.
4.2 Trace the development of the brain and the nervous system during the first two years.
4.3 Summarize the research about the effects of television on the developing brain.
4.4 Describe the reflexes and behavioral states of an infant.
4.5 Describe the development of muscles, bones, lungs, and the heart, and their impact on motor skills during infancy.
4.6 Identify the health issues of infants.
4.7 Identify the factors influencing infant mortality.
4.8 Trace the development of vision during infancy.
4.9 Trace the development of hearing and the other senses.
4.10 Summarize the arguments about perceptual development for the nativist position, the empiricist position, and the interactionist position.
4.11 Describe the "looking" behavior of infants.
4.12 Summarize the research on babies' preferences for attractive faces.
4.13 Describe the "listening" behavior of infants.
4.14 Explain the importance of intersensory integration and cross-modal transfer.
4.15 Summarize the research on when preterm infants catch up with full-term infants.

AS YOU READ . . . TERM IDENTIFICATION

Adaptive reflexes (p. 89)
Auditory acuity (p. 100)
Colic (p. 91)
Cross-modal perception (p. 108)
Dishabituation (p. 103)
Empiricists (p. 102)
Habituation (p. 103)
Infant mortality (p. 96)
Intersensory integration (p. 108)
Myelinization (p. 88)
Nativists (p. 102)

Plasticity (p. 88)
Preference technique (p. 103)
Primitive reflexes (p. 90)
Pruning (p. 87)
Reticular formation (p. 88)
States of consciousness (p. 90)
Sudden infant death syndrome (SIDS) (p. 96)
Synapses (p. 87)
Synaptogenesis (p. 87)
Tracking (p. 99)
Visual acuity (p. 99)

AS YOU READ . . . GUIDED STUDY QUESTIONS

PHYSICAL CHANGES

The Real World: A Day in the Life of Two Babies (p. 86)

Objective 4.1: Summarize the typical daily routine of a six-month-old baby and a nine-month-old baby.

1. How does the daily routine of a six-month-old baby compare to that of a nine-month-old baby?

The Brain and the Nervous System (pp. 87-88)

Objective 4.2: Trace the development of the brain and the nervous system during the first two years.

2. What do the midbrain and the medulla regulate?

3. What are the most fully developed parts of the brain at birth? What is the least-developed part of the brain?

4. Define the following terms:
    a. synapses (p. 87)

    b. synaptogenesis (p. 87)

    c. pruning (p. 87)

    d. plasticity (p. 88)

5. Describe the pattern of brain development (creation of synapses and pruning).

6. List and explain two implications from the information about neurological development.

7. Define the following terms:
    a. myelinization (p. 88)

    b. reticular formation (p. 88)

8. Give examples of how the sequence of myelinization follows both cephalocaudal and proximodistal patterns.

9. When is myelinization most rapid?

Development in the Information Age: Is Television Harmful to the Developing Brain? (p. 89)

Objective 4.3: Summarize the research about the affects of television on the developing brain.

10. List possible flaws in the research about the relationship between television watching and ADHD (attention-deficit hyperactivity disorder).

Reflexes and Behavioral States (pp. 88-91)

Objective 4.4: Describe the reflexes and behavioral states of an infant.

11. Define the following terms:
    a. adaptive reflexes (p. 89)

    b. primitive reflexes (p. 90)

12. Give examples of the two types of reflexes.

13. Weak or absent adaptive reflexes in neonates suggest that _____.

14. Define the following terms:
   a.   states of consciousness (p. 90)

   b.   colic (p. 91)

15. List the states of consciousness, and describe the characteristics of each.

State	Characteristics

16. Describe the differences in an infant's cry for pain, for anger, and for hunger.

17. Research suggests that prompt attention to a crying baby in the first three months actually leads to

_____.

Developing Body Systems and Motor Skills (pp. 91-93)

Objective 4.5: Describe the development of muscles, bones, lungs, and the heart, and their impact on motor skills during infancy.

18. How do bones change during infancy?

19. Explain how motor development is dependent on ossification.

20. Describe the changes in muscle composition during infancy.

21. How is stamina related to the lungs and heart?

22. Trace the development of motor skills by completing the following table:

Age (in months)	Locomotor Skills (Gross Motor Skills)	Nonlocomotor Skills	Manipulative Skills (Fine Motor Skills
1			
2-3			
4-6			

Age (in months)	Locomotor Skills (Gross Motor Skills)	Nonlocomotor Skills	Manipulative Skills (Fine Motor Skills
7-9			
10-12			
13-18			

23. The _____ of motor skill development is virtually the same for all children, even those with serious physical or mental handicaps.

24. List some gender differences during infancy.

Health and Wellness (pp. 93-96)

Objective 4.6: Identify the health issues of infants.

25. What are the benefits of breast milk over bottle-feeding?

26. Describe some special circumstances in which breast milk may need to be supplemented or replaced?

27. How can malnutrition in infancy impair an infant's brain?

28. Define the following terms and describe how each is harmful to children:

Nutritional Problem	Definition	Potential Harm to Child
Macronutrient Malnutrition		
Marasmus		
Kwashikor		
Micronutrient Malnutrition		

29. List the immunizations included in a "full set."

30. How can the timing of respiratory infections that lead to ear infections be important?

Infant Mortality (pp. 96-98)

Objective 4.7: Identify the factors influencing infant mortality.

31. Define the following terms:
    a. infant mortality (p. 96)

    b. sudden infant death syndrome (SIDS) (p. 96)

32.   List some of the evidence or recommendations physicians have found as to the causes of SIDS.

Contributor	Evidence or Recommendation
Season of the Year	
Apnea	
Sleeping Position	
Smoking in the Home	
Delayed Brain Maturation	

33.   Discuss the factors related to racial group differences in infant mortality.

AFTER YOU READ . . . PRACTICE TEST #1
PHYSICAL CHANGES

1.   **What is "pruning" as it relates to development?**
        a.   a surgical technique for compensating for brain damage
        b.   elimination of redundant neural pathways
        c.   slowly easing the child off of the bottle and onto solid food
        d.   a surgery that may alleviate epileptic seizures

2.   **The connections between neurons are called _____.**
        a.   synapses
        b.   pruning
        c.   glial cells
        d.   myelin sheaths

3.   **Reflexes such as sucking are called _____.**
        a.   states of consciousness
        b.   primitive reflexes
        c.   adaptive reflexes
        d.   neurological reflexes

4.   **The typical sequence of the infant's behavioral states is _____.**
        a.   deep sleep, crying and fussing, active sleep, quiet awake, active awake
        b.   active sleep, deep sleep, crying and fussing, active awake, quiet awake
        c.   active awake, quiet awake, active sleep, quiet sleep, crying and fussing
        d.   deep sleep, active sleep, quiet awake, active awake, crying and fussing

5.   **The process of bone hardening is called _____.**
        a.   the proximodistal pattern
        b.   locomotor skills
        c.   stamina
        d.   ossification

6.   _____ are also called fine motor skills.
    a.   Manipulative skills
    b.   Locomotor skills
    c.   Nonlocomotor skills
    d.   Gross motor skills

7.   **Which of the following statements about infant nutrition is TRUE?**
    a.   Viruses cannot be transmitted through breast milk.
    b.   Babies need solid foods to supplement breast milk or formula beginning at two months of age.
    c.   Breast milk provides important antibodies for the infant against many kinds of diseases.
    d.   Solid foods encourage babies to sleep through the night.

8.   **Infants _____ are more likely than their peers to have learning disabilities and language deficits during the school years.**
    a.   who have been exposed to measles
    b.   who have chronic ear infections
    c.   who have not had flu shots
    d.   who attend day care

9.   **Brief periods when a baby's breathing stops is called _____.**
    a.   apnea
    b.   an adaptive reflex
    c.   marasmus
    d.   ossification

10.   **Each of the following is a factor related to SIDS (sudden infant death syndrome) EXCEPT:**
    a.   sleeping position
    b.   smoking in the home
    c.   children who attend day care
    d.   season of the year

(Check you answers to Practice Test #1 on p. 88.)

SENSORY SKILLS

Vision (pp. 99-100)

Objective 4.8: *Trace the development of vision during infancy.*

34.   Define the following terms:
    a.   visual acuity (p. 99)

    b.   tracking (p. 99)

35.   Describe the changes in an infant's visual acuity during the first two yeas after birth.

36.   Why is "tracking" an important skill for infants to develop?

Hearing and Other Senses (pp. 100-101)

Objective 4.9: Trace the development of hearing and the other senses.

37.   Define auditory acuity (p. 100).

38.   How does the auditory acuity of a infant compare to that of an adult?

39.   Describe how the ability to determine the location of a sound develops during infancy.

40.   Summarize the development of the following senses by completing the table.

Sense	Summary of Development in Infancy
Smell	
Taste	
Touch and Motion	

AFTER YOU READ . . . PRACTICE TEST #2
SENSORY SKILLS

Indicate whether each of the following statements is true or false.

_____ 1.   Although the newborn has poorer visual skills than older children, few are definitely born blind.

_____ 2.   Most children reach the level of 20/20 vision by about two years of age.

_____ 3.   The fact that infants lack visual acuity is a negative factor that they must overcome.

_____ 4.   Infants younger than two months show some tracking for brief periods if the target is moving slowly.

_____ 5.   Children's hearing improves up to adolescence.

_____ 6.   Because your two ears are separated from one another, sounds arrive at one ear slightly before the other, which allows you to judge location.

_____ 7.   Newborns cannot tell the difference between their mother's and other women's smells until about two months after birth.

_____ 8.   Reflexes related to feeding are associated with the sense of touch.

(Check your answers to Practice Test #2 on p. 88.)

PERCEPTUAL SKILLS

Explaining Perceptual Development (pp. 102-103)

Objective 4.10: Summarize the arguments about perceptual development for the nativist position, the empiricist position, and the interactionist position.

41.   Define the following terms:
        a.   nativists (p. 102)

        b.   empiricists (p. 102)

        c.   preference technique (p. 103)

        d.   habituation (p. 103)

        e.   dishabituation (p. 103)

42.   State the arguments for each of the following positions.

Nativism	*Empiricism*	*Interactionist*

43.   Describe the three basic techniques to study what babies experience.

Looking (pp. 103-106)

Objective 4.11: Describe the "looking" behavior of infants.

44.   Why does an infant need depth perception?

45.   Distinguish among the three kinds information that may used to judge depth.

46.   Trace the ages in which depth perception develops.

47.   Trace the development of what babies look at in the first few months, including faces.

Research Report: Langlois' Studies of Babies' Preferences for Attractive Faces (p. 106)

Objective 4.12: Summarize the research on babies' preferences for attractive faces.

48.　　What were the results of Langlois' study of babies' preferences for attractive faces?

Listening (pp. 106-107)

Objective 4.13: Describe the "listening" behavior of infants.

49.　　Trace the development of infants' abilities to discriminate speech sounds, including individual voices.

50.　　Describe the evidence that infants pay attention to patterns or sequences of sounds.

Combining Information from Several Senses (pp. 108-110)

Objective 4.14: Explain the importance of intersensory integration and cross-modal transfer.

51.　　Define the following terms:
　　　　a.　　intersensory integration (p. 108)

　　　　b.　　cross-modal transfer (p. 108)

52.　　Describe the development of intersensory integration and cross-modal transfer.

No Easy Answers: When Do Preterm Infants Catch Up with Full-Term Infants? (p. 109).

Objective 4.15: Summarize the research on when preterm infants catch up with full-term infants.

53.　　Give an example of "corrected age."

54.　　List four factors that predict development in preterm infants for many years following birth.

55.　　How do the parents' responses to the child contribute to how rapidly she develops?

56.　　List two factors that shape parental responses to preterm infants.

AFTER YOU READ . . . PRACTICE TEST #3
PERCEPTUAL SKILLS

1. **_____ argue that perceptual skills are learned.**
    a.   Interactionists
    b.   Nativists
    c.   Habituationists
    d.   Empiricists

2. **Learning to respond to a familiar stimulus as if it is new is called _____.**
    a.   dishabituation
    b.   interposition
    c.   intersensory integration
    d.   habituation

3. **Pictorial information, sometimes called _____, requires input from only one eye.**
    a.   linear perspective
    b.   binocular cues
    c.   monocular cues
    d.   kinetic cues

4. **If you move your head, objects near you seem to move more than objects further away, a phenomenon called _____.**
    a.   linear perspective
    b.   motion parallax
    c.   monocular cues
    d.   binocular cues

5. **A baby's visual attention is focused on where objects are in his world _____.**
    a.   in the first two months
    b.   between two and three months
    c.   between four and six months
    d.   after six months

6. **Before two months, babies seem to look mostly at _____.**
    a.   a person's mouth
    b.   a person's eyes
    c.   the internal part of a face
    d.   the edges of faces

7. **By age _____, a baby's ability to discriminate non-heard consonant contrasts begins to fade**
    a.   one year
    b.   six months
    c.   three months
    d.   two months

8. **The transfer of information from one sense to another is called _____.**
    a.   intersensory perception
    b.   motion parallax
    c.   cross-modal perception
    d.   habituation

(Check your answers to Practice Test #3 on p. 88.)

AFTER YOU READ . . . CRITICAL REFLECTION EXERCISES

What Babies Do

1. How would you respond to the following comment from a student colleague? "Babies drive me nuts; all they can do is eat and sleep. They can't do anything for themselves."

2. Your friend has a 10-month old girl whom she is trying to get to feed herself. She is expressing her frustration to you because her daughter keeps throwing her food utensils on the floor. Explain to her why her child might be doing this. What suggestions would you have for how your friend can encourage the child to learn, yet keep the floor clean?

3. How could you design a study to see if an infant remembers a toy she saw an hour ago?

Advice for Young Parents

Imagine that you are a social worker. You have been assigned the following case. Sara and her husband Jim are both seventeen. They are the proud parents of Katie, a four-month-old daughter. Sara and Jim do not have much money, but they are interested in providing as well as possible for their girl. Utilizing information from the chapter, give at least five pieces of advice to these young parents. For each piece of advice you give, cite specific information from the textbook to support that advice.

AFTER YOU READ . . . COMPREHENSIVE PRACTICE TEST
MULTIPLE CHOICE QUESTIONS

1. **The part of the newborn brain that is the LEAST developed is the _____.**
   a. brainstem
   b. hypothalamus
   c. cortex
   d. thyroid

2. **Neurons that are insulated with the myelin sheath _____.**
   a. cannot form new neural connections
   b. can conduct the neural impulse faster
   c. become nerve muscle cells
   d. become rigid and less efficient

3. **If an infant's primitive reflexes do not disappear by around six months of age, _____.**
   a. we might suspect a neurological problem
   b. there is nothing to worry about since they never disappear
   c. the infant is more likely to be a boy since boys mature more slowly
   d. it means the infant is not getting enough intellectual stimulation

4. **The ability to maintain activity is called _____.**
   a. nativism
   b. auditory acuity
   c. cross-modal transfer
   d. stamina

5. **When an infant's diet contains almost enough calories, but not enough protein, it may lead to _____.**
   a. micronutrient malnutrition
   b. macronutrient malnutrition
   c. marasmus
   d. kwashikor

6. **The leading cause of death between one month and one year of age is _____.**
   a. ossification
   b. micronutrient malnutrition
   c. sudden infant death syndrome
   d. habituation

7. **The ability to see details at a distance is called _____.**
   a. visual acuity
   b. dishabituation
   c. myelinization
   d. auditory acuity

8. **Each of the following is one of the four basic tastes registered by the tongue EXCEPT:**
   a. salty
   b. bland
   c. sweet
   d. bitter

9. **Babies appear to be especially sensitive to touches on each of the following EXCEPT:**
    a. the abdomen
    b. the soles of the feet
    c. the face
    d. the legs

10. **_____ claim that most perceptual abilities are inborn.**
    a. Nativists
    b. Behaviorists
    c. Empiricists
    d. Interactionists

11. **Which of the following correctly illustrates the concept of habituation?**
    a. learning habits simply by being exposed to them
    b. no longer noticing a ticking clock after a few moments of exposure
    c. hearing someone whisper your name across a loud and crowded room
    d. learning how to categorize information into schemes through practice

12. **Each of the following is a possible way to judge depth EXCEPT:**
    a. binocular cues
    b. pictorial information
    c. habituation
    d. kinetic cues

13. **Babies seem to prefer the mother's face _____.**
    a. from the earliest hours of life
    b. from one month after birth
    c. from three months after birth
    d. from six months after birth

14. **Knowing which mouth movements go with which sounds is an example of _____.**
    a. cross-modal transfer
    b. motion parallax
    c. kinetic cues
    d. intersensory integration

15. **Empirical findings show that cross-modal transfer is possible as early as _____ and becomes common by _____.**
    a. three months; one year
    b. six months; one year
    c. one month; nine months
    d. one month; six months

TRUE-FALSE QUESTIONS

_____ 1. The reticular formation is the part of the brain responsible for keeping your attention on what you are doing and for helping you sort out important and unimportant information.

_____ 2. Sixty to eighty percent of infants develop colic.

_____ 3. One of the most important elements of well baby care is vaccination of the infant against a variety of diseases.

_____ 4. Infants' ability to sense color, even in the earliest weeks after birth, is almost identical to that of adults.

_____ 5. Newborns' auditory acuity is better than their visual acuity.

_____ 6. The preference technique is used to keep track of how long a baby listens to each pattern of sounds.

_____ 7. Babies are actually better at discriminating some kinds of speech sounds than adults are.

_____ 8. Four- to five-month-old babies will spend the same amount of time looking at a face of a person mouthing a vowel that the baby hears spoken over a loudspeaker as they do looking at the face of a person mouthing another vowel.

ESSAY QUESTIONS

1. Discuss the relationship between brain development and good nutrition for infants.

2. How is visual acuity related to synaptogenesis, pruning, and myelinization?

3. Discuss the relationship between the fading of infants' ability to discriminate non-heard consonant contrasts and synaptogenesis and pruning.

(Check your answers to the Comprehensive Practice Test on p. 88.)

WHEN YOU HAVE FINISHED . . . PUZZLE IT OUT

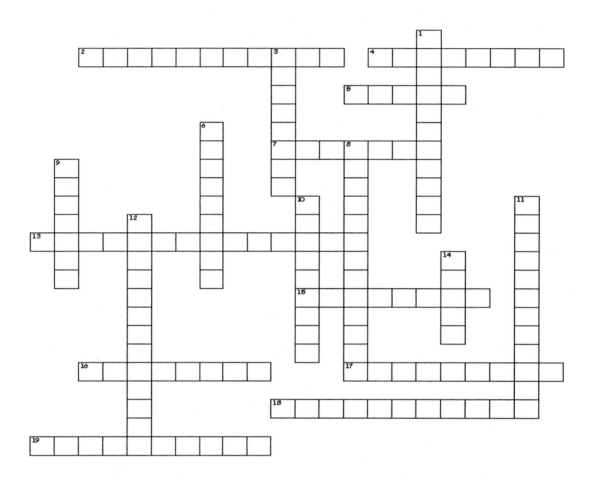

Across

2. Claim that perceptual abilities are learned
4. Reflexes such as sucking
5. Intense daily bouts of crying
7. The ability to maintain activity
13. Responding to a familiar stimulus as if new
15. Visually following a moving object
16. Disease resulting from severe calorie deficiency
17. Claim that perceptual abilities are inborn
18. Disease resulting from insufficient protein
19. The ability of the brain to change in response to experience

Down

1. Decline in attention to a familiar stimulus
3. Connections between neurons
6. Also called gross motor skills
8. The sheaths of axons are covered and insulated
9. The process of eliminating unused synapses
10. Reflexes that disappear during the first year after birth
11. Skills such as controlling head movements
12. Malnutrition resulting from a diet with too few calories
14. Brief periods when breathing stops

Created by Puzzlemaker at DiscoverySchool.com

(Check your answers on p. 88.)

WHEN YOU HAVE FINISHED . . . RESEARCH PROJECT

Student Project 6: Observation In A Newborn Nursery

You can get a feeling for what newborn babies are like, as well as learn something about observational techniques, by arranging to visit a newborn nursery in a local hospital. Your instructor will have made arrangements with one or more hospitals for permission for such observations. You will need to sign up for a specific observation time. At all times, remember that newborn nurseries are complex, busy, and they cannot tolerate lots of questions or extra getting in the way. So be unobtrusive, non-demanding, and do what you are told.

Procedure

Position yourself at one side of the window outside the newborn nursery, leaving room at the window for others to see their newborns. From this vantage point, observe one baby for approximately half an hour. Proceed in the following way:

BABY'S STATES

30-second intervals	Deep Sleep	Active Sleep	Quiet Awake	Active Awake	Crying & Fussing
1					
2					
3					

1. Set up a score sheet that looks something like the one shown above, continuing the list for sixty 30-second intervals.

2. Reread the material in Table 4.1 (p. 90) in the text until you know the main features of the five states as well as possible. You will need to focus on the eyes (open versus closed, rapid eye movement), the regularity of the baby's breathing, and the amount of body movement.

3. Select an infant in the nursery and observe that infant's state every 30 seconds for half an hour. For each interval, note on your score sheet the state that best describes the infant. Do not select an infant to observe who is in deep sleep at the beginning. Pick an infant who seems to be in an in-between state (active sleep or quiet awake), so that you can see some variation over the half hour observation.

4. If you can arrange it, you might do this observation with a partner, each of you scoring the same infant's state independently. When the half hour is over, compare notes. How often did you agree on the infant's state? What might have been producing the disagreements?

5. When you discuss or write about the project, consider the following issues: Did the infant appear to have cycles of states? What were they? What effect, if any, do you think the nursery environment might have had on the baby's state?

You may find yourself approached by family members of the babies in the nursery, asking what you are doing, why you have a clipboard and a stopwatch. Reassure the parents or grandparents that your presence does not in any way suggest that there is anything wrong with any of the babies. Let them know that you are doing a school project on observation. You may even want to show them the text describing the various states.

Alternate Project

The same project can be completed in a home setting with any infant under one or two months of age, with appropriate permission obtained from the baby's parents. You should observe the infant when he or she is lying in a crib or another sleeping location where it is possible for the child to move fairly freely (an infant seat won't do, nor will a baby carrier of any kind).

CHAPTER 4 ANSWER KEY

Practice Test #1 Physical Changes

1. b   2. a   3. c   4. d   5. d   6. a   7. c   8. b   9. a   10. c

Practice Test #2 Sensory Skills

1. T   2. T   3. F   4. T   5. T   6. T   7. F   8. T

Practice Test #3 Perceptual Skills

1. d   2. a   3. c   4. b   5. a   6. d   7. a   8. c

Comprehensive Practice Test

Multiple Choice Questions

1. c   2. b   3. a   4. d   5. d   6. c   7. a   8. b   9. d   10. a
11. b   12. c   13. a   14. d   15. c

True-False Questions

1. T   2. F   3. T   4. T   5. T   6. F   7. T   8. F

Essay Questions

1.
   - The nervous system is the most rapidly developing body system in the first two years after birth.
   - Adequate nutrition is essential for the brain's development.

2.
   - Visual acuity improves rapidly during the first year as a result of synaptogenesis, pruning, and myelinization in the neurons that serve the eyes and the brain's vision processing centers.

3.
   - At about six months, infants begin to lose the ability to distinguish pairs of vowels that do not occur in the language they are hearing.
   - By age one, the ability to discriminate non-heard consonants begins to fade.
   - These findings are consistent with what we know about the pattern of rapid, apparently preprogrammed, growth of synapses in the early months after birth, followed by synaptic pruning.
   - Many connections are initially created, permitting discriminations along all possible sound continua, but only those pathways that are actually used in the language the child hears are strengthened or retained.

Puzzle It Out

Across
2. Empiricists
4. Adaptive
5. Colic
7. Stamina
13. Dishabituation
15. Tracking
16. Marasmus
17. Nativists
18. Kwashiorkor
19. Plasticity

Down
1. Habituation
3. Synapses
6. Locomotor
8. Myelinization
9. Pruning
10. Primitive
11. Nonlocomotor
12. Macronutrient
14. Apnea

CHAPTER 5

COGNITIVE DEVELOPMENT IN INFANCY

BEFORE YOU READ . . . CHAPTER SUMMARY

Cognitive development in infancy includes thinking changes, learning and remembering, and the emergence of language skills. Measuring intelligence in infancy is also discussed.

Cognitive Changes

- In Piaget's sensorimotor stage, infants begin with schemes they are born with and accommodate them to their experiences. The development of object permanence is the most important cognitive milestone.
- Recent research suggests that Piaget underestimated infants' capabilities and their inborn abilities.
- Developmentalists such as Spelke and Baillargeon have studied object permanence within the context of infants' global understanding of objects. Their research shows that Piaget underestimated how much younger infants know about objects and their movements.

Learning, Categorizing, and Remembering

- From the first moments following birth, babies are capable of learning in a variety of ways, such as classical and operant conditioning and schematic learning.
- Infants use categories to organize information.
- Babies as young as three months of age can remember specific objects and their own actions with those objects over periods of as long as a week. With age, their memories become less and less tied to specific cues or contexts.

The Beginnings of Language

- Behaviorists claim that babies learn language by being reinforced for making word-like sounds. Nativists, on the other hand, argue that children's comprehension and production of language is innate. Constructivists say that language development is a sub-process of cognitive development.
- An eclectic approach includes elements of all three perspectives, and seems to fit with research showing that both environmental and internal variables affect language development.
- Babies' earliest sounds are cries, followed by cooing, then by babbling. At nine months, babies typically use meaningful gestures and can understand more words than they can produce.
- The first spoken words typically occur at about one year, after which children acquire words slowly. At about 24 months, they add new words rapidly and generalize them to many more situations.
- Simple two-word sentences appear in children's expressive language at about 18 months of age.
- The rate of language development varies from one child to another. Some toddlers display an expressive style in early word learning while others show a referential style.
- The sequence of language development seems to hold true for babies in all cultures. The child's word order of a child's telegraphic speech depends on which language she is speaking.

Measuring Intelligence in Infancy

▪ Infant intelligence tests are not strongly related to later measures of intelligence. Basic information-processing skills, such as the rate of habituation at four months, are correlated with later intelligence test scores.

AS YOU READ . . . LEARNING OBJECTIVES

After completing Chapter 5, you should be able to:

5.1   Summarize the research on what babies learn from watching television.
5.2   Explain Piaget's view of sensorimotor intelligence.
5.3   Identify the challenges to Piaget's view.
5.4   Summarize the alternative approaches to Piaget's research.
5.5   Give examples of the ways infants learn through classical conditioning, operant conditioning, and modeling.
5.6   Give examples of schematic learning.
5.7   Summarize the recent research on infants' memory.
5.8   Distinguish among the theoretical perspectives of the development of language.
5.9   Explain the eclectic approach to language development.
5.10   Summarize the research on the importance of reading to toddlers.
5.11   Trace the pattern of pre-language development in infants.
5.12   Summarize the research on language of children of deaf parents.
5.13   Describe the research about the infant's first words.
5.14   Describe the development of a child's first sentences.
5.15   Discuss the research about individual differences in language development.
5.16   Summarize the advantages and disadvantages of learning two languages.
5.17   Describe the cross-cultural similarities and differences in language development in infancy.
5.18   Summarize the research on measuring intelligence in infancy.

AS YOU READ . . . TERM IDENTIFICATION

Babbling (p. 127)
Bayley Scales of Infant Development (p. 134)
Constructivists (p. 125)
Cooing (p. 127)
Deferred imitation (p. 117)
Expressive language (p. 129)
Expressive Style (p. 132)
Holophrases (p. 129)
Inflections (p. 130)
Language acquisition device (LAD) (p. 124)
Mean length of utterance (MLU) (p. 131)
Means-end behavior (p. 115)

Motherese (infant directed speech) (p. 124)
Naming explosion (p. 129)
Object concept (p. 118)
Object permanence (p. 116)
Primary circular reaction (p. 114)
Receptive language (p. 128)
Referential style (p. 132)
Schematic learning (p. 122)
Secondary circular reaction (p. 115)
Sensorimotor stage (p. 114)
Telegraphic speech (p. 130)
Tertiary circular reaction (p. 115)

AS YOU READ . . . GUIDED STUDY QUESTIONS

COGNITIVE CHANGES

Development in the Information Age: What Do Babies Really Learn from Watching Television? (p. 115)

Objective 5.1: Summarize the research on what babies learn from watching television.

1.   What do infants really learn from watching television?

Piaget's View of the First Two Years (pp. 114-117)

Objective 5.2 Explain Piaget's view of sensorimotor intelligence.

2.   Define the following terms:
        a.   sensorimotor stage (p. 114)

        b.   primary circular reactions (p. 114)

        c.   secondary circular reactions (p. 115)

        d.   means-end behavior (p. 115)

        e.   tertiary circular reactions (p. 115)

        f.   object permanence (p. 116)

        g.   deferred imitation (p. 116)

3.   Fill in the following table indicating the name of each of the sensorimotor substages and characteristics of each:

Substage	Characteristic
1 (0-1 month)	
2 (1-4 months)	
3 (4-8 months)	

Substage	Characteristic
4 (8-12 months)	
5 (12-18 months)	
6 (18-24 months)	

4.   Trace the development of object permanence across the first year.

5.   Trace the development of deferred imitation in infancy.

Challenges to Piaget's View (pp. 117-118)

Objective 5.3: Identify the challenges to Piaget's view.

6.   Describe the recent research about object permanence that challenges Piaget's findings.

7.   List two important exceptions to the general confirmation of Piaget's sequence of imitation.

8.   List three reasons why the findings about deferred imitation are significant.

Alternative Approaches (pp. 118-121)

Objective 5.4: Give examples of the ways infants learn through classical conditioning, operant conditioning, and modeling.

9.   Define object concept (p. 118).

10.   Describe Elizabeth Spelke's research on the object concept.

11.   Describe Renee Baillargeon's research on the object concept.

AFTER YOU READ . . . PRACTICE TEST #1
COGNITIVE CHANGES

Match the term in the right hand column with its definition in the left column.

_____ 1. The many simple repetitive actions that center around a baby's own body.

_____ 2. An infant's understanding of the nature of objects and how they behave.

_____ 3. Repeating a behavior in the absence of the model who first demonstrated it.

_____ 4. The baby repeats some action in order to trigger a reaction outside her own body.

_____ 5. Assumption that when two exterior areas are joined to each other, they belong to the same object.

_____ 6. Stage marked by the ability to manipulate mental symbols.

_____ 7. The ability to keep a goal in mind and devise a plan to achieve it.

_____ 8. The understanding that objects continue to exist when they can't be seen.

a. accommodation
b. assimilation
c. connected surface principle
d. deferred imitation
e. means-end behavior
f. object concept
g. object permanence
h. primary circular reactions
i. secondary circular reactions
j. sensorimotor stage
k. substage 2
l. substage 3
m. substage 4
n. substage 5
o. substage 6
p. tertiary circular reactions

(Check your answers to Practice Test #1 on p. 105.)

LEARNING, CATEGORIZING, AND REMEMBERING

Conditioning and Modeling (p. 121)

Objective 5.5: Give examples of the ways infants learn through classical conditioning, operant conditioning, and modeling.

12. Give examples of the ways infants learn through classical conditioning, operant conditioning, and modeling.

Classical Conditioning	Operant Conditioning	Modeling

Schematic Learning (p. 122)

Objective 5.6: Give examples of schematic learning.

13.   Define schematic learning (p. 122).

14.   Describe how infants build and use categories as they take in information, including the concepts of superordinates and hierarchical categorization.

Memory (pp. 122-123)

Objective 5.7: Summarize the recent research on infants' memory.

15.   Briefly describe the research on infants' memory. What do the findings demonstrate?

AFTER YOU READ . . . PRACTICE TEST #2
LEARNING, CATEGORIZING, AND REMEMBERING

Indicate whether each of the following statements is true or false.

_____ 1.   Generally, the term learning is used to denote temporary changes in behavior that result from experience.

_____ 2.   Learning of emotional responses through classical conditioning processes may begin as early as the first week of life.

_____ 3.   Both the sucking response and head turning have been successfully increased by the use of reinforcements such as sweet liquids or the sound of the mother's voice.

_____ 4.   The mother's voice and the father's voice are equally effective reinforcers for virtually all babies.

_____ 5.   Schemes help the baby to distinguish between the familiar and the unfamiliar.

_____ 6.   By seven months of age, infants actively use categories to process information.

_____ 7.   Infants respond to superordinate categories before they display reactions to basic-level categories.

_____ 8.   The concept that smaller categories are nested within larger ones is demonstrated to some degree by one-year-olds.

_____ 9.   Babies as young as three months can remember specific objects and their own actions with those objects over periods as long as a week.

_____ 10.   With age, babies' memories become more and more tied to specific cues or contexts.

(Check your answers to Practice Test #2 on p. 105.)

THE BEGINNINGS OF LANGUAGE

Theoretical Perspectives (pp. 123-125)

Objective 5.8: Distinguish among the theoretical perspectives of the development of language.

16.　Define the following terms:
　　a.　language acquisition device (LAD) (p. 124)

　　b.　motherese (or infant-directed speech) (p. 124)

　　c.　constructivists (p. 125)

17.　Distinguish among the following perspectives on the development of language. Include examples of each.

Theory	*Proponent(s)*	*Description and Examples*
Behaviorist		
Nativist		
Constructivist		

18.　List two examples of evidence in support of the constructivists view.

An Eclectic Approach to Language Development (pp. 125-127)

Objective 5.9: Explain the eclectic approach to language development

19.　Describe the effects of poverty on exposure to language.

20.　How does the sheer quantity of language a child hears impact language development?

21.　Give examples of how adults use expansion (or recasting) when talking to infants.

22.　List characteristics of motherese that seem to be attractive to babies.

23.　List four steps of language development that support the integration of the nativist and constructivist positions.

The Real World: The Importance of Reading to a Toddler (p. 126)

Objective 5.10: Summarize the research on the importance of reading to toddlers.

24.   Describe and give examples of dialogic reading.

Sounds, Gestures, and Word Meanings (pp. 127-129)

Objective 5.11: Trace the pattern of pre-language development in infants.

25.   Define the following terms:
        a.   cooing (p. 127)

        b.   babbling (p. 127)

        c.   receptive language (p. 128)

26.   List two important reasons for babies' babbling.

27.   List the series of changes that seem to come together at nine or ten months.

Research Report: Early Gestural Language in the Children of Deaf Parents (p. 128)

Objective 5.12: Summarize the research on language of children of deaf parents.

28.   Describe the language development of deaf children of deaf parents, and of hearing children of deaf parents.

The First Words (pp. 129-130)

Objective 5.13: Describe the research about the infant's first words.

29.   Define the following terms and give examples of each:
        a.   expressive language (p. 129)

        b.   holophrases (p. 129)

        c.   naming explosion (p. 129)

30.   Distinguish expressive language from receptive language.

The First Sentences (p. 130)

Objective 5.14: Describe the development of a child's first sentences.

31.   Define the following terms:
    a.   telegraphic speech (p. 130)

    b.   inflections (p. 130)

32.   List the distinguishing features of babies' first sentences.

Individual Differences in Language Development (pp. 131-133)

Objective 5.15: Discuss the research about individual differences in language development.

33.   Define the following terms:
    a.   mean length of utterance (MLU) (p. 131)

    b.   expressive style (p. 132)

    c.   referential style (p. 132)

34.   Describe the subset of children who talk late and who do not catch up.

35.   Distinguish between expressive style and referential style, and give examples of how they are related to a child's cognitive development.

No Easy Answers: One Language or Two? (p. 131)

Objective 5.16: Summarize the advantages and disadvantages of learning two languages.

36.   List at least five advantages of growing up bilingual.

37.   List at least three disadvantages of growing up bilingual.

Language Development across Cultures (pp. 133-134)

Objective 5.17: Describe the cross-cultural differences in language development in infancy.

38.   List four similarities in language development across cultures.

39.   Give examples of cross-cultural differences

AFTER YOU READ . . . PRACTICE TEST #3
THE BEGINNINGS OF LANGUAGE

1.   **Chomsky called the innate language processor _____.**
        a.   receptive language
        b.   expressive language
        c.   dialogic device
        d.   the language acquisition device

2.   **Another name for motherese is _____.**
        a.   infant-directed speech
        b.   metalinguistic ability
        c.   babbling
        d.   referential style

3.   **Each of the following is a characteristic of children whose parents talk to them often and read to them regularly EXCEPT:**
        a.   learn to read more easily when they reach school age
        b.   develop larger vocabularies
        c.   use simpler sentences
        d.   talk sooner

4.   **When adults repeat the child's own sentences but in slightly longer, more grammatically correct forms, the speech is called _____.**
        a.   the language acquisition device
        b.   receptive style
        c.   recasting
        d.   expressive style

5.   **Which of following is the typical sequence of language development in infancy?**
        a.   babbling, cooing, telegraphic speech, holophrases
        b.   crying, cooing, babbling, gestural language, holophrases
        c.   gestural language, babbling, telegraphic speech, cooing
        d.   holophrases, gestural language, cooing, telegraphic speech

6.   **Which of the following is TRUE about babbling?**
        a.   Babbling is preparation for spoken language.
        b.   Babbling includes only the sounds that the baby hears.
        c.   Babbling is repetitive vowel sounds.
        d.   Babbling begins at about two months.

7.   **Each of the following is part of the series of changes in language that converge by about nine or ten months EXCEPT:**
        a.   imitative gestural games
        b.   the first comprehension of individual words
        c.   the beginning of meaningful gestures
        d.   the drift of babbling toward the non-heard language sounds

8.   **Between 16 and 24 months, most children begin to add new words rapidly. This is called _____.**
      a.   expressive language
      b.   the naming explosion
      c.   telegraphic speech
      d.   expressive style

9.   **Inflections are _____.**
      a.   examples of the dialogic reading style
      b.   grammatical markers
      c.   metalinguistic ability
      d.   recasting

10.   **The average sentence length is referred to as _____.**
      a.   a referential style
      b.   a holophrase
      c.   the mean length of utterance
      d.   adult-directed speech

(Check your answers to Practice Test #3 on p. 105.)

MEASURING INTELLIGENCE IN INFANCY (pp. 134-135)

Objective 5.18: Summarize the research on measuring intelligence in infancy.

40.   Define the Bayley Scales of Infant Development (p. 134), and state its usefulness and its drawbacks.

41.   How have habituation tasks been of value as measures of infant intelligence?

42.   Describe the usefulness of the Fagan Test of Infant Intelligence for special populations.

AFTER YOU READ . . . PRACTICE TEST #4
MEASURING INTELLIGENCE IN INFANCY

Indicate whether each of the following statements is true or false.

_____ 1.   It is extremely difficult to measure intelligence in infants.

_____ 2.   Infant intelligence tests are used to identify infants who require special interventions.

_____ 3.   The Bayley Scales of Infant Development measure primary reflexes.

_____ 4.   What is being measured on typical infant intelligence tests is not the same as what is tapped by the commonly used childhood or adult intelligence tests.

_____ 5.   Individual differences in rate of habituation in the early months of life are unlikely to predict later intelligence test scores.

(Check your answers to Practice Test #4 on p. 105.)

AFTER YOU READ . . . COMPREHENSIVE PRACTICE TEST
MULTIPLE CHOICE QUESTIONS

1. Piaget's first stage during which infants use information from their senses and motor actions to learn about the world is called _____.
    a. sensorimotor stage
    b. preoperational stage
    c. concrete operational stage
    d. formal operational stage

2. The understanding that a toy exists even if we roll it under the couch is called _____.
    a. object permanence
    b. conservation
    c. concept consistency
    d. schematic processing

3. Each of the following statements is TRUE of the recent findings about deferred imitation EXCEPT:
    a. Infants can and do learn specific behaviors through modeling, even when they have no change to imitate the behavior immediately.
    b. Babies may be more skillful than Piaget thought.
    c. Deferred imitation begins at 14 months.
    d. More abilities than Piaget suggested may be built in from the beginning and may develop continuously, rather than in stages, throughout infancy.

4   An infant's understanding of the nature of objects and how they behave is called _____.
    a. means-end behavior
    b. object concept
    c. deferred imitation
    d. object permanence

5. Infants learn by each of the following methods EXCEPT:
    a. modeling
    b. classical conditioning
    c. operant conditioning
    d. expressive imitation

6. Schematic learning assumes that _____.
    a. babies attempt to categorize their experiences
    b. children cannot learn unless the information is organized for them
    c. babies will only learn if they are reinforced for exploring
    d. learning is sequential and orderly

7. Which of the following is an accurate statement about infant memory?
    a. Infants younger than six months do not retain memories.
    b. The expansion of memory is preprogrammed.
    c. Infants develop very general memories for information.
    d. Early infant memory is specific to the context in which it was learned.

8.   **Theorists who argue that language development is part of the broader process of cognitive development are called _____.**
      a.   nativists
      b.   constructivists
      c.   behaviorists
      d.   psychoanalysists

9.   **A child understands a word that is spoken before she can say the word. This is called _____.**
      a.   expressive language
      b.   receptive language
      c.   imitation
      d.   innate vocalization

10.   **Combinations of gestures and single words that convey more meaning than just the word alone are termed _____.**
      a.   expressive linguistics
      b.   babbles
      c.   holophrases
      d.   infant-directed speech

11.   **Telegraphic speech typically includes each of the following parts of speech EXCEPT:**
      a.   nouns
      b.   verbs
      c.   adjectives
      d.   adverbs

12.   **Children's early vocabulary that uses words linked to social relationships rather than objects is called _____.**
      a.   hierarchical style
      b.   referential style
      c.   expressive style
      d.   metalinguistic ability

13.   **Each of the following statements about language development across cultures is true EXCEPT:**
      a.   babies the world over coo before they babble
      b.   telegraphic speech precedes holophrases in every language
      c.   all babies understand language before they can speak it
      d.   babies in all cultures begin to use their first words at about 12 months

14.   **Which of the following is an accurate statement about infant intelligence tests?**
      a.   Babies who habituate quickly when they are four or five months old are likely to have higher intelligence test scores at later ages.
      b.   The Bayley Scales of Infant Development accurately predict a child's intelligence at age ten.
      c.   None of the infant intelligence tests correlate with intelligence test scores at later ages.
      d.   Infant intelligence tests are based on individual differences in cognitive abilities.

15.   **Tests of _____ are also known as novelty preference and visual recognition.**
      a.   reflex tests
      b.   habituation
      c.   motor skills
      d.   expressive style

TRUE-FALSE QUESTIONS

Indicate whether each of the following statements is true or false.

_____ 1.   One consequence of the drive to explore is means-end behavior, or the ability to keep a goal in mind and devise a plan to achieve it.

_____ 2.   Piaget argued that deferred imitation was possible as early as substage three.

_____ 3.   The concept that smaller categories are nested within larger ones, or hierarchical categorization, is demonstrated to some degree by two-year-olds.

_____ 4.   Newborns do not appear to be able to remember auditory stimuli to which they are exposed while sleeping.

_____ 5.   Expressive language is the ability to produce as well as understand and respond to words.

_____ 6.   Children who use a referential style have vocabularies made up predominantly of names for things or people.

_____ 7.   The Bayley Scales of Infant Development measure primarily language development.

_____ 8.   Individual differences in rate of habituation in the early months after birth may predict later intelligence test scores.

ESSAY QUESTIONS

1.   Using Piaget's six sensorimotor substages as your guide, trace the cognitive development of infants. Include the approximate ages of each substage and the distinguishing characteristics of each. Include specific examples of each.

2.   Discuss the importance of reading to toddlers.

3.   Discus the pros and cons to measuring intelligence in infancy.

(Check your answers to the Comprehensive Practice Test on p. 105.)

WHEN YOU HAVE FINISHED . . . PUZZLE IT OUT

Across
1. View that language is learned by reinforcement
3. Learning by watching others
4. Learning involving the organization of experiences into expectancies, often called schemas
9. Categorization of smaller categories nested within larger ones
10. Adults expand on a child's own sentence in a more grammatically correct form
13. Ability to understand language
14. Conditioning in which infants learn by reinforcement
15. Piaget's first stage
16. Grammatical markers

Down
1. Repetition of combination of consonant and vowel sounds
2. Combinations of gestures and single words
5. Speech that uses simple, two-word sentences
6. Conditioning in which infants learn emotional responses
7. Repetition of vowel sounds
8. View that language comprehension and production is innate
11. View that language development is a sub-process of cognitive development
12. Language style made up of names for things or people

Created by Puzzlemaker at DiscoverySchool.com

(Check your answers on p. 106.)

WHEN YOU HAVE FINISHED . . . RESEARCH PROJECT

Student Project 7: Development of the Object Concept

For this project, you will need to locate an infant between 6 and 12 months of age. Obtain permission from the baby's parents, following whatever procedure your instructor requires, and ask one of them to be there while you present materials to the baby.

Procedure

Obtain from the parents one of the baby's favorite toys. Place the baby in a sitting position or on his stomach in such a way that he can reach for the toy easily (as in figure 5.2). Then perform the following steps:

Step 1: While the baby is watching, place the toy in full view and easy to reach. See if the infant reaches for the toy.

Step 2: In full view of the infant, cover part of the toy with a handkerchief, so that only part is visible. Does the baby reach for the toy?

Step 3: While the infant is reaching for the toy (you'll have to pick your moment), cover it completely with the handkerchief. Does the baby continue reaching?

Step 4: In full view of the baby, while he is still interested in the toy, cover the whole toy with the cloth. Does the baby try to pull the cloth away or search for the toy in some way?

You may need to use more than one toy to keep the baby's interest and/or spread the test over a period of time.

Analysis and Report

Jackson, Campos, and Fischer (1978) report that step 2 (continuing to reach for the partly covered toy) is typically "passed" at about 26 weeks, step 3 at about 28 or 29 weeks, and the final step (reaching for the toy that was fully covered before the child began to reach) at about 30 or 31 weeks. The closer to these ages your infant is, the more interesting your results are likely to be.

Did your subject's performance conform to those expectations? If not, why do you think it was different? You might read the Jackson, Campos, and Fischer paper to see some of the reasons they give for differences in results from several studies. Do you think it mattered, for example, that a familiar toy was used? Did it matter that the mother or father was present?

Reference

Jackson, E., Campos, J. J., & Fischer, K. W. (1978). The question of decalage between object permanence and person permanence. *Developmental Psychology, 14*, 1-10.

CHAPTER 5 ANSWER KEY

Practice Test #1 Cognitive Changes

1. h 2. f 3. d 4. i 5. c 6. o 7. e 8. g

Practice Test #2 Learning, Categorizing, and Remembering

1. F 2. T 3. T 4. F 5. T 6. T 7. T 8. F 9. T 10. F

Practice Test #3 The Beginnings of Language

1. d 2. a 3. c 4. c 5. b 6. a 7. d 8. b 9. b 10. c

Practice Test #4 Measuring Intelligence in Infancy

1. T 2. T 3. F 4. T 5. F

Comprehensive Practice Test

Multiple Choice Questions

1. a 2. a 3. c 4. b 5. d 6. a 7. d 8. b 9. b 10. c
11. d 12. c 13. b 14. a 15. b

True-False Questions

1. T 2. F 3. T 4. F 5. T 6. T 7. F 8. T

Essay Questions

1.
   - Substage 1: Birth to on month. Built-in reflexes.
   - Substage 2: One to four months. Primary circular reactions—repeating pleasurable actions involving the infant's own body. Beginning of coordination between looking and listening, between reaching and looking, and between reaching and sucking.
   - Substage 3: Four to eight months. Secondary circular reactions—repeating some action to trigger a reaction outside the baby's body.
   - Substage 4: Eight to 12 months. Beginning of causal connections resulting in mean-end behavior.
   - Substage 5: Twelve to 18 months. Tertiary circular reactions—trying out variations of original behavior. Purposeful, experimental behavior.
   - Substage 6: Eighteen to 24 months. Ability to manipulate mental symbols, such as words or images, allowing the infant to generate solutions to problems simply by thinking about them.

2.
   - Children gain a wide range of words in their speech. They talk sooner, develop larger vocabularies, use more complex sentences, and learn to read more readily when they reach school age.

3.
   - Pro: Helps heath care professionals identify infants who require special interventions to support cognitive development.
   - Con: Can result in "labeling" children as "smart" or "slow."

Puzzle It Out

Across	Down
Across	**Down**
1. Behaviorist	1. Babbling
3. Modeling	2. Holophrases
4. Schematic	5. Telegraphic
9. Hierarchical	6. Classical
10. Recasting	7. Cooing
13. Receptive	8. Nativist
14. Operant	11. Constructivist
15. Sensorimotor	12. Referential
16. Inflections	

CHAPTER 6

SOCIAL AND PERSONALITY DEVELOPMENT IN INFANCY

BEFORE YOU READ . . . CHAPTER SUMMARY

Developmentalists of diverse theoretical orientations agree that the formation of a strong emotional connection to a primary caregiver early in life is critical to healthy child development and has important implications across the entire lifespan.

Theories of Social and Personality Development

- Freud believed that the weaning process in the oral stage of development influenced the development of personality. Erikson emphasized the role of the family in providing for all of the infant's needs, thereby instilling a sense of trust.
- Ethologists believe that the first two years constitute a sensitive period for attachment in human infants and that infants who fail to form a close relationship with a primary caregiver are at risk for future social and personality problems.

Attachment

- The development of synchrony, a set of mutually reinforcing and interlocking behaviors that characterize most interactions between parent and infant, is essential to the development of the parents' attachment to the infant.
- According to Bowlby, the baby's attachment to the parents emerges gradually across three stages.
- Children differ in the security of their first attachments and in the internal working model that they develop. The secure infant uses the parent as a safe base for exploration and can be readily consoled by the parent.
- Caregiver characteristics such as age, depression, and a history of abuse can affect attachment quality.
- Children who were securely attached to their mothers in infancy are more sociable and more positive in their behavior toward friends and siblings than those who were insecurely attached. The internal model of attachment that individuals develop in infancy affects how they parent their own babies.
- Studies in many countries suggest that a secure attachment is the most common pattern everywhere, but cultures differ in the frequency of different types of insecure attachment.

Personality, Temperament, and Self-Concept

- A few key dimensions appear in the lists of dimensions described by many of the key researchers. They are activity level, approach/positive emotionality, inhibition, negative emotionality, and effortful control/task persistence.
- Both nature and nurture contribute to individual differences in temperament as the child's built-in temperament shapes the child's interactions with the world and affects others' responses to the child.
- Infant temperament may affect security of attachment. The goodness-of-fit between an infant's temperament and the ways her environment responds to her is the real factor in correlations between temperament and attachment.

- The infant develops the awareness of a separate self and the understanding of self-permanence (called the subjective self), and an awareness of himself as an object in the world (the objective self). An emotional self develops in the first year as the range of emotions develops, as well as the ability to use information about emotions.

Effects of Nonparental Care

- Comparing parental care to nonparental care is difficult because there are so many kinds of nonparental care arrangements.
- High-quality day care has beneficial effects on many children's overall cognitive development, especially on disadvantaged children.
- Some studies show that children with a history of day care are more aggressive in their social relationships whereas other studies show them to be more socially skillful.
- Factors such as stress hormones, individual differences, and gender differences may affect a child in nonparental care.

AS YOU READ . . . LEARNING OBJECTIVES

After completing Chapter 6, you should be able to:

6.1   Describe the psychoanalytic perspective of social and personality development.
6.2   Describe the ethological perspective of social and personality development.
6.3   Summarize the issues involved with adoption and development.
6.4   Describe the development of the parent's bond to the infant.
6.5   Describe the development of the infant's bond to the parents.
6.6   List and describe the variations in attachment quality.
6.7   Describe how the characteristics of the caregiver influence attachment.
6.8   Summarize the research on the long-term consequences of attachment quality.
6.9   Summarize the research on attachments in different cultures.
6.10   Explain the dimensions of temperament.
6.11   Describe the research on the origins and stability of temperament.
6.12   Explain the relationship between temperament and development.
6.13   Summarize the gender differences in temperament.
6.14   Trace the steps in the process of the development of the self-concept.
6.15   List the issues involved in studying nonparental care.
6.16   State the advantages and disadvantages of day care on cognitive development.
6.17   Describe the issues involved in determining the effects of nonparental care on social development.
6.18   Describe the variables that should be included when interpreting research on nonparental care.
6.19   Identify the criteria for choosing a high-quality day-care setting.

AS YOU READ . . . TERM IDENTIFICATION

Affectional bond (p. 140)
Affective dysregulation (p. 144)
Attachment (p. 140)
Attachment theory (p. 140)
Goodness-of-fit (p. 154)
Insecure/ambivalent attachment (p. 145)
Insecure/avoidant attachment (p. 145)
Insecure/disorganized attachment (p. 145)
Niche-picking (p. 152)

Objective (categorical self) (p. 156)
Personality (p. 150)
Secure attachment (p. 145)
Separation anxiety (p. 144)
Social referencing (p. 144)
Stranger anxiety (p. 144)
Subjective self (p. 154)
Synchrony (p. 142)
Temperament (p. 150)

AS YOU READ . . . GUIDED STUDY QUESTIONS

THEORIES OF SOCIAL AND PERSONALITY DEVELOPMENT

Psychoanalytic Perspectives (pp. 139-140)

Objective 6.1: Describe the psychoanalytic perspective of social and personality development.
1.   What was Freud's belief about the importance of the oral stage? Why was the weaning process important?

2.   Describe the importance of the symbiotic relationship between the mother and the infant.

3.   How does Erikson's theory differ from Freud's? Why is the trust versus mistrust stage so important?

Ethological Perspectives (p. 140)

Objective 6.2: Describe the ethological perspective of social and personality development.
4.   Define the following terms:
      a.   attachment theory (p. 140)

      b.   affectional bond (p. 140)

      c.   attachment (p. 140)

5.   What was Bowlby's argument?

6.   Distinguish between affectional bonds and attachment. Give examples of each.

7.   Describe the ethologists perspective.

No Easy Answers: Adoption and Development (p. 141)

Objective 6.3: Summarize the issues involved with adoption and development.
8.   Why are the child's circumstances prior to adoption important to consider?

9.   In spite of the potential difficulties of parenting the adopted children at risk, there are a few important facts parents who adopt them should keep in mind. List three of the facts.

AFTER YOU READ . . . PRACTICE TEST #1
THEORIES OF SOCIAL AND PERSONALITY DEVELOPMENT

Indicate whether each of the following statements is true or false.
_____ 1.   Freud proposed a series of psychosexual stages that extend from birth through old age.

_____ 2.   According to Freud, the consequences of overgratification or undergratification at the oral stage would be fixation.

_____ 3.   Freud emphasized the symbiotic relationship between the mother and the young infant, in which the two behave as if they were one.

_____ 4.   Erikson claimed that responding to the infant's needs by talking to her and comforting her were just as important to development as nursing and weaning.

_____ 5.   Ethologists claim that attachment behaviors are learned behaviors, not instinctive.

_____ 6.   An attachment is a type of affectional bond in which a person's sense of security is bound up in the relationship.

_____ 7.   When you are securely attached, you can use the other as a "safe base" from which to explore the rest of the world.

(Check your answers to Practice Test #1 on p. 128.)

ATTACHMENT

The Parents' Attachment to the Infant (pp. 141-143)

Objective 6.4: Describe the development of the parent's bond to the infant.

10.   Define synchrony (p. 142), and give examples.

11.   Give an example of how the degree of synchrony in parent-infant interactions seems to contribute to cognitive development.

12.   Past the first few weeks, what are the signs of a kind of specialization of parental behaviors with infants and toddlers?

The Infant's Attachment to the Parents (pp. 143-144)

Objective 6.5: Describe the development of the infant's bond to the parents.

13.   Complete the following table with information about the three stages that Bowlby suggested in the development of the infant's attachment:

Stage	Name of Stage	Age	Attachment Behaviors
1			
2			
3			

14.   Define the following terms:
      a.   stranger anxiety (p. 144)

      b.   separation anxiety (p. 144)

      c.   social referencing (p. 144)

      d.   affect dysregulation (p. 144)

15.   How do infants express stranger anxiety?

16.   How do infants express separation anxiety?

17.   Give an example of social referencing.

18.   How do infants use social referencing to regulate their own emotions?

Variations in Attachment Quality (pp. 144-146)

Objective 6.6: List and describe the variations in attachment quality.

19.   Give examples of internal models.

20.   List, in order, the eight episodes in the Strange Situation.

21.   Define the following terms:
      a.   secure attachment (p. 145)

      b.   insecure/avoidant attachment (p. 145)

      c.   insecure/ambivalent attachment (p. 145)

      d.   insecure/disorganized attachment (p. 145)

22.   List and describe two key ingredients for secure attachment.

23.   Describe how each of the following factors affect attachment:

Factor	Affect
Parental Responsiveness	
Avoidant Pattern	
Ambivalent Pattern	
Disorganized/Disoriented Pattern	

24.   What may happen to the consistency of security or insecurity if the child's circumstances change in some major way? Give examples.

25.   How does the quality of the child's relationship with each parent determine the child's security with that specific adult?

Caregiver Characteristics and Attachment (pp. 146-148)

Objective 6.7: Describe how the characteristics of the caregiver influences attachment.

26.   How might marital status affect attachment?

27.   How might the caregiver's age predict the attachment quality?

28.   How might a mother's depression affect an infant's nutrition?

29.   Identify four ways that depressed mothers might interact with their infants and the responses of the babies.

Category	Mother's Behavior toward Infant	Children's Response
Withdrawn or detached		
Overly involved with infant		
Overreaction and anger		
Sensitive and responsive		

30.   How does the behavior of a mother with panic disorder affect the synchrony with her infant?

Long-Term Consequences of Attachment Quality (p. 148)

Objective 6.8: Summarize the research on the long-term consequences of attachment quality.

31.   List six behaviors of children who were rated as securely attached to their mothers in infancy.

32.   List five behaviors of adolescents who were rated as securely attached to their mothers in infancy.

33.   List two behaviors of adolescents who were rated as insecure attachments—particularly those with avoidant attachments—in infancy.

34.   How does attachment in infancy predict sociability in adulthood?

35.   Give examples of how an adult's internal model of attachment affects his or hr parenting behaviors.

36.   How does attachment history affect parental attitudes?

Cross-Cultural Research on Attachment (pp. 148-150)

Objective 6.9: Summarize the research on attachments in different cultures.

37.   What does the research show about secure attachment in a culture in which the child's early care is much more communal?

AFTER YOU READ . . . PRACTICE TEST #2
ATTACHMENT

1.   **Each of the following is part of the distinctive pattern of interactive behavior that adults automatically display in the presence of an infant EXCEPT:**
       a.   low-pitched voice
       b.   smiling
       c.   raised eyebrows
       d.   very wide-open eyes

2.   **For an adult, the critical ingredient for the formation of a bond with an infant seems to be the opportunity to develop _____.**
       a.   affect dysregulation
       b.   nonfocused orienting
       c.   synchrony
       d.   contingent responsiveness

3.   **During which of Bowlby's phases in the development of the infant's attachment will the baby use a set of innate behavior patterns that orient her toward others and signal her needs?**
       a.   phase 4, reactive attachment
       b.   phase 3, secure base behavior
       c.   phase 2, focus on one or more figures
       d.   phase 1, nonfocused orienting and signaling

4.   **Expressions of discomfort, such as crying, when separated from an attachment figure is called _____.**
       a.   stranger anxiety
       b.   separation anxiety
       c.   social referencing
       d.   separation distress

5.   **Researchers use the term _____ to refer to the interaction pattern in which a caregiver responds to an infant's anger with anger of her own.**
       a.   affect dysregulation
       b.   reactive attachment
       c.   secure base behavior
       d.   stranger anxiety

6.   **An infant's internal model includes each of the following elements EXCEPT:**
       a.   the child's sense of assurance that the other is really a safe base for exploration
       b.   the child's expectation of rebuff or affection
       c.   the child's anticipation of affect dysregulation
       d.   the child's confidence (or lack of it) that the attachment figure will be available or reliable

7. **Each of the following is a problematic behavior pattern in depressed mothers EXCEPT:**
    a. mothers overreact and respond angrily to babies' undesirable behaviors
    b. mothers are sensitive to the babies' needs
    c. mothers are overly involved with their infants
    d. mothers are withdrawn or detached

8. **_____ is more common when the primary caregiver is inconsistently or unreliably available to the child.**
    a. A disorganized/disoriented pattern
    b. An ambivalent pattern
    c. An avoidant pattern
    d. A low level of parental responsiveness

9. **Each of the following behaviors of children is correlated to secure attachment in infancy EXCEPT:**
    a. more sociable
    b. more positive in their behavior towards friends and siblings
    c. more aggressive and disruptive
    d. more empathetic

10. **Secure attachment in infancy has been linked to _____ in adolescence.**
    a. self-esteem problems
    b. rebellious backlash
    c. earlier sexual experience
    d. more intimate friendships

(Check your answers to practice Test #2 on p. 128.)

PERSONALITY, TEMPERAMENT, AND SELF-CONCEPT

Dimensions of Temperament (pp. 150-151)

Objective 6.10: Explain the dimensions of temperament.

38. Define the following terms:
    a. personality (p. 150)

    b. temperament (p. 150)

39. List and describe the three types of temperament proposed by Thomas and Chess.

40. How do researchers who examine temperament from a trait rather than an categorical perspective view an infant's temperament?

41. Describe each of the following key dimensions of temperament:

Dimension	Description
Activity Level	
Approach/Positive Emotionality	

Dimension	Description
Inhibition	
Negative Emotionality	
Effortful Control/ Task Persistence	

Origins and Stability of Temperament (pp. 151-153)

Objective 6.11: Describe the research on the origins and stability of temperament.

42.   Describe the evidence that temperamental differences are inborn.

43.   Explain how each of the following physiological patterns might explain temperamental differences.
a.   differing thresholds for arousal in parts of the brain
b.   function of the neurotransmitters dopamine and serotonin
c.   frontal lobe asymmetry

44.   Define niche-picking (p. 152), and give examples.

45.   List three temperament/environment interactions that tend to strengthen built-in qualities, and give examples of each.

46.   List the characteristics of temperament that seem to be consistent over rather long periods of infancy and childhood.

Temperament and Development (p. 154)

Objective 6.12: Explain the relationship between temperament and development.

47.   How do temperamental differences contribute to cognitive development?

48.   Define goodness-of-fit (p. 154), and give examples of its importance in attachment.

Research Report: Gender Differences in Temperament (p. 155)

Objective 6.13: Summarize the gender differences in temperament.

49.   List the gender differences in temperament found in some research studies.

50.   Describe how temperamental stereotyping may affect the quality of the parent-infant relationship.

115

Self-Concept (pp. 154-157)

Objective 6.14: Trace the steps in the process of the development of the self-concept.

51.   Define the following terms:
    a.   subjective self, or existential self (p. 154)

    b.   objective self, or categorical self (p. 156)

52.   Describe the research to determine just when a child has developed the initial self-awareness that defines the beginning of the objective self.

53.   Trace the development of the emotional self by completing the following table:

Age	Behavior	Emotions Expressions
2-3 months		
5-7 months		
End of the first year		
Near the middle of the second year		

AFTER YOU READ . . . PRACTICE TEST #3
PERSONALITY, TEMPERAMENT, AND SELF-CONCEPT

Match the letter of the term in the right column with its description in the left column.

_____ 1.   A tendency to respond with fear or withdrawal to new people, new situations, new objects—the flip side of approach.

_____ 2.   Try new foods without much fuss, regular sleeping and eating cycles, usually happy, adjust easily to change.

_____ 3.   The process of selecting experiences on the basis of temperament.

_____ 4.   Inborn predispositions that form the foundations of personality.

_____ 5.   The degree to which an infant's temperament is adaptable to his or her environment, and vice versa.

_____ 6.   A pattern of responding to people and objects in the environment.

_____ 7.   Sometimes called the categorical self.

_____ 8.   Exhibit higher levels of arousal in the right frontal lobe than the left hemisphere.

_____ 9.   Neurotransmitters that regulate the brain's responses to new information and unusual situations.

_____ 10.   Sometimes called the existential self.

a. Activity level
b. Approach/positive emotionality
c. Difficult child
d. Dopamine and serotonin
e. Easy child
f. Effortful control/task persistence
g. Emotional self
h. Frontal lobe asymmetry
i. Goodness-of-fit
j. Inhibition
k. Negative emotionality
l. Niche-picking
m. Objective self
n. Personality
o. Slow-to-warm-up child
p. Subjective self
q. Temperament

(Check your answers to Practice Test #3 on p. 128.)

EFFECTS OF NONPARENTAL CARE

Difficulties in Studying Nonparental Care (pp. 157-159)

Objective 6.15: List the issues involved in studying nonparental care.

54.   List at least four factors that may be involved in the issue of day care that confound the question of how much impact nonparental care has on infants and young children.

55.   What is the most common pattern of nonparental care?

Effects on Cognitive Development (p. 159)

Objective 6.16: State the advantages and disadvantages of day care on cognitive development.

56.   Describe the evidence that high-quality day care has beneficial effects on many children's overall cognitive development.

57.   Describe the studies that point to possible negative effects of day care experience on cognitive development in some children, particularly middle-class children.

58.   How can these conflicting findings be reconciled?

Effects on Social Development (pp. 159-160)

Objective 6.17: Describe the issues involved in determining the effects of nonparental care on social development.

59.   What evidence is there that nonparental care has a negative impact on social development?

60.   What seems to be the critical variable that increases the risk for affecting social relationships?

Interpreting Research on Nonparental Care (pp. 160-161)

Objective 6.18: Describe variable that should be included when interpreting research on nonparental care.

61.   List and describe at least three variables that may affect the interpretation of research on nonparental care.

The Real World: Choosing a Day-Care Center (p. 161)

Objective 6.19: Identify the criteria for choosing a high-quality day-care setting.

62.   Identify and describe six criteria for choosing a high-quality day-care center.

Criteria	Description

63.   Why are preterm and low-birth-weight babies who are very ill at a significantly greater risk for developing insecure attachments than those who are healthy?

64.   Give examples of the temperamental characteristics of preterm infants that place them at risk of insecure attachment.

65.   Why is insecure attachment an additional risk for preterm and low-birth-weight babies?

AFTER YOU READ . . . PRACTICE TEST #4
EFFECTS OF NONPARENTAL CARE

Indicate whether each of the following statements is true or false.

_____ 1.   The mother's attitudes toward child care arrangements may affect the overall experience.

_____ 2.   Children in nonparental care from poor families are most likely to have negative affects on cognitive development than children from higher socio-economic backgrounds.

_____ 3.   Infants whose parents exhibit behaviors associated with insecure attachment, such as poor sensitivity to the child's needs, are more likely to be negatively affected by nonparental care.

_____ 4.   Children who have spent ten hours or more per week in nonparental care appear to be at low risk from difficulties in social relationships.

_____ 5.   The levels of the stress hormone cortisol increased from morning to afternoon in infants who were enrolled in center-based care.

_____ 6.   Family variables are more important than the type of day-care arrangements a family chooses.

(Check your answers to Practice Test #4 on p. 128.)

AFTER YOU READ . . . CRITICAL REFLECTION EXERCISE

Attachment

Imagine that you work in a day-care center. You notice that one parent is having a difficult time dropping off his son. The child clings to the father in apparent fear about being dropped off, kicks and screams when the father walks away, and then seems fine. You also notice that the child seems very "mad" at his father when the father returns to pick him up. The boy refuses to look his father in the eye, does not want to be picked up, and will not answer the father's questions about how the boy's day went. Utilizing information from the text, provide answers for the following questions:

1. According to Ainsworth's categories of attachment, what kind of attachment bond seems to have developed between this parent and child?

2. What types of interactions between the parent and child seem to lead to this type of attachment bond?

3. What effects might this attachment bond have on the child's developing sense of self? Why?

4. What things might you do when interacting with this child in the day care to ensure that this same type of relationship does not develop between you and this child? Discuss at least four things that you might do.

AFTER YOU READ . . . COMPREHENSIVE PRACTICE TEST
MULTIPLE-CHOICE QUESTIONS

1. **The theorist who proposed that infants must resolve the conflict of trust versus mistrust was _____.**
    a.   Ainsworth
    b.   Bowlby
    c.   Erikson
    d.   Freud

2. **A relatively long-enduring tie in which the partner is important as a unique individual and is interchangeable with none other is called _____.**
    a.   trust versus mistrust
    b.   an affectional bond
    c.   personality theory
    d.   reactive attachment

3. **The mutual, interlocking pattern of attachment behaviors between a parent and an infant is called _____.**
    a.   synchrony
    b.   attachment
    c.   temperament
    d.   conversation

4. **During which phase of attachment will the child show attachment behaviors that are more narrowly focused on select persons?**
    a.   Phase 4, reactive attachment
    b.   Phase 3, secure base attachment
    c.   Phase 2, focus on one or more figure phase
    d.   Phase 1, non-focused orienting and signaling

5. **A child who does not seek much contact with the mother after she returns from a short absence is probably _____.**
    a.   securely attached
    b.   insecurely attached/avoidant
    c.   insecurely attached/ambivalent
    d.   insecurely attached/disorganized/disoriented

6. **Which of the following statements about the relationship between the mother's age and attachment is accurate?**
    a.   The mother's age is not a factor in attachment.
    b.   Adolescent mothers are more likely to describe their babies as "difficult."
    c.   Mothers in their 30s are more likely to describe their babies as "difficult."
    d.   Training in child development has no effect on the mother's ability to interpret an infant's behavior.

7. **An adult's _____ of attachment affect his or her parenting behaviors.**
    a.   internal model
    b.   activity level
    c.   nonfocused orientation
    d.   symmetry

8. **What type of attachment is the most common across cultures?**
    a. It differs greatly from culture to culture.
    b. It depends on the gender of the children.
    c. insecure attachment
    d. secure attachment

9. **Each of the following is a dimension of temperament described by many of the key researchers EXCEPT:**
    a. activity level
    b. emotional maturity
    c. inhibition
    d. negative emotionality

10. **Which statement is an accurate statement about where temperament qualities come from?**
    a. Temperament is developed in response to parental style.
    b. Gender differences can account for most differences in temperament.
    c. Temperament differences in infancy appear to be genetically based.
    d. Early differences in temperament are a combination of the infant's mood and parental style.

11. **People of all ages choose their experiences, a process Sandra Scarr calls _____.**
    a. temperament
    b. niche-picking
    c. affectional bonds
    d. heredity

12. **Another name for the objective self is ____.**
    a. existential self
    b. categorical self
    c. emotional self
    d. subjective self

13. **Each of the following is an issue impacting the study of nonparental care EXCEPT:**
    a. most children have the same nonparental care arrangements for many years
    b. an enormous range of different care arrangements are all lumped under the title of "nonparental care"
    c. infants enter nonparental care arrangements at different ages and stay for varying lengths of time
    d. nonparental care varies widely in quality

14. **What has been discovered about the effects of day care on cognitive development?**
    a. Children spending time in day care exhibit more emotional problems.
    b. Children from poorer families are especially disadvantaged by day care.
    c. There are no consistent findings about the effects of day care.
    d. Cognitively enriched day-care experiences tend to positively affect children.

15. **When children reach school age, those who entered nonparental care during the early months of life and who spent 20 or more hours per week in such care throughout early childhood are more likely to experience _____ than children who spent less time in nonparental care.**
    a. increased activity level
    b. increased emotionality
    c. increased social problems
    d. increased intelligence

TRUE-FALSE QUESTIONS

Indicate whether each of the following statements is true or false.

_____ 1.   Freud believed that the weaning process should be managed in such a way that the infant's need to suck is neither frustrated nor overgratified.

_____ 2.   Ethologists claim that the first five years constitute a sensitive period for attachment in human infants.

_____ 3.   The father's bond seems to depend more on the development of synchrony than on contact immediately after birth.

_____ 4.   By about ten months, babies will look first at Mom's or Dad's face to check for the adult's emotional expression.

_____ 5.   Generally speaking, difficult infants, as defined by Thomas and Chess, are more likely to be securely attached than babies in those theorists' other two categories.

_____ 6.   Near the middle of the first year, such self-conscious emotional expressions as embarrassment, pride, or shame emerge.

_____ 7.   The most common pattern of nonparental care is for a child to be cared for by a family member in her own or in a relative's home.

_____ 8.   When a day-care setting provides more enrichment than the child would have received at home, then day-care attendance has some beneficial cognitive effects.

ESSAY QUESTIONS

1.   Discuss the importance of synchrony with the infant.

2.   Thomas and Chess found that "easy" babies were more likely to be securely attached than "difficult" babies or "slow-to-warm-up" babies. Discuss the factors that might contribute to that attachment.

3.   Based on the research about nonparental care in the text and your own experience, what conclusions can you draw?

(Check your answers to Practice Test # on p. 128.)

WHEN YOU HAVE FINISHED . . . PUZZLE IT OUT

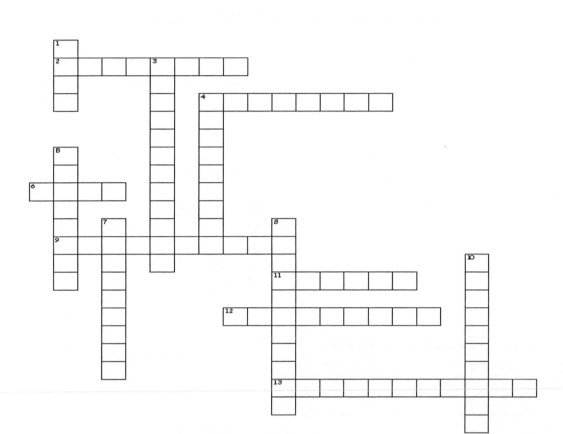

Across

2. Pattern of insecure attachment in which an infant shows no preference for the parent over others
4. Neurotransmitter that regulates the brain's response to unusual situations
6. First stage of Freud's theory
9. Also known as the existential self
11. Pattern of attachment in which the infant uses the parent as a safe base for exploration
12. A mutual, interlocking pattern of attachment behaviors
13. Inborn predispositions that form the foundations of personality

Down

1. Infants who approach new events positively and have good sleeping and eating cycles
3. Pattern of insecure attachment in which the infant shows contradictory behavior
4. Infants who are slow to develop regular sleeping and eating cycles
5. Stress hormone
7. Also known as the categorical self
8. A pattern of responding to people and objects in the environment
10. The emotional tie to a parent from which an infant derives security

Created by Puzzlemaker at DiscoverySchool.com

(Check your answers on p. 128.)

WHEN YOU HAVE FINISHED . . . INVESTIGATIVE PROJECT

Student Project 8: Observation of Turn Taking

This observation is designed to examine "turn taking" in the feeding interaction. You will observe a single feeding—breast or bottle—of an infant not older than one month, preferably younger. Naturally, you will need to obtain the appropriate written permission from the parents for this observation. Tell them that the purpose of your observation is simply for you to develop better observational skills. You will not be interfering in any way, and there are no "right" or "wrong" ways to go about the task.

Procedure

Observe for a total of about ten minutes, keeping a running record of behaviors by the child and by the parent. To make the task manageable, focus on only three behaviors for each member of the pair, listed below with an appropriate abbreviation letter for each:

Infant Behaviors	*Parent Behaviors*
▪ sucking (S) ▪ fussing or crying (C) ▪ other vocalizing (grunt, any other non-crying sounds) (V)	▪ jiggling (J) ▪ vocalizing (any talking to the infant, other sounds such as singing or cooing) (V) ▪ stroking or touching (T)

To record these behaviors, you will need a sheet with two columns of boxes on it: one column for the infant and one for the parent, such as:

Infant	Parent

Begin your observation a few minutes after the feeding has begun so that the infant and parent can adapt a bit to your presence and settle into some kind of pattern of interaction. Then start recording whatever behavior is occurring.
- If the infant is doing nothing, but the parent is jiggling or talking or touching, then put the relevant letter in the parent box for the first row.
- If the infant is doing something and the parent is simultaneously doing something, record each in the adjacent boxes in a single row.
- If the infant is doing something but the parent is not, then put the relevant letter in the infant box for that row and leave the parent box blank.

When either member of the pair changes behavior, move to the next row in your record sheet.
- If the baby sucks and then stops, and after the baby stops the mother jiggles and then says something, and then the baby sucks again, the chart would look like this:

Infant	Parent
S	
	J
	V

- If the baby sucks and the mother talks at the same time, and then the infant stops sucking and the mother keeps talking, it would look like this:

Infant	Parent
S	V
	V

For this observation, you should pay no attention to the duration of an activity. For the purposes of this exercise, it doesn't matter if the child sucks for three seconds or for 30 seconds before some change occurs.

When you have completed ten minutes of observation, or when the feeding is completed, whichever comes first, stop recording. You will need to remain seated and quiet until the feeding is over so as not to distract the parent or the infant. Be sure to thank the parent, and feel free to show the parent your observational record if he or she asks.

Analysis and Report

In examining your observational record, see if you can detect any signs of "turn taking" in the patterns of interaction. Does the parent jiggle or talk primarily in the pauses of the infant's sucking? Or does the parent talk and jiggle at the same time as the sucking? Can you devise some way of scoring the sequence of interactions that would yield a measure of "turn taking?" What are the difficulties involved in such a score?

WHEN YOU HAVE FINISHED . . . RESEARCH PROJECT

Student Project 9: Assessment of Day-Care Centers

You will have a far better sense of the variation in quality of day-care centers if you visit some yourself. Your instructor may have arranged for visits to several such centers, and you may need to sign up for designated times. If you have a choice, try to visit a least one for-profit center and at least one that is run by a charitable or educational organization (e.g., a church-run or university center).

Procedure

You should, of course, present yourself to the office in each center when you arrive, identifying yourself as a student in Professor _____'s _____ class. Find out whether there are any special ground rules, such as places you may not go.

Arrange to spend at least an hour in each center, sitting as unobtrusively as possible at the side of the room or on the edge of the playground. If you need to walk around so that you can see the full setting, feel free to do so, but do not intrude on the process. As you observe, imagine that you are a parent of a youngster, and you are looking for a care setting for that child.

With that frame of reference, record the following information for each center:
- What is the teacher/child ratio? Does this vary depending on the age of the child?
- How many children are cared for in each group in the center? (Some centers will care for all children as a single "group." Others will have separate rooms for children of different ages. What you want to know is the number of children cared for together.)

In addition, you should rate each center on a series of five-point scales, where a score of 1 always means "poor" or "low" and a score of 5 always means "optimum" or "high":

	Rating
Amount of individual one-on-one contact between adults and children	1 2 3 4 5
Amount of verbal stimulation from adults to children	1 2 3 4 5
Richness and complexity of verbal stimulation from adults to children	1 2 3 4 5
Cleanliness of environment	1 2 3 4 5

	Rating
Colorfulness of environment	1 2 3 4 5
Adequacy of space	1 2 3 4 5
Summary rating of center	1 2 3 4 5

Analysis

Compare the results for several centers which you observed. If you had a young child, would you be willing to place your child in any of these centers? Why or why not? Having observed these centers, can you suggest other criteria that might be helpful for a parent? What sort of research would be needed to determine the importance of any of these features for a child's development?

WHEN YOU HAVE FINISHED . . . INVESTIGATIVE PROJECT

Student Project 10: Investigation of Day-Care Options

Any parent can tell you that it is not easy to obtain good information about available day-care options. The purpose of this investigation project is therefore not only to discover as much as possible about the options in your community, but to identify good sources and good strategies for obtaining such information.

Basic Questions to Answer
- What center-care settings are available?
- Who runs the centers? For-profit companies? Churches? Schools? Others?
- How many and what ages of children do these centers accommodate? What are the costs of such center care?
- What is the best way for someone to find out about these care options?
- What family day-care options are available, and how does one locate them? Is there a registry? A licensing process? Are all family day-care providers listed in such registries or licensed?
- Are after-school care settings available as well? Who runs them? How much do they cost?
- Is care available for children in the evening and at night (as might be needed by a parent who works evenings or on the night shift)?

Sources
Much of the information you'll need can be gleaned on the phone, or from the phone book. The Yellow Pages will list day-care centers, usually under "Child-Care." Data on family day-care is much more difficult to come by (both for you and for parents). For information on licensing, especially the licensing of home-care or family day-care providers, you will want to talk to local or state government agencies. To locate individual care providers, bulletin boards are often the best data source—those located in places parents are likely to be, such as colleges or universities, on grocery store bulletin boards, in laundromats, etc. A person or group doing this project will need to sample such stores in some systematic fashion, and then call the providers whose names they find in this way to find out how many children are cared for, what age, for what hours, and what fee is charged.

Analysis and Report
Your instructor may want you to prepare an oral or a written report for your class. In any case, you should prepare a written description of the steps you followed and the answers to the questions listed above.

CHAPTER 6 ANSWER KEY

Practice Test #1 Theories of Social and Personality Development

1. F   2. T   3. T   4. T   5. F   6. T   7. T

Practice Test #2 Attachment

1. a   2. c   3. d   4. b   5. a   6. c   7. b   8. b   9. c   10. d

Practice Test #3 Personality, Temperament, and Self-Concept

1. j   2. e   3. l   4. q   5. i   6. n   7. m   8. h   9. d   10. p

Practice Test #4 Effects of Nonparental Care

1. T   2. F   3. T   4. F   5. T   6. T

Comprehensive Practice Test

Multiple Choice Questions

1. c   2. b   3. a   4. c   5. b   6. b   7. a   8. d   9. b   10. c
11. b   12. b   13. a   14. d   15. c

True-False Questions

1. T   2. F   3. T   4. T   5. F   6. F   7. T   8. T

Essay Questions

1. • Bonding of the adult with the infant.
   • Imitative conversation style—language development
   • Cognitive development

2. • Difficult babies actively resist comfort, consequently, synchrony may lead a parent to make less effort to establish a nurturing relationship with a difficult infant.
   • Slow-to-warm-up babies are less responsive to parental behaviors directed toward them. Synchrony causes the parents of these unresponsive infants to reduce the frequency of behaviors.
   • The kind of give-and-take relationships most easy infants experience with their parents never develop for babies who are difficult or slow-to-warm-up.

3. • Children who enter day care before their first birthday may be at greater risk for insecure attachment.
   • Children who stay in nonparental care for more than two hours per week are at greater risk for negative affects to social development.
   • The quality of the nonparental care is essential.
   • Quality care is likely to be especially beneficial to children from poor families.

Puzzle It Out

Across
2. Avoidant
4. Dopamine
6. Oral
9. Subjective
11. Secure
12. Synchrony
13. Temperament

Down
1. Easy
3. Disorganized
4. Difficult
5. Cortisol
7. Objective
8. Personality
10. Attachment

CHAPTER 7

PHYSICAL AND COGNITIVE DEVELOPMENT IN EARLY CHILDHOOD

BEFORE YOU READ . . . CHAPTER SUMMARY

In the years from two to six, the period known as early childhood, the child changes from being a dependent toddler, able to communicate only in very primitive ways, to being a remarkably competent, communicative social creature, ready to begin school. Subtle physical changes happen during this period as well as a number of advances in cognitive and language development. Issues involved in intelligence testing are also discussed.

Physical Changes

- Changes in height and weight are far slower in the preschool years than in infancy. Motor skills continue to improve gradually, with marked improvement in large muscle skills and slower advances in small muscle skills.
- Brain growth, synapse formation, and myelinization continue in early childhood, although at a pace slower than in infancy. Neurological milestones, such as lateralization and handedness, happen between two and six.
- Health and wellness issues include diet, illness, stress, and accidents.
- Two- to nine-year-olds are more likely to be abused or neglected than infants or older children. Characteristics of the child and the abuser increase the risk of abuse. Education, identification of families at risk, and keeping abused children from further injury are three ways to prevent abuse.

Cognitive Changes

- According to Piaget, the 18- to 24-month-old child begins to use symbols and enters the preoperational stage. Despite this advance, the preschool child still lacks many sophisticated cognitive characteristics. This age child is still egocentric and lacks an understanding of conservation.
- Research challenging Piaget's findings makes it clear that young children are less egocentric than Piaget thought.
- By age four or five, the child has developed a new and quite sophisticated theory of mind. They understand that other people's actions are based on their thoughts and beliefs.
- Information-processing theory explains early childhood cognitive development in terms of limitations on young children's memory systems. Vygotsky's socio-cultural theory asserts that children's thinking is shaped by social interaction through the medium of language.

Changes in Language

- Fast-mapping enables language development to increase at a rapid pace between ages two and four
- Between ages three and four, children's advances in grammar are extraordinary. Inflections, questions and negatives, and overregularization lead to the use of complex sentences.
- Phonological awareness, a child's sensitivity to the sound patterns that are specific to her own language, is key to the child's ability to learn to read and write. Children seem to acquire this skill through word play.

Differences in Intelligence

- Scores on early childhood intelligence tests are predictive of later school performance and are at least moderately consistent over time.
- Arguments about the origins of difference in IQ nearly always boil down to a dispute about nature versus nurture.
- Several kinds of racial differences in IQ or test performance have been consistently found. Such differences seem most appropriately attributed to environmental variation, rather than genetics.

AS YOU READ . . . LEARNING OJECTIVES

After completing Chapter 7, you should be able to:

7.1   Summarize the changes in growth and motor development in preschool children.
7.2   List and describe the developmental milestones of the brain and the nervous system in early childhood.
7.3   Identify the most common health issues of children in early childhood.
7.4   Summarize the research on sleep problems in early childhood.
7.5   Summarize the issues involved in abuse and neglect of children.
7.6   Describe Piaget's view of cognitive development during the preschool period.
7.7   List and describe five kinds of play behaviors.
7.8   Summarize the challenges to Piaget's view.
7.9   Summarize the research on theories of mind.
7.10   Describe the alternative theories of early childhood thinking.
7.11   Explain how preschoolers use fast-mapping to increase their vocabularies.
7.12   Summarize the increase in grammar in the preschool years.
7.13   Describe the development of phonological awareness in the preschool years.
7.14   Identify the issues involved in measuring intelligence.
7.15   Describe the issues surrounding the origins of the differences in intelligence.
7.16   State the pros and cons involved in using the computer to teach young children.
7.17   Summarize the research findings on racial differences in IQ.
7.18   Identify the pros and cons of intelligence testing of preschool children.

AS YOU READ . . . TERM IDENTIFICATION

Centration (p. 175)
Conservation (p. 175)
Corpus callosum (p. 168)
Egocentrism (p. 173)
False belief principle (p. 177)
Fast-mapping (p. 182)
Handedness (p. 168)
Hippocampus (p. 168)
Intelligence quotient (IQ) (p. 186)
Inverted spelling (p. 185)
Lateralization (p. 168)

Metacognition (p. 180)
Metamemory (p. 180)
Operational efficiency (p. 179)
Overregularization (p. 183)
Phonological awareness (p. 184)
Preoperational stage (p. 173)
Reaction range (p. 191)
Semiotic (symbolic) function (p. 173)
Short-term storage space (STSS) (p. 179)
Theory of mind (p. 178)

AS YOU READ . . . GUIDED STUDY QUESTIONS

PHYSICAL CHANGES

Growth and Motor Development (pp. 166-168)

Objective 7.1: Summarize the changes in growth and motor development in preschool children.

1.   What are the typical changes in height and weight in the preschool years?

2.   Compare the milestones of motor development from age two to age six by completing the following table:

Age	*Locomotor*	*Non-locomotor*	*Manipulative*
18-24 months			
2-3 years			
3-4 years			
4-5 years			
5-6 years			

3.   How does training in writing and drawing affect physical and cognitive development?

The Brain and Nervous System (pp. 168-169)

Objective 7.2:   List and describe the developmental milestones of the brain and the nervous system in early childhood.

4.   Define the following terms:
     a.   corpus callosum (p. 168)

     b.   lateralization (p. 168)

     c.   hippocampus (p. 168)

     d.   handedness (p. 168)

5.   Describe the interaction of maturation and experience in the development of lateralization.

6.   How is the hippocampus involved in memory?

7.   How does handedness develop?

Health and Wellness (pp. 169-171)

Objective 7.3: Identify the most common health issues of children in early childhood.

8.   For each of the following health issues of children in early childhood, identify possible causes of concern:

Issue	Possible Causes of Concern
Medical Check-ups	
Diet	
Illness	
Stress	
Accidents	

The Real World: Sleep Problems in Early Childhood (p. 170)

Objective 7.4: Summarize the research on sleep problems in early childhood.

9.   List and give examples of reasons why children's sleep patterns often increase after the child's second birthday.

10.   Distinguish between nightmares and night terrors.

11.   Explain how operant conditioning may be involved in children sleeping in their parents' bed.

12.   List five recommended sleep hygiene practices

Abuse and Neglect (pp. 171-173)

Objective 7.5: Summarize the issues involved in abuse and neglect of children.

13.   Define child abuse using the legal definition.

14.   List at least two reasons why it is difficult to define child abuse and neglect in a practical sense.

15.   List six types of child abuse.

16.   Give examples of each of the following broad categories of explanations of why abuse happens.

Categories	Examples
Socio-cultural Factors	
Characteristics of the Child	
Characteristics of the Abuser	
Family Stresses	

17.   Describe post-traumatic stress disorder (PTSD), and explain why some abused children develop it.

18.   List ways each of the following may help prevent abuse:

Categories	Ways to Prevent Abuse
Education	
Identification of families at risk	
Protection from further injury	

AFTER YOU READ . . . PRACTICE TEST #1
PHYSICAL CHANGES

1.   **During the preschool years, children add about _____ in height and about _____ in weight.**
   a.   1-3 inches; 4 pounds
   b.   2-4 inches; 8 pounds
   c.   2-3 inches; 6 pounds
   d.   3-5 inches; 10 pounds

2.   **Running, jumping, hopping, and skipping are examples of _____.**
   a.   fine-muscle skills
   b.   large-muscle skills
   c.   manipulative skills
   d.   nonlocomotor skills

3. **The brain structure through which the left and right sides of the cerebral cortex communicate is called _____.**
   a.   the corpus callosum
   b.   lateralization
   c.   handedness
   d.   brain maturation

4. **The process through which brain functions are divided between the two hemispheres of the cerebral cortex is called _____.**
   a.   brain maturation
   b.   myelinization
   c.   the corpus callosum
   d.   lateralization

5. **The tendency to rely primarily on the right or left hand is called _____.**
   a.   the reticular formation
   b.   handedness
   c.   brain maturation
   d.   myelinization

6. **Children living in single-parent homes are more likely than children living with both biological parents to experience each of the following EXCEPT:**
   a.   more headaches
   b.   more asthma
   c.   less stress
   d.   higher vulnerability to illness

7. **Each of the following is a type of child abuse EXCEPT:**
   a.   providing adequate supervision
   b.   drugging or poisoning children
   c.   failure to obtain medical attention for an illness or injury
   d.   underfeeding an infant

8. **Post-traumatic stress disorder involves each of the following EXCEPT:**
   a.   nightmares
   b.   flashback memories
   c.   sleep disturbances
   d.   low levels of anxiety

(Check your answers to Practice Test #1 on p. 150.)

COGNITIVE CHANGES

Piaget's Preoperational Stage (pp. 173-175)

Objective 7.6: Describe Piaget's view of cognitive development during the preschool period.

19. Define the following terms, and give examples of each:
    a. semiotic (symbolic) function (p. 173)

    b. preoperational stage (p. 173)

    c. egocentrism (p. 173)

    d. centration (p. 175)

    e. conservation (p. 175)

20. Explain Piaget's use of the following terms, and give examples of each:
    a. locomotion
    b. animism

21. Explain how children demonstrate their understanding of conservations by using each of the characteristics listed in the table.

Characteristic	Explanation of Conservation
Identity	
Compensation	
Reversibility	

Research Report: Children's Play and Cognitive Development (p. 174)

Objective 7.7: List and describe five kinds of play behaviors.

22. Complete the following table with a description of each of the six play behaviors:

Type of Play	Play Behaviors
Constructive Play	
First Pretend Play	
Substitute Pretend Play	
Sociodramatic Play	
Rule-Governed Play	

Challenges to Piaget's View (pp. 175-177)

Objective 7.8: Summarize the challenges to Piaget's view.

23. List and give examples of the two levels of perspective-taking ability proposed by John Flavell.

24. Give an example of how preschoolers' understanding of emotion has challenged Piaget's description of the young child's egocentrism.

25. Define the false belief principle (p. 177), and give an example.

Theories of Mind (pp. 178-179)

Objective 7.9: Summarize the research on theories of mind.

26. Define theory of mind (p. 178).

27. Describe the progression of children's understanding of thoughts, desires, and beliefs by completing the following table:

Age	Examples of Understanding
3	
4-5	
6	
5-7	

28. List at least four correlates of a child's theory of mind.

29. Give examples of how certain aspects of theory of mind develop across cultures.

Alternative Theories of Early Childhood Thinking (pp. 179-181)

Objective 7.10: Describe the alternative theories of early childhood thinking.

30. Define the following terms:
    a. short-term storage space (STSS) (p. 179)

    b. operational efficiency (p. 179)

    c. metamemory (p. 180)

    d. metacognition (p. 180)

31. How does Robbie Case's Neo-Piagetian theory explain why the seven-year-old is better able to handle the processing demands of conservation than the four-year-old?

32.   Describe the research on training children in matrix classification skills.

33.   Give examples of how children's metamemory and metacognitive skills improve during the early childhood period.

34.   Briefly describe Vygotsky's views on development using the example of the puzzle.

35.   Vygotsky proposed four stages that represent steps toward the child's internalization of the ways of thinking used by adults in her society. Complete the following table to trace this development:

Stage	Examples of Internalization
Primitive Stage	
Naive Psychology Stage	
Private Speech Stage	
Ingrowth Stage	

AFTER YOU READ . . . PRACTICE TEST #2
COGNITIVE CHANGES

Match the letter of the term in the right column with its description in the left column.

_____ 1.   A set of ideas constructed by a child or adult to explain other people's ideas, beliefs, desires, and behavior.

_____ 2.   Play that develops by age 5 or 6 in which children prefer formal games.

_____ 3.   The understanding that one subject or behavior can represent another.

_____ 4.   The capacity to mentally compare the transformed appearance of a given quantity of matter to its original appearance.

_____ 5.   An understanding that enables a child to look at a situation from another person's point of view and cause that person to have a false belief.

_____ 6.   A neo-Piagetian term that refers to the maximum number of schemes that can be processed in working memory at one time.

_____ 7.   The knowledge about how the mind thinks and the ability to control and reflect on one's own thought processes.

_____ 8.   The stage of Vygotsky's theory in which the child learns to use language to communicate but still does not understand its symbolic character.

_____ 9.   Product of preoperational logic when children believe that objects are alive.

_____ 10.   Play between ages 2 and 3 when children begin to use objects to stand for something altogether different.

a. Animism
b. Centration
c. Compensation
d. Constructive
e. Conservation
f. Egocentrism
g. False belief principle
h. First pretend
i. Matrix classification
j. Metacognition
k. Metamemory
l. Naïve psychology
m. Operational efficiency
n. Primitive
o. Reversibility
p. Rule-governed
q. Semiotic function
r. Short-term storage space
s. Sociodramatic
t. Substitute pretend
u. Theory of mind

(Check your answers to Practice Test #2 on p. 150.)

CHANGES IN LANGUAGE

Fast-Mapping (p. 182)

Objective 7.11: *Explain how preschooler's use fast-mapping to increase their vocabularies.*

36.   Define fast-mapping (p. 182), and explain how it enables preschool children to learn new words.

The Grammar Explosion (pp. 182-184)

Objective 7.12: *Summarize the increase in grammar in the preschool years.*

37.   Children seem to add inflections and more complex word orders in fairly predictable sequences. Give examples of each of the following:

Inflection	Example
Adding –ing to a Verb	
Preposition	
Plural	
Irregular Past Tense	
Possessives	
Articles	
Plural to Third-Person Verbs	
Regular Past Tense	
Auxiliary Verbs	

38.   List the sequence in the child's developing use of questions and negatives.

39.   Define overregularization (p. 183), or overgeneralization, and give examples.

Phonological Awareness (pp. 184-185)

Objective 7.13: *Describe the development of phonological awareness in the preschool years.*

40.   Define the following terms, and give examples of each:
   a.   phonological awareness (p. 184)

   b.   invented spelling (p. 185)

41.   What are the benefits to the child of developing phonological awareness in early childhood?

42. Describe how phonological awareness develops through word play.

43. What are the benefits to the child of using invented spelling as a preschooler?

AFTER YOU READ . . . PRACTICE TEST #3
CHANGES IN LANGUAGE

Indicate whether each of the following statements is true or false.

_____ 1. By the time a child goes to school at age 5 or 6, her total vocabulary has risen to perhaps 50,000 words.

_____ 2. Referents are the real objects and events to which words refer.

_____ 3. Children learning English typically add the –s to third person verbs before they add –ing to a verb.

_____ 4. When a child says, "I go-ed to the store with Mommy," he is using overregularization.

_____ 5. Phonological awareness in the early childhood years is related to rate of literacy in languages as varied as English, Punjabi, and Chinese.

_____ 6. Reciting nursery rhymes is an example of word play that contributes to phonological awareness.

(Check your answers to Practice Test #3 on p. 150.)

DIFFERENCES IN INTELLIGENCE

Measuring Intelligence (pp. 185-188)

Objective 7.14: Identify the issues involved in measuring intelligence.

44. Define intelligence quotient, or IQ (p. 186).

45. Who designed the first modern intelligence test that was published in 1905?

46. What was the practical purpose of the first test?

47. How was IQ computed from the Stanford-Binet? State the formula and give examples.

48. What is the current process for IQ score calculations?

49. What are the scores for "gifted" and for "retarded"?

50. Describe the Wechsler Intelligence Scale for Children (WISC-IV).

51. Describe how a child's high IQ adds to the child's resilience.

52. What negative long-term outcomes are associated with low intelligence?

53. Describe how IQ scores can be stable, yet show wide fluctuations in individual scores.

54. List at least three limitations of IQ tests.

Origins of Individual Differences in Intelligence (pp. 188-191)

Objective 7.15: Describe the issues surrounding the origins of the differences in intelligence.

55.   What do both twin studies and studies of adopted children show?

56.   List five behaviors of family interactions that foster higher scores.

57.   How do programs like Head Start or other quality preschool experiences supplement home environments and family interactions? Include IQ scores as well as other measures in your answer.

58.   Define reaction range (p. 191), and give examples.

Development in the Information Age: Computers and Early Childhood Learning (p. 190)

Objective 7.16: State the pros and cons involved in using the computer to teach young children.

59.   List three positive outcomes of using computers to teach young children.

60.   List and describe four important questions about using computers that remain to be answered.

61.   List three suggestions for using computers as an additional learning opportunity rather than as a replacement for traditional activities.

Racial Differences in Intelligence Test Scores (pp. 191-193)

Objective 7.17: Summarize the research findings on racial differences in IQ.

62.   How do many developmentalists use reaction range to explain differences in IQ scores of African-American and white children?

63.   Describe the Flynn effect, and give examples.

64.   Give examples of Flynn's belief that many theorists have neglected a consideration of cultural beliefs in their search for a heredity basis for intelligence.

No Easy Answers: To Test or Not to Test? (p. 193)

Objective 7.18: Identify the pros and cons of intelligence testing of preschool children.

65.   How can intelligence testing benefit children?

66.   Why is routine testing of young children who have no disabilities more controversial?

AFTER YOU READ . . . PRACTICE TEST #4
DIFFERENCES IN INTELLIGENCE

1. **Psychologists can devise tests of intelligence for preschoolers that measure _____.**
    a. vocabulary and reasoning skills
    b. only vocabulary
    c. mathematical ability
    d. reasoning skills and mathematical ability

2. **The practical use of the first modern intelligence test was to _____.**
    a. sort out children who were gifted and needed extra assignments
    b. label children as "smart" and "not smart"
    c. place children in "tracks" for their school career
    d. identify children who might have difficulty in school.

3. **Children who score above _____ are often called gifted.**
    a. 100
    b. 110
    c. 120
    d. 130

4. **The two subgroups of the _____ are the verbal scale and the performance scale.**
    a. Case Scales of Intelligence in Early Childhood
    b. Flynn Measure of Intelligence
    c. Wechsler Intelligence Scales for Children
    d. Simon Intelligence Test

5. **Intelligence is likely to add to a child's _____.**
    a. resilience
    b. secular effect
    c. reaction range
    d. Flynn effect

6. **Low intelligence is associated with each of the following negative long-term outcomes EXCEPT:**
    a. delinquency in adolescence
    b. increased self-esteem
    c. adult illiteracy
    d. criminal behavior in adulthood

7. **Children who go through Head Start or other quality preschool experience _____**
    a. are more likely to be placed in special education classes than their peers
    b. have poorer immunization rates than their peers
    c. are more likely to repeat a grade than their peers
    d. have better school adjustment than their peers

8. **_____ is a range between upper and lower boundaries for traits such as intelligence, which is established by one's genes; one's environment determines where, within those limits, one will be.**
    a. Flynn effect
    b. Reaction range
    c. Intelligence quotient
    d. The gifted-retarded dichotomy

(Check your answers to Practice Test #4 on p. 150.)

AFTER YOU READ . . . CRITICAL REFLECTION EXERCISES

Kindergarten

You are about to enter your first day of teaching kindergarten. Based on the information provided in the text, provide detailed responses to the following questions:

1.   At what level of language development will most of these children be? What language skills will they have?

2.   How might the child's perception of you and the classroom experience be related to culture? What things might you do to minimize any potential negative effects of cultural differences, yet support these differences at the same time?

3.   How would a child's cognitive development influence his or her play?

Intelligence

Based on the discussion of intelligence in the text, how would you define "intelligence"? There is not a "right versus wrong" definition. Utilizing the concepts discussed, what definition makes sense to you? Why? How would you utilize this definition if you were raising a child in the two to six age range?

AFTER YOU READ . . . COMPREHENSIVE PRACTICE TEST
MULTIPLE CHOICE QUESTIONS

1. **Which of the following statements is TRUE concerning growth and motor skill development in the preschool years?**
    a.   Changes in height and weight are at the same rate as in infancy.
    b.   Changes in motor development are as dramatic as in infancy.
    c.   The most impressive changes are in small muscle skills.
    d.   Changes in height and weight are far slower in the preschool years.

2. **The _____ is involved in the transfer of information to long-term memory.**
    a.   corpus callosum
    b.   hippocampus
    c.   cerebral cortex
    d.   cerebellum

3. **_____ are the major cause of death in preschool and school-age children.**
    a.   Accidents
    b.   Chronic illnesses
    c.   Acute illnesses
    d.   Stressful situations

4. **Each of the following is one of the four broad categories of abuse EXCEPT:**
    a.   socio-cultural factors
    b.   family stresses
    c.   responsive parenting
    d.   characteristics of the child

5. **According to Piaget, the preschool child is in the _____ stage of cognitive development.**
    a.   sensorimotor
    b.   preoperational
    c.   concrete operational
    d.   formal operational

6. **An understanding that enables a child to look at a situation from another person's point of view and determine what kind of information will cause that person to have a false belief is called _____.**
    a.   the theory of mind
    b.   conservation
    c.   egocentrism
    d.   the false belief principle

7. **A set of ideas that explains other people's ideas, beliefs, desires, and behaviors is called _____.**
    a.   false belief principle
    b.   theory of mind
    c.   metamemory
    d.   matrix classification

8.   **Knowledge about how memory works and the ability to control and reflect on one's own memory function is called _____.**
   a.   metamemory
   b.   metacognition
   c.   metaprocessing
   d.   metaknowledge

9.   **The ability to categorically link new worlds to real-world referents is called _____.**
   a.   fast-tracking
   b.   categorizing
   c.   fast-mapping
   d.   invented spelling

10.   **Which of the following inflections is the child likely to add first to his words?**
   a.   the suffix *–ing*
   b.   the suffix *–ed*
   c.   auxiliary verbs
   d.   plurals

11.   **A child who says "foots" instead of "feet" is _____.**
   a.   probably in danger of developing language deficits
   b.   exhibiting overregularization
   c.   not a native speaker of English
   d.   at least five years old

12.   **A child's sensitivity to the sound patterns that are specific to her own language is called _____.**
   a.   metacognition
   b.   overregularization
   c.   metamemory
   d.   phonological awareness

13.   **Which of the following correctly illustrates the formula use to calculate IQ?**
   a.   chronological age + mental age ÷ 100
   b.   mental age ÷ chronological age x 100
   c.   chronological age – mental age + 100
   d.   chronological age ÷ mental age - 100

14.   **Which of the following family characteristics tends to lead to children having higher IQs?**
   a.   families that avoid excessive restrictiveness
   b.   families that set extremely high performance standards
   c.   families that do not place high demands on their children
   d.   families that encourage competition between siblings

15.   **Which of the following statements is TRUE about IQ testing?**
   a.   IQ testing is seldom beneficial to any child.
   b.   IQ testing of children is always reliable.
   a.   IQ tests are important tools for identifying children who have special educational needs.
   b.   Labeling non-disabled young children on the basis of IQ scores is strongly recommended.

TRUE-FALSE QUESTIONS

Indicate whether each of the following statements is true or false.

_____ 1.   Brain growth, synapse formation, and myelinization continue in early childhood at the same rate as in infancy.

_____ 2.   Obesity in early childhood is common.

_____ 3.   Piaget used the term animism to refer to the aspect of preoperational logic in which children believe that inanimate objects are alive.

_____ 4.   Robbie Case theorized that there is a limit on how many schemes can be attended to in short-term storage space (STSS).

_____ 5.   After children have figured out inflections and the basic sentence forms using negatives and questions, they begin to create remarkably complex sentences.

_____ 6.   Children who use invented spelling strategies before school-based instruction in reading and writing are more likely to become poor spellers and poor readers later in childhood.

_____ 7.   When an enrichment program such as Head Start is begun in infancy rather than at age 3 or 4, IQ scores remain elevated into adulthood.

_____ 8.   Many developmentalists emphasize that the environments in which African-American and white children are typically reared differ sufficiently to account for the average difference in IQ score.

ESSAY QUESTIONS

1.   The text states that the difference between abusive and non-abusive parents is the presence of a number of risk factors that show how the parents respond to the ordinary stresses of parenting. Discuss the risk factors and how they interact to affect whether or not parents abuse their children.

2.   Compare Piaget's concept of egocentrism with the theory of mind. Are they mutually exclusive or can a child be egocentric as well as the theory of mind? Give examples to support your answer.

3.   Choose a book, story, or nursery rhyme that preschoolers might enjoy that uses word play to increase their phonological awareness. Give examples of how it would increase a child's phonological awareness.

(Check your answers to the Comprehensive Practice Test on p. 150.)

WHEN YOU HAVE FINISHED . . . PUZZLE IT OUT

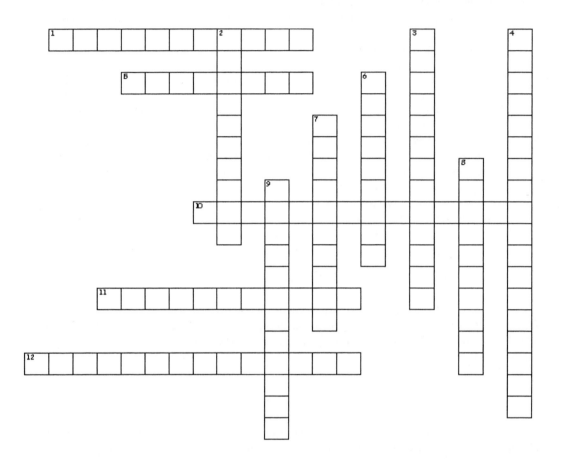

Across

1. A brain structure that is important in learning
5. Range between upper and lower boundaries which is established by one's genes
10. Piaget's second stage of cognitive development
11. The young child's belief that everyone sees the world the way she does
12. The process through which brain functions are divided between the two hemispheres of the cerebral cortex

Down

2. Knowledge about how memory works
3. Knowledge about how the mind thinks
4. Attachment of regular inflections to irregular words
6. A dream that includes a frightening experience
7. A strong preference for using one hand or the other
8. The young child's tendency to think of the world in terms of one variable at a time
9. The understanding that matter can change in appearance without changing in quantity

Created by Puzzlemaker at DiscoverySchool.com

(Check your answers on p. 150.)

WHEN YOU HAVE FINISHED . . . INVESTIGATIVE PROJECT

Student Project 11: Assessing the Child's Theory of Mind

For this project, you will need to locate a child between the ages of three and five. You must obtain written permission from the child's parents, following whatever procedure your instructor specifies. The testing should be done in a quiet place in the child's home.

The task that has most often been used to assess the child's theory of mind has been called the Smarties task because it uses a box of a type of candy called "Smarties," common in England and Canada where much of this research has been done. United States children, however, are not going to be familiar with Smarties, so we need to revise the procedure, using an M&M bag filled with small rocks.

Procedure

Find a quiet place where you and the child can sit down at a table or on the floor. Tell the child:

> *We're going to play a game where I show you some things and ask you questions about them.*

Bring out your M&M bag and ask the child to look at it. Then open the bag and show the child that there are rocks inside. Ask:

> *What's inside the bag?*

If the child doesn't say "rocks," ask again, *What are they?* When it is clear that the child knows that they are really rocks, put the rocks in the bag and close it. Now ask the child the following questions (all adapted from the procedure used by Gopnik & Astington, 1988) and write down the child's answers carefully.

> *Does it look like this bag has rocks in it or does it look like it has candies in it?*
>
> *What's really inside the bag? Are there really rocks inside it, or are there really candies inside it?*
>
> *When you first saw the bag, before we opened it, what did you think was inside it? Did you think there were rocks inside it, or did you think there were candies inside it?*
>
> *Your Mom hasn't seen inside this bag. If your Mom sees the bag all closed up like this, what will she think is inside it? Will she think there are rocks inside it, or will she think there are candies inside it?*

When you are done, thank the child, compliment the child on his or her answers, and stay long enough to play with the child at some game the child chooses.

Analysis and Report

In analyzing and reporting on your result, compare your child's answers to those reported in the text. Did your child understand the difference between appearance and reality? Did she or he understand false belief?

Reference

Gopnik, A., & Astington, J. W. (1988). Children's understanding of representational change and its relation to the understanding of false belief and the appearance-reality distinction. *Child Development, 59,* 26-37.

WHEN YOU HAVE FINISHED . . . RESEARCH PROJECT

Student Project 12: Beginning Two-Word Sentences

Some of you have been around young children a lot, and already have some sense for the delightful quality of their early language, but all of you would benefit from some additional listening. Locate a child who is still in the earliest stages of sentence formation, or just beginning to add a few inflections. This is most likely to be a child of 20 to 24 months, but a child between 24 and 30 months may do fine, too. The one essential aspect is that the child must be speaking at least some two-word sentences. If you are unsure, ask the parent; they can nearly always tell you whether the child has reached this stage or not.

Procedure

As usual, begin by following whatever procedures your instructor requires for obtaining appropriate informed consent from the parents of your subject for you to observe. Then arrange to spend enough time with the child at his or her home, or in any other convenient setting, so that you can collect a list of 50 different spontaneous utterances, including both one-word and two-word sentences. By spontaneous, I mean those that the child speaks without prompting; try to avoid getting into a situation in which the mother or some other adult actively tries to elicit language from the child, although it is certainly acceptable if you collect a sample from a time when the child is playing with an adult, or doing some activity with a parent or older sibling. The most fruitful time is likely to be when the child is playing with someone, and it is fine to ask the mother to play with the child, but not to play the sort of game in which the object is to get the child to talk. Whenever you can, make notes about the context in which each sentence occurred so that you can judge the meaning more fully.

Analysis and Report

When you have your list of 50 utterances, try describing the child's language in any terms from the text. For example, is the child using any grammatical inflections? Which ones? Does the pattern conform to what was described? What about questions or negatives? And what about the different meanings expressed? What is the child's mean length of utterance (MLU)? To calculate the MLU you will need to count the number of meaningful units in each sentence. Each word is a meaningful unit, but so is each grammatical inflection, like the -*s* for a plural, the -*ed* ending for a past tense, etc. Some specific rules to follow in calculating the MLU are:

1.   Do not count such sounds as "uh," or " "um," "oh," but do count "no," "yeah," and "hi."
2.   All compound words, like "birthday," "choo-choo," "night-night," and "pocketbook" should be counted as single words.
3.   Count all irregular past tenses as single words, such as "got," "did," "want," and "saw," but count as two words any regular past tense, such as "play-ed," or any erroneous extension of the past tense, such as "went-ed."
4.   Count as one all diminutives, such as "doggie" or "mommy."
5.   Count as one all combinations, such as "gonna," "wanna," or "hafta."
6.   Count as one each auxiliary, such as "is," "have," "will," "can," and "must," and as one each inflection, such as the "s" for plural or possessive, the "s" for third person singular verb form, and the "ing" on a verb.

WHEN YOU HAVE FINISHED . . . RESEARCH PROJECT

Student Project 13: Conversation between Mother and Child

This project focuses on the social environment—what is said to the child as well as the child's response. Again, find a child around age two, though it's acceptable to go up to about three and a half. (It can be the same child you listened to in project 12, but you should collect the two sets of observations separately.)

Procedure

After obtaining the appropriate informed consent, spend some time with the child while the mother or father is around. As with project 12, the interaction should be as spontaneous as possible. It is fine if the adult and child play together as long as they aren't playing "repeat after me" naming games.

Record the conversation between the parent and the child, making sure that you have the sentences of the two people in the right order. Continue to record the conversation until you have at least 25 sentences for each. You may use a tape recorder if you wish, but you'll find it helpful to write down the sentences as they occur as well.

Analysis and Report

Did the adult adapt his or her language to that of the child? Did the adult repeat the child's utterances with minor modifications? Was there any obvious reinforcement or shaping going on? Did the adult attempt to correct the child's speech, and if so, what was the effect? Include your record of the conversation in your report, along with a page or two of comments.

CHAPTER 7 ANSWER KEY

Practice Test #1 Physical Changes

| 1. c | 2. b | 3. a | 4. d | 5. b | 6. c | 7. a | 8. d | | |

Practice Test #2 Cognitive Changes

| 1. u | 2. p | 3. q | 4. o | 5. g | 6. m | 7. j | 8. l | 9. a | 10. t |

Practice Test #3 Changes in Language

| 1. F | 2. T | 3. F | 4. T | 5. T | 6. T | | | | |

Practice Test #4 Differences in Intelligence

| 1. a | 2. d | 3. d | 4. c | 5. a | 6. b | 7. d | 8. b | | |

Comprehensive Practice Test

Multiple Choice Questions

| 1. d | 2. b | 3. a | 4. c | 5. b | 6. d | 7. b | 8. a | 9. c | 10. a |
| 11. b | 12. d | 13. b | 14. a | 15. c | | | | | |

True-False Questions

| 1. F | 2. F | 3. T | 4. T | 5. T | 6. F | 7. T | 8. T |

Essay Questions

1.
   - Socio-cultural factors: Personal or cultural values that regard physical abuse of children as morally acceptable.
   - Characteristics of the child: Children with physical or mental disabilities or those who have difficult temperaments.
   - Characteristics of the abusers: Parents who are depressed, lack parenting skills and knowledge, have a history of abuse themselves, or are substances abusers.
   - Family stresses: Factors such as poverty, unemployment, and inter-parental conflict

2.
   - Egocentrism: The preoperational child's tendency to look at things entirely from her own point of view.
   - Theory of mind: A set of ideas constructed by a child or adult to explain other people's ideas, beliefs, desires, and behavior.

3.
   - Choose a favorite and include specific examples.

Puzzle It Out

Across
1. Hippocampus
5. Reaction
10. Preoperational
11. Egocentrism
12. Lateralization

Down
2. Metamemory
3. Metacognition
4. Overregularization
6. Nightmare
7. Handedness
8. Centration
9. Conservation

CHAPTER 8

SOCIAL AND PERSONALITY DEVELOPMENT IN EARLY CHILDHOOD

BEFORE YOU READ . . . CHAPTER SUMMARY

Children between ages two and six undergo remarkable changes in their social skills. They go from being nay-saying, oppositional toddlers who spend most of their play times alone to being skilled, cooperative playmates by age five or six.

Theories of Social and Personality Development

- Freud and Erikson each described two stages of personality development in early childhood. Both suggest that the key to this period is the balance between the child's emerging skills and desire for autonomy, and the parent's need to protect and control the child's behavior. More recent psychoanalytic approaches, however, include relationships with peers and siblings.
- Social-cognitive theorists emphasize that advances in social and personality development are associated with cognitive development. They focus on three areas of interest: person perception, understanding of intentions, and understanding of different kinds of rules.

Family Relationships and Structure

- Although the child's attachment to the parents remains strong, many attachment behaviors become less visible. Young preschoolers may show more refusals and defiance of parental influence attempts than infants, but as they gain language and cognitive skills, they generally comply fairly readily.
- Different approaches to parenting result in differences in children's development. Authoritative parenting, combining warmth, clear rules, and communication with high maturity demands, is associated with the most positive results.
- Ethnicity and socioeconomic class are linked to parenting style. Studies of parenting style and developmental outcomes suggest that in some situations, authoritative parenting may not always be the "best" style for Asian Americans, African Americans, and children of poor parents.
- Family structure affects social and personality development. Data from studies in the United States indicate that more positive outcomes are associated with two biological parents than any other family structure.
- Following a divorce, children typically show declines in school performance and show more aggressive, negative, or depressed behavior. Many effects of divorce are associated with problems that existed before the marriage ended.
- A number of variables are involved with family structure and divorce, such as a change in family income, the upheaval of subtracting or adding new adults to the family system, and the possible shift away from authoritative parenting. Ultimately, it is the process within the family, rather than any particular disruption, that is significant for the child.

Peer Relationships

- Preschoolers participate in various kinds of play that are related to the development of social skills. Children who are unskilled at the social skill of group entry are often rejected by their peers.

- Physical aggression toward peers increases and then declines during these years, whereas verbal aggression increases among older preschoolers. Some children develop a pattern of aggression that creates problems for them throughout childhood and adolescence.
- Children display prosocial behavior as young as age two, and the behavior seems to grow as the child's ability to take another's perspective increases. Parents and teachers can encourage the development of altruistic behavior.

Personality and Self-Concept

- As young children gain more understanding of the social environment, their temperaments ripen into true personalities.
- Two aspects of self-concept, the categorical self and the emotional self, continue to develop between ages two and six, and the social self is added. Children make major strides in self-control and in their understanding of their own social roles.

The Gender Concept and Sex Roles

- Neither Freud's nor Erikson's explanations of gender development has fared well. Social learning theory explanations are more persuasive but ignore the role of cognitive development. Social-cognitive theories explain and predict gender-related understanding and behavior better then psychoanalytic or learning theories.
- Children seem to develop gender constancy, the understanding that gender is an innate characteristic that cannot be changed, in three steps: labeling their own and others' gender, understanding the stability of gender, and comprehending the constancy of gender at about age five or six.
- In these same years, children begin to learn what goes with being a boy or a girl in a given culture. By age five or six, most children have developed fairly rigid rules about what boys or girls are supposed to do or be.
- Sex-typed behavior, different patterns of behavior among girls and boys, develops earlier than ideas about sex roles, beginning as early as 18 to 24 months of age. Girls tend to adopt an enabling style of behavior whereas boys are likely to show a constricting or restrictive style.

AS YOU READ . . . LEARNING OBJECTIVES

After completing Chapter 8, you should be able to:
8.1 Summarize the key points of the psychoanalytic theories that are relevant to early childhood.
8.2 Summarize the key points of the social-cognitive perspective that are relevant to early childhood.
8.3 Describe how racial attitudes may be formed in the preschool classroom.
8.4 Describe the preschool-aged child's attachment to his or her parents.
8.5 Discuss the impact of styles of parenting on the social and personality development of the preschool child.
8.6 Summarize the research on spanking children.
8.7 Identify the ethnicity and socioeconomic variables that interact with parenting styles.
8.8 Explain how the structure of children's families may influence their development.
8.9 Describe the impact of divorce on children in the preschool years.
8.10 Identify explanations for the effects of family structure and divorce.
8.11 List six suggestions for softening the effects of divorce.
8.12 Trace a child's changing relationship with his or her peers through play.
8.13 Identify the key factors in aggressive behavior in preschool children.
8.14 Trace the development of prosocial behavior through the preschool years.
8.15 Explain the relationship between a young child's temperament and his or her developing personality.
8.16 Trace the development of the self-concept during early childhood.
8.17 Distinguish among the theories explaining gender concept and sex-role development.
8.18 Identify the steps in the development of gender constancy.
8.19 Describe how preschoolers acquire knowledge of sex roles.
8.20 Describe the sex-typed behavior of young children.

AS YOU READ . . . TERM IDENTIFICATION

Aggression (p. 214)
Authoritarian parenting style (p. 202)
Authoritative parenting style (p. 203)
Cross-gender behavior (p. 225)
Emotional regulation (p. 218)
Empathy (p. 219)
Extended family (p. 211)
Gender concept (p. 220)

Gender constancy (p. 221)
Gender constancy theory (p. 221)
Gender identity (p. 222)
Gender schema theory (p. 221)
Gender stability (p. 222)
Hostile aggression (p. 214)
Inductive discipline (p. 204)
Instrumental aggression (p. 214)

Permissive parenting style (p. 202)
Person perception (p. 198)
Prosocial behavior (p. 216)
Sex role (p. 220)
Sex-typed behavior (p. 224)
Social skills (p. 213)
Social-cognitive theory (p. 198)
Uninvolved parenting style (p. 202)

AS YOU READ . . . GUIDED STUDY QUESTIONS

THEORIES OF SOCIAL AND PERSONALITY DEVELOPMENT

Psychoanalytic Perspectives (pp. 197-198)

Objective 8.1: Summarize the key points of the psychoanalytic theories that are relevant to early childhood.

1. List and describe the two stages of Freud's theory during the preschool years.

Stage	*Description*

2. List and describe the two stages of Erikson's theory during the preschool years.

Stage	*Description*

3. List and describe the two kinds of relationships that Hartup emphasized. Why does he suggest that both kinds of relationships are needed for the child to develop effective social skills?

Relationship	*Description*

Social-Cognitive Perspectives (pp. 198-200)

Objective 8.2: Summarize the key points of the social-cognitive perspective that are relevant to early childhood.

4.   Define the following terms:
        a.   social-cognitive theory (p. 198)

        b.   person perception (p. 198)

5.   Give examples of how young children's observations and people categories are far less consistent than those of older children.

6.   Describe how children demonstrate the cross-race effect.

7.   Give examples of how preschoolers use classification skills to begin to understand the difference between social conventions and moral rules.

8.   Give examples of how young children demonstrate their understanding of intentions.

Research Report: Racism in the Preschool Classroom (p. 199)

Objective 8.3: Describe how racial attitudes may be formed in the preschool classroom.

9.   How do young children form race schemas?

10.   What is the key to preventing racial awareness from developing into racism? Give examples.

AFTER YOU READ . . . PRACTICE TEST #1
THEORIES OF SOCIAL AND PERSONALITY DEVELOPMENT

Fill in the blanks with the best answer.

1.   Freud described two stages during the preschool years, the _____ stage and the _____ stage.

2.   Erikson described two stages in the preschool period, the _____ stage and the _____ stage.

3.   Hartup suggested that preschoolers need experience in two kinds of relationships: _____ and _____ .

4.   The theoretical perspective that asserts that social and personality development in early childhood are related to improvements in the cognitive domain is called the _____ theory.

5.   _____ is the ability to classify others according to categories such as age, gender, and race.

6.   A phenomenon in which individuals are more likely to remember the faces of people of their own race than those of a different race is called the _____.

7. A _____ is a rule that serve to regulate behavior but has not moral implications; _____ are regulations based on a fundamental sense of right and wrong.

(Check your answers to Practice Test #1 on p. 171.)

FAMILY RELATIONSHIPS AND STRUCTURE

Attachment (p. 201)

Objective 8.4: Describe the preschool-aged child's attachment to his or her parents.

11. Compare a two- or three-year-old child's attachment to her parents with that of an infant.

12. Give examples of how attachment quality predicts behavior during the preschool years.

13. According to Bowlby, how does the attachment relationship change at about age four? Give examples.

14. How do advances in the internal working model lead to new conflicts?

Parenting Styles (pp. 201-204)

Objective 8.5: Discuss the impact of styles of parenting on the social and personality development of the preschool child.

15. Complete the following table by listing the four aspects of family functioning, and stating how each is related to various child behaviors:

Aspect of Family Functioning	*Relationship to Child Behaviors*

16. Define the following terms:
    a. permissive parenting style (p. 202)

    b. authoritarian parenting style (p. 202)

    c. authoritative parenting style (p. 202)

    d. uninvolved parenting style (p. 202)

155

17.   According to Maccoby and Martin, what are the two dimensions of family characteristics?

18.   Complete the following table to describe how parenting style affects the child's behavioral outcomes:

Parenting Style	Likely Behavioral Outcomes
Authoritarian	
Permissive	
Authoritative	
Uninvolved	

19.   Describe some of the complexities of the effects of parenting styles.

20.   Define inductive discipline (p. 204), and give examples.

The Real World: To Spank or Not to Spank? (p. 205)

Objective 8.6: Summarize the research on spanking children.

21.   List two negative side effects in the short term of spanking.

22.   List four longer term negative effects of spanking.

23.   Why is yelling a poor alternative to spanking?

24.   Give evidence of why some developmentalists argue that the effects of spanking should be examined within the context in which it occurs.

Ethnicity, Socio-Economic Status, and Parenting Styles (pp. 204-207)

Objective 8.7: Identify the ethnicity and socio-economic variables that interact with parenting styles.

25.   Summarize the results of the study of 10,000 high school students representing four ethnic groups.

26.   List some reasons why Asian-American parents and African-American parents tend to use the authoritarian parenting style.

Family Structure (pp. 207-210)

Objective 8.8: Explain how the structure of children's families may influence their development.

27.   Describe the diversity in two-parent families.

28.   List and describe two reasons why single-parent families are far more common among African Americans and Native-Americans.

Reason	Description

29.   List the negative effects of children growing up in single-parent families.

30.   Describe the type of research available on custodial grandparenting.

31.   Describe the research available on gay and lesbian parenting.

32.   Describe the research available on children who were conceived by artificial insemination.

Divorce (pp. 210-211)

Objective 8.9: Describe the impact of divorce on children in the preschool years.

33.   List four divorce-related factors that may affect the results of research.

34.   List several negative effects of divorce for children, adolescents, and adults.

35.   How might divorce affect boys and girls differently?

Understanding the Effects of Family Structure and Divorce (p. 211)

Objective 8.10: Identify explanations for the effects of family structure and divorce.

36.   Define extended family (p. 211), and give examples of how it assists single-parent families.

37.   List and describe three key reasons explaining the negative findings about divorce.

Reason	Description

No Easy Answers: When Divorce is Unavoidable (p. 212)

Objective 8.11: List six suggestions for softening the effects of divorce.

38. List and describe six specific things that parents can do that are likely to soften or shorten the effects of divorce.

Action	*Description*

AFTER YOU READ . . . PRACTICE TEST #2
FAMILY RELATIONSHIPS AND STRUCTURE

1. **Four- and five-year-olds who are securely attached to their parents are _____ to have positive relationships with their preschool teachers than their insecurely attached peers.**
    a. equally as likely
    b. ten times as likely
    c. more likely
    d. less likely

2. **Developmental psychologists believe that two-year-olds _____.**
    a. are more compliant than at any other age
    b. comply with parents' requests more often than not
    c. are more likely to comply with self-care requests than other requests
    d. will generally say "no" to everything but then comply

3. **The permissive parental style includes _____.**
    a. low nurturance and high communication
    b. high control and low communication
    c. low maturity demands and low nurturance
    d. high nurturance and low control

4. **In a large-scale study of 10,000 high school students representing four ethnic groups, the _____ was more common among white families and more common among the middle class.**
    a. authoritative parenting style
    b. authoritarian parenting style
    c. uninvolved parenting style
    d. permissive parenting style

5.   **Each of the following is a negative effect of spanking EXCEPT:**
   a.   children learn to use physical force as a method of solving problems
   b.   children who are spanked at later ages show lower levels of aggression
   c.   parents undermine their own positive value for the child
   d.   spanking frequently carries a strong underlying emotional message

6.   **A traditional cultural value sociologists call _____ views parenting as the responsibility of the child's entire extended family.**
   a.   uninvolved parenting
   b.   inductive discipline
   c.   kin orientation
   d.   interactional synchrony

7.   **What do we know about the effects of different family structures?**
   a.   The structure does not matter, but the temperament of the child does.
   b.   The optimum family structure appears to be being reared by both natural parents.
   c.   Who reared the child does not matter, but how the child is reared does.
   d.   Family structure appears to affect girls more negatively than it does boys.

8.   **Each of the following is a negative effect of divorce on children EXCEPT:**
   a.   declines in school performance
   b.   increased aggression
   c.   more defiance
   d.   decreased likelihood of depression

(Check your answers to Practice Test #2 on p. 171.)

PEER RELATIONSHIPS

Relating to Peers Through Play (pp. 212-213)

Objective 8.12: Trace a child's changing relationship with his or her peers through play.

39.   List and distinguish among the four types of play:

Type of Play	*Description*

40.   Define social skills (p. 213).

41.   How does the social skill of group entry predict children's relationships with their peers?

42.   What are the sex differences in the reasons for and consequences of poor group-entry skills?
a.   for girls
b.   for boys

43.   Describe social-skills training.

Aggression (pp. 214-216)

Objective 8.13: Identify the key factors in aggressive behavior in preschool children.

44.   Define the following terms:
a.   aggression (p. 214)

b.   instrumental aggression (p. 214)

c.   hostile aggression (p. 214)

45.   How does the emergence of dominance hierarchies affect the display of physical aggression? Why?

46.   Summarize the findings about the key factors in aggressive behaviors by completing the following table:

Factor	Research Findings
Frustration	
Reinforcement	
Modeling	

47.   Describe the research about causes of trait aggression by completing the following table:

Cause	Research Findings
Genetic Basis	
Aggressive Environment	
Reinforcement of Behavior	
Understanding of Others' Intentions	

Prosocial Behavior and Friendships (pp. 216-217)

Objective 8.14: Trace the development of prosocial behavior through the preschool years.

48.   Define prosocial behavior (p. 216).

49.   Give examples of prosocial behavior at age two or three and older children.

Age	Example
2	
3	

50.   Define attributions.

51.   Describe examples of parental behavior that contributes to the development of prosocial behavior by completing the following table:

Parental Behavior	Examples
Loving and Warm Climate	
Providing Prosocial Attributions	
Looking for Opportunities for Children to do Helpful Things	
Parental Modeling of Prosocial Behavior	

AFTER YOU READ . . . PRACTICE TEST #3
PEER RELATIONSHIPS

Match the letter of the term in the right column with its description in the left column.

_____ 1.   Aggression used to hurt another person or gain an advantage.

_____ 2.   Another term for "pecking order."

_____ 3.   A set of behaviors that usually lead to being accepted as a play partner or a friend by peers.

_____ 4.   Play in which several children work together to accomplish a goal.

_____ 5.   Behavior intended to help another person.

_____ 6.   Play in which toddlers pursue their own activities but also engage in spontaneous, though short-lived, social interactions.

_____ 7.   Behavior intended to harm another person or an object.

_____ 8.   Aggression used to gain or damage an object.

a. Aggression
b. Associative play
c. Attributions
d. Cooperative play
e. Dominance hierarchy
f. Group entry
g. Hostile aggression
h. Instrumental aggression
i. Parallel play
j. Prosocial behavior
k. Social skills
l. Solitary play

(Check your answers to Practice Test #3 on p. 171.)

PERSONALITY AND SELF-CONCEPT

From Temperament to Personality (pp. 217-218)

Objective 8.15: Explain the relationship between a young child's temperament and his or her developing personality.

52.   Describe the link between a difficultness of temperament and concurrent and future behavior problems.

53.   Give an example of the processes through which temperament becomes modified into personality during the early preschool years.

54.   How is the transition from temperament to personality influenced by parental responses to a young child's temperament?

Self-Concept (pp. 218-220)

Objective 8.16: Trace the development of the self-concept during early childhood.

55.   Describe and give examples of the development of the categorical self in the preschool years.

56.   Define the emotional regulation (p. 218).

57.   How does a child's temperament affect the process of gaining emotional regulation?

58.   How are parents' age-based expectations and parenting behaviors important in the process of gaining self-control?

59.   Define empathy (p. 218), and list its two aspects.

60.   Give an example of a social "script."

61.   Give examples of how role scripts help young children become more independent.

AFTER YOU READ . . . PRACTICE TEST #4
PERSONALITY AND SELF-CONCEPT

Fill in the banks with the best answer.

1.   Preschoolers with a difficult temperament at more likely to show heightened _____, _____, and other forms of behavior problems in school, as teenagers, and as adults.

2.   _____ represents the combination of the temperament with which children are probably born and the knowledge they gain about temperament-related behavior during childhood.

3.   The transition from temperament to personality is also influenced by _____ to the young child's temperament.

4.   The self-concept of preschool children tends to focus on their own _____ rather than on more enduring qualities.

5. _____ is the ability to control emotional states and emotion-related behavior.

6. The process of acquiring emotional regulation is one in which control shifts slowly from the _____ to the _____.

7. Empathy involves two aspects: _____
   and then _____.

8. _____ help young children become more independent as they gain an increasing awareness of themselves as players in the social game.

(Check your answers to practice Test #4 on p. 171.)

THE GENDER CONCEPT AND SEX ROLES

Explaining Gender Concept and Sex-Role Development (pp. 220-222)

Objective 8.17: Distinguish among the theories explaining gender concept and sex-role development.

62. Define the following terms:
    a. gender concept (p. 220)

    b. sex role (p. 220)

    c. gender constancy theory (p. 221)

    d. gender constancy (p. 221)

    e. gender schema theory (p. 221)

63. Summarize the theoretical views of gender concept and sex role development by completing the following table:

Psychoanalytic Theories
Freud
Difficulty of Freud's Theory

Social Learning Theory
Role of Parents
Evidence that Social-Learning Theory is Insufficient

Social-Cognitive Theories
Kohlberg's Theory
Difficulty with Gender Constancy Theory

Gender Schema Theory
Gender Schema Theory
Key Difference Between Gender Schema and Kohlberg's Theory

The Gender Concept (p. 222)

Objective 8.18: Identify the steps in the development of gender constancy.

64.   Define the following terms:
  a.   gender identity (p. 222)

  b.   gender stability (p. 222)

65.   Describe the three steps in the development of gender constancy.

66.   How is gender constancy related to the concept of conservation?

Sex-Role Knowledge (pp. 222-224)

Objective 8.19: Describe how preschoolers acquire knowledge of sex roles.

67.   What are sex-role stereotypes? Give examples of commonly stereotyped traits for men and for women.

Sex-Typed Behavior (pp. 224-226)

Objective 8.20: Describe the sex-typed behavior of young children.

68.   Define sex-typed behavior (p. 224).

69.   Give examples of girls' use of the enabling style, and boys' use of the restrictive style.

70.   Define cross-gender behavior (p. 225), and give examples of cross-gender behavior of girls and boys, and adults' reactions to it.

71.   It cannot be assumed that the prevalence of sex-typed play among boys is strictly the result of adult and peer influence. List four pieces of evidence for the statement.

AFTER YOU READ . . . PRACTICE TEST #5
THE GENDER CONCEPT AND SEX ROLES

Indicate whether each of the following statements is true or false.

_____ 1.　Preschooler's learn gender constancy (a cognitive task) and their appropriate sex role (a social task).

_____ 2.　According to Freud, children learn both the gender concept and sex roles through the process of rationalization.

_____ 3.　Social learning theorists emphasize the role of parents in shaping children's sex-role behavior and attitude.

_____ 4.　Kohlberg suggested that the crucial aspect of the process of explaining gender concept and sex-role development is the child's understanding of his sex role.

_____ 5.　Gender constancy is the understanding that gender is an innate characteristic that can't be changed.

_____ 6.　The gender scheme begins to develop as soon as the child notices the differences between male and female, knows her own gender, and can label the two groups with some consistency.

_____ 7.　The final step is the development of true gender constancy, the recognition that someone stays the same gender even though he may appear to change by changing his hair length.

_____ 8.　Different patterns of behavior exhibited by boys and girls is called sex-typed behavior.

(Check your answers to Practice Test #5 on p. 171.)

CRITICAL REFLECTION EXERCISE

Social and Personality Development

Based on the information in the text, respond to the following question about social and personality development during the age range of two to six years:

1.　Why is the development of self-control so important during these ages? Be sure to include evidence from the text to support your answer.

2.　How would you utilize the information from this chapter of the text in a preschool? What kind of issues would you confront as the teacher (discuss at least three issues)? How would you utilize the information from this chapter to address these issues?

AFTER YOU READ . . . COMPREHENSIVE PRACTICE TEST
MULTIPLE CHOICE QUESTIONS

1. **The two preschool stages that Erikson identified are _____.**
   a. trust versus mistrust and autonomy versus shame and doubt
   b. initiative versus guilt and identity versus role confusion
   c. autonomy versus shame and doubt and initiative versus guilt
   d. ego integrity versus despair and trust versus mistrust

2. **_____ is a rule that serves to regulate behavior but has no moral implications.**
   a. A moral rule
   b. A social convention
   c. Person perception
   d. Social-cognitive perception

3. **Baumrind focused on the following four aspects of family functioning: warmth or levels of nurturance, level of expectations or "maturity demands," clarity and consistency of rules, and _____.**
   a. communication
   b. responsibilities
   c. friendliness
   d. standards

4. **A discipline strategy in which parents explain to children why a punished behavior is wrong is called _____.**
   a. inductive discipline
   b. authoritarian parenting
   c. uninvolved discipline
   d. attachment

5. **A family structure that includes parents, grandparents, aunts, uncles, cousins, and so on is called _____.**
   a. involved parenting
   b. single parenting
   c. an extended family
   d. inductive discipline

6. **Each of the following is a method of softening the effects of divorce EXCEPT:**
   a. The custodial parent should help children stay in touch with the non-custodial parent.
   b. Use the children as a go-between with the ex-spouse.
   c. Keep the conflict to a minimum.
   c. Try to keep the number of separate changes the child has to cope with to a minimum.

7. **A set of behaviors that usually lead to being accepted as a play partner or friend by peers is called _____.**
   a. trait aggression
   b. altruism
   c. solitary play
   d. social skills

8. **When groups of children arrange themselves in well understood orders of leaders and followers, it is called _____.**
    a. leader-follower dichotomies
    b. dominance hierarchies
    c. role management
    d. interactional synchrony

9. **"You're such a helpful child!" is an example of _____.**
    a. a dominance hierarchy
    b. interactional synchrony
    c. role management
    d. a prosocial attribution

10. **The ability to control emotional states and emotion-related behavior is called _____.**
    a. inductive discipline
    b. emotional regulation
    c. deductive discipline
    d. empathy

11. **The process of acquiring self-control requires _____.**
    a. the ability to role-play
    b. sensorimotor thought
    c. shifting control from the parents to the child
    d. a rapid shift in maturity level on the part of the child

12. **The knowledge of what behaviors go with being a boy or a girl is called _____.**
    a. gender concept
    b. gender constancy
    c. gender identity
    d. the sex role

13. **The understanding that gender is an innate characteristic that cannot be changed is called _____.**
    a. sex role
    b. gender schema
    c. gender constancy
    d. cross-gender behavior

14. **The first step in developing gender constancy is _____.**
    a. gender stability
    b. gender identity
    c. sex-role behavior
    d. gender scripts

15. **Girls tend to use an enabling style when interacting. This means _____.**
    a. fostering equality and intimacy
    b. critiquing the partner so improvements can be made
    c. discussing one's own attributes more than the partner's
    d. contradicting, interrupting, boasting, and other forms of self-display

TRUE-FALSE QUESTIONS

Indicate whether each of the following statements is true or false.

_____ 1.   Both Freud and Erikson emphasized the role of the child's peers in development.

_____ 2.   Children who are securely attached to their parents experience fewer behavior problems.

_____ 3.   The most consistently positive outcomes have been associated with an authoritative parenting pattern in which the parents are high in both control and acceptance.

_____ 4.   Children growing up in single-parent families are less likely to drop out of high school than their peers in two-parent families.

_____ 5.   Teaching aggressive children how to think about others' intentions reduces aggressive behavior.

_____ 6.   Like aggression, prosocial behavior is intentional and voluntary, but its purpose is to help another person in some way.

_____ 7.   The development of empathy is preceded by the development of sympathy.

_____ 8.   The most clearly stereotyped traits for women are weakness, gentleness, appreciativeness, and soft-heartedness.

ESSAY QUESTIONS

1.   Discuss the importance of the four aspects of family functioning identified by Diana Baumrind.

2.   Research indicates that aggressive school-aged children seem to reason more like two- to three-year-olds about others' intentions. Using what you've learned about development in early childhood, design a training program for preschoolers to help decrease aggressive behavior.

3.   Which of the gender concept theories do you believe is most accurate? Defend your answer.

(Check your answers to the Comprehensive Practice Test on p. 171.)

WHEN YOU HAVE FINISHED . . . PUZZLE IT OUT

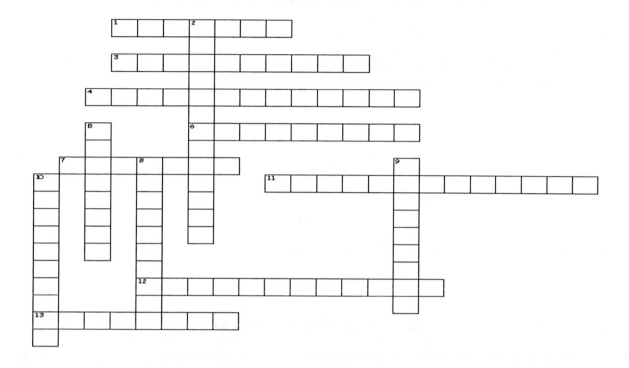

Across

1. Aggression used to hurt another person or gain an advantage
3. Parenting style high in nurturance and low in maturity demands, control, and communication
4. Parenting style high in nurturance, maturity demands, control, and communication
6. Discipline strategy in which parents explain to children why a punished behavior is wrong
7. The ability to identify with another person's emotional state
11. Parenting style low in nurturance and communication, but high in control and maturity demands
12. Aggression used to gain or damage an object
13. Family structure that includes grandparents, aunts, uncles, cousins, and so on

Down

2. Girls' preference for activities that are more typical for boys
5. A general feeling of sorrow or concern for another person
8. Behavior intended to harm another person or an object
9. Behavior intended to help another person
10. Parenting style low in nurturance, maturity demands, control, and communication

Created by Puzzlemaker at DiscoverySchool.com

(Check your answers on p. 172.)

WHEN YOU HAVE FINISHED . . . INVESTIGATIVE PROJECT

Student Project 14: Observation of Altruistic Behavior

In this project, take an "anthropological" approach to an observation of preschool-age children. Your instructor will have arranged for you to observe in a preschool or other group-care setting containing children between 18 months and four years of age. Permission will ordinarily have been obtained though the center itself, but you will need to follow whatever process is required to obtain the appropriate informed consent.

Procedure

For this observation, assume you are a researcher who has become interested in the earliest forms of altruistic behavior in children, and that there has not yet been any research on this subject. You want to begin simply by observing without preconceived ideas about how frequently this type of behavior might occur under what circumstances.

Observe for at least two hours in a group-care setting. Note in narrative form any episode that appears to you to fit some general criteria of "altruistic" or "compassionate" behavior. For each episode, record the circumstances involved, the gender of the child, the approximate age of the child, the other children present, and the words used (if any).

Analysis and Report

After the observation, look over your notes and try to answer the following questions:

1. What definition of altruism guided your observations? Did your definition change as a result of observing the children? Were there several types of observed "altruistic" actions that seem to be conceptually distinct?

2. Based on the episodes you have observed, what tentative hypotheses about the early development of altruism might you propose for further study? For example, are there hints of sex differences or age differences? Did the specific setting seem to have an effect? Was such behavior more common in pairs of children than in larger groups? Did this behavior occur primarily when one child was hurt or upset, or did it occur in other situations as well?

3. How might you test these tentative hypotheses with further research?

CHAPTER 8 ANSWER KEY

Practice Test #1 Theories of Social and Personality Development

1. anal; phallic
2. autonomy versus shame and doubt; initiative versus guilt
3. attachment to someone who has greater knowledge and social power; reciprocal relationships with others
4. social-cognitive
5. Person perception
6. cross-race effect
7. social convention; moral rules

Practice Test #2 Family Relationships and Structure

1. c   2. b   3. d   4. a   5. b   6. c   7. b   8. d

Practice Test #3 Peer Relationships

1. g   2. e   3. k   4. d   5. j   6. b   7. a   8. h

Practice Test #4 Personality and Self-Concept

1. aggressiveness; delinquency
2. Personality
3. parental responses
4. visible characteristics
5. Emotional regulation
6. parents; child
7. apprehending another person's emotional stage or condition; matching that emotional state oneself
8. Role scripts

Practice Test #5 The Gender Concept and Sex Roles

1. T   2. F   3. T   4. F   5. T   6. T   7. T   8. T

Comprehensive Practice Test

Multiple Choice Questions

1. c   2. b   3. a   4. a   5. c   6. b   7. d   8. b   9. d   10. b
11. c   12. d   13. c   14. b   15. a

True-False Questions

1. F   2. T   3. T   4. F   5. T   6. T   7. F   8. T

Essay Questions

1.
   - Warmth or nurturance: Children show higher self-esteem, more empathy, more altruism, higher IQs, and less delinquent behavior.
   - Clarity and consistency of rules: Children are less likely to be defiant or non-compliant, are more competent and sure of themselves, and are less aggressive.
   - Levels of expectations (maturity demands): Children have higher self-esteem and show more altruism.
   - Communication between parent and child: Children are more emotionally and socially mature.

2.
   - The training could include the following concepts: reinforcement, modeling, parenting style, emotional regulation, etc.

3.
   - Answers should include the key principles of the theory and rationale as to why it was selected.

Puzzle It Out

Across

1. Hostile
3. Permissive
4. Authoritative
6. Inductive
7. Empathy
11. Authoritarian
12. Instrumental
13. Extended

Down

2. Tomboyishness
5. Sympathy
8. Aggression
9. Prosocial
10. Uninvolved

POLICY QUESTION II

"DEADBEAT DADS:" IRRESPONSIBLE PARENTS OR POLITICAL SCAPEGOATS?

Learning Objective: Summarize the issues about "deadbeat dads" (pp. 228-229).

1.   Define deadbeat dad.

2.   List two consequences of the efforts to keep up with child support obligations.

3.   Give examples of how custodial mothers are forced to cooperate with government officials.

4.   How has the general public been enlisted to find deadbeat dads?

5.   List two criticisms of deadbeat dad policies.

6.   State two examples of how the courts are biased against fathers.

7.   According to fathers' rights organizations and empirical research, what lies at the heart of the child support issue?

8.   Give examples of issues involved with child support awards exceeding what a non-custodial father can realistically pay.

9.   List three reforms of the judicial process that would improve child support compliance.

10.   Federal welfare reform legislation in 1992 and 1996 required every state to take steps to improve enforcement of child support orders. The states have complied in a variety of ways. Use your Internet skills to find the answers to the following questions.

    a.   What are the penalties in your state for non-payment of child support?

    b.   What efforts have been made by officials in your state to locate deadbeat dads?

    c.   Can an alleged deadbeat dad or a non-custodial father seeking a reduction in a child support award represent himself in court in your state? If not, are there agencies that provide low-cost legal assistance to such men?

    d.   Does your state have policies requiring custodial mothers to cooperate in identifying their children's fathers?

    e.   Do welfare statistics in your state indicate that deadbeat dad policies have reduced the welfare rolls?

    f.   Do you agree with your state's current approach to the deadbeat dad issue? Why or why not?

CHAPTER 9

PHYSICAL AND COGNITIVE DEVELOPMENT IN MIDDLE CHILDHOOD

BEFORE YOU READ . . . CHAPTER SUMMARY

Development in middle childhood, ages six to twelve, is marked by major physical changes, including those in the brain. Cognitive advances occur in these years, and the patterns and habits established during this time affect not only adolescent experiences, but also adulthood. Formal education impacts development and a variety of factors—such as learning disabilities, attention problems, language proficiency, sex, race, and culture—shape academic achievement.

Physical Changes
- Growth from six to twelve is steady and slow. Coordination of both large muscles and fine motor continue to improve. Sex differences in bone and skeletal maturation may lead boys and girls to pursue different activities.
- Major growth spurts occur in the brain in six- to eight-year-olds and in ten- to twelve-year-olds. Neurological development leads to improvements in selective attention, information-processing speed, and spatial perception.
- Accidents and obesity are among the most significant health hazards of this age group.

Cognitive Changes
- Language development continues at an astonishing rate with vocabulary growth, improvements in grammar, and an understanding of the social uses of language.
- The school-aged child discovers or develops a set of immensely powerful schemes that Piaget called concrete operations, such as reversibility, addition, subtraction, multiplication, division, and serial ordering. The child develops the ability to use inductive logic but does not yet use deductive logic.
- Piaget understood that it took children some years to apply the new cognitive skills to all kinds of problems, that he called horizontal decalage. The "operations" may be rules for solving specific types of problems.
- Children in middle childhood clearly make improvements in processing efficiency, automaticity, executive and strategic processes, and expertise.

Schooling
- Literacy, the ability to read and write, is the focus of education in the six- to twelve-year-old period. Reading skills include improvements in phonological awareness, automaticity, learning word parts, comprehension strategies, and exposure to good literature. Writing techniques include outlining, paragraph development, language mechanics, as well as how to edit their own and others' written work.
- Achievement tests are designed to assess specific information learned in school. IQ tests are also used in schools to assess and group children for instruction. Both types of tests may ignore important aspects of intellectual functioning.
- Effective schools have many of the same qualities of authoritative parenting, such as clear rules and goals, good control, good communication, and high nurturance. Parent involvement is important in high-quality schools. Some parents choose to educate their children at home; research examining the cognitive and social effects of homeschooling is sparse.
- Language proficiency, sex, race, and culture affect school performance.

Children with Special Needs

- In the United States, 12 to 13 percent of all school children receive special education services; most of them are classified as learning disabled.
- Many children with attention-deficit hyperactivity disorder (ADHD) have problems in school but do not fit well into typical special education categories. The cause of ADHD is unknown. The two types of ADHD are the hyperactive/impulsive type, and the inattentive type.

AS YOU READ . . . LEARNING OBJECTIVES

After completing Chapter 9, you should be able to:

9.1   Identify the changes in growth and motor development from ages six to twelve.
9.2   Describe how the growth spurts of the brain in middle childhood affect cognitive development.
9.3   Identify the health risks to children in middle childhood.
9.4   Trace the pattern of language development in the school years.
9.5   Explain Piaget's view of the concrete operational stage.
9.6   Summarize the research testing Piaget's ideas.
9.7   Explain advances in information-processing skills in the school years.
9.8   Describe the skills involved in learning to read and write.
9.9   Describe how tests are used to measure and predict achievement and intelligence.
9.10 Summarize the issues involved in IQ testing in the schools.
9.11 List the characteristics of effective schools.
9.12 Summarize the research on the homeschooling movement.
9.13 Describe the affects of language proficiency, sex, race, and culture on school performance.
9.14 Describe the issues involved with children with learning disabilities.
9.15 Summarize the issues involved with attention-deficit hyperactivity disorder.

AS YOU READ . . . TERM IDENTIFICATION

Achievement test (p. 244)
Analytical style (p. 250)
Association areas (p. 233)
Asthma (p. 234)
Attention-deficit hyperactivity disorder (ADHD) (p. 254)
Automaticity (p. 240)
Bilingual education (p. 249)
Class inclusion (p. 237)
Concrete operational stage (p. 236)
Conservation (p. 237)
Decentration (p. 236)
Deductive logic (p. 237)
Dyslexia (p. 252)

English-as-a-second-language (ESL) (p. 249)
Executive processes (p. 241)
Inductive logic (p. 237)
Learning disability (p. 252)
Memory strategies (p. 241)
Obesity (p. 234)
Processing efficiency (p. 240)
Relational style (p. 250)
Relative right-left orientation (p. 233)
Reversibility (p. 236)
Selective attention (p. 233)
Spatial cognition (p. 233)
Spatial perception (p. 233)

AS YOU READ . . . GUIDED STUDY QUESTIONS

PHYSICAL CHANGES

Growth and Motor Development (p. 232)

Objective 9.1: Identify the changes in growth and motor development from ages six to twelve.

1.   Between six and twelve, children grow _____ inches and add about _____ pounds each year.

2.   List some of the skills that improve as a result of gains in large muscle coordination and in fine muscle coordination.

3.   Give examples of how the sex differences in skeletal and muscular maturation cause girls to be better-coordinated but slower and somewhat weaker than boys.

The Brain and Nervous System (pp. 232-233)

Objective 9.2: Describe how the growth spurts of the brain in middle childhood affect cognitive development.

4.   Define the following terms:
       a.   selective attention (p. 233)

       b.   association areas (p. 233)

       c.   spatial perception (p. 233)

       d.   relative right-left orientation (p. 233)

       e.   spatial cognition (p. 233)

5.   Describe the site and result of the two growth spurts by completing the following table:

Site of Growth Spurt	Area of Improvement

6.   Give an example of how the myelinization of linkages between the frontal lobes and the reticular formation work together to develop selective attention.

7.   How does the myelinization of the association areas contribute to increases in information-processing speed?

8. Give an example of the development of the lateralization of spatial perception, and describe a behavioral test of spatial perception lateralization that neuroscientists often use.

9. What evidence suggests that visual experience affects the development of spatial perception? Give an example of how visual experiences might explain sex differences in spatial perception and spatial cognition.

Health and Wellness (pp. 234-235)

Objective 9.3: Identify the health risks to children in middle childhood.

10. Define the following terms:
    a. asthma (p.)234

    b. obesity (p. 234)

11. What are the two most common causes of head injuries in children?

12. Describe the "step" approach to treating asthma.

13. What is the purpose of the body mass index (BMI)?

14. List the likely causes of obesity in middle childhood.

15. Describe how to successfully help children lose weight.

16. What can parents do to encourage children to be more physically active?

AFTER YOU READ . . . PRACTICE TEST #1
PHYSICAL CHANGES

1. **Between ages six and twelve, children grow _____ inches and add about _____ pounds each year.**
   a. one to two; ten
   b. two to three; six
   c. two to four; eight
   d. three to five; four

2. **The primary sites of brain growth during the first spurt of middle childhood are the _____.**
   a. occipital lobes and parietal lobes
   b. frontal lobes and temporal lobes
   c. sensory and motor areas
   d. medulla and the cerebellum

3. **Parts of the brain where sensory, motor, and intellectual functions are linked are called _____.**
   a. association areas
   b. frontal lobes
   c. cerebellum and brainstem
   d. parietal lobes

4. **The ability to identify and act on relationships between objects in space is called _____.**
    a. metamemory
    b. spatial cognition
    c. metacognition
    d. spatial perception

5. **The ability to understand the difference between statements such as, "It's on YOUR right," and "It's on MY right," is called _____.**
    a. handedness
    b. spatial cognition
    c. an executive process
    d. relative right-left orientation

6. **Head injuries are more common among _____ than any other age group.**
    a. infants
    b. preschoolers
    c. school-aged children
    d. teenagers

7. **Obesity is most often defined as a body weight that is _____ or more above the normal weight for a particular height.**
    a. 10%
    b. 20%
    c. 5%
    d. 50%

8. **Each of the following is a way parents can encourage children to be more physically active EXCEPT:**
    a. limiting time playing outside
    b. limiting time watching television
    c. limiting time on computers
    d. limiting time playing video games

(Check your answers to Practice Test #1 on p. 198.)

COGNITIVE CHANGES

Language (p. 236)

Objective 9.4: Trace the pattern of language development in the school years.

17. How many words do children add to their vocabularies per year between ages six and 12?

18. Give examples of derived words.

19. According to Anglin, what do children learn about the structure of language at about age eight or nine?

Piaget's Concrete Operational Stage (pp. 236-237)

Objective 9.6: Explain Piaget's view of the concrete operational stage.

20. Define the following terms:
    a. concrete operational stage (p. 236)

    b. decentration (p. 236)

    c. reversibility (p. 236)

    d. inductive logic (p. 237)

    e. deductive logic (p. 237)

21. To what is the concrete operational stage devoted?

22. Give examples of decentration and reversibility.

23. Why did Piaget believe that the concept of reversibility was the most important?

24. Distinguish between inductive logic and deductive logic by giving examples of each.

Direct Tests of Piaget's View (pp. 237-240)

Objective 9.6: Summarize the research testing Piaget's ideas.

25. Define class inclusion (p. 237), and give an example.

26. What is horizontal decalage?

27. Give examples of research that has found that Piaget was correct in his assertions that concrete operational schemes are acquired gradually across the six- to twelve-year-old period.

28. Describe Robert Siegler's research with a balance scale to discover the rules for problem solving.

29. Describe the four steps of rule formation Siegler found.

Rule	Description
Rule I	
Rule II	
Rule III	
Rule IV	

30. According to Siegler, what determines the progression from one rule to the next?

Advances in Information-Processing Skills (pp. 240-242)

Objective 9.7: Explain advances in information-processing skills in the school years.

31. Define the following terms and give an example of each:
    a. processing efficiency (p. 240)

    b. automaticity (p. 240)

    c. executive process (p. 241)

    d. memory strategies (p. 241)

32. Give evidence that cognitive processing becomes more efficient.

33. Explain why automaticity is critical to efficient information-processing.

34. Give an example of how executive processes increase during middle childhood.

35. Explain how expertise can make a difference in how efficiently the information-processing system works.

AFTER YOU READ . . . PRACTICE TEST #2
COGNITIVE CHANGES

Match the letter of the term in the right column with its description in the left column.

_____ 1. The ability to make efficient use of short-term memory capacity.

_____ 2. Words that have a basic root to which some prefix or suffix is added.

_____ 3. The inability to think of some transformed object as it was prior to the transformation.

_____ 4. Thinking that takes multiple variables into account.

_____ 5. Learned methods for remembering information.

_____ 6. Piaget's third stage of cognitive development.

_____ 7. A type of reasoning based on hypothetical premises that requires predicting a specific outcome from a general principle.

_____ 8. The understanding that subordinate classes are included in larger, superordinate classes.

_____ 9. The ability to recall information from long-term memory without using short-term memory capacity.

_____ 10. Knowing about knowing or thinking about thinking.

a. automaticity
b. centration
c. class inclusion
d. concrete operational stage
e. decentration
f. deductive logic
g. derived words
h. executive processes
i. horizontal decalage
j. inductive logic
k. irreversibility
l. memory strategies
m. metacognition
n. processing efficiency
o. reversibility

(Check your answers to Practice Test #2 on p. 198.)

SCHOOLING

Literacy (pp. 242-243)

Objective 9.8: Describe the skills involved in learning to read and write.

36.   What is literacy?

37.   Why is phonological awareness a significant skill?

38.   Complete the following table by providing an example of each of the following skills:

Skill	*Example*
Automaticity	
Oral Reading	
Word Parts	
Comprehension Strategies	
Good Literature	

39.   Describe the skills involved in learning to write.

40.   Describe some techniques to assist poor readers.

Achievement and intelligence Tests (pp. 243-246)

Objective 9.9: Describe how tests are used to measure and predict achievement and intelligence.

41.   Define achievement test (p. 244), and distinguish it from an intelligence test.

42.   List at least two objections to using IQ tests in schools.

43.   Complete the following table by listing and briefly describing the seven types of intelligence, according to Howard Gardner:

Type of Intelligence	*Description*

Type of Intelligence	Description

44. List and give an example of the three components of Sternberg's triarchic theory of intelligence by completing the following table:

Component	Example

45. List and describe the three components of Goleman's theory of emotional intelligence, and explain why it is important.

Component	Description

No Easy Answers: IQ Testing in the Schools *(p. 246)*

Objective 9.: Summarize the issues involved in IQ testing in the schools.

46. What is a legitimate use for IQ testing in schools?

47. List and describe three strong reasons usually given against using IQ tests to group elementary school children for instruction.

48. State the arguments about IQ testing in schools by completing the following table:

Pro	Con

Effective Schools (pp. 246-247)

Objective 9.11: List the characteristics of effective schools.

49.   What is an effective school? List its characteristics.

50.   How are the characteristics of an effective school similar to those of authoritative parenting?

51.   List the benefits of parent participation in school activities.

Research Report: The Homeschooling Movement (p. 248)

Objective 9.12: Summarize the research on the homeschooling movement.

52.   List reasons why some parents choose to homeschool their children.

53.   List some special circumstances that contribute to the decision to homeschool.

54.   List ways that parents of homeschoolers differ from other families.

Group Differences in Achievement (pp. 247-248)

Objective 9.13: Describe the affects of language proficiency, sex, race, and culture on school performance.

55.   Define the following terms:
       a.   bilingual education (p. 249)

       b.   English-as-a-second-language (ESL) program (p. 249)

56.   What does LEP stand for?

57.   Why is most bilingual education for Spanish-speaking children? Why is it logistically impossible for most LEP children?

58.   Why is submersion probably not the best approach for learning English?

59.   How do LEP students' performances in school compare to that of English-speaking children?

60.   State the cautionary note, and explain why it is necessary.

61.   What sex differences in test scores exist?

62.   State the environmental factors that shaped the sex differences in mathematics.

63.   Define the following terms:
       a.   analytical style (p. 250)

       b.   relational style (p. 250)

64.   How does an analytical style or a relational style affect achievement? Give an example.

65.   Describe how achievement differences may be due to philosophical beliefs.

66.   How might feelings of hopelessness on the part of some disadvantaged students be a factor?

67.   How might cultural beliefs affect achievement?

68.   Complete the following table to describe the differences in how teaching methods differ between Asian teachers and U.S. teachers:

Asian Teaching Method	*U.S. Teaching Method*

69.   Give an example of computational fluency.

AFTER YOU READ . . . PRACTICE TEST #3
SCHOOLING

1.   **Each of the following is a step in the process of learning to read EXCEPT:**
        a.   automaticity with respect to identifying sound-symbol connections
        b.   learning about word parts, such as prefixes and suffixes
        c.   attaining computational fluency
        d.   instruction in comprehension strategies

2.   **A test designed to assess specific information learned in school is called _____.**
        a.   an achievement test
        b.   an intelligence test
        c.   metacognition
        d.   computational fluency

3.   **The type of multiple intelligence that deals with the ability to use language effectively is called _____ intelligence.**
        a.   linguistic
        b.   naturalistic
        c.   spatial
        d.   logical/mathematical

4.   **The type of multiple intelligence that is the ability to understand oneself is called _____ intelligence.**
        a.   musical
        b.   bodily kinesthetic
        c.   intrapersonal
        d.   interpersonal

5. **Each of the following is a characteristic of an effective school EXCEPT:**
   a. high self-esteem
   b. high scores on standardized tests
   c. a high rate of disruptive classroom behavior and delinquency
   d. a high rate of later college attendance

6. **An approach to second-language education in which children receive instruction in two different languages is called _____.**
   a. submersion
   b. bilingual education
   c. immersion
   d. aversion

7. **A tendency to focus on the details of a task is called _____.**
   a. computational style
   b. relational style
   c. cognitive style
   d. analytical style

8. **The degree to which an individual can automatically produce solutions to simple calculation problems is called _____.**
   a. executive processes
   b. computational fluency
   c. metamemory
   d. metacognition

(Check your answers to Practice Test #3 on p. 198.)

CHILDREN WITH SPECIAL NEEDS

Learning Disabilities (pp. 252-254)

Objective 9.14: Describe the issues involved with children with learning disabilities.

70. Define the following terms:
    a. learning disability (p. 252)

    b. dyslexia (p. 252)

71. Describe how a neurological explanation of learning disabilities might occur.

72. Describe reciprocal teaching.

Attention-Deficit Hyperactivity Disorder (pp. 254-256)

Objective 9.15: Summarize the issues involved with attention-deficit hyperactivity disorder.

73. Define attention-deficit hyperactivity disorder (ADHD) (p. 254).

74. Give examples of evidence that children with ADHD are neurologically different from their peers.

75.　List four factors that are unlikely to cause ADHD.

76.　List and describe the two types of ADHD.

Type	Description

77.　List the kinds of problems ADHD children may have in school.

78.　Describe parent training that may be useful in helping parents cope with children who have ADHD.

79.　Identify the pros and cons of giving children ADHD stimulant medication, like methylphenidate (Ritalin), by completing the following table:

Pros	Cons

AFTER YOU READ . . . PRACTICE TEST #4
CHILDREN WITH SPECIAL NEEDS

Fill in the blanks with the best answer.

1.　A disorder in which a child has difficulty mastering a specific academic skills, even though she possesses normal intelligence and no physical or sensory handicaps is said to have a _____.

2.　In _____ programs, children with learning disabilities work in pairs or groups. Each child takes a turn summarizing and explaining material to be learned to the others in the group.

3.　_____ is a mental disorder that causes children to have difficulty attending to and completing tasks.

4.　Psychologists are fairy sure that _____, _____, or _____ is not the cause of ADHD.

5.　There are two types of ADHD: _____ and _____.

(Check your answers to Practice Test #4 on p. 198.)

AFTER YOU READ . . . CRITICAL REFLECTION EXERCISE

Developing Cognitive Skills

Imagine that you are a school teacher working with children ranging in age from six to eight years. You want to make sure that you develop classroom activities that provide children with practice with their developing cognitive skills. First, describe three skills that children are developing during these ages. Second, suggest one activity for each of these skills that you could use in the classroom to enhance the child's use of each skill.

AFTER YOU READ . . . COMPREHENSIVE PRACTICE TEST

MULTIPLE CHOICE QUESTIONS

1. **School age children will show the most dramatic increase in _____.**
   a. jumping ability
   b. intelligence
   c. running speed
   d. fine motor coordination

2. **The ability to focus cognitive activity on the important elements of a problem or situation is called _____.**
   a. selective attention
   b. myelinization
   c. relative right-left orientation
   d. spatial cognition

3. **Aside from head injuries and asthma, the most significant health risk of the middle childhood period is _____.**
   a. obesity
   b. difficulty sleeping
   c. coordination of vision with body movements
   d. anorexia

4. **A derived word is one that _____.**
   a. was slang but is now considered acceptable
   b. has a basic root to which a prefix or suffix is added
   c. means dramatically different things in different cultures
   d. is offensive to individuals of particular cultural groups

5. **The understanding that both physical actions and mental operations can be reversed is called _____.**
   a. addition and subtraction
   b. conservation
   c. reversibility
   d. reverse object rotation

6. **Piaget understood that it took children some years to apply their new cognitive skills to all kinds of problems, a phenomenon he called _____.**
   a. automaticity
   b. executive processes
   c. class inclusion
   d. horizontal decalage

7. **The ability to recall information from long-term memory without using short-term memory capacity is called _____.**
   a. horizontal decalage
   b. conservation
   c. automaticity
   d. memory strategies

8. **The ability to read and write is called _____.**
   a. phonological awareness
   b. literacy
   c. long-term memory
   d. intelligence

9. **The three components of Sternberg's triarchic theory of intelligence are _____.**
   a. contextual intelligence, experimental intelligence, and componential intelligence
   b. interpersonal intelligence, intrapersonal intelligence, and musical intelligence
   c. logical/mathematical intelligence, spatial intelligence, and interpersonal intelligence
   d. linguistic intelligence, emotional intelligence, and bodily kinesthetic intelligence

10. **The text suggests that effective schools do most of the things that _____.**
    a. allow the children maximum freedom to explore and learn
    b. authoritative parents do
    c. allow children to learn rule-governed behavior
    d. the parents should be doing but are not

11. **An approach to second-language education in which children attend English classes for part of the day and receive most of their academic instruction in English is called _____.**
    a. computational fluency
    b. emotional intelligence
    c. horizontal decalage
    d. English-as-a-second-language (ESL)

12. **Focusing attention on the "big picture" instead of an individual bits of information is called a(n) _____.**
    a. individualistic style
    b. collectivist style
    c. relational style
    d. analytical style

13. **The degree to which an individual can automatically produce solutions to simple calculation problems is called _____.**
    a. computational fluency
    b. executive processes
    c. horizontal decalage
    d. metacognition

14. **The total absence of reading is the technical term for _____.**
    a. literacy
    b. dyslexia
    c. learning disability
    d. limited English proficient

15. **Which of the following is a possible cause of attention-deficit hyperactivity disorder?**
    a. environmental toxins
    b. diet
    c. cultural factors
    d. brain damage

TRUE-FALSE QUESTIONS

Indicate whether each of the following statements is true or false.

_____ 1. The ability to infer rules from and make predictions about the movement of objects in space is called spatial cognition.

_____ 2. The most frequent cause of school absence for six- to 12-year-olds is head injuries.

_____ 3. Children develop the ability to use deductive logic before inductive logic.

_____ 4. The understanding that subordinate classes are included in larger, superordinate classes is called class inclusion.

_____ 5. The three components of emotional intelligence are awareness of one's own emotions, the ability to express one's emotions appropriately, and the capacity to channel emotions into the pursuit of worthwhile goals.

_____ 6. On average, studies in the United States show that girls do slightly better on verbal tasks and at arithmetic computation and that boys do slightly better at numerical reasoning.

_____ 7. When reading is the problem skill, the term dyslexia is often used.

_____ 8. Medication always improves the grades of children with ADHD.

ESSAY QUESTIONS

1. How can parents and teachers help school-aged children gain expertise?

2. Choose one of the theories of intelligence (Gardner's, Sternberg's, or Goleman's) and give reasons why you believe it accurately represents human intelligence.

3. Compare the analytical style to the relational style. Suggest reasons why the cognitive style may impact success in school.

(Check your answers to the Comprehensive Practice Test on p. 198.)

WHEN YOU HAVE FINISHED . . . PUZZLE IT OUT

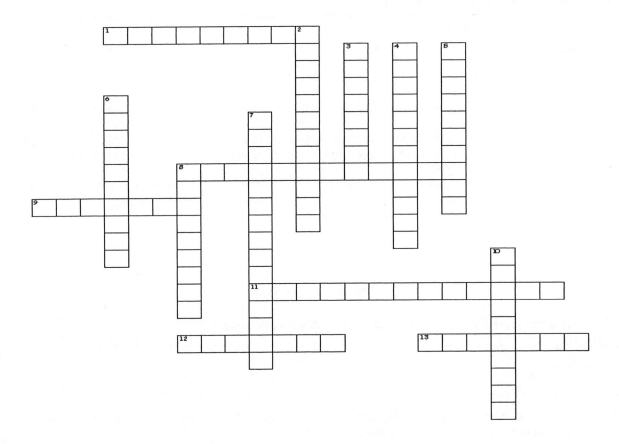

Across
1. Reasoning in which general principles are inferred from specific experiences
8. Thinking that takes multiple variables into account
9. Words that have a basic root to which some prefix or suffix is added
11. The ability to understand oneself
12. The ability to appreciate spatial relationships
13. Facility with numbers and logical problem-solving

Down
2. Intelligence that is measured by IQ tests
3. Problems in reading or the inability to read
4. The ability to recall information from long-term memory without using short-term memory capacity
5. Style that focuses on the "big picture"
6. Style that focuses on the details of a task
7. The inability to think of some transformed object as it was prior to the transformation
8. Reasoning based on hypothetical premises that requires predicting a specific outcome from a general principle
10. The ability to use language effectively

Created by Puzzlemaker at DiscoverySchool.com

(Check your answers on p. 198.)

192

WHEN YOU HAVE FINISHED . . . RESEARCH PROJECT

Student Project 15: The Game of Twenty Questions

For this project you will need to locate a child between the ages of six and ten, and obtain permission from the parent to research their child using the procedure specified by your instructor. Be sure to reassure the parents that you are not "testing" the child.

Procedure

Arrange a time to be alone with the child if at all possible. Having the mother, father, or siblings there can be extremely distracting, both for the child and for you. Come prepared with the equipment you will need. Tell the child that you have some games you would like to play. Play with the child for a while to establish some kind of rapport before you begin your experiment. At the appropriate moment, introduce your "game" by saying:

> *I am thinking of something in this room, and your job is to figure out what I am thinking of. To do this, you can ask any questions at all that I can answer by saying yes or no, but I can't give you any answer other than yes or no. You can ask as many questions as you need, but try to find out in as few questions as you can.*

Choose "the door to the room" as the answer to your first game. (If there is more than one door, select one particular door as correct; if there is no door, use a particular window.) If the child asks questions that cannot be answered yes or no, remind him or her that you can't answer that kind of question, and restate the kind of question that can be asked. Allow the child as many questions as needed (more than 20 if necessary). Write down each question verbatim. When the child has reached the correct answer, praise her or him and then say:

> *Let's try another one. I'll try to make it harder this time. I'm thinking of something in the room again. Remember, you ask me questions that I can answer yes or no. You can ask as many questions as you need, but try to find out in as few questions as possible.*

Use your pencil or pen as the correct answer this time. After the child has solved the problem, praise her or him. If the child has not been successful, find something to praise (i.e., "You asked some good questions, but it's a really hard problem, isn't it?") When you are satisfied that the child's motivation is still reasonably high, continue.

> *Now we're going to play another question-asking game. In this game, I will tell you something that happened, and your job is to find out how it happened by asking questions I can answer yes or no. Here's what happened: A man is driving down the road in his car. The car goes off the road and hits a tree. You have to find out how it happened by the way I answer questions you ask me about it. But I can only answer yes or no. The object of the game is to find out the answer in as few questions as possible. Remember, here's what happened: A man is driving down the road in his car, and the car goes off the road and hits a tree. Find out what happened.*

If the child asks questions that cannot be answered yes or no, remind her or him that you cannot answer that kind of question and that you can only answer yes or no. If the child can't figure out the answer, urge him or her to try until you are persuaded that you are creating frustration, at which point you should quit with lots of positive statements. The answer to the problem is that it had been raining, the car skidded on a curve, went off the road, and hit a tree.

Scoring

Score each question asked by the child on each of the three problems as belonging to one of two categories:

1. **Hypothesis**: A hypothesis is essentially a guess that applies to only one alternative. A yes answer to a hypothesis solves the problem; with a no answer, all that has been accomplished is to eliminate one possibility. In the first two problems, a hypothesis would be any question that applied to only one alternative, only one object in the room, i.e., "Is it your hair?" or "Is it the picture?" In the third problem, a hypothesis would be any question that covered only one alternative: "Did the man get stung in the eye by a bee?" "Did he have a heart attack?" "Was there a big snow bank in the middle of the road that the car ran into so that it skidded?"

2. **Constraint**: A constraint question covers at least two possibilities, often many more. A yes answer to a constraint question must be followed up ("Is it a toy?" "Yes." "Is it a truck?") A no answer to a constrain question allows the questioner to eliminate a whole class of possibilities. On the first two problems, any of the following would be constraints: "Is it in that half of the room?" "Is it something big?" "Is it a toy?" "Is it something red?" (Assuming that there is more than one red thing in the room). For the third problem, any of the following (or equivalent) would be constraints: "Was there something wrong with the car?" "Was the weather bad?" "Did something happen to the man?"

Analysis and Report

You should examine at least the following aspects of your results.

1. How many questions did the child ask for each problem?
2. On each problem, how many of the child's questions were hypotheses, and how many were constraints?
3. Did the child do better (ask more constraints) on the "concrete operations" problems (the first two) than on the "formal operations" problem (the story)? Or was the performance the same on both?

Reference

Mosher, F. A., & Hornsby, J. R. (1966). On asking questions. In J. S. Bruner, R. R. Oliver, & P. M. Greenfield (Eds.), *Studies in cognitive growth*, pp. 68-85. New York: Wiley.

WHEN YOU HAVE FINISHED . . . RESEARCH PROJECT

Student Project 16: Conservation of Mass, Number, and Weight

For this project you need to locate a child between the ages of six and ten, and obtain permission from the parents, or from both the parents and the child, following the procedures specified by your instructor. You will be testing this child for three kinds of conservation: mass, number, and weight. Recall that the concept of conservation involves the understanding that some features of objects remain invariant despite changes in other features. The weight of an object remains the same regardless of how its shape is changed; the number of objects in a row remain the same regardless of how widely spaced the objects are. Typically, number and mass conservation are learned (or discovered) at about age five or six, while conservation of weight is learned later, at perhaps eight or nine. So if you are able to find a child between six and eight, you may find out later that he or she can manage the first two conservation tasks, but not the last.

Procedure

The testing can ordinarily be done most easily in the child's home, although other settings are also acceptable. Present the child with the three tasks in the order given here, following instructions precisely.

Conservation of Mass

You will need two equal balls of clay or play dough, each a size that can be readily handled by a child's palm. Handle them yourself, rounding them into balls, and then hand them to the child, asking: *Is there the same amount of clay in each of these balls? Are they the same?*

If the child agrees that they are the same, proceed. If not, say to the child: "Make them the same." The child may want to squish them a little or may actually shift some clay from one ball to the other. That is all right. When the child is ready, ask again: *Is there the same amount of clay in each of these balls? Are they the same?*

Once the child has agreed that they are the same, say: *Now I'm going to squash this one into a pancake.*

Squash one of the two balls into a pancake and place the two objects—the remaining ball and the pancake—in front of the child. Read the following questions exactly as written and record precisely what the child says: *Is there the same amount of clay in this one* (pointing to the ball) *as there is in this one* (pointing to the pancake), *or is there more here* (pointing to the ball) *or more here* (pointing to the pancake)?

Depending on the child's answer to the first question, follow up by asking: *Why are they the same? or Why is there more here?*

Now mold the pancake back into a ball and set the two balls aside for the moment.

Conservation of Number

For this part of the process you will need 14 pennies or identical buttons. Start with ten items and place them between yourself and the child (preferably on a table, but the floor will do), spaced in two rows of five as follows:

X X X X X
X X X X X

Ask the child: *Are there the same number of pennies* (buttons) *in this row as there are in this row, or are there more here* (pointing to the child's row) *or more here* (pointing to your row)?

The child may want to move the objects around a bit before he agrees that the two rows are the same, which is fine. Once the child has agreed that they are the same, spread the objects in your row so that it is now noticeably longer than the child's row but still contains only five objects, i.e.:

X   X   X   X   X
X X X X X

Now ask the following questions, and record the child's exact answers: *Are there the same number of pennies in this row as there are in this row, or are there more here, or more here?*

Depending on the child's answer, ask either of the following probe questions: *Why are they the same?* or *Why are there more here?*

Now spread out the child's row and add two objects to each row, so that your row and the child's row are again exactly matched, with seven items equally spaced in each. Repeat the questions above, and record the child's answer precisely. Now move the objects in your row closer together, so that the child's row is now longer. Ask the questions again, and record the answers.

Conservation of Weight

Put away the pennies (or give them to the child), and bring out the two balls of clay again, saying; *Now we're going to play with the clay again.*

Hand the balls to the child and ask: *Do these two balls weigh the same? Do they have the same amount of weight?*

If the child agrees that they weigh the same, proceed. If not, say "Make them the same," and let her manipulate the balls until she agrees. Once she has agreed say: *Now I am going to make this ball into a hot dog.*

Roll one of the two balls into a hot dog shape. When you have completed the transformation, put the two pieces of clay in front of the child and ask: *Does this one* (pointing to the hot dog) *weigh the same as this one* (pointing to the ball), *or does this one weigh more, or does this one weigh more?*

Depending on the child's answer to the question, ask one of the following probe questions and record the answers carefully: *Why do they weigh the same?* or *Why does this one weigh more?*

This ends the procedure, so you should praise and thank the child. You might also want to play a bit with the child with some other toy of the child's choosing, to make sure that the whole process is pleasant for the child.

Analysis and Report

For each of the crucial questions, decide whether or not the child "conserved." To be regarded as having conserved, the child must have said (1) the two objects were the same after transformation and (2) she must also give a valid reason, such as:

> You haven't added any or taken any away, so they have to be the same.
> One is longer, but it is also skinnier, so it is still the same.
> If I made it back into a ball, it would be the same.

Compare the child's performance on the three types of conservation. Did the child conserve in all three exercises? If not, was the child's performance consistent with the typically observed sequence of acquisition? (If the child conserved weight, but not mass or number, that would be contrary to research data). What else, other than the child's basic comprehension of conservation, might affect the child's answers in the test of this kind? Was the child interested or bored? Were there distractions in the environment? Might the sequence in which the items were given have any effect? Do you think it would have mattered, for example, if conservation of weight had been tested before conservation of mass? If one were designing a study to examine the acquisition of these conservations, would one want to have all children given the items in the same order, or should the order be randomized?

If several students have completed this project, you may want to combine your data and analyze children's success on these three conservations as a function of age. Do your collective findings match the results of existing research?

WHEN YOU HAVE FINISHED . . . INVESTIGATIVE PROJECT

Student Project 17: Investigation of IQ Testing in Local Schools

As a follow-up to the information given in the text on the pros and cons of using IQ test scores in the schools, one student, or a small group of students, may wish to investigate the policies on the uses of IQ and achievement test in your own local school districts.

Basic Questions to Answer

- Is there a state-wide policy on the use of IQ tests in public schools? Is there a local district policy instead of, or in addition to, a state policy?

- Is there a state or local policy on the use of achievement tests? Are they routinely given in specific grades? How are the scores used?

- If individual IQ tests are used in the district, who administers them? Are the scores used to help in the placement of children in special programs? What other types of information are also used as part of any placement process?

Sources

The best source will be the state department of education and local school district administrative offices. At the state level there is likely to be a public information office; large school districts may also have such a service. In smaller districts, you will have to use some ingenuity to figure out which person is the best to talk to. Naturally, you should identify yourself as a student and make it clear that this information is for a report for your class.

CHAPTER 8 ANSWER KEY

Practice Test #1 Physical Changes

1. b 2. c 3. a 4. d 5. d 6. c 7. b 8. a

Practice Test #2 Cognitive Changes

1. n 2. g 3. k 4. e 5. l 6. d 7. f 8. c 9. a 10. m

Practice Test #3 Schooling

1. c 2. a 3. a 4. c 5. c 6. b 7. d 8. b

Practice Test #4 Children with Special Needs

1.   learning disability
2.   reciprocal teaching
3.   attention-deficit hyperactivity disorder (ADHD)
4.   diet, environmental toxins, brain damage
5.   hyperactive/impulsive type; inattentive type

Comprehensive Practice Test

Multiple Choice Questions

1. d 2. a 3. a 4. b 5. c 6. d 7. c 8. b 9. a 10. b
11. d 12. c 13. a 14. b 15. c

True-False Questions

1. T 2. F 3. F 4. T 5. T 6. T 7. T 8. F

Essay Questions

1.   ▪ Answers will vary, but should include helping the child learn the basic skills, practicing the skills, and opportunities to share the skills with others.

2.   ▪ Answer should include basic premise of the selected theory and reasons for its selection.

3.   ▪ Analytical: focus on the details of a task.
         ▪ Relational: focus on the "big picture" and ignore the details.
         ▪ Teachers often

Puzzle It Out

Across
1. Inductive
8. Decentration
9. Derived
11. Intrapersonal
12. Spatial
13. Logical

Down
2. Experiential
3. Dyslexia
4. Automaticity
5. Relational
6. Analytical
7. Irreversibility
8. Deductive
10. Linguistic

CHAPTER 10

SOCIAL AND PERSONALITY DEVELOPMENT IN MIDDLE ADOLESCENCE

BEFORE YOU READ . . . CHAPTER SUMMARY

The social and personality development in children ages six to twelve includes changes in social relationships and the expansion of the self-concept. Influences beyond the family and school include after-school care, poverty, and television.

Theories of Social and Personality Development

- Freud believed that children repress sexual desires between ages six and twelve, a period he called the latency stage. Erikson claimed that children in middle childhood acquire a sense of industry by achieving goals determined by their culture.
- Between ages six and twelve, children's understanding of others' stable, internal traits improve.

Dimensions of Moral Development

- Psychoanalytic theorists emphasize emotions, such as guilt, shame, and pride in explaining moral development.
- Cognitive-development theorists focus on moral reasoning. Piaget and Kohlberg claim that moral reasoning develops in stages within correlate with Piaget's cognitive stages.
- According to learning theorists, moral development is a function of reward, punishment, and modeling.

Social Relationships

- Middle childhood is a period of increasing independence of the child from the family, yet attachment to parents and siblings continues to be important.
- The biggest shift in relationships in the middle childhood years is the increasing importance of peers, particularly close friendships.
- Gender segregation of peer groups is at its peak in the school-aged years. Boys' and girls' friendships differ in specific ways.
- Although physical aggression decreases in middle childhood, relational aggression increases, especially in girls.
- There are three groups of social status: popular children, rejected children, and neglected children. Aggressive children are often rejected, but some are popular. Neglected children may suffer from loneliness and depression.

Personality and Self-Concept

- The Big Five personality traits are identifiable and stable in middle childhood. They may be useful in identifying children who are in need of interventions to prevent delinquency.
- The psychological self develops in middle childhood. As a result, self-descriptions begin to include traits such as intelligence and friendliness along with physical characteristics.
- The self-concept of the six- to twelve-year-old contains an evaluative aspect called self-esteem. It is shaped by the degree of discrepancy a child experiences between goals and achievements, and the degree of perceived social support from peers and parents.

Influences Beyond Family and School

- Self-care is associated with many negative effects, but children who have parental monitoring are less likely to be affected.
- Children who grow up in poverty do worse in school and drop out at far higher rates. Protective factors, such as secure attachment, higher IQ, authoritative parenting, and effective schools can counterbalance the effects of poverty for some children.
- Television has positive educational effects, such as learning vocabulary and prosocial behavior, but heavy TV watching is associated with lower scores on achievement tests. Experts agree that watching violence on television also increases the level of personal aggression shown by a child.

AS YOU READ . . . LEARNING OBJECTIVES

After completing Chapter 10, you should be able to:

10.1 Describe the key points of the psychoanalytic perspectives relevant to middle childhood.
10.2 Summarize the key points of the social-cognitive perspectives relevant to middle childhood.
10.3 Trace the development of moral emotions across the middle childhood period.
10.4 Trace the development of moral reasoning across the school-aged period.
10.5 List suggestions for helping children learn mature moral reasoning.
10.6 Summarize how learning theory explains the development of moral behavior.
10.7 Describe the changes in family relationships across the school years.
10.8 Trace the development of the friendships of the elementary school child.
10.9 Describe gender segregation in middle childhood.
10.10 Identify the patterns of aggression in school-aged children.
10.11 Summarize the research on bullies and victims.
10.12 Describe the characteristics of children that influence their social status in middle childhood.
10.13 Discuss the long-term consequences of childhood aggression and peer rejection.
10.14 Summarize the research on the Big Five personality traits.
10.15 Trace the development of the psychological self during middle childhood.
10.16 Describe the development of the evaluative aspect of the self-concept in middle childhood.
10.17 Explain how after-school care affects the social and personality development of school-aged children.
10.18 Discuss the effects of poverty on the development of the child.
10.19 Identify the influences that television has on the development of children.
10.20 Summarize the issues involved with video games.

AS YOU READ . . . TERM IDENTIFICATION

The Big Five (p. 275)
Conscience (p. 262)
Ego ideal (p. 262)
Industry versus inferiority stage (p. 260)
Latency stage (p. 260)

Moral realism stage (p. 263)
Moral relativism stage (p. 263)
Psychological self (p. 277)
Relational aggression (p. 271)
Retaliatory aggression (p. 271)

Self-care children (p. 280)
Self-esteem (p. 278)
Self-regulation (p. 266)
Social status (p. 273)

AS YOU READ . . . GUIDED STUDY QUESTIONS

THEORIES OF SOCIAL AND PERSONALITY DEVELOPMENT

Psychoanalytic Perspectives (p. 260)

Objective 10.1: Describe the key points of the psychoanalytic perspectives relevant to middle childhood.

1.   Define the following terms:
     a.   latency stage (p. 260)

     b.   industry versus inferiority stage (p. 260)

2.   What is the focus of Freud's psychosexual theory during middle childhood?

3.   What is the focus of Erikson's psychosocial theory during middle childhood?

Social-Cognitive Perspectives (pp. 260-261)

Objective 10.2: Summarize the key points of the social-cognitive perspectives relevant to middle childhood.

4.   Give examples of how the child's description of others moves from the concrete to the abstract during middle childhood.

5.   How do behavioral comparisons and psychological constructs change throughout the school-years?

AFTER YOU READ . . . PRACTICE TEST #1
THEORIES OF SOCIAL AND PERSONALITY DEVELOPMENT

Fill in the blanks with the best answer.

1.   Psychological theories explain social and emotional development in terms of a struggle between _____ and _____.

2.   Freud called the period of development in middle childhood the _____.

3.   Like their understanding of the physical world, six- to 12-year-olds' descriptions of other people move from the _____ to the _____.

4.   A _____ was any description that involved comparing a child's behaviors or physical features with those of another child or with a norm.

5.   Any statement that involved some internal personality trait was referred to as a _____.

(Check your answers to Practice Test #1 on p. 223.)

DIMENSIONS OF MORAL DEVELOPMENT

Moral Emotions (pp. 261-262)

Objective 10.3: Trace the development of moral emotions across the middle childhood period.

6. Define the following terms:
    a. conscience (p. 262)

    b. ego ideal (p. 262)

7. According to Freud, how does a child learns moral rules?

8. According to Freud, what causes a child to feel guilt? What causes a child to feel shame?

9. How does Erikson's view of moral development differ from Freud's?

10. How does cognitive development impact the connection between moral emotions and moral behavior?

Moral Reasoning (pp. 263-264)

Objective 10.4: Trace the development of moral reasoning across the school-aged period.

11. Define the following terms:
    a. moral realism stage (p. 263)

    b. moral relativism stage (p. 263)

12. Describe Piaget's two-stage theory of moral development, and give examples of each stage.

13. Briefly describe Kohlberg's theory of moral development.

The Real World: Encouraging Moral Reasoning (p. 264)

Objective 10.5: List suggestions for helping children learn mature moral reasoning.

14. Give examples of each of Lickona's ten suggestions to help children achieve more mature levels of moral reasoning.

Suggestion	*Example*

Suggestion	Example

Moral Behavior (pp. 264-265)

Objective 10.6: Summarize how learning theory explains the development of moral behavior.

15.   According to Skinner, how do consequences teach children to obey moral rules? Give examples.

16.   Give examples of how punishment may actually interfere with moral development.

17.   How would parents who use inductive discipline respond to a seven-year-old child who has stolen a candy bar?

18.   How does social-learning theorist Albert Bandura explain how children learn moral reasoning?

AFTER YOU READ . . . PRACTICE TEST #2
DIMENSIONS OF MORAL DEVELOPMENT

Indicate whether each of the following statements is true or false.

_____ 1.   According to Freud, the child learns moral rules by identifying with the same-sex parent during the phallic stage.

_____ 2.   According to Freud, the superego has two parts: a conscience and an ego integrity.

_____ 3.   Erikson claimed that pride is just as important to moral development as guilt and shame.

_____ 4.   Moral reasoning is the process of making judgments about the rightness or wrongness of specific acts.

_____ 5.   In the moral realism stage, children understand that many rules can be changed through social agreement.

_____ 6.   Learning theorist B. F. Skinner proposed that consequences teach children to obey moral rules.

_____ 7.   According to Skinner, punishment may actually interfere with moral development.

_____ 8.   According to Albert Bandura, children learn more from observing others than from either rewards or punishments.

(Check your answers to Practice Test #2 on p. 223.)

SOCIAL RELATIONSHIPS

Family Relationships (pp. 265-267)

Objective 10.7: Describe the changes in family relationships across the school years.

19.   Give an example of how school-aged children are better than younger children at predicting family roles and relationships.

20.   Describe the attachment between parents and school-aged children.

21.   Why does the agenda of issues between parent and child change during middle childhood?

22.   Define self-regulation (p. 266).

23.   Give an example of cultural differences in parental expectations of self-regulation.

24.   Give an example of sex differences in parental expectations of self-regulation.

25.   List two parenting variables that contribute to the development of self-regulation.

26.   Give an example of how the parenting variables are associated with the authoritative style of parenting.

27.   List and give an example of each of the five patterns, or styles, of sibling relationships by completing the following table:

Pattern/Style	Example

Friendships (pp. 268-269)

Objective 10.8: Trace the development of the friendships of the elementary school child.

28.   Give an example of how preschoolers and young school-aged children would describe the way that people make friends. Give an example of how a ten-year-old would describe the way people make friends.

29.   List several examples of evidence of the centrality of friends to social development in middle childhood.

Gender Segregation (pp. 269-270)

Objective 10.9: Describe gender segregation in middle childhood.

30.   Give examples of how shared interests and activities play a critical part of friendship in the early years of middle childhood.

31.   Compare ways that girls' and boys' friendships differ, and list characteristics that they have in common by completing the following table:

Differences	Commonalties

32.   Define "controlling speech," and give examples.

Patterns of Aggression (pp. 270-273)

Objective 10.10: Identify the patterns of aggression in school-aged children.

33.   What happens to the level of physical aggression during the middle childhood years? Describe the exception to the general pattern.

34.   Define the following terms:
a.   relational aggression (p. 271)

b.   retaliatory aggression (p. 271)

35.   How do girls tend to express aggression?

36.   How does the level of retaliatory aggression change across the middle childhood years?

37.   Describe a technique to help children learn non-aggressive ways to manage the kinds of situations that lead to retaliatory aggression.

No Easy Answers: Bullies and Victims (p. 272)

Objective 10:11: Summarize the research on bullies and victims.

38.   List the consistent roles related to bullies and victims children assume in middle childhood.

39.   List the characteristics of victims.

40.   What are the consequences of victimization?

41.   List four characteristics of bullies.

42.   List four child-rearing factors that lie behind the development of bullying behavior.

Social Status (pp. 273-275)

Objective 10.12: Describe the characteristics of children that influence their social status in middle childhood.

43.   Define social status (p. 273), and list the three groups of social status.

44.   How do developmentalists measure popularity and rejection?

45. Give characteristics of each of the following groups of children by completing the following table. Include behavior as well as looks or temperament.

Group	Characteristics
Popular Children	
Withdrawn/Rejected Children	
Aggressive/Rejected Children	
Neglected Children	

46. Describe the friends of aggressive boys.

Research Report: Long-Term Consequences of Childhood Aggression and Peer Rejection (p. 274)

Objective 10.13: Discuss the long-term consequences of childhood aggression and peer rejection.

47. Describe the relationship between childhood aggression and social difficulties in adulthood.

48. Give examples of how the risk of future problems may be greatest for boys who are both aggressive and rejected.

AFTER YOU READ . . . PRACTICE TEST #3
SOCIAL RELATIONSHIPS

1. **Key issues of attachment in middle childhood include each of the following EXCEPT:**
   a. standards of school performance
   b. whether the child will receive an allowance or be paid for chores
   c. disciplinary interactions
   d. household responsibilities

2. **Which of the following statements is TRUE about sex differences in mothers' expectations of self-regulatory behavior?**
   a. Mothers give girls more autonomy over their own behavior than boys.
   b. Mothers hold boys to a higher standard of accountability for failure than girls.
   c. Mothers provide more guidance for girls than for boys.
   d. Mothers make different kinds of demands on boys and girls.

3.   **Which parental style is linked to self-regulation in school-aged children?**
   a.   permissive
   b.   authoritative
   c.   authoritarian
   d.   neglecting

4.   **The pattern of sibling relationship which includes teasing, quarreling, and attempts by one sibling to dominate the other is called a _____ pattern.**
   a.   caregiver
   b.   critical
   c.   rival
   d.   casual

5.   **Rival or critical relationships are more likely when siblings are _____.**
   a.   close together in age
   b.   of the opposite gender
   c.   far apart in age
   d.   of the same gender

6.   **Boys' friendship groups _____ than girls'.**
   a.   play more indoors
   b.   are more likely to play in pairs
   c.   are larger and more accepting of newcomers
   d.   spend more time near home or school

7.   **In middle childhood, _____ becomes even less common as children learn the cultural rules about when it is acceptable to display anger or aggression and how much of a display is acceptable.**
   a.   physical aggression
   b.   verbal aggression
   c.   hostile aggression
   d.   instrumental aggression

8.   **Aggression to get back at someone who hurt you is called _____.**
   a.   relational aggression
   b.   retaliatory aggression
   c.   hostile aggression
   d.   instrumental aggression

9.   **An individual child's classification as popular, rejected, or neglected is called _____.**
   a.   self-regulation
   b.   self-esteem
   c.   social status
   d.   psychological self

10.   **_____ realize that they are disliked by peers.**
   a.   popular children
   b.   aggressive/rejected children
   c.   retaliatory children
   d.   withdrawn/rejected children

(Check your answers to Practice Test #3 on p. 223.)

PERSONALITY AND SELF-CONCEPT

The Big Five Personality Traits (pp. 275-277)

Objective 10.14: Summarize the research on the Big Five personality traits.

49.   Define the Big Five (p. 275).

50.   Describe each of the dimensions of the Big Five personality traits.

Dimension	*Description*

51.   Give examples of how school-aged children's scores on the dimensions of the Big Five personality traits predict academic achievement and social skills in adolescence and adulthood.

The Psychological Self (p. 277)

Objective 10.15: Trace the development of the psychological self during middle childhood.

52.   Define the psychological self (p. 277), and give examples of how it becomes increasingly complex and abstract during middle childhood.

The Valued Self (pp. 277-280)

Objective 10.16: Describe the development of the evaluative aspect of the self-concept in middle childhood.

53.   Define self-esteem (p. 278).

54.   Describe the two internal judgments that make up a child's level of self-esteem.

55.   What is the key to self-esteem?

56.   How stable are self-esteem judgments over time?

57.   Describe the correlation between the child's level of self-esteem and depression.

58.   List and describe the four sources of differences in self-esteem.

Source	Description

AFTER YOU READ . . . PRACTICE TEST #4
PERSONALITY AND SELF-CONCEPT

Match the letter of the term in the right column with its description in the left column.

_____ 1.   An understanding of one's stable, internal traits.

_____ 2.   Personality traits of efficient, organized, prudent, reliable, responsible.

_____ 3.   A set of five major dimensions of personality.

_____ 4.   Personality traits of anxious, self-pitying, tense, touchy, unstable, worrying.

_____ 5.   A global evaluation of one's own worth.

_____ 6.   Personality traits of active, assertive, enthusiastic, outgoing persons.

a. Agreeableness
b. The Big Five
c. Conscientiousness
d. Extraversion
e. Neuroticism
f. Openness/intellect
g. Psychological self
h. Self-esteem

(Check your answers to Practice Test #4 on p. 223.)

INFLUENCES BEYOND FAMILY AND SCHOOL

After-School Care (pp. 280-281)

Objective 10.17: Explain how after-school care affects the social and personality development of school-aged children.

59.   Define the term self-care children (p. 280).

60.   List the variables associated with the effects of self-care on a child's development.

61.   Why is parental monitoring so important in self-care arrangements? Give examples of effective parental monitoring.

Poverty (pp. 281-284)

Objective 10.18: Discuss the effects of poverty on the development of the child.

62.   Give examples of how child poverty is unequally distributed across ages, races, and family structures.

63.   List ways that poverty reduces options for parents.

64.   How might parents living in poverty treat their children differently than do working-class or middle-class parents?

65.   Why are the negative effects of poverty exacerbated for children growing up in poverty-ravaged urban areas?

66.   List the symptoms of post-traumatic stress disorder from which children may suffer.

67.   List the seven key protective factors of resilient children, and give an example of how each factor may offer protection.

Protective Factor	*Example*

Television (pp. 284-285)

Objective 10.19: Identify the influences that television has on the development of children.

68.   Describe three types of research evidence of a causal link between television and aggression by completing the following table:

Research Type	Evidence

69.   What is the clear message to parents from the research on television?

Development in the Information Age: The Effects of Video Games (p. 286)

Objective 10.20: Summarize the issues involved with video games.

70.   How does playing video games relate to math achievement?

71.   Describe the relationship between violent video games and aggression.

AFTER YOU READ . . . PRACTICE TEST #5
INFLUENCES BEYOND FAMILY AND SCHOOL

Indicate whether each of the following statements is true or false.

_____ 1. Self-care children are those who are at home by themselves after school for an hour each week.

_____ 2. Self-care has the most negative effects for children in low-income neighborhoods with high crime rates.

_____ 3. Child poverty is equally distributed across ages, races, and family structures.

_____ 4. Parents living in poverty in the United States tend to treat their children differently than do working-class or middle-class parents.

_____ 5. Many children living in poor, inner-city neighborhoods show all the symptoms of post-traumatic stress disorder.

_____ 6. Television is an educational medium.

(Check your answers to Practice Test #5 on p. 223.)

AFTER YOU READ . . . CRITICAL REFLECTION EXERCISE

Self-Concept

Utilizing information from the text, provide detailed answers to the following questions:

1. What three factors do you think are the most important in influencing the child's developing self-concept during the six- to twelve-year-old age range? What role does each of these factors play? Why do you think they are so important?

2. You have been hired to teach a parenting class. Design an exercise that you could do with this class to illustrate the important effect that parents have on the developing self-concept of their children. List and discuss three things that parents might do that would have a negative effect on the child's self-concept. Provide suggestions for how to alter each of these negative effects into a positive one.

AFTER YOU READ . . . COMPREHENSIVE PRACTICE TEST
MULTIPLE CHOICE QUESTIONS

1.   **According to Erikson, the psychosocial task of children between the ages of six and twelve is the development of _____, or the willingness to accomplish tasks.**
   a.   identity
   b.   industry
   c.   isolation
   d.   initiative

2.   **According to Freud, the superego has two parts, _____.**
   a.   an ego ideal and a Freudian slip
   b.   the id and the conscience
   c.   the ego and the id
   d.   a conscience and an ego ideal

3.   **According to Piaget, children learn that people can agree to change rules if they want to. This is called the _____ stage.**
   a.   moral emotional
   b.   moral realism
   c.   moral judgmental
   d.   moral relativism

4.   **How would a parent who uses inductive discipline help a child learn that stealing a candy bar is wrong?**
   a.   Severely punish the child for stealing.
   b.   Embarrass the child in front of her friends.
   c.   Require the child to admit the crime and pay for the candy.
   d.   Publicly spank the child to teach him a lesson.

5.   **A child's ability to maintain friendships with peers is strongly related to _____.**
   a.   the number of siblings in the family
   b.   attachment to his parents
   c.   the stability of the parents' marriage
   d.   her grades in school

6.   **Selman suggested that elementary school children begin to view friends as persons who _____.**
   a.   are similar to them
   b.   will do good things for them
   c.   help and trust one another
   d.   will protect each other

7.   **Which of the following illustrates "controlling speech?"**
   a.   "Let's work on this together."
   b.   "If you let me borrow your toy, you can look at mine."
   c.   "That's not right!"
   d.   "I wish I had that toy, too."

8.   **Which of the following is an example of relational aggression?**
    a.   "What a nut."
    b.   "Bite your tongue."
    c.   "You're stupid."
    d.   "What's your problem?"

9.   **A combination of rejection and aggressiveness in childhood _____.**
    a.   has negative effects but can be easily overcome
    b.   is primarily a function of whether the child feels he fits in
    c.   has been linked to continuing aggression in adulthood
    d.   is directly linked to parental attitudes

10.   **The Big Five personality traits are _____.**
    a.   openness/intellect, reciprocity, neuroticism, agreeableness, curious
    b.   extraversion, agreeableness, conscientiousness, neuroticism, openness/intellect
    c.   conscientiousness, efficiency, organization/control, responsibility, persistence
    d.   enthusiasm, extraversion, sociability/sympathy, emotionality, insightfulness

11.   **Children's "Who am I?" responses become more _____ across middle childhood.**
    a.   positive
    b.   rigid
    c.   focused on physical characteristics
    d.   complex and comparative

12.   **A global evaluation of one's own worth is called _____.**
    a.   self-perception
    b.   self-esteem
    c.   self-concept
    d.   self-evaluative maintenance

13.   **Harter suggests that self-esteem is influenced by the _____.**
    a.   discrepancy between who a child feels he ought to be and who he thinks he is
    b.   sum total of the assessments the child makes about her skills
    c.   addition of all the positive assessments minus the negative ones
    d.   relationship between physical abilities and cultural expectations

14.   **Self-care children who are monitored closely are _____.**
    a.   more likely to be involved in criminal behavior
    b.   more likely to make poor grades
    c.   less likely to experience the negative effects of self-care
    d.   less likely to complete their homework

15.   **Which of the following could protect a child from the effects of a stressful environment?**
    a.   secure initial attachment to the parent
    b.   being of high socioeconomic status
    c.   authoritarian parenting
    d.   permissive parenting

TRUE-FALSE QUESTIONS

Indicate whether each of the following statements is true or false.

_____ 1.   Beginning at about age seven or eight, the child begins to focus more on the inner traits or qualities of another person and to assume that those traits will be visible in many situations.

_____ 2.   Moral reasoning is the process of making judgments about the rightness or wrongness of specific areas.

_____ 3.   Because school-aged children are more independent than they were when they were younger, the parent-child attachment relationship has weakened.

_____ 4.   As a general rule, sibling relationships seem to be more central to the lives of children in middle childhood than relationships with either friends or parents.

_____ 5.   Possibly the most striking thing about peer group interactions in the elementary school years is how gender-segregated they are.

_____ 6.   At every age, boys show more physical aggression and more assertiveness than do girls.

_____ 7.   Attractive children and physically small children are more likely to be popular.

_____ 8.   The lower a child's self-esteem score, the more depressed they child describes himself to be.

ESSAY QUESTIONS

1.   What are the parenting variables that contribute to self-regulation, and why are they important?

2.   Discuss the sex differences in aggression.

3.   What behavior is characteristic of popular children?

(Check your answers to the Comprehensive Practice Test on p. 223.)

WHEN YOU HAVE FINISHED . . . PUZZLE IT OUT

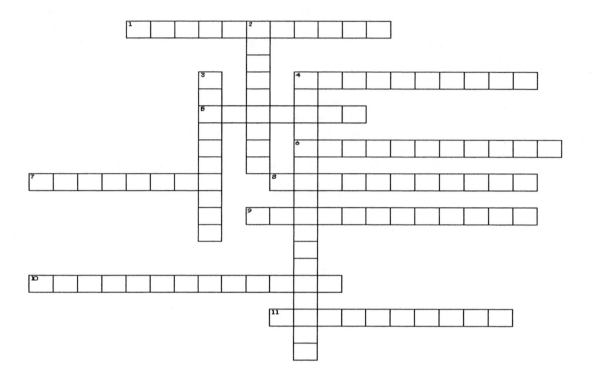

Across

1. Aggression to get back at someone who has hurt you
4. The list of "don'ts" in the superego
5. The fourth of Freud's psychosexual stages
6. Speech that includes rejecting comments, ordering, manipulating, challenging, defiance
7. Internal moral judge
8. Traits such as self-pitying, tense, touchy, unstable, worrying
9. Traits such as active, assertive, enthusiastic, outgoing
10. Traits such as affectionate, forgiving, generous, kind, trusting
11. Comparison with a description that involved comparing a child's behavior or physical features with those of another child or with a norm

Down

2. Discipline that is combined with instruction
3. Aggression aimed at damaging another person's self-esteem
4. Traits such as efficient, organized, prudent, reliable

Created by Puzzlemaker at DiscoverySchool.com

(Check your answers on p. 224.)

WHEN YOU HAVE FINISHED . . . RESEARCH PROJECT

Student Project 18: Understanding of Friendship

For this project you will need to locate a child between the ages of six to twelve. After obtaining the appropriate permission(s), arrange with the parents to spend some time with the child, explaining that you want to talk to the child for a school project, and that this is not a "test" of any kind. Try to find a time and a place to be alone with your subject; it will not work as well if siblings or parents are present.

Procedure

After chatting for a while to establish rapport, say to the child something like:

I'd like to talk to you about friends. Let me tell you a story about some children who were friends.

Then read the following story:

> Kathy and Becky have been best friends since they were five years old. They went to the same kindergarten and have been in the same class ever since. Every Saturday they would try to do something special together, such as go to the park or the store, or play something special at home. They always had a good time with each other.
>
> One day a new girl, Jeanette, moved into their neighborhood and soon introduced herself to Kathy and Becky. Right away, Jeanette and Kathy seemed to hit it off very well. They talked about where Jeanette was from and the things she could be doing in her new town. Becky, on the other hand, didn't seem to like Jeanette very well. She thought Jeanette was a show-off, but was also jealous of all the attention Kathy was giving Jeanette.
>
> When Jeanette left the other two alone, Becky told Kathy how she felt about Jeanette. "What did you think of her, Kathy? I thought she was kind of pushy, butting in on us like that."
>
> "Come on, Becky. She's new in town and just trying to make friends. The least we can do is be nice to her."
>
> "Yeah, but that doesn't mean we have to be friends with her," replied Becky. "Anyway, what would you like to do this Saturday? You know those old puppets of mine? I thought we could fix them up and make our own puppet show."
>
> "Sure, Becky, that sounds great," said Kathy. "I'll be over after lunch. I'd better go home now. See you tomorrow."
>
> Later that evening, Jeanette called Kathy and surprised her with an invitation to the circus, the last show before it left town. The only problem was that the show happened to be at the same time Kathy had promised to go to Becky's. Kathy didn't know what to do: go to the circus and leave her best friend alone, or stick with her best friend and miss a good time (Selman, 1980, pp. 321-322).

219

After reading the child the story, ask the following open-ended questions, and then probe the child's understanding of friendship:

1.   What do you think the problem is in this story?

2.   What do you think Kathy will do, choose to be with her old friend Becky, or go with the new girl, Jeanette? Why? Which do you think is more important: to be with an old friend or to make new friends? Why?

3.   Do you have a best friend? What kind of friendship do you have with that person? What makes that person your best friend?

Based on the child's answers, you may then want or need to probe as follows (you probably will not need to ask all of these questions; be selective, depending on your child's comments):

1.   What kind of friendship do you think Kathy and Becky have? Do you think it is a good, close relationship? What is a really good, close relation? Does it take something special to have a very good friendship? What kinds of things do friends know about each other?

2.   What does being friends for a long time, like Kathy and Becky have been, do for a friendship?

3.   What makes good, close friendships last?

4.   What kinds of things can good friends talk about that other friends sometimes can't? What kinds of problems can they talk over?

5.   What makes two friends feel really close to each other?

6.   What is the difference between the kind of friendship Becky and Kathy have and Kathy and Jeanette's friendship? Are there different kinds of friendship? What is the difference between "regular" and "best" friendships?

7.   Is it better when close friends are like each other or different from each other friendships? Why? In what way should good friends be the same? In what way should they be different?

8.   Which is better to have (be with), one close friend or a group of regular friends? Why? (Selman, 1980, pp. 321-333).

Analysis and Report

Transcribe your child's answers as close to verbatim as you can (tape them, if that will help). Describe the child's understanding of friendship and compare it to the description of friendships in the text.

Reference

Selman, R. L. (1980). *The Growth of Interpersonal Understanding.* New York: Academic Press.

WHEN YOU HAVE FINISHED . . . AT-HOME PROJECT

Student Project 19: Television Aggression

You may want to combine this project with the next one, which involves observing sex role presentations on TV. If so, you or your instructor may wish to modify the following instructions somewhat. But if you are doing this in isolation, proceed as follows:

Procedure

Using the definition of violence offered by George Gerbner ("the overt expression of physical forces against others or self, or the compelling of action against one's will on pain of being hurt or killed"), select a minimum of four half-hour television programs normally watched by children and count the number of aggressive or violent episodes in each. Extend Gerbner's definition somewhat, however, to count verbal aggression as well as physical aggression.

You may select any four (or more) programs, but consider distributing them in the following way:
- At least one "educational" television program, such as *Sesame Street* or *Mr. Rogers' Neighborhood.*
- At least one Saturday morning cartoon.
- At least one early evening adult program that is watched by young children: a family comedy, a western, a crime film, or one of each.

For each program that you watch, record the number of violent episodes, separating the instances of verbal and physical violence.

Analysis and Report

In thinking of writing about the details of your observations, consider the following questions:

1.	What kind of variation in the number of violent episodes is there among the programs that you watched?

2.	Are some programs more verbally aggressive, some more physically aggressive?

3.	Do the numbers of violent episodes per program correspond to the numbers found by Gerbner?

4.	What about the consequences of aggression in the television films? Are those who act violently rewarded or punished? How often do reward and punishment occur?

5.	What behaviors other than aggression might a child learn from watching the programs you viewed? This question is particularly relevant for *Sesame Street* or *Mr. Rogers' Neighborhood*, but applies to more traditional entertainment as well.

6.	In view of the material in this chapter, and your own observations for this project, what rules or limits (if any) would you place on TV viewing for your own child? Why?

WHEN YOU HAVE FINISHED . . . AT-HOME PROJECT

Student Project 20: Sex Roles on TV

If you combine this with the preceding project, recording both aggressive episodes and sex role behavior on TV programs, you will gain a very good sense of portrayals of "real life" given on TV.

Procedure

You can gain some experience designing your own research by selection among the following options:

Option 1. Watch at least five hours of TV, spread over several time periods, and record the number of male and female characters and whether they are the central character or a minor character.

Option 2. Watch four to six hours of TV, selecting among several different types of programs, and note the activities of each male and female character in the following categories: aggression, nurturance, problem solving, conformity, and physical exertion.

Option 3. Watch and analyze the commercials on at least ten programs, making sure that the programs cover the full range of types, from sports to soap operas. You might count the number of male and female participants in the commercials and the nature of their activity in each case, using some of the same categories listed in option 2.

Analysis and Report

In preparing your report, you need to specify clearly which of these options (or some other) you chose, which programs you watched, how often you defined your terms, and what results you obtained. What do you think these results mean for the average viewer of TV?

CHAPTER 10 ANSWER KEY

Practice Test #1 Theories of Social and Personality Development

1. internal drives; cultural demands
2. latency stage
3. concrete; abstract
4. behavioral comparison
5. psychological construct

Practice Test #2 Dimensions of Moral Development

1. T   2. F   3. T   4. T   5. F   6. T   7. T   8. T

Practice Test #3 Social Relationships

1. c   2. d   3. b   4. b   5. a   6. c   7. a   8. b   9. c   10. d

Practice Test #4 Personality and Self-Concept

1. g   2. c   3. b   4. e   5. h   6. d

Practice Test #5: Influences Beyond Family and School

1. F   2. T   3. F   4. T   5. T   6. T

Comprehensive Practice Test

Multiple Choice Questions

1. b   2. d   3. d   4. c   5. b   6. c   7. c   8. c   9. c   10. b
11. d   12. b   13. a   14. c   15. a

True-False Questions

1. T   2. T   3. F   4. F   5. T   6. T   7. F   8. T

Essay Questions

1.
   - The parents' own ability to self-regulate provides the child with models of good or poor self-regulation.
   - The degree of self-regulation expected by parents influences the child's self-regulatory behavior. Higher expectations, together with parental monitoring to make certain the expectations are met, are associated with greater self-regulatory competence.

2.
   - Boys friendships are more focused on competition and dominance than girls.
   - Girls' friendships include more agreement, more compliance, and more self-disclosure than boys.
   - More "controlling" speech among boys.

3.
   - Popular children behave in positive, supportive, non-punitive, and non-aggressive ways toward most other children.
   - They explain things, take their playmates' wishes into consideration, take turns in conversation, and are able to regulate the expression of their strong emotions.
   - They are usually good at regulating their own emotions and accurately assessing others' feelings.

Puzzle It Out

Across

1. Retaliatory
4. Conscience
5. Latency
6. Controlling
7. Superego
8. Neuroticism
9. Extraversion
10. Agreeableness
11. Behavioral

Down

2. Inductive
3. Relational
4. Conscientiousness

CHAPTER 11

PHYSICAL AND COGNITIVE DEVELOPMENT IN ADOLESCENCE

BEFORE YOU READ . . . CHAPTER SUMMARY

Development in adolescence is marked by strides, as well as challenges. Along with physical maturity comes new health risks. Advances in cognitive functioning enable teenagers to function almost as well as adults. School experiences are critical to adolescent development.

Physical Changes

- Puberty is triggered by a complex set of hormones, beginning at about age seven or eight. Menarche, a girl's first menstrual period, typically occurs two years after the beginning of other visible changes. In boys, the peak of the growth spurt typically comes fairly late in the sequence of physical development.
- Each teenager has an internal model, or mental image, of the "normal" or "right" timing for puberty. Discrepancies between an adolescent's expectation and what actually happens determine the psychological effect of puberty.
- There are two major growth spurts in the teenaged years: the first occurs between ages 13 and 15, the second from 17 to 19. An adolescent may grow three to six inches a year for several years, then continue to add height and weight slowly until he or she reaches their adult size. Boys add more muscle than girls; girls add more fat than boys.

Adolescent Health

- In general, teenagers show heightened levels of risky behavior, such as unprotected sex, drug use, and reckless driving.
- Sexual activity among teens has increased in recent decades in the United States, but many do not use contraception consistently.
- Long-term consequences for teenaged mothers are generally negative, although some girls are able to overcome the challenges.
- Alcohol, drugs, and tobacco are more likely to be used by teens who show other forms of deviant or problem behavior. Sensation-seeking interacts with parenting style to increase the likelihood of drug use.
- Eating disorders such as bulimia and anorexia are among the most significant mental health problems during adolescence. Body image may be a causal factor. A general tendency toward mental illness may also be a factor in eating disorders.
- The contributing factors in completed suicides include depression, aggression, and a family history of psychiatric disorders or suicide or drug or alcohol abuse.

Changes in Thinking and Memory

- In Piaget's fourth stage of cognitive development, the formal operational period, teenagers learn to reason logically about abstract concepts. It is characterized by the ability to apply basic operations to ideas and possibilities—systematic problem solving—in addition to actual objects.
- There is clear evidence of some advanced forms of thinking in at least some adolescents, but formal operational thinking is not universal, nor is it consistently used even by those who possess the ability.

- Adolescents process information faster, use processing resources more efficiently, understand their own memory processes better, and have more knowledge than do elementary school children.

Schooling
- The transition to middle school may be accompanied by changes in children's goal orientation that result in achievement and self-esteem losses.
- Girls seem to be at particular risk for achievement losses after the transition to high school, especially in science and math. The ethnic variations in math performance are wide, partly because not all teens receive the necessary the encouragement and/or preparation for advanced high school math classes.
- Adolescents who succeed academically in high school are typically from authoritative families. Those who drop out are more likely to be poor, or to be doing poorly in school.

AS YOU READ . . . LEARNING OBJECTIVES

After completing Chapter 11, you should be able to:
11.1   Identify the changes in the endocrine system and the reproductive system that occur during adolescence.
11.2   Discuss the psychological issues involved in the timing of pubertal development.
11.3   Describe the changes in other body systems that allow adolescents to acquire new cognitive and motor skills.
11.4   Describe how risky behavior affects teenagers.
11.5   Identify the issues involved with the sexual behavior of adolescents.
11.6   Summarize the issues involved in teenaged pregnancy.
11.7   List and describe the stages of the crisis intervention model for pregnant teens.
11.8   Describe the use of drugs, alcohol, and tobacco among adolescents.
11.9   Identify the issues involved with body image and eating disorders among teenagers.
11.10   Identify the issues involved in adolescent depression and suicide.
11.11   Describe Piaget's stage of formal operational thought.
11.12   Summarize Elkind's research on adolescent egocentrism.
11.13   Describe the direct tests of Piaget's view of formal operational thinking.
11.14   Summarize the advances in information-processing skills during the teenage years.
11.15   Describe the issues involved in adolescents' transition to secondary school.
11.16   Identify the gender and ethnicity issues involved in achievement in science and math among adolescents.
11.17   Summarize the research on teenagers who drop out of school.
11.18   Describe programs designed to reach the high school drop-out.

AS YOU READ . . . TERM IDENTIFICATION

Ability goals (p. 309)
Adolescence (p. 289)
Anorexia nervosa (p. 301)
Bulimia (p. 301)
Endocrine glands (p. 290)
Formal operational stage (p. 304)
Gonadotrophic hormones (p. 290)
Hypothetico-deductive reasoning (p. 305)

Menarche (p. 291)
Pituitary gland (p. 291)
Primary sex characteristics (p. 291)
Secondary sex characteristics (p. 291)
Secular trend (p. 291)
Systematic problem-solving (p. 304)
Task goals (p. 309)

AS YOU READ . . . GUIDED STUDY QUESTIONS

PHYSICAL CHANGES

The Endocrine and Reproductive Systems (pp. 289-292)

Objective 11.1: Identify the changes in the endocrine system and the reproductive system that occur during adolescence.

1. Define the following terms:
   a. adolescence (p. 289)

   b. endocrine glands (p. 290)

   c. pituitary gland (p. 290)

   d. gonadotrophic hormones (p. 290)

   e. primary sex characteristics (p. 291)

   f. secondary sex characteristics (p. 292)

   g. menarche (p. 292)

   h. secular trend (p. 292)

2. List the major hormones that contribute to physical growth and development.

3. Trace the events of sexual development of boys and girls.

Timing of Puberty (pp. 292-293)

Objective 11.2: Discuss the psychological issues involved in the timing of pubertal development.

4. Describe why the discrepancies between an adolescent's expectation and what actually happens determine the psychological effects of puberty. Give examples for girls and for boys.

Other Body Systems (pp. 293-294)

Objective 11.3: Describe the changes in other body systems that allow adolescents to acquire new cognitive and motor skills.

5. List and describe the two major brain growth spurts in the teenaged years.

Age	Area of Brain Growth	Result of Growth
13-15		
17-19		

6. Give examples of how the cephalocaudal and proximodistal patterns of development are reversed in adolescence.

7. Distinguish between the development of joints in girls and in boys.

8. Compare the gains in muscles of boys and girls.

9. How does the increase in the size of the heart and lungs affect endurance, size, strength, and speed?

AFTER YOU READ . . . PRACTICE TEST #1
PHYSICAL CHANGES

Match the letter of the term in the right column with its description in the left column.

_____ 1.	Changes in body parts during puberty such as breasts and body hair.	a. Adolescence
		b. Endocrine glands
_____ 2.	The beginning of menstrual cycles.	c. Estradiol
		d. Gonadotrophic hormone
_____ 3.	The transitional period between childhood and adulthood.	e. Menarche
		f. Pituitary gland
_____ 4.	Hormones responsible for the development of the sex organs.	g. Primary sex characteristics
_____ 5.	Glands that secrete hormones.	h. Secondary sex characteristics
_____ 6.	Gland that triggers other glands to release hormones; called the master gland.	i. Secular trend
		j. Testosterone

(Check your answers to Practice Test #1 on p. 243.)

ADOLESCENT HEALTH

Sensation-Seeking (p. 295)

Objective 11.4: Describe how risky behavior affects teenagers.

10. Give examples of adolescent sensation-seeking behavior.

11. Why are risky behaviors more common in adolescence than other periods?

12. Give examples of how television and other forms of the popular media may influence teens' risky behavior.

Sexual Behavior (pp. 295-298)

Objective 11.5: Identify the issues involved with the sexual behavior of adolescents.

13. Give examples of how sexual experience varies across racial and ethnic groups, and across age and ethnic groups.

14. List the social factors that predict teenagers' sexual activity.

15.   Give examples of the finding that teens lack knowledge about sexually transmitted diseases (STDs).

16.   Describe a comprehensive sex education program.

Teenaged Pregnancy (pp. 298-299)

Objective 11.6: Summarize the issues involved in teenaged pregnancy.

17.   List the factors that predict sexual activity in general as well the likelihood that she will become pregnant.

18.   How are the children of teenaged mothers at risk?

The Real World: Crisis Intervention for the Pregnant Teen (p. 299)

Objective 11.7: List and describe the stages of the crisis intervention model for pregnant teens.

19.   List the characteristics of each phase of the intervention model, and provide suggested caregiver techniques.

Phase	Characteristics of Phase	Caregiving Techniques
Initial Phase		
Escalation Phase		
Redefinition Phase		
Dysfunctional Phase		

20.   What is the goal of crisis intervention?

Drugs, Alcohol, and Tobacco (pp. 300-201)

Objective 11.8: Describe the use of drugs, alcohol, and tobacco among adolescents.

21.   What is binge drinking?

22.   How does sensation-seeking interact with parenting style?

23.   What are the ages during which teens seem to be most susceptible to peer influence with regard to smoking?

24.   Give examples of how parents influence teenagers' smoking habits.

Body Image and Eating Disorders (pp. 301-303)

Objective 11.9: Identify the issues involved with body image and eating disorders among teenagers.

25. Define and distinguish between the following eating disorders:
    a. bulimia, or bulimia nervosa (p. 301)

    b. anorexia nervosa (p. 301)

26. List and describe three possible theoretical explanations for eating disorders.

27. Give an example of how the general tendency toward mental illness may be a factor in eating disorders.

28. What is an obsessive-compulsive personality disorder?

Depression and Suicide (pp. 303-304)

Objective 11.10: Identify the issues involved in adolescent depression and suicide.

29. Give examples of family stresses that might impact adolescent depression.

30. How does low self-esteem impact teenagers' depression?

31. Give examples of how depression can hinder academic achievement.

32. List and describe six factors that contribute to completed suicides.

Factor	*Description*

33. Describe suicide prevention programs.

AFTER YOU READ . . . PRACTICE TEST #2
ADOLESCENT HEALTH

1. _____ leads to recklessness, which, in turn, leads to markedly increased rates of accidents and injuries in the teen years.
   a. Sensation seeking
   b. Bulimia
   c. Adolescent egocentrism
   d. Playing violent video games

2. Social factors that predict teenagers' risky sexual behavior include each of the following EXCEPT:
   a. they come from poorer families
   b. they come from families in which sexual activity is condoned and dating rules are lax
   c. they were abused and/or neglected in early childhood
   d. they are less likely to use alcohol

3. Factors that predict teenage pregnancy include each of the following EXCEPT:
   a. they younger the girl is when she becomes sexually active
   b. they come from single-parent families
   c. they come from well-educated families
   d. they come from poor families

4. Consuming five or more drinks on a single occasion is called _____.
   a. social drinking
   b. binge drinking
   c. independent drinking
   d. extracurricular drinking

5. Teens who are high sensation-seekers choose friends _____.
   a. who are low sensation-seekers
   b. who are similar
   c. who have more money than they do
   d. to impress with their adventures

6. The period between ages _____ seems to be the time during which a teenager is most susceptible to peer influences with regard to smoking.
   a. 15 and 17
   b. 13 and 15
   c. 11 and 13
   d. 9 and 11

7. An eating disorder characterized by binge eating and purging is called _____.
   a. major depression
   b. obsessive-compulsive personality disorder
   c. anorexia nervosa
   d. bulimia

8.   **Each of the following is a proposed cause for eating disorders EXCEPT:**
      a.   operant conditioning
      b.   biological
      c.   psychoanalytical
      d.   discrepancy between a teens' internal image of a desirable body and her (or his) perception of her (or his) own body

9.   **Teenaged girls are _____ as likely as boys to report feelings of depression.**
      a.   just
      b.   three times
      c.   twice
      d.   not

10.   **Each of the following is a contributing factor in completed suicides EXCEPT:**
      a.   an opportunity
      b.   special training in coping abilities
      c.   an altered mental state
      d.   some triggering stressful event

(Check your answers to Practice Test # 2 on p. 243.)

CHANGES IN THINKING AND MEMORY

Piaget's Formal Operational Stage (pp. 304-305)

Objective 11.11: Describe Piaget's stage of formal operational thought.

34.   Define the following terms:
      a.   formal operational stage (p. 304)

      b.   systematic problem solving (p. 304)

      c.   hypothetico-deductive reasoning (p. 305)

35.   Describe the methods Piaget used to test for systematic problem-solving skills. Include the pendulum problem.

36.   How would an adolescent using a formal operational approach differ from a concrete-operational thinker in attempting to solve the pendulum problem?

37.   Give examples of deductive reasoning, and explain how deductive reasoning is related to the scientific process.

Research Report: Elkind's Adolescent Egocentrism (p. 306)

Objective 11.12: Summarize Elkind's research on adolescent egocentrism.

38.   What is adolescent egocentrism?

39.   Give examples of the two components of adolescent egocentrism by completing the following table:

Component	Example

40.   Describe the new look theory, and explain how projection is involved.

Direct Tests of Piaget's View (pp. 305-308)

Objective 11.13: Describe the direct tests of Piaget's view of formal operational thinking.

41.   Give examples of how adolescents gain formal operational skills in the pendulum problem and in understanding figurative language.

42.   Give examples of how formal operational thinking alters the ways teenagers make decisions.

Advances in Information-Processing (pp. 308-309)

Objective 11.14: Summarize the advances in information-processing skills during the teenage years.

43.   List the gains in information-processing skills of adolescents as compared to elementary school children.

44.   Give examples of how the metacognitive and metamemory skills of adolescents far exceed those of younger children.

45.   Give examples to illustrate the difference between younger children's and adolescents' processing of a memory for text. Include the four rules that participants used in writing summaries.

AFTER YOU READ . . . PRACTICE TEST #3
CHANGES IN THINKING AND MEMORY

Indicate whether each of the following statements is true or false.

_____ 1.   The formal operational stage is defined as the period during which adolescents learn to reason logically about concrete concepts.

_____ 2.   Systematic problem solving is the ability to search methodically for the answer to a problem.

_____ 3.   Inductive reasoning involves considering hypotheses or hypothetical premises and then deriving logical outcomes.

_____ 4.   Formal operational reasoning seems to enable adolescents to understand figurative language, such as metaphors, to a greater degree.

_____ 5. The capacity to apply memory strategies selectively continues to improve throughout adolescence.

_____ 6. The ability to summarize a text improves significantly during the early half of adolescence.

(Check your answers to Practice Test #3 on p. 243.)

SCHOOLING

Transition to Secondary School (pp. 309-311)

Objective 11.15: Describe the issues involved in adolescents' transition to secondary school.

46. Define the following terms:
   a. task goals (p. 309)

   b. ability goals (p. 309)

47. Describe two models of transitional schools from elementary school to high school.

48. Explain how a student's goal (task or ability) influences his or her behavior.

49. Describe two strategies to address the shift in goal structure by completing the following table.

Strategy	*Description and Examples of Strategy*
Mentoring	
Grade-level Teams	

50. How can electives in high school make the transition more positive?

Gender, Ethnicity, and Achievement in Science and Math (pp. 311-313)

Objective 11.16: Identify the gender and ethnicity issues involved in achievement in science and math among adolescents.

51. Give examples of how girls are at risk for achievement losses in science after the transition to high school. Include suggestions for lessening the gap.

52. Give examples of ethnic variations in mathematics achievement. Include examples of preparation for college-preparatory courses.

Dropping Out of High School (pp. 313-314)

Objective 11.17: Summarize the research on teenagers who drop out of school.

53.   Describe the characteristics of the parents of students who achieve in high school.

54.   Give examples of the following influences that predict school completion.

Influence	Examples
Social class	
History of academic failure	
Pattern of aggressive behavior	
Decisions about risky behavior	
Peer influence	
Family variables	

55.   List the long-term consequences of dropping out of high school.

No Easy Answers: Reaching the High School Drop-out (p. 314)

Objective 11.18: Describe programs designed to reach the high school drop-out.

56.   Define a charter school, and give examples of how it may reach the high school drop-out.

AFTER YOU READ . . . PRACTICE TEST #4
SCHOOLING

Fill in the blanks with the best answer.

1.   _____ are goals based on a desire for improvement; _____ are goals based on a desire to be superior to others.

2.   Task goals are associated with a greater sense of _____ and more positive attitudes about school.

3.   Students with ability goals adopt _____ —that is, they view performance on a given academic task as good as long as it is better than someone else's.

4. Some schools provide students with _____, either a teacher or a volunteer from the community, to whom middle-school students are assigned.

5. One approach aimed at making middle schools truly transitional involves organizing students and teachers into _____.

6. _____ seem to be a particular risk for achievement losses after the transition to high school.

7. _____ high school students earn twice as many high school credits in advanced math courses as white students, and three to four times as many as African-American and Hispanic-American students.

8. Despite ethnic differences in drop-out rates, _____ is a better predictor of school completion than is ethnicity.

9. Longitudinal studies show that students who have _____, _____, and _____ are most likely to drop out of high school.

10. One recent educational innovation, the _____, seems to be especially promising with regard to meeting the educational needs of drop-outs.

(Check your answers to Practice Test #4 on p. 243.)

AFTER YOU READ . . . CRITICAL REFLECTION EXERCISE

Puberty and Adolescence

Utilizing information from the text, provide answers to the following questions. Be sure and provide specific examples and evidence from the chapters to support your answers.

1. What effect does the timing of the onset of puberty have on the developing adolescent? Name and discuss three factors that influence the type of effects on early or later onset of puberty will have.

2. Why are physical and cognitive changes so closely linked during adolescent development? Provide at least three possible reasons.

3. You are conducting a parents-as-teachers session. You have been asked to explain some of the factors that influence why teens might turn to drugs and alcohol. Provide four reasons that adolescents might start drinking or using other drugs. In addition, provide four pieces of advice to these parents on how to approach the concept with their children.

AFTER YOU READ . . . COMPREHENSIVE PRACTICE TEST
MULTIPLE CHOICE QUESTIONS

1. **The pituitary gland _____.**
   a. regulates bodily systems such as temperature and hunger
   b. provides the trigger for the release of hormones from other glands
   c. produces and releases thyroxin which regulates sexual growth
   d. triggers the development of primary and secondary sex characteristics

2. **What effect does early pubertal development have on boys?**
   a. It has significant negative effects on self-esteem.
   b. There are no consistent effects of the timing of pubertal development.
   c. It tends to have positive effects on body image and the number of friends.
   d. It has minor negative effects on body image and school-related problems.

3. **After puberty, _____ in endurance as well as in size, strength, and speed.**
   a. boys have a clear advantage over girls
   b. boys have a limited advantage over girls
   c. boys and girls have an equal advantage
   d. girls have a clear advantage over boys

4. **A desire to experience increased levels of arousal, such as those that accompany fast driving or the "highs" that are associated with drugs, is called _____.**
   a. an extracurricular activity
   b. socializing
   c. independence
   d. sensation-seeking

5. **Which of the following statements about the sexual behavior of teens is TRUE?**
   a. The proportion of sexually experienced teens decreases across grades 9 to 12.
   b. Sexual experience is consistent across racial and ethnic groups.
   c. Boys are more sexually active than girls.
   d. Teens consistently use effective contraceptive methods.

6. **The children of teenaged mothers are more likely than children born to older mothers to _____.**
   a. grow up in poverty
   b. complete high school
   c. achieve high self-esteem
   d. delay having children of their own

7. **Which of the following parenting styles seems to offer teens some protection from their sensation-seeking tendencies?**
   a. permissive parental style
   b. authoritarian parental style
   c. authoritative parental style
   d. neglecting parental style

8. **Which of the following is TRUE about anorexia nervosa?**
   a. It is less common than bulimia.
   b. It is more common in underdeveloped countries than industrialized ones.
   c. It is fatal in about five percent of the cases.
   d. It involves bingeing but not purging.

9. **Which of the following statements is TRUE about teenage suicide?**
    a. Native-American teenagers are the least likely to complete a suicide attempt.
    b. Hispanic-American youths are the most likely to complete a suicide attempt.
    c. Boys are more likely than girls to use self-poisoning in a suicide attempt.
    d. Boys are more likely than girls to complete a suicide attempt.

10. **The ability to derive conclusions from hypothetical premises is called _____.**
    a. hypothetico-deductive reasoning
    b. formal deductive reasoning
    c. inductive reasoning
    d. abstract thinking

11. **Which of the following statements about formal operational reasoning is TRUE?**
    a. Piaget was overly pessimistic about adolescents' thinking abilities.
    b. People develop formal operational thinking even if their life situations or cultures do not require it.
    c. In adulthood, rates of formal operational thinking decrease with education.
    d. Piaget was overly optimistic about adolescents' thinking abilities.

12. **Each of the following is an advance in the information-processing abilities of teenagers EXCEPT:**
    a. understanding their own memory
    b. processing information faster
    c. using processing resources less efficiently
    d. metacognitive and metamemory skills

13. **Goals based on personal standards and a desire to become more competent at something are called _____.**
    a. metacognition
    b. ability goals
    c. task goals
    d. metamemory

14. **Which of the following statements about gender, ethnicity, and achievement in science and math is TRUE?**
    a. Gender differences in achievement in math are greater than ethnic differences.
    b. Ethnic differences in achievement in math are greater than gender differences.
    c. Girls excel in math but not science.
    d. Intellectually talented girls are encouraged to take courses in sciences such as chemistry and physics rather than zoology or botany.

15. **Which of the following statements about dropping out of school is TRUE?**
    a. Few variables are involved in school completion.
    b. Ethnicity is the strongest predictor of school completion.
    c. Academic failure is not a predictor of school completion.
    d. Social class is a better predictor of school completion than ethnicity.

TRUE-FALSE QUESTIONS

Indicate whether each of the following statements is true or false.

_____ 1. Changes in primary sex characteristics include breast development in girls, changing voice pitch and beard growth in boys, and the growth of body hair in both sexes.

_____ 2. Major changes in brain organization show up between ages 13 and 15 and qualitative shifts in cognitive functioning appear after age 15.

_____ 3. Risky behaviors may be more common in adolescence than other periods because they help teenagers gain peer acceptance and establish autonomy with respect to parents and other authority figures.

_____ 4. Despite their high levels of sexual activity, teenagers know remarkably little about physiology and reproduction.

_____ 5. A child in the concrete operational stage working on the pendulum problem will usually try out many different combinations of length, weight, force, and height in an inefficient way.

_____ 6. In adulthood, rates of formal operational thinking decrease with education.

_____ 7. Ability-goal-oriented students are more likely than others to attribute success and failure to forces outside themselves.

_____ 8. Alcohol and drug use better predict a high school student's grades than do the student's grades in elementary or middle school.

ESSAY QUESTIONS

1. Discuss how the popular media may influence teenagers' sensation-seeking behavior.

2. Discuss how Elkind's adolescent egocentrism is helpful in explaining a variety of adolescents' everyday behaviors. Give specific examples.

3. Discuss the long-term consequences that correlate with dropping out of high school.

(Check your answers to the Comprehensive Practice Test on p. 243.)

WHEN YOU HAVE FINISHED . . . PUZZLE IT OUT

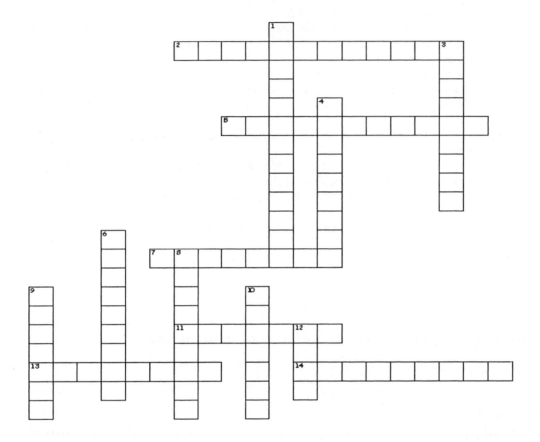

Across

2. A sex hormone in males
5. The transitional period between childhood and adulthood
7. The beginning of menstrual cycles
11. Goals based on a desire to be superior to others
13. An eating disorder characterized by self-starvation
14. Sex characteristics that involve body parts such as breasts and body hair

Down

1. Hormones responsible for the development of the sex organs
3. Glands that secrete hormones that govern growth and other aspects of physical development
4. Reasoning that involved considering hypotheses and then deriving logical outcomes
6. Gland that triggers other glands to release hormone
8. A sex hormone in girls
9. Sex characteristics that involve the growth of the sex organs
10. An eating disorder characterized by binge eating and purging
12. Goals based on a desire for self-improvement

Created by Puzzlemaker at DiscoverySchool.com

(Check your answers on p. 244.)

WHEN YOU HAVE FINISHED . . . RESEARCH PROJECT

Student Project 21: The Pendulum

This is a simplified version of the Inhelder and Piaget pendulum problem. To complete this project, you should locate a child between roughly age eight and 16, obtaining the parents' permission for the testing in the prescribed way.

Equipment

Because the physical objects are so important for this problem, you need to collect your equipment carefully and test it before you start. You will need three pieces of strong, flexible string (one about 25 cm, one about 37 cm, and one 50 cm long). You will also need three similar objects of varying weights. Fishing sinkers work well, as do keys, but the lightest one should be heavy enough so that it will weigh down the string and allow it to swing.

If you can complete the testing in some location in which you have a chance to tie all three strings to some overhead rod or other object, that would be the best, since it leaves you free to write down what your subject does. Otherwise, you will have to hold the top of each string when your subject wishes to use that string in the test.

Procedure

Tell your subject:

> *I am doing a class project about how different people go about solving a problem. The problem I would like you to solve is to find out what makes a pendulum swing faster or slower.*

Pause at this point and demonstrate how you can attach a weight to the string, then push the weight to start the pendulum swinging. Demonstrate this with more than one weight/string combination so that it is clear that there is variability in the speed of the pendulum swing. Then say:

> *You need to figure out what makes the pendulum swing faster or slower. You can use any of these strings and these three weights to help you figure this out. I'll be taking notes about what you do and say while you are working on the problem.*

Record each combination the subject tries, in the order of the attempts. If you can, you should also record any comments the subject makes in the process. Allow the subject to continue until he or she gives you an answer; if no answer is forthcoming, after a period of time, you may ask some questions like, *"Can you figure out what makes the pendulum move fast or slow?"* If that does not elicit an answer, or if the subject seems very frustrated or bored, you may terminate the procedure and thank the subject for his or her help. If the subject has not solved the problem, you will want to reassure him or her by pointing out that this is a really hard problem and that lots of kids have a hard time figuring it out.

Analysis and Report

In reporting on your project, make sure to discuss the following points:

- Did your subject solve the problem? (That is, did he or she figure out that it is the length of the string and not the weight that determines the speed of the pendulum?)
- How many separate swing/weight combination tests did it take to reach some conclusion, whether the conclusion was correct or not?
- Did the subject try various string/weight combinations in any systematic order? Or were the various attempts more random?
- Did the subject talk to himself or herself while working on the problem? Was this self-talk directed at keeping track of things that had been tried, or at thinking through the problem?
- Did your subject's performance fit the findings form Piaget's and others' studies on the age at which formal operations develop?

WHEN YOU HAVE FINISHED . . . AT-HOME PROJECT

Student Project 22: Plotting Your Own Growth

This project will work best if your parents are among those who routinely stood you up against a convenient doorjamb and measured you—and if you still live in the house with the marked-up doorjamb. Alternatively, you may have a friend or an acquaintance who has access to doorjamb data you could use. Assuming you can locate such a set of measurements, you should plot your own (or your friend's) rate of growth over the years of childhood. Calculate the inches you grew each year (estimating when needed), plot the ages and the height, and draw a curve.

When was your maximum height spurt (the year in which you grew the most inches)? During elementary school, did you grow about the same number of inches per year? If you are a female, add to the graph a point that represents your first menstruation (to the best of your recollection). Where did menarche fall on the curve; that is, did menarche occur after your major growth spurt?

CHAPTER 11 ANSWER KEY

Practice Test #1 Physical Changes

1. h   2. e   3. a   4. d   5. b   6. f

Practice Test #2 Adolescent Health

1. a   2. d   3. c   4. b   5. b   6. a   7. d   8. a   9. c   10. b

Practice Test #3 changes in Thinking and Memory

1. F   2. T   3. F   4. T   5. T   6. F

Practice Test #4 Schooling

1.   task goal; ability goal
2.   personal control
3.   relative standards
4.   an adult mentor
5.   teams
6.   Girls
7.   Asian American
8.   social class
9.   a history of academic failure, a pattern of aggressive behavior, poor decisions about risky behavior
10. charter school

Comprehensive Practice Test

Multiple Choice Questions

1. b   2. c   3. a   4. d   5. c   6. a   7. c   8. a   9. d   10. a
11. d   12. c   13. c   14. b   15. d

True-False Questions

1. F   2. T   3. T   4. T   5. T   6. F   7. T   8. T

Essay Questions

1.   ▪ In the United States teens spend more time watching TV, listening to music, and playing video games than they do in school.
     ▪ Teens who are highest in sensation-seeking behaviors are those who are most strongly influenced by media portrayals of risky behavior.
     ▪ Television programs have an abundance of sexual incidents and the use of drug and alcohol.

2.   ▪ Examples of the personal fable could include ones similar to these: "You don't understand what it's like to be a teenager in love." "I can drink a six-pack of beer and drive safely—no problem." I'm not at risk for HIV/AIDS; only those other people et that."
     ▪ Examples of the imaginary audience could include ones similar to these: "I can't go to school with my hair looking like this—everyone will laugh." "I have to have the perfect shirt to wear to the party."

3.   ▪ Answers should include the following: higher unemployment, lower wages, increased likelihood of depression, boys with poor self-regulatory skills are more likely to become involved in criminal behavior in early adulthood.

Puzzle It Out

Across
2. Testosterone
5. Adolescence
7. Menarche
11. Ability
13. Anorexia
14. Secondary

Down
1. Gonadotrophic
3. Endocrine
4. Deductive
6. Pituitary
8. Estradiol
9. Primary
10. Bulimia
12. Task

CHAPTER 12

SOCIAL AND PERSONALITY DEVELOPMENT IN ADOLESCENCE

BEFORE YOU READ . . . CHAPTER SUMMARY

The social and personality development of adolescents is strongly influenced by the process of identity development. Other factors influencing development include changes in adolescents' self-concept and social relationships. The development of moral reasoning is also considered.

Theories of Social and Personality Development

- For Freud, the primary developmental task of the genital stage is to channel the libido into a healthy sexual relationship, whereas Erikson emphasizes the development of the identity.
- James Marcia's study of identity statuses is based on Erikson's ideas, and it includes two key parts—a crisis and a commitment. Combining these elements, four identity statuses are possible.

Self-Concept and Personality

- In adolescence, the teen's self-concept becomes more abstract and differentiated. More emphasis is placed on enduring, internal qualities and ideology.
- Gender-related aspects of the psychological self are termed sex-role identity.
- Self-esteem drops somewhat at the beginning of adolescence and then rises steadily throughout the teen years.
- Minority teenagers, especially those of color in a predominantly white culture, face the task of creating two identities in adolescence: a sense of individual identity that sets them apart from others and an ethnic identity that includes self-identification as a member of their specific group.
- Teens who are introverted, neurotic, and pessimistic and who blame their problems on forces outside themselves encounter more difficulties than peers who have a more positive outlook.

Social Relationships

- Adolescents have two, apparently contradictory, tasks in their relationships with their parents; to establish autonomy from them and to maintain a sense of relatedness with them.
- Peer relationships become far more significant in adolescence than they have been at any earlier period, and perhaps than they will be at any time later in life. Perhaps the most profound change in social relationships is the shift toward the inclusion of heterosexual relationships that prepare teens for assuming a full adult sexual identity.
- Teens who are homosexual or who are unsure about their sexual orientation face many obstacles in the formation of an identity.

Moral Development

- Kohlberg proposed six stages of moral reasoning, organized into three levels. These levels are loosely correlated with age, develop in a specified order, and appear in this same sequence in all cultures studied so far.
- The acquisition of cognitive role-taking skills is important to moral development, but the social environment is important as well.

- Kohlberg's theory has been criticized by theorists who place more emphasis on learning moral behavior and others who believe that moral reasoning may be based more on emotional factors than on ideas about justice and fairness.
- Delinquent teens are usually found to be far behind their peers in both role-taking and moral reasoning. Other factors, such as parenting style, may be equally important in delinquency.
- Adolescents who work more than ten to fifteen hours per week get lower grades and engage in more risky behavior than those who work less. Work can be beneficial if it is of a type that allows the teenager to acquire work-related skills she will need in adulthood.

AS YOU READ . . . LEARNING OBJECTIVES

After completing Chapter 12, you should be able to:
12.1 Describe the key points in the psychoanalytic perspective relevant to adolescence.
12.2 Explain Marcia's theory of identity achievement.
12.3 Discuss the issues involved in teenagers who are employed.
12.4 Describe the changes in self-understanding during the teenage years.
12.5 Summarize the development of sex-role identity.
12.6 Describe the development of self-esteem during adolescence.
12.7 Discuss the issues involved in ethnic identity.
12.8 Summarize the issues involved in the search for minority role models.
12.9 Discuss the issues involved with locus of control.
12.10 Describe the changing relationships of adolescents with their parents.
12.11 Discuss the issues involved in adolescents' relationships with peers.
12.12 Discuss the issues involved in homosexuality among adolescents.
12.13 Explain Kohlberg's theory of moral reasoning.
12.14 Identify the causes and consequences of moral development.
12.15 Identify the criticisms of Kohlberg's theory.
12.16 Describe the relationship between moral development and antisocial behavior.
12.17 Discuss the effectiveness of the efforts at preventing youth violence.

AS YOU READ . . . TERM IDENTIFICATION

Clique (p. 332)
Conventional morality (p. 337)
Crowd (p. 332)
Delinquency (p. 342)
Ethnic identity (p. 324)
Foreclosure (p. 319)
Genital stage (p. 318)
Identity (p. 318)
Identity achievement (p. 319)

Identity crisis (p. 318)
Identity diffusion (p. 319)
Identity versus role confusion (p. 318)
Locus of control (p. 327)
Moratorium (p. 319)
Postconventional morality (p. 338)
Preconventional morality (p. 336)
Role-taking (p. 339)
Sex-role identity (p. 323)

AS YOU READ ... GUIDED STUDY QUESTIONS

THEORIES OF SOCIAL AND PERSONALITY DEVELOPMENT

Psychoanalytic Perspectives (p. 318)

Objective 12.1: Describe the key points in the psychoanalytic perspective relevant to adolescence.

1.   Define the following terms:
    a.   genital stage (p. 318)

    b.   identity (p. 318)

    c.   identity versus role confusion (p. 318)

    d.   identity crisis (p. 318)

2.   For Freud, what is the primary developmental task of the genital stage?

3.   According to Erikson, what is the central crisis of adolescence?

4.   Explain why Erikson states that an identity crisis is inevitable during adolescence.

5.   According to Erikson, what is the function of the peer group?

Marcia's Theory of Identity Achievement (pp. 318-320)

Objective 12.2:   Explain Marcia's theory of identity achievement.

6.   Define the following terms:
    a.   identity achievement (p. 319)

    b.   moratorium (p 319)

    c.   foreclosure (p. 319)

    d.   identity diffusion (p. 319)

7.   What are the two key parts of adolescent identity formation? Give examples of each.

Key Part	*Example*

8.   What is the relationship between identity formation and the development of logical thinking?

9.   How do extreme stressors affect identity achievement?

Research Report: The Effects of Teenaged Employment (p. 321)

Objective 12.3: Discuss the issues involved in teenagers who are employed.

10.   The more hours adolescents work, the more likely they were to experience negative consequences. List the negative effects.

11.   How does the kind of work teenagers do as well as how many hours they spend on the job affect them?

AFTER YOU READ . . . PRACTICE TEST #1
THEORIES OF SOCIAL AND PERSONALITY DEVELOPMENT

Indicate whether each of the following statements is true or false.

_____ 1.   According to Freud, the primary developmental task of the latency stage is to channel the libido into a healthy sexual relationship.

_____ 2.   Freud believed that fixation at the phallic stage could lead to sexual deviance or dysfunction.

_____ 3.   In Erikson's model, the central crisis of adolescence is identity versus role confusion.

_____ 4.   According to Erikson, the teenaged group forms a base of security from which the young person can move toward an integrated view of herself, including her patterns of beliefs, occupational goals, and relationships.

_____ 5.   In Marcia's theory, identity achievement is the status of a person who has been through a crisis and reached a commitment to ideological or occupational goals.

_____ 6.   In Marcia's theory, foreclosure is the status of a person who is in a crisis but who has made no commitment.

_____ 7.   The quest for personal identity is complete at the end of adolescence.

_____ 8.   Teens facing extreme stressors, such as life-threatening illness, seem to be most optimally adjusted when they adopt the status of foreclosure.

(Check your answers to Practice Test #1 on p. 263.)

SELF-CONCEPT AND PERSONALITY

Self-Understanding (pp. 320-322)

Objective 12.4: Describe the changes in self-understanding during the teenage years.

12.   Compare the school-aged child's self-understanding with that of the adolescent.

13.   Give examples of how an adolescent's self-concept becomes differentiated as she comes to see herself somewhat differently in each of several roles.

14. Give examples of how the adolescents' academic self-concepts seem to come both from internal comparisons of their performance to a self-generated ideal and from external comparisons to peer performance.

Source	Example
Internal	
External	

15. Give examples of how social self-concepts predict behavior.

16. Compare how girls and boys construct various components of self-concept differently.

Sex-Role Identity (pp. 322-324)

Objective 12.5: Summarize the development of sex-role identity.

17. Define sex-role identity (p. 323).

18. List and describe the four basic sex-role types.

Type	Description

Self-Esteem (pp. 323-324)

Objective 12.6: Describe the development of self-esteem during adolescence.

19. Either an androgynous or a masculine sex-role identity is associated with higher self-esteem in both boys and girls. Why might this be explained by the existence of a "masculine bias?"

20. Give an example of how the adoption of an androgynous or masculine orientation by a girl can lead to lower self-esteem in some cultures.

21. What is the overall trend of self-esteem during the years of adolescence?

22. List and describe the four groups based on the stability of their self-esteem rating across adolescence.

Ethnic Identity (pp. 324-328)

Objective 12.7 Discuss the issues involved in ethnic identity.

23.   Define ethnic identity (p. 324).

24.   Describe the task facing minority teenagers in creating two identities.

25.   According to Jean Phinney, describe the stages in the development of a complete ethnic identity by completing the following table.

Stage	Equivalent Stage in Marcia's Theory	Example
Unexamined ethnic identity		
Ethnic identity search		
Resolution of the conflicts and contradictions		

26.   Give examples of a "bicultural orientation."

27.   How is the search of personal identity affected by ethnicity and culture?

Development in the Information Age: The Search for Minority Role Models (p. 326)

Objective 12.8: Summarize the issues involved in the search for minority role models.

28.   Give examples of why ethnic minority teens have problems when it comes to finding role models that can help with a quest for identity.

Locus of Control and Other Traits (pp. 327-328)

Objective 12.9: Discuss the issues involved with locus of control.

29.   Define locus of control (p. 327).

30.   Distinguish between external locus of control and internal locus of control by giving examples of each.

Internal Locus of Control	External Locus of Control

31.   Give examples of correlations between locus of control and behavior.

32.   List the cluster of personality variables associated with external locus of control, and describe their characteristics. What is the outlook for teens with these characteristics?

AFTER YOU READ . . . PRACTICE TEST #2
SELF-CONCEPT AND PERSONALITY

1.   **In adolescence, self-definition _____.**
        a.   becomes more abstract
        b.   becomes more concrete
        c.   continues to be concrete, as in middle childhood
        d.   becomes more focused on external characteristics

2.   **Adolescents' academic self-concepts come from _____.**
        a.   internal comparisons only
        b.   external comparisons only
        c.   neither internal or external comparisons
        d.   both from internal and external comparisons

3.   **An androgynous individual is likely to _____.**
        a.   be homosexual
        b.   have more feminine than masculine personality traits
        c.   have both masculine and feminine personality traits
        d.   have neither masculine nor feminine personality traits

4.   **Cross-cultural research suggests that adoption of an androgynous or masculine orientation by a girls can lead to _____.**
        a.   higher self-esteem
        b.   lower self-esteem
        c.   lower academic achievement
        d.   increased likelihood of homosexuality

5.   **To study the relationship of self-esteem to developmental outcomes such as school achievement, researchers often divide teens into four groups based on the stability of their self-esteem ratings across adolescence. Each of the following is one of the groups EXCEPT:**
        a.   self-esteem increases steadily throughout adolescence
        b.   self-esteem is consistently low throughout adolescence
        c.   self-esteem decreases dramatically during adolescence
        d.   self-esteem is consistently high throughout adolescence

6.   **The first stage in Jean Phinney's model of ethnic identity is _____.**
        a.   unexamined ethnic identity
        b.   ethnic moratorium
        c.   ethnic identity search
        d.   identity resolution

7. **Someone with _____ views personal variables, such as ability and effort, as responsible for outcomes.**
   a. a strong work ethic
   b. high self-esteem
   c. an external locus of control
   d. an internal locus of control

8. **An external locus of control is sometimes correlated with _____.**
   a. agreeableness and introversion
   b. introversion and neuroticism
   c. neuroticism and conscientiousness
   d. openness and agreeableness

(Check your answers to Practice Test #2 on p. 263.)

SOCIAL RELATIONSHIPS

Relationships with Parents (pp. 328-331)

Objective 12.10: Describe the changing relationships of adolescents with their parents.

33. Describe the two, apparently contradictory, tasks teenagers have in their relationships with their parents.

34. Give examples of research on teenagers' emotional attachment to their parents.

35. What is the relationship between teens who remain closely attached to their parents and their academic success, the likelihood of antisocial behavior, and the likelihood of drug use in later adolescence and early adulthood?

36. Give examples of why the authoritative parenting style is associated with more positive outcomes during adolescence.

37. How does family structure affect teenagers?

Relationships with Peers (pp. 331-334)

Objective 12.11: Discuss the issues involved in adolescents' relationships with peers.

38. Give examples of how the similarity of psychological characteristics and attitudes take on new significance in adolescence.

39. Give examples of how adolescent friendships are more stable than are those of younger children.

40. Trace the pattern of peer group conformity across adolescence.

41. Describe how the structure of the peer group changes over the years of adolescence.

42. Define the following terms, and give an example of each:
   a. clique (p. 332)

   b. crowd (p. 332)

43.   Give examples of how the term crowd is used to refer to the reputation-based group with which a young person is identified, either by choice or by peer designation.

44.   What is an identity prototype? Give examples.

45.   What is the most profound change in social relationships in adolescence?

46.   Why is the sense of being in love an important factor in adolescent dating patterns?

Homosexuality (pp. 334-335)

Objective 12.12: Discuss the issues involved in homosexuality among adolescents.

47.   State the concordant rates of homosexuality for the following groups:

Group	Concordant Rate
Identical Twins	
Fraternal Twins	
Biologically Unrelated Boys Adopted into the Same Family	

48.   Describe the evidence to support the hypothesis that homosexuality is programmed in at birth.

49.   Give examples of similar concerns which homosexual adolescents share with heterosexual adolescents.

AFTER YOU READ . . . PRACTICE TEST #3
SOCIAL RELATIONSHIPS

Fill in the blanks with the best answers.

1.   Teenagers have two, apparently contradictory, tasks in their relationships with their parents: to
        _____ and to _____.

2.   Teenagers' underlying emotional attachment to their parents _____ on average.

3.   For adolescents, as for younger children, _____ parenting is consistently associate with more positive outcomes.

4.   In contrast to younger children, among adolescents, it is _____ who show more distress when parents divorce.

5.   Despite the importance of family relationships to adolescents, it is an undeniable fact that
        _____ become far more significant in adolescence than they have been at any earlier period.

6.   Similarity of _____ and _____ takes on new significance during the teenaged years.

7.   A _____ is four to six young people who appear to be strongly attached to another.

8.   The word crowd refers to the _____ group with which a young person is identified, either by choice or by peer designation.

9.   The sense of _____ is an important factor in adolescent dating patterns.

10.   Taken together, _____,
_____, and _____
are consistent with the hypothesis that homosexuality is programmed in at birth.

(Check your answers to Practice Test #3 on p. 263.)

MORAL DEVELOPMENT

Kohlberg's Theory of Moral Reasoning (pp. 335-339)

Objective 12.13: Explain Kohlberg's theory of moral reasoning.

50.   Define the following terms:
       a.   preconventional morality (p. 336)

       b.   conventional morality (p. 337)

       c.   postconventional morality (p. 338)

51.   Describe Kohlberg's research method.

52.   What is the relationship between age and the stages?

53.   List and describe the three levels and six stages of Kohlberg's theory by completing the following table:

Level	Stages	Description

Level	Stages	Description

Causes and Consequences of Moral Development (pp. 339-340)

Objective 12.14: Identify the causes and consequences of moral development.

54.   Describe how cognitive development affects Kohlberg's stages and chronological age.

55.   Define role-taking (p. 339), and explain why it is related to cognitive development and Kohlberg's stages.

56.   How is the social environment involved in the development of moral reasoning?

57.   How do parenting style and family climate relate to the levels of moral reasoning?

58.   Give examples of how teenagers' levels of moral reasoning appear to be positively correlated with prosocial behavior and negatively related to antisocial behavior.

Criticisms of Kohlberg's Theory (pp. 340-342)

Objective 12.15: Identify the criticisms of Kohlberg's theory.

59.   Give an example of the aspects of moral reasoning found in non-Western cultures that do not fit in well with Kohlberg's approach.

60.   How does Nancy Eisenberg uses empathy to connect moral reasoning and moral emotions?

61.   Explain Carol Gilligan's claim that justice and care are involved in moral reasoning.

62.   What are the sex differences in moral reasoning, according to Gilligan?

63.   To explain inconsistencies between reasoning and behavior, learning theorists suggest that moral reasoning is situational rather then developmental. List two examples of research that learning theorists give to support this assertion.

Moral Development and Antisocial Behavior (pp. 342-344)

Objective 12.16: Describe the relationship between moral development and antisocial behavior.

64.   Define delinquency (p. 342).

65. Give an example of how delinquents seem to be behind their peers in moral reasoning because of deficits in role-taking skills.

66. List and describe the two sub-varieties of delinquents.

Sub-variety	Definition	Description of Developmental Pathway

No Easy Answers: Preventing Youth Violence (p. 343)

Objective 12.17: Discuss the effectiveness of the efforts at preventing youth violence.

67. What percentage of all violent crimes in the United States are committed by individuals under age 18?

68. Describe the Fast Track Project, including the effects among children in the experimental group.

AFTER YOU READ . . . PRACTICE TEST #4
MORAL DEVELOPMENT

Match the letter of the term in the right column with its description in the left column.

_____ 1. The ability to took at a situation from another person's perspective.

_____ 2. Stage 6 of Kohlberg's theory that involves balancing equally valid, but conflicting, moral principles against one another to determine which should be given precedence with respect to a specific moral issue.

_____ 3. Stage 3 of Kohlberg's theory; sometimes called the good boy/nice girl stage.

_____ 4. The ability to identify with others' emotions.

_____ 5. Stage 4 of Kohlberg's theory; sometimes called the law-and-order orientation.

_____ 6. Deliberately breaking laws that are believed to be immoral.

_____ 7. Stage 2 of Kohlberg's theory; sometimes called naïve hedonism stage.

_____ 8. Antisocial behavior that includes law-breaking.

a. civil disobedience
b. conventional morality
c. delinquency
d. empathy
e. individualism, instrumental purpose, and exchange
f. mutual interpersonal expectations, relationships, and interpersonal conformity
g. preconventional morality
h. punishment and obedience orientation
i. role-taking
j. social contract orientation
k. social system and conscience
l. universal ethical principles orientation

(Check your answers to Practice Test #4 on p. 263.)

AFTER YOU READ . . . CRITICAL REFLECTION EXERCISE

Sense of Self

Utilizing information from the text, provide detailed answers to the following questions:

1. You are a teacher at an inner city school. You firmly believe that one of the most important things you can provide for youth is a sense of self-worth and purpose. Develop a program that you could use to help adolescents develop a positive image of themselves. Why did you design the program this way? What impact(s) will this program have on these youth as they mature into adulthood?

2. What does self-concept look like? Draw a diagram or picture that illustrates self-concept and how it develops. It does not matter what you draw as long as you could explain to someone else how the drawing illustrates the major factors that determine self-concept and feelings of self-worth. Write out an explanation of how your drawing illustrates these factors.

3. Choose any characteristic of your self. Consider how this characteristic has developed in the fashion that it has. Are you pleased with this development? Why or why not? If you are not pleased, what would you do to change it? Why would you change it?

AFTER YOU READ ... COMPREHENSIVE PRACTICE TEST
MULTIPLE-CHOICE QUESTIONS

1. **A period during which an adolescent is troubled by his lack of identity is called the _____.**
   a. identity crisis
   b. identity shift
   c. identity commitment
   d. identity status

2. **According to Marcia, a _____ is a period of decision-making when old values and old choices are reexamined.**
   a. conviction
   b. crisis
   c. curiosity-seeking experience
   d. commitment

3. **Adolescent moratorium means that the adolescent _____.**
   a. is in a stage of rigid identity acceptance
   b. stops seeking self-related feedback
   c. adopts an identity that is unhealthy
   d. is in a state of crisis, but no firm identity has been adopted

4. **In comparison to younger children, the adolescent's self-concept may be described as _____.**
   a. centering more on ideology than in childhood
   b. less differentiated than in childhood
   c. centering more on external characteristics than in childhood
   d. centering more on physical characteristics than in childhood

5. **Gender-related aspects of the psychological self are referred to as _____.**
   a. gender characteristics
   b. sex-role identity
   c. the genital stage
   d. sexually-active behavior

6. **Self-esteem levels during adolescence _____.**
   a. go down dramatically for girls but up for boys
   b. stay relatively the same as in childhood
   c. go up steadily for both boys and girls
   d. go up for girls but down for boys

7. **An ethnic identity search parallels _____.**
   a. a crisis in Marcia's theory
   b. ego integrity in Erikson's theory
   c. identification in Freud's theory
   d. cognitive dissonance in Maslow's theory

8. **Someone with _____ attributes the causes of experiences such as school failure to factors outside himself.**
   a. a strong work ethic
   b. high self-esteem
   c. an internal locus of control
   d. an external locus of control

9. **Teenagers must establish autonomy from their parents and _____.**
   a. prove to the their parents that they can do things on their own
   b. maintain their sense of relatedness with their parents
   c. sever their attachment bonds for the transition into adulthood
   d. display the differences between themselves and their peers

10. **What is a clique?**
    a. groups of ten to twelve persons who really are not attached to each other
    b. four to six young people strongly attached to one another
    c. a group of adolescents together because there is power in numbers
    d. a street gang that terrorizes the neighborhood

11. **The concordance rate for homosexuality in identical twins suggests that homosexuality _____.**
    a. is heavily driven by the environment
    b. is still completely unexplainable
    c. has a strong biological base
    d. is on the rise

12. **Which of the following illustrates Stage 4 moral development, according to Kohlberg's theory?**
    a. Moral actions are defined by expectations from a significant group.
    b. Moral actions are defined by a larger social group, such as society.
    c. Moral actions are defined by whether or not the outcome is positive or negative.
    d. Moral actions are defined by universal ethical principles.

13. **The term _____ is used to refer to the ability to look at a situation from another person's perspective.**
    a. role-taking
    b. sympathy
    c. empathy
    d. civil disobedience

14. **According to Gilligan, the two distinct moral orientations involved in moral reasoning are _____.**
    a. justice and empathy
    b. justice and care
    c. honesty and sincerity
    d. right and wrong

15. **Delinquency is defined as _____.**
    a. disobedience
    b. intentional law-breaking
    c. age-appropriate activities
    d. mischief

TRUE-FALSE QUESTIONS

Indicate whether each of the following statements is true or false.

_____ 1. According to Freud, the genital stage is the period during which psychosexual maturity is reached.

_____ 2. According to Marcia, a young person who is not in the midst of a crisis and has not made a commitment is in the moratorium status.

_____ 3. The adolescents' self-concept becomes more differentiated as she comes to see herself somewhat differently in each of several roles: as a student, with friends, with parents, and in romantic relationships.

_____ 4. A girl who adopts a traditional feminine sex role is adopting a less-valued role, with attendant risks of lower self-esteem and a reduced sense of competence.

_____ 5. On average, teenagers' underlying emotional attachment to their parents increases across adolescence.

_____ 6. Like friendships, peer groups are very unstable in adolescence.

_____ 7. The most common types of moral reasoning among adolescents are stage 2 and stage 3.

_____ 8. There are at least two important sub-varieties of delinquents, distinguished by the age at which the delinquent behavior begins.

ESSAY QUESTIONS

1. James Marcia describes four identity statuses, and states that they are based on the notion of crisis and commitment. Give examples of crisis and commitment for each of the four statuses.

2. Discuss the three stages in the formation of an ethnic identity proposed by Jean Phinney. Give examples of each.

3. Describe the developmental pathway for early-onset delinquency.

(Check your answers to the Comprehensive Practice Test on pp. 263-264.)

WHEN YOU HAVE FINISHED . . . PUZZLE IT OUT

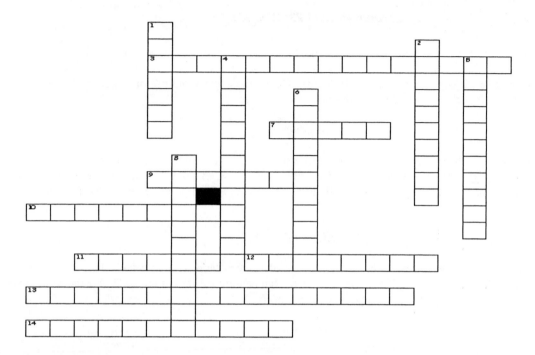

Across

3. Level of moral reasoning in which judgments are based on authorities outside the self
7. A combination of cliques which includes both males and females
9. In Freud's theory, the period during which people reach psychosexual maturity
10. Identity status in which the young person is not in the midst of a crisis and has not made a commitment
11. Four to sex young people who appear to be strongly attached to one another
12. An understanding of one's own unique characteristics
13. Level of moral reasoning in which judgments are based on the integration of individual rights and the needs of society
14. Individuals who see themselves as having both masculine and feminine personality traits

Down

1. The ability to identify with others' emotions
2. Identity status in which a crisis is in progress, but no commitment has yet been made
4. Level of moral reasoning in which judgments are based on rules or norms of a group
5. Identity status in which a person has been through a crisis and has reached commitment
6. Identity status in which the person has made a commitment without have gone through a crisis
8. Antisocial behavior that includes law-breaking

Created by Puzzlemaker at DiscoverySchool.com

(Check your answers on p. 264.)

WHEN YOU HAVE FINISHED . . . RESEARCH PROJECT

Student Project 23: Who Am I?

The purpose of this project is to replicate, on a small scale, the research by Montemayor and Eisen (1977). For the project you will need to find three or four teenagers, preferably one or two who are in early adolescence (12 to 14) and several who are near the end of high school (16 to 18). Obtain the appropriate informed consent from each of these youngsters, following whatever guidelines your instructor specifies.

Procedure

For each student, prepare a sheet of paper with 20 numbered spaces on it. At the top, write the instructions: *In the spaces below, write 20 different answers to the question, "Who am I?"* Each subject should be interviewed alone. Hand the teenager the sheet, and ask him or her to fill out all 20 blanks, each time giving one answer to the "Who am I" question.

Analysis and Report

Analyze the answers your subjects give using the categories of physical appearance and ideology (or any other categories you may identify). Do your subjects' answers match the pattern reported in the text? Are there any other differences in the responses given by your younger and older subjects?

Reference

Montemayor, R., & Eisen, M. (1977). The development of self-conceptions from childhood to adolescence. *Developmental psychology, 13,* 314-319.

CHAPTER 12 ANSWER KEY

Practice Test #1 Theories of Social and Personality Development
1. F   2. T   3. T   4. T   5. T   6. F   7. F   8. T

Practice Test #2 Self-Concept and Personality
1. a   2. d   3. c   4. b   5. c   6. a   7. d   8. b

Practice Test #3 Social Relationships
1. establish autonomy from them; maintain a sense of relatedness with them
2. remains strong
3. authoritative
4. girls
5. peer relationships
6. psychological characteristics; attitudes
7. clique
8. reputation-based
9. being in love
10. prenatal hormone exposure studies, research examining early childhood activity preferences, and studies comparing the process of physical maturation in heterosexuals and homosexuals.

Practice Test #4 Moral Development
1. i   2. l   3. f   4. d   5. k   6. a   7. e   8. c

Comprehensive Practice Test
Multiple Choice Questions
1. a   2. b   3. d   4. a   5. b   6. c   7. a   8. d   9. b   10. b
11. c   12. b   13. a   14. b   15. b

True-False Questions
1. T   2. F   3. T   4. T   5. F   6. F   7. T   8. T

Essay Questions
1.
- Identity achievement: The person has been through a crisis and has reached a commitment to ideological, occupational, or other goals.
- Moratorium: A crisis is in progress, but no commitment has yet been made.
- Foreclosure: The person has made a commitment without having gone through a crisis. No reassessment of old positions has been made. Instead, the young person has simply accepted a parentally or culturally defined commitment.
- Identity diffusion: The young person is not in the midst o f crisis (although there may have been one in the past) and has not made a commitment. Diffusion may this represent either an early stage in the process (before a crisis) or a failure to reach a commitment after a crisis.

2.
- Unexamined ethnic identity: Includes the negative images and stereotypes common in the wider culture.
- Ethnic identity search: Typically triggered by some experience that makes ethnicity relevant. The young person begins to compare his own ethnic group with others, to try to arrive at his own judgments.
- Resolution of the conflicts and contradictions: Often a difficult process. Some may take on the values of the dominant culture, and risk being ostracized by their friends. Some create two identities. Some wholeheartedly choose their own ethnic group's patterns and values.

3.
- Directed by factors inside the child, such as temperament and personality.
- In early life, they throw temper tantrums and defy parents. They may also develop insecure attachments.
- Once the defiance appears, if the parents are not up to the task of controlling the child, the child's behavior worsens. He may display overt aggression toward others, who then reject him, which aggravates the problem.
- The seriously aggressive child is pushed in the direction of other children with similar problems, who then become the child's only supportive peer group.
- In adolescence, they may exhibit serious disturbances in thinking. Most have friends who are also delinquent teens. The situation is reinforced by frequent rejection by non-delinquent peers.
- Parents have histories of antisocial behavior.
- Cluster of other problem behaviors, such as drug and alcohol use, truancy or dropping out of school, and early and risky sexual behavior.

Puzzle It Out

Across
3. Preconventional
7. Crowd
9. Genital
10. Diffusion
11. Clique
12. Identity
13. Postconventional
14. Androgynous

Down
1. Empathy
2. Moratorium
4. Conventional
5. Achievement
6. Foreclosure
8. Delinquency

POLICY QUESTION III

HAS TEST-BASED REFORM IMPROVED SCHOOLS IN THE UNITED STATES?

Learning Objective: Summarize the issues involved in test-based school reform (pp. 346-347).

1.   Define the test-based school reform movement.

2.   Briefly trace the history of test-based school reform.

3.   What is meant by the term "standards"?

4.   Complete the table to describe the criticisms of test-based school reform from each of the following perspectives:

Perspective	Description of Criticism
Teaching the Test	
Textbook Quality	
Quality of the Tests	
Claims of Cultural Bias	

5.   Give examples of the positive impact of test-based reform.

6.   Give examples of the negative impact of test-based reform.

7.   You should be able to learn more about test-based school reform in your state by doing the following:
      a.   Talk to public school teachers and administrators about your state's testing program. How has No child Left Behind affected their schools?

      b.   Check your state education agency's Web site for information on standards and testing.

      c.   Locate newspaper articles that report on what your governor and state legislators think about test-based reform. Do they support a national test?

      d.   Find links to parent organizations in your state that oppose test-based reform at http://www.fairtest.org/parents.html.

      e.   Visit http://nces.ed.gov/nationsreportcard/about/statehistorypublic.asp to learn about your state's history of participation in the NAEB.

CHAPTER 13

PHYSICAL AND COGNITIVE DEVELOPMENT IN EARLY ADULTHOOD

BEFORE YOU READ . . . CHAPTER SUMMARY

Young adulthood, the period from 20 to 40, is the time in life when individuals' developmental pathways begin to diverge significantly.

Physical Functioning

- Primary aging is caused by basic biological forces. Secondary aging is the result of illness and lifestyle choices.
- There is a major growth spurt in the brain across the late teens and early twenties. Some neuroscientists believe that there is another significant spurt in the mid to late twenties.
- The body's other systems, such as the heart and lungs, the reproductive system, and the immune system, are at their peak level of functioning during early adulthood.

Health and Wellness

- Sexually transmitted diseases are one of the major health concerns of the early adult years.
- Individual differences in health habits and personality variables begin to affect physical functioning in these years.
- Intimate partner abuse is another health risk of early adulthood; women are at greater risk than are men. Many young adults, especially women, are also victimized by sexual violence.
- Mental health problems are more prevalent in early adulthood than in later periods, perhaps because young adults' expectations in intimate relationships and in other areas of life are often in conflict with their actual experiences.

Cognitive Changes

- Young adults more often exhibit formal operational thinking than do adolescents, and many psychologists believe there are even more advanced levels of thought than Piaget's final stage of cognitive development.
- Longitudinal studies show that IQ scores change little across early and middle adulthood. Likewise, memory skills are fairly stable in young and middle-aged adults.

Post-Secondary Education

- Young adults who attend college experience greater economic success in later years and display more advanced cognitive skills than those who do not go do college.
- Traditional students, those who go to college full-time directly after high school, are more likely to attain degrees than those who possess many "nontraditional" factors such as having children prior to entering post-secondary education.
- Modifications help many students with disabilities succeed in college.
- Women are more successful in college than men, but still tend to avoid traditionally male fields of study such as mathematics and engineering.

- Members of many minority groups are less likely to drop out of college than whites; however, many African-American students who leave college report that experiences with overt racism in the college environment influenced their decision.

AS YOU READ . . . LEARNING OBJECTIVES

After completing Chapter 13, you should be able to:

13.1   Distinguish between primary and secondary aging.
13.2   List habits associated with good health.
13.3   Summarize the changes in the brain and nervous system in early adulthood.
13.4   Identify the physical changes that take place in early adulthood.
13.5   Trace the pattern of age and peak sports performance.
13.6   Summarize the research on assisted reproductive technology.
13.7   Describe the risk of acquiring sexually transmitted diseases during early adulthood.
13.8   Identify health habits and personal factors that have long-term effects.
13.9   Identify the issues involved in intimate partner abuse.
13.10   Identify the risks to mental health in young adulthood.
13.11   Summarize the theories of cognitive change in adulthood.
13.12   Summarize the research on the course of intelligence and memory in early adulthood.
13.13   Describe the developmental impact of post-secondary education.
13.14   Summarize the issues involved in distance learning.
13.15   Distinguish between traditional and non-traditional post-secondary students.
13.16   Describe the issues that students with disabilities face in post-secondary classes.
13.17   Summarize the gender differences in the college experience.
13.18   Identify how race affects the college experience.

AS YOU READ . . . TERM IDENTIFICATION

Crystallized intelligence (p. 369)
Dialectical thought (p. 358)
Fluid intelligence (p. 370)
Intimate partner abuse (p. 362)
Limbic system (p. 351)
Maximum oxygen uptake (VO_2 max) (p. 353)
Nontraditional post-secondary student (p. 373)
Pelvic inflammatory disease (p. 358)
Personality disorder (p. 366)

Phobia (p. 365)
Post-secondary education (p. 371)
Primary aging (p. 350)
Schizophrenia (p. 367)
Secondary aging (p. 350)
Self-efficacy (p. 361)
Sexual violence (p. 364)
Traditional post-secondary student (p. 372)

AS YOU READ . . . GUIDED STUDY QUESTIONS

PHYSICAL FUNCTIONING

Primary and Secondary Aging (pp. 350-351)

Objective 13.1: Distinguish between primary and secondary aging.

1.   Define the following terms, and give examples of each to distinguish between them:
    a.   primary aging (p. 350)

    b.   secondary aging (p. 350)

2.   Give examples of how social class differences in health may be due to secondary aging.

No Easy Answers: There Is No Fountain of Youth (p. 352)

Objective 13.2: List habits associated with good health.

3.   List and describe four important changes a person can make to prevent the effects of secondary aging.

Changes	Description

The Brain and Nervous System (pp. 351-353)

Objective 13.3: Summarize the changes in the brain and nervous system in early adulthood.

4.   List and describe the two spurts in brain growth in early adulthood.

5.   What is meant by response inhibition? How is the limbic system involved?

6.   Define limbic system (p. 351).

7.   Give examples of bodily functions that undergo the gradual loss of speed as a result of very gradual changes at the neuronal level.

8. Distinguish between the following types of brain tissue, and give examples of how they may cause sex differences in the adult brain:

Type of Tissue	Examples of Sex Differences
Gray Matter	
White Matter	

Other Body Systems (pp. 353-358)

Objective 13.4: Identify the physical changes that take place in early adulthood.

9. Compare young adults in their 20s and 30s to middle-aged or older adults on physical measures.

10. List the bodily functions that show a gradual decline in physical functioning through the years of adulthood (from Table 13.1, p. 354).

11. Define maximum oxygen uptake (VO_2 max) (p. 353), and give examples of changes as a person ages:

12. Give examples of changes in strength and speed with age.

13. Compare women's and men's reproductive capacity.

14. List the two key organs in the immune system, and explain how they are involved in immune system functioning.

15. Distinguish between B cells and T cells.

The Real World: Age and Peak Sports Performance (p. 355)

Objective 13.5: Trace the pattern of age and peak sports performance.

16. Give examples of how researchers study top performers in sports to learn about aging.

Research Report: Assisted Reproductive Technology (p. 357)

Objective 13.6 Summarize the research on assisted reproductive technology.

17. How do physicians define infertility?

18. How are fertility drugs used?

19. Distinguish between artificial insemination and in vitro fertilization.

20. List some of the problems for the couple if in vitro fertilization is unsuccessful.

21.   List the risks to babies born as a result of in vitro fertilization.

AFTER YOU READ . . . PRACTICE TEST #1
PHYSICAL FUNCTIONING

Fill in the blanks with the best answers.

1.   The basic, underlying inevitable aging process is called _____. In contrast, _____ is the product of environmental influences.

2.   Regardless of income level, _____ may prevent or even reverse the effects of aging.

3.   Just as is true in childhood and adolescence, a _____ probably supports brain development.

4.   Neuropsychologists hypothesize that the _____ that emerge in the middle of the early adulthood period seem to depend on changes in the brain.

5.   The most common measure of overall aerobic fitness is _____, which reflects the ability of the body to take in and transport oxygen to various body organs.

6.   The collective effect of changes in muscles and cardiovascular fitness is a general loss _____ and _____ with age.

7.   The end point of reproductive aging for women involves a _____ of the capacity for reproduction.

8.   The two key organs in the immune system are the _____ and the _____.

9.   _____ fight against external threats by producing antibodies against such disease organisms as viruses or bacteria; _____ defend against essentially internal threats, such as transplanted tissue, cancer cells, and viruses that live within the body's cells.

10.   The functioning of the immune system is highly responsive to _____ and _____.

(Check your answers to Practice Test #1 on p. 287.)

HEALTH AND WELLNESS

Sexually Transmitted Diseases (pp. 358-359)

Objective 13.7: Describe the risk of acquiring sexually transmitted diseases during early adulthood.

22.   Define pelvic inflammatory disease (p. 358).

23.   What is the major difference between bacterial STDs and viral STDs?

24.   Complete the following table with information about sexually transmitted diseases.

Bacterial STD	Description of Affects
Chlamydia	
Pelvic Inflammatory Disease	
Gonorrhea	
Syphilis	

Viral STD	Description of Affects
Genital Herpes	
Genital Warts	
HIV/AIDS	

25.   What is the key to STD prevention?

26.   List the possible high risk behaviors linked to STDs that young adults may engage in.

Health Habits and Personal Factors (pp. 359-362)

Objective 13.8: Identify health habits and personal factors that have long-term effects.

27.   List the seven good health habits that researchers identified from the Alameda County Study. Which two were unrelated to mortality?

28.   Give examples of how a person's perception of the adequacy of social contacts and emotional support is more strongly related to physical and emotional health than are the actual number of such contacts.

29.   Give examples of the benefits of social support when an individual is under high stress.

30.   Define self-efficacy (p. 361).

31.   Describe each of the following terms, identify the researcher associated with each, and explain how it is related to a sense of control in a person's life.

Term	Researcher	Relationship to a Sense of Control
Perceived Control		
Self-efficacy		
Optimism		
Helplessness		

Intimate Partner Abuse (pp. 362-364)

Objective 13.9: Identify the issues involved in intimate partner abuse.

32.   Define intimate partner abuse (p. 362).

33.   Briefly summarize the prevalence of intimate partner abuse in the United States.

34.   Give examples of how each of the following can contribute to the rates of intimate partner abuse:

Factor	Example
Cultural Attitudes	
Gender-Role Prescriptions	

35.   List the characteristics of intimate partner abusers.

36.   List the characteristics of intimate partner abuse victims.

37.   Describe the effects of intimate partner abuse on women.

38.   List ways to prevent intimate partner abuse.

39.   Define sexual violence (p. 364).

40.   Describe the psychological effects of being a victim of sexual violence.

41.   What is date rape, and what are two causes of it?

42.   How can sexual violence be prevented?

Mental Health Problems (pp. 364-367)

Objective 13.10: Identify the risks to mental health in young adulthood.

43.   List the possible causes of mental disorders in young adulthood.

44.   What are the most common mental disorders?

45.   Define phobias (p. 365).

46.   Give examples of how phobias are learned and how they can be unlearned.

47.   Explain why the rates of depression are higher in early adulthood than in either adolescence or middle age.

48.   What is binge drinking, and what are the problem behaviors associated with it?

49.   Define personality disorder (p. 366).

50.   List the five most common types of personality disorders.

51.   Define schizophrenia (p. 367).

52.   Distinguish between delusions and hallucinations.

AFTER YOU READ . . . PRACTICE TEST #2
HEALTH AND WELLNESS

1.   _____ STDs are those that are caused by microorganisms that can be eradicated through the use of antibiotic medications.
   a.   Sensitive
   b.   Contagious
   c.   Viral
   d.   Bacteria

2.   The primary symptom of _____ is the presence of growths in the genitals.
   a.   genital warts
   b.   genital herpes
   c.   syphilis
   d.   gonorrhea

3.   Each of the following is a method of transmission of HIV EXCEPT:
   a.   sexual intercourse with a person with HIV
   b.   sharing needles with an intravenous drug user with HIV
   c.   drinking after a person with HIV

d.   a blood transfusion from someone with HIV

4.   **Each of the following is one of the seven good health habits EXCEPT:**
a.   not smoking
b.   skipping breakfast
c.   getting physical exercise
d.   getting regular sleep

5.   **The social network index reflected an objective measure of each of the following EXCEPT:**
a.   membership at an exercise facility
b.   number of contacts with friends and relatives
c.   marital status
d.   church and group membership

6.   **The _____ believes that setbacks are temporary and usually caused by circumstances.**
a.   helpless person
b.   pessimist
c.   optimist
d.   person with low self-efficacy

7.   **The term _____ refers only to incidents of abuse involving individuals who live in the same household.**
a.   partner abuser
b.   domestic abuse
c.   intimate partner abuse
d.   sexual abuse

8.   **Each of the following is a characteristic of an abuser EXCEPT:**
a.   sudden mood swings
b.   a need for dependency in the partner
c.   a tendency toward irrational jealousy
d.   a slow temper

(Check your answers to Practice Test #2 on p. 287.)

COGNITIVE CHANGES

Formal Operations and Beyond (pp. 367-368)

Objective 13.11: Summarize the theories of cognitive change in adulthood.

53.   Define dialectical thought (p. 368).

54.   Describe three concepts of new structures of stages in thinking that occur in adulthood.

Theorist	*Concept*	*Description*
Gisela Labouvie-Vief	*Contextual validity*	

Theorist	Concept	Description
Michael Basseches	*Dialectical thought*	
Patricia Arlin	*Problem finding/ creativity*	

Intelligence and Memory (pp. 368-370)

Objective 13.12: Summarize the research on the course of intelligence and memory in early adulthood.

55.   Give examples of how IQ scores remain stable across middle childhood, adolescence, and early adulthood. Include the results of Werner Schaie's Seattle Longitudinal Study in your examples.

56.   Define the following terms, and give examples to distinguish them:
        a.   crystallized intelligence (p. 369)

        b.   fluid intelligence (p. 370)

57.   Describe the pattern of results from studies of memory ability, including the encoding and retrieval of long-term memories.

AFTER YOU READ . . . PRACTICE TEST #3
COGNITIVE CHANGES

Fill in the blanks with the best answers.
1.   Like most aspects of physical functioning, _____ are at their peek in early adulthood. The intellectual peak lasts longer than originally thought and the rate of decline is quite slow.

2.   Formal operational thinking is more characteristic of adults than of adolescents and is strongly tied to _____.

3.   Adults learn how to solve the problems associated with the particular social roles they occupy, or the particular jobs they hold. In the process, they trade the deductive thoroughness of formal operations for _____.

4.   _____ is a form of thought involving recognition and acceptance of paradox and uncertainty.

5.   Patricia Arlin proposes a further stage characterized by _____, which includes much of what is normally called _____.

6.   Examination of intelligence and memory in early adulthood suggests that both _____ and _____ characterize these components of cognitive functioning.

7.   There is good support for the temptingly optimistic view that intellectual ability remains _____ through most of adulthood.

8.   _____ depends heavily on education and experience; _____, in contrast, involves more "basic" abilities—it is the aspect of intelligence that depends more on the efficient functioning of the central nervous system and less on specific experience.

(Check your answers to Practice Test #3 on p. 287.)

POST-SECONDARY EDUCATION

Developmental Impact (p. 371)

Objective 13.13: Describe the developmental impact of post-secondary education.

58.   Define post-secondary education (p.), and describe its economic impact.

59.   How does post-secondary education provide socialization opportunities?

Development in the Information Age: Distance Learning (p. 372)

Objective 13.14: Summarize the issues involved in distance learning.

60.   What is distance learning?

61.   What is a virtual college?

62.   List the pros and cons of distance learning.

Traditional and Non-Traditional Students (pp. 372-374)

Objective 13.15: Distinguish between traditional and non-traditional post-secondary students.

63.   Define the following terms, and give examples to distinguish between them:
       a.   traditional post-secondary students (p. 372)

       b.   non-traditional post-secondary students (p. 373)

64.   List the seven criteria used to classify students as non-traditional post-secondary students.

65.   Explain how the three categories of students (minimally, moderately, and highly non-traditional) are used to clarify the traditional and non-traditional status of students.

66.   Give examples to describe the differences in support for non-traditional students in four-year institutions and two-year institutions.

Students with Disabilities (pp. 374-375)

Objective 13.16: Describe the issues that students with disabilities face in post-secondary classes.

67.   Describe how the Americans with Disabilities Act (1990) affected college students in the United States.

Gender and the College Experience (p. 375)

Objective 13.17: Summarize the gender differences in the college experience.

68.   List differences in the attitudes and behaviors of men and women that significantly affect the likelihood of graduation.

Race and the College Experience pp. 376)

Objective 13.18: Identify how race affects the college experience.

69.   Briefly summarize the drop-out rates of minority groups compared to whites.

70.   List differences experienced by African-American students that may contribute to the drop-out rate.

71.   List characteristics of high-achieving African-American college students.

72.   Describe the advantages for African-American students of attending historically black institutions.

AFTER YOU READ . . . PRACTICE TEST #4
POST-SECONDARY EDUCATION

Indicate whether each of the following statements is true or false.

_____ 1.   People who succeed in completing a college degree have no income advantage over those who have only some college.

_____ 2.   During their years of college enrollment, students' academic and vocational aspirations rise.

_____ 3.   Advances in moral and social reasoning, as well as increases in the capacity to empathize with others' feelings, are also linked to college attendance.

_____ 4.   Traditional post-secondary students have a low graduation rate.

_____ 5.   The more nontraditional factors a student possesses, the less likely he is to graduate from college.

_____ 6.   Women have higher graduation rates then men at all degree levels and in both traditional and nontraditional post-secondary groups.

_____ 7.   College women are more likely to cheat than men.

_____ 8.   A strong sense of racial identity is associated with persistence and academic performance in college for African-American students.

(Check your answers to Practice Test #4 on p. 287.)

AFTER YOU READ . . . CRITICAL REFLECTION EXERCISES

Crystallized Intelligence and Fluid Intelligence

Give three examples of crystallized intelligence and three examples of fluid intelligence. What profession are you pursuing and which of these intelligences will you rely on more in that profession? Why?

Social Stress

Describe the concept of social stress. Why is this type of stress so potentially damaging? Discuss three things a person could do to minimize the negative effects of social stress.

AFTER YOU READ . . . COMPREHENSIVE PRACTICE TEST
MULTIPLE CHOICE QUESTIONS

1. **Age-related changes that are due to environmental influences, poor health habits, or disease are called _____.**
   a. primary aging
   b. auxiliary aging
   c. secondary aging
   d. maturation

2. **The part of the brain that regulates emotional responses is the _____.**
   a. pituitary gland
   b. thymus
   c. limbic system
   d. gray matter

3. **When VO$_2$ max is measured in a person at rest, it _____.**
   a. begins to decline gradually at about age 35
   b. does not change as we get older
   c. increases gradually starting at age 40
   d. declines for women and goes up for men as a function of aging

4. **In contrast to other types of disease, most _____ is(are) more common among young adults than in any other age group.**
   a. sexually transmitted diseases
   b. colds and the flu
   c. coronary heart disease
   d. osteoporosis

5. **Undiagnosed chlamydia increases the risk of _____, which can cause infertility.**
   a. malaria
   b. pelvic inflammatory disease
   c. cancer
   d. schizophrenia

6. **The belief in one's capacity to cause an intended event to occur or to perform a task are called _____.**
   a. hardiness
   b. pessimism
   c. helplessness
   d. self-efficacy

7. **Physical acts or other behaviors intended to intimidate or harm an intimate partner is called _____.**
   a. pessimism
   b. intimate partner abuse
   c. helplessness
   d. depression

8. **An irrational fear of an object, a person, a place, or a situation is called _____.**
   a. schizophrenia
   b. a panic attack
   c. a phobia
   d. depression

9. **A person with _____ is suspicious of others' behavior and is emotionally guarded and highly sensitive to minor violations of personal space or perceived rights.**
   a.   paranoid personality disorder
   b.   antisocial personality disorder
   c.   borderline personality disorder
   d.   histrionic personality disorder

10. **Dialectical thought deals with _____.**
   a.   fact
   b.   declarative memories
   c.   uncertainty
   d.   how and why we develop accents in our speaking

11. **Which of the following is an example of fluid intelligence?**
   a.   a reaction time test
   b.   technical job skills
   c.   knowledge about your culture
   d.   the ability to read

12. **Any formal educational experience that follows high school is called _____.**
   a.   formal operational thinking
   b.   dialectical learning
   c.   post-secondary education
   d.   the virtual college

13. **Each of the following is one of the factors used to classify non-traditional post-secondary students EXCEPT:**
   a.   delay in entering college for more than one year after high school
   b.   are enrolled full-time
   c.   are employed while enrolled in college
   d.   are single parents

14. **Which of the following statements is TRUE regarding gender and the college experience?**
   a.   Women are more likely to be accepted into honors programs.
   b.   Men display a greater number of study strategies than women.
   c.   Men are more likely to be admitted to selective institutions.
   d.   Women are more likely to pursue difficult majors.

15. **Which of the following groups is likely to have the highest drop-out rate from college?**
   a.   European Americans
   b.   Hispanic Americans
   c.   Asian Americans
   d.   African Americans

TRUE-FALSE QUESTIONS

Indicate whether each of the following statements is true or false.

_____ 1.   No matter what age an individual is, new synapses are forming, myelinization is occurring, and old connections are dying off.

_____ 2.   Men's reproductive capacity declines at the same rate as women's.

_____ 3.   The most prevalent of the bacterial STDs is chlamydia.

_____ 4.   Adults with adequate social support have lower risk of disease, death, and depression than do adults with weaker social networks or less supportive networks.

_____ 5.   Formal operational thinking is more characteristic of adolescents than adults.

_____ 6.   IQ scores remain quite stable across middle childhood, adolescence, and early adulthood.

_____ 7.   College graduates earn more than non-graduates.

_____ 8.   The most common modification for a disability is a large-print version of the exams.

ESSAY QUESTIONS

1.   Give examples of how secondary aging is related to social class.

2.   Behavioral change is the key to STD prevention. How could you convince young adults to modify their behavior to prevent acquiring a sexually transmitted disease such as HIV/AIDS?

3.   Discuss the characteristics of women who are victims of abuse. How might social support and a sense of control assist her?

(Check your answers to the Comprehensive Practice Test on pp. 287-288.)

WHEN YOU HAVE FINISHED . . .PUZZLE IT OUT

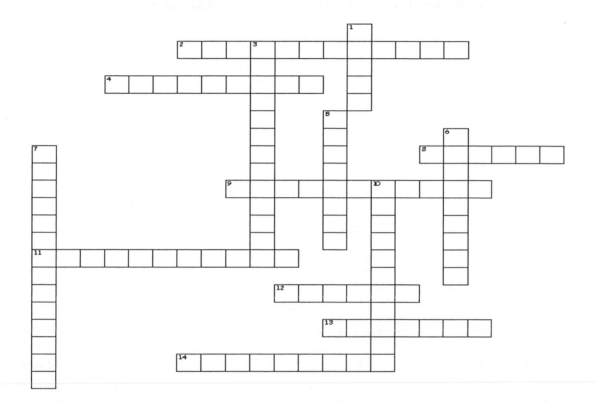

Across

2. Intelligence that depends heavily on education and experience
4. A bacterial STD that is very resistant to antibiotics
8. An irrational fear of an object, a person, a place, or a situation
9. Post-secondary students who attend college full-time immediately after graduating from high school
11. Thought involving recognition and acceptance of `□`□`□`□`□`□`□`□`□`□`□`□`□
12. System of the brain that regulates emotional responses
13. Age-related physical changes that have a biological basis and are inevitable
14. Age-related changes that are due to environmental influences, poor health habits, or disease

Down

1. Intelligence that involves "basic" abilities
3. A serious mental disorder characterized by delusions and hallucinations
5. A bacterial STD that can lead to serious mental disorders and death if not treated in the early stages
6. STD that is a bacterial infection three times more common to women than men
7. Post-secondary student who either attends college part-time or delays enrollment after high school graduation
10. The failure to conceive after twelve consecutive months of unprotected intercourse

Created by Puzzlemaker at DiscoverySchool.com

Check your answers on p. 288.)

WHEN YOU HAVE FINISHED . . .AT-HOME PROJECT

Student Project 24: Estimating Your Own Longevity

Given the importance of health habits in longevity (the length of expected life), you may be interested in estimating your own longevity, based on your own habits and other factors that we know affect the length of life. Respond to each of the following items honestly and sum the various negative and positive factors. The average 20-year-old male in the United States can expect to live to age 72.8; the average 20-year-old female can expect to live to age 79.4, so add or subtract your total number from this expectation to find your estimated length of life. (Remember, please, that this will provide only a very rough estimate; it is not a guarantee that you will live as long or as short a time as the formula suggests.)

Health Habits

1. *Weight*: Using the following table, determine the number of years to subtract (if any):

	10% to 30% heavier than standard weight tables		30% or more above standard weight tables	
	Women	Men	Women	Men
Age 20-29	-5	-10	-6.5	-13
Age 30-49	-4	-4	-5	-6
Age 50 +	-2	-2	-4	-4

2. *Diet*: If your diet is truly low in fat and sugar, and you never eat to the point past fullness, +1

3. *Smoking*: If you smoke less than a pack a day, -2; between 1 and 2 packs a day, -7; more than 2 packs a day, -12.

4. *Drinking*: Heavy drinkers, -8; moderate drinkers, +2; light or abstainer, +1 1/2.

5. *Exercise*: If you do some aerobic exercise for 20 to 30 minutes at least 3 times a week, + 3.

6. *Sleep*: If you sleep more than 10 or less than 7 hours a night, -2

Health History

1. If you have any chronic health condition, such as high blood pressure, diabetes, cancer, or ulcers, or are frequently ill, -5.

2. If your mother was older than 35 or younger than 18 at your birth, -1.

3. If you are the oldest child in your family. +1.

4. If you have an annual physical examine, +2.

5. Women only: If you have no children (or plan to have none), -1/2.

Heredity

1. For each of your grandparents who has lived past age 80, +1. (If your grandparents have not yet reached this age, simply ignore the item.)

2. For each grandparent who have lived past 70, but not 80, +1/2.

3. If your mother lived past 80, +4.

4. If your father lived past 80, +2.

5. For each sibling, parent, or grandparent who died of heart disease before age 50, -4.

6. For each sibling, parent, or grandparent who died of heart disease between age 50 and 60, -2

7. Women only: For each mother or sister who died of breast cancer before age 60, -1.

Social Class, Personality, and Other Characteristics

1. If your intelligence is superior, +2.

2. If you have only an eighth grade education or less, -2
    If you have completed high school but no further, +1
    If you have completed 1 to 3 years of college, +2
    If you have 4 or more years of college, +3

3. If your occupation is professional, technical, or managerial, +1; if it is unskilled, -4.

4. If your income is above average for your education and occupation, +1; if it is below average, -1.

5. If your job is sedentary, -2; if it is physically active, +2.

6. If you have lived in urban areas most of your life, -1; if you have lived mostly in a rural area, +1.

7. If you are married and living with your spouse, +1.

8. If you are separated or divorced, -4 if you are a women, -9 if you are a man.

9. If you are widowed, -4 if you are a women, -7 if you are a man.

10. Women: If you have never been married. -1 for each decade unmarried past the age of 25.

11. Men: if you have never married and are living with your family, -1 for each decade unmarried past age 25; if you live alone, -2 for each decade unmarried past age 25.

12. If you have at least two close confidants, +1.

13. If your personality is noticeably hostile and aggressive, and you regularly feel under time pressure, subtract between 2 and 5 years, depending on how well the description fits.

14. If you easy-going, relaxed, and calm, and adapt easily to changing circumstances, add between 1 and 3 years, depending on how well the description fits.

15.   If you have a lot of fun in life and are basically happy, +2.

16.   If you have had at least one period of a year or more in your life when you were depressed, very tense, very worried, or guilty, subtract between 1 and 3, depending on how severe the depression was.

17.   If you live in a high crime neighborhood, or take physical risk regularly, -2.

18.   If you generally avoid risk and wear seatbelts regularly, +1.

When you have calculated the score, think about the result. How many of the factors that affect longevity do you have control over? Make a list of specific steps you could take today that might increase your longevity.

Reference

Adapted from D. S. Woodruff-Pak (1988), *Psychology and aging*. Englewood Cliffs, NJ: Prentice-Hall, pp. 145-154.

CHAPTER 13 ANSWER KEY

Practice Test #1 Physical Functioning

1. primary aging; secondary aging
2. changes in behavior
3. challenging environment
4. cognitive skills
5. maximum oxygen uptake (VO_2 max)
6. strength; speed
7. total loss
8. thymus gland; bone marrow
9. B cells; T cells
10. psychological stress; depression

Practice Test #2 Health and Wellness

1. d   2. a   3. c   4. b   5. a   6. c   7. b   8. d

Practice Test #3 Cognitive Changes

1. intellectual processes
2. educational experiences
3. contextual validity
4. dialectical thought
5. problem finding; creativity
6. continuity; change
7. essentially stable
8. crystallized intelligence; fluid intelligence

Practice Test #4 Post-Secondary Education

1. F   2. T   3. T   4. F   5. T   6. T   7. F   8. T

Comprehensive Practice Test

Multiple Choice Questions

1. c   2. c   3. b   4. a   5. b   6. d   7. b   8. c   9. a   10. c
11. a   12. c   13. b   14. c   15. d

True-False Questions

1. T   2. F   3. T   4. T   5. F   6. T   7. T   8. F

Essay Questions

1.
   - Differences among young adults across social class are fairly small, but increase with age.
   - Better-educated adults and those with higher incomes have longer life expectancies and better health than do those with less education or lower incomes.
   - Social class differences in health result from income-related variations in both social environments and individual behavior. Doctors in low-income neighborhoods tend to have less training and less access to hospitals equipped with advanced diagnostic and treatment facilities.
   - The same factors that contribute to economic differences are also related to health habits. Among individuals who drop out of high school, physical activity rates decline significantly during the late teens and remain low in adulthood. Physical activity is a predictor of cardiovascular health, and educational level is associated with income.
   - The emotions underlying individuals' perceptions of their social class may be more important than their actual economic status. People who are unhappy with their economic situation are more likely to be sick than those who are relatively satisfied.

2.
   - Answers will vary, but should include sexual behavior (i.e., abstinence, monogamy, condom use, HIV testing, etc.), bodily fluids, intravenous needles, etc.

3.
   - Characteristics of women who are victims of abuse: likely to have been abused as children, young, lack of education and/or work experience, young women may be caring for infants and young children for whom they do not have access to day care.
   - A person's perception of the adequacy of her social contacts and emotional support is more strongly related to physical and emotional health than are the actual number of such contacts.
   - Self-efficacy is the belief in one's capacity to cause an intended event to occur or to perform a task. It is affected by one's experiences with mastering tasks and overcoming obstacles.
   - Optimists believes that setbacks are temporary and usually caused by circumstances.
   - Those with a more helpless attitude or a low sense of self-efficacy are more likely to become depressed or physically ill.

Puzzle It Out

Across
2. Crystallized
4. Gonorrhea
8. Phobia
9. Traditional
11. Dialectical
12. Limbic
13. Primary
14. Secondary

Down
1. Fluid
3. Schizophrenia
5. Syphilis
6. Gonorrhea
7. Nontraditional
10. Infertility

CHAPTER 14

SOCIAL AND PERSONALITY DEVELOPMENT IN EARLY ADULTHOOD

BEFORE YOU READ . . . CHAPTER SUMMARY

In early adulthood, individuals turn away from the preoccupation with self that is characteristic of social relationships in adolescence. For most, the formation of an intimate relationship with a long-term partner is a theme that dominates this period of development.

Theories of Social and Personality Development

- Erikson proposed that the crisis of intimacy versus isolation is the defining theme of early adulthood.
- Levinson's theory suggests that adult development is characterized by alternating periods of stability and instability, such as the young adult's moving away from home. Through these periods of instability, adults redefine what Levinson calls their *life structures*.
- Evolutionary theories of mate selection suggest that women are more interested in long-term relationships and are more selective than are men in choosing partners because their investment in parenting is greater.
- Social role theory emphasizes factors such as gender roles, similarity, and economic exchange in explaining sex differences in mating.

Intimate Relationships

- Attachment, love, and personality contribute to marital success. Marriage has many health benefits; divorce increases the likelihood of depression.
- Numerous factors contribute to the relationship between premarital cohabitation and divorce.
- Factors that contribute to relationship satisfaction are similar across homosexual and heterosexual couples. Monogamy is not as important to gay male couples as it is to lesbian or heterosexual couples.
- Singles rely on family and friends for intimacy. After many years of singlehood, single adults tend to incorporate "singleness" into their sense of identity.

Parenthood and Other Relationships

- The transition to parenthood is stressful and is made more so by perceived inequities in the division of labor between mother and father and several by other factors.
- Young adults' social networks are important sources of support. These networks include friends as well as an intimate partner and other family members.

The Role of Worker

- Career choice is influenced by family history, intelligence, resources, personality, gender, and other variables.
- Job satisfaction rises during early adulthood. The work role appears to have two stages: a trial stage in which different types of work are explored, and an establishment stage, in which the career path becomes stable.
- Women's patterns of work are less continuous because many take time out from their careers to bear and raise children. Women with more continuous work histories are more economically successful. In dual-earner families, women often carry a heavier load of responsibility for child-care and household tasks.

AS YOU READ . . . LEARNING OBJECTIVES

After completing Chapter 14, you should be able to:

14.1   Describe the key points in the Erickson's theory relevant to early adulthood.
14.2   Summarize Levinson's theory of life structures.
14.3   Explain the evolutionary theory of mate selection.
14.4   Explain the social role theory of mate selection.
14.5   Identify the factors involved in marital success, and discuss the impact of divorce.
14.6   Summarize the issues involved in avoiding bridal stress disorder.
14.7   Summarize the research on the sex differences in the impact of marriage.
14.8   Identify the relationship between cohabitation and subsequent success in marriage.
14.9   Summarize the research comparing satisfaction and stability in heterosexual and homosexual partnerships.
14.10   Describe how singlehood affects intimacy.
14.11   Identify the changes brought about by becoming a parent.
14.12   Identify the role of social networks in early adulthood.
14.13   Summarize the issues involved in Internet relationships.
14.14   List the influences that affect a young person's choice of job or career.
14.15   Trace the issues in keeping jobs over time.
14.16   Discuss the sex differences in work patterns.
14.17   List strategies for coping with conflict between work and family life.

AS YOU READ . . . TERM IDENTIFICATION

Assortative mating (p. 383)	Intimacy (p. 380)	Parental investment theory (p. 382)
Avoidant couples (p. 386)	Intimacy versus isolation (p. 380)	Social role theory (p. 382)
Career ladder (p. 398)	Kin-keeper (p. 395)	Validating couples (p. 386)
Hostile/detached couples (p. 386)	Life structure (p. 380)	Volatile couples (p. 386)
Hostile/engaged couples (p. 386)		

AS YOU READ . . . GUIDED STUDY QUESTIONS

THEORIES OF SOCIAL AND PERSONALITY DEVELOPMENT

Erikson's Stages of Intimacy versus Isolation (p. 380)

Objective 14.1: Describe the key points in the Erickson's theory relevant to early adulthood.

1.   Define the following terms:
        a.   intimacy versus isolation (p. 380)

        b.   intimacy (p. 380)

2.   According to Erikson, what does the successful resolution of intimacy versus isolation depend upon?
        Why?

Levinson's Life Structures (pp. 380-381)

Objective 14.2: Summarize Levinson's theory of life structures.

3.   Define life structure (p. 380), and explain how it changes over the course of adulthood.

4.   List and describe the three phases of each life structure. Give an example to support the definitions.

Phase	Description	Example
Novice		
Mid-Era		
Culmination		

Evolutionary Theory and Mate Selection (pp. 381-382)

Objective 14.3: Explain the evolutionary theory of mate selection.

5.   How do evolutionary explanations of behavior explain mate selection?

6.   Define parental investment theory (p. 382), and give examples of how it explains mate selection.

Social Role Theory and Mate Selection (pp. 382-383)

Objective 14.4: Explain the social role theory of mate selection.

7.   Define the following terms:
     a.   social role theory (p. 382)

     b.   assortative mating, or homogamy (p. 383)

8.   Distinguish social role theory from evolutionary theory.

AFTER YOU READ . . . PRACTICE TEST #1
THEORIES OF SOCIAL AND PERSONALITY DEVELOPMENT

Match the letter of the term in the right column with its description in the left column.

_____ 1.　Theory that sex differences in mate preferences and mating behavior are adaptations to gender roles.

_____ 2.　The underlying pattern or design of a person's life at a given time, which includes all the roles, relationships, and behavior patterns

_____ 3.　The capacity to engage in a supportive, affectionate relationship without losing one's own sense of self

_____ 4.　Term for the tendency to mate with someone who has traits similar to one's own.

_____ 5.　Phase of Levinson's theory that is the period of adjustment.

_____ 6.　Theories that focus on survival value.

_____ 7.　Phase of Levinson's theory in which adults become more competent at meeting the new challenges through reassessment and reorganization of the life structure.

_____ 8.　Theory that sex differences in mate preferences and mating behavior are based on the different amounts of time and effort men and women must invest in child-rearing.

a. Assortative mating
b. Culmination
c. Evolutionary
d. Intimacy
e. Intimacy versus isolation
f. Life structures
g. Mate-switching
h. Mid-era
i. Novice
j. Parental investment
k. Social role

(Check your answers to Practice Test #1 on p. 308.)

INTIMATE RELATIONSHIPS

Marriage (pp. 383-387)

Objective 14.5: Identify the factors involved in marital success, and discuss the impact of divorce.

9.　What is the probability of divorce for a couple who has been married for eight years?

10.　List the heath benefits for married adults.

11.　Give an example of each of the following influences on marital success.

Factor	Example
Personality Characteristics	
Attachment to Family of Origin	
Emotional affection	
Management of Conflict	

12.   List and define the three components of Robert Sternberg's theory of love.

Component	Definition

13.   List and describe all the combinations of the components of Sternberg's theory.

Relationship	Description

14.   Describe the three types of stable or enduring marriages and two types of unsuccessful marriages by completing the following tables:

Type of Stable or Enduring Marriage	Description
Validating Couples	
Volatile Couples	
Avoidant Couples	

Type of Unsuccessful Marriage	Description
Hostile/Engaged Couples	
Hostile/detached Couples	

15. Describe the possible negative stressors of divorce.

16. Explain how the economic effects of divorce may be worse for women than for men.

17. How might divorce affect the sequence and timing of family roles?

No Easy Answers: Avoiding Bridal Stress Disorder (p. 385)

Objective 14.6: Summarize the issues involved in avoiding bridal stress disorder.

18. Explain how to balance problem-focused coping and emotional-focused coping by giving examples of each.

19. What is marriage insurance?

Research Report: Sex Differences in the Impact of Marriage (p. 387)

Objective 14.7: Summarize the research on the sex differences in the impact of marriage.

20. How do self-selection and health practices why married adults appear to be healthier and happier than their single counterparts?

21. Arrange the following list in order with "1" being greatest health and longest life, and "4" being the least healthy with the shortest life.

_____ Unmarried men

_____ Unmarried women

_____ Married men

_____ Married women

22. Give examples of how the levels of cortisol explain the quality of a person's marriage, including the sex differences.

Cohabiting Heterosexual Couples (pp. 387-388)

Objective 14.8: Identify the relationship between cohabitation and subsequent success in marriage.

23.   Give three explanations of the relationship between premarital cohabitation and divorce.

24.   The critical variable at work in the cohabitation-divorce relationship is the fact that a large proportion of cohabitants have been in prior cohabiting or sexual relationship. Explain why.

Gay and Lesbian Couples (pp. 388-389)

Objective 14.9: Summarize the research comparing satisfaction and stability in heterosexual and homosexual partnerships.

25.   List the similarities and differences between satisfaction and stability of heterosexual and homosexual relationships.

Similarities	*Differences*

Singlehood (pp. 389-390)

Objective 14.10: Describe how singlehood affects intimacy.

26.   Why does the impact of singlehood on an adult's life often depend on the reason for his or her relationship status?

27.   How does singleness affect a person's relationship with family and friends?

28.   Trace the development of singleness as a positive component of the individual's identity.

AFTER YOU READ . . . PRACTICE TEST #2
INTIMATE RELATIONSHIPS

1. **Each of the following is a benefit of marriage EXCEPT:**
   a. increased happiness
   b. greater health
   c. lower rates of psychiatric problems
   d. lower income

2. **Each of the following is an influence in the quality of the marriage relationship EXCEPT:**
   a. emotional affection
   b. socio-economic status
   c. the personality characteristics of the partners
   d. the security of each partner's attachment to his or her family of origin

3. **What is companionate love?**
   a. love that is long lasting, but is non-emotional
   b. love that is without passion
   c. love that will definitely evolve into romantic love
   d. very similar to empty love

4. **Which of the following marriage represents volatile couples?**
   a. The couple has no humor or affection.
   b. The couple agrees to disagree.
   c. The couple does not listen to each other well during arguments.
   d. The couple expresses mutual respect for each other.

5. **Each of the following is associated with recent separation or divorce EXCEPT:**
   a. less likely to become depressed
   b. more automobile accidents
   c. more likely to commit suicide
   d. lose more days at work because of illness

6. **The critical variable at work in the cohabitation-divorce relationship is _____**
   a. the individuals' relationship with their family of origin
   b. the individual's religious beliefs
   c. the fact that a large proportion of cohabitants have been in prior cohabiting or sexual relationships
   d. the fact that cohabitants are homogamous

7. **Similarities between homosexual and heterosexual couples include each of the following EXCEPT:**
   a. attachment quality
   b. neuroticism in one or both partners
   c. both partners are committed to the relationship
   d. closeness to their families of origin

8. **A single person's self-affirmation _____.**
   a. may increase the likelihood of depression
   b. may protect singles from some of the negative health consequences associated with singlehood
   c. may decrease the likelihood of individual autonomy
   d. may decrease the likelihood for personal growth

(Check your answers to Practice Test #2 on p. 308.)

PARENTHOOD AND OTHER RELATIONSHIPS

Parenthood (pp. 390-393)

Objective 14.11: Identify the changes brought about by becoming a parent.

29.   Summarize the statistics about the desire to become a parent.

30.   What is postpartum depression (PPD)?

31   List the characteristics of women who are likely to develop postpartum depression. What is the best predictor of postpartum depression?

32.   Describe the transition experience for new parents.

33.   What is the positive impact of the transition to parenthood?

34.   List the variables that may affect marital satisfaction as a result of the transition to parenthood.

35.   How does childlessness affect the shape of an adult's life?

Social Networks (pp. 393-396)

Objective 14.12: Identify the role of social networks in early adulthood.

36.   Summarize young adults' relationships with their parents.

37.   How does proximity affect a young adult's contact with his or her family?

38.   Give examples of how cultural differences impact young adults' involvement with their families.

39.   Describe the sex differences in both the number and quality of friendships in the social networks of young adults.

40.   Define the kin-keeper role (p. 395), and give examples of the behavior of a person who is a kin-keeper.

Development in the Information Age: Internet Relationships (p. 395)

Objective 14.13: Summarize the issues involved in Internet relationships.

41.   Describe the reasons people use Internet dating.

42.   Describe the drawbacks of Internet dating.

AFTER YOU READ . . . PRACTICE TEST #3
PARENTHOOD AND OTHER RELATIONSHIPS

Fill in the blanks with the best answers.

1. Despite the opportunistic attitude toward mating that evolutionary theory ascribes to men, the percentage of _____ who feel strongly that they want to become parents and who view parenting as a life-enriching experience is actually greater than the percentage of _____ who feel this way.

2. The best predictor of postpartum depression is _____ during pregnancy.

3. Despite its inherent stressfulness, the transition to parenthood is associated with _____ behavior change.

4. Marital satisfaction tends to _____ after the birth of a child.

5. The amount and kind of contact an adult has with kin is strongly influenced by _____.

6. Beyond the basic requirement of similarity, close friendships seem to rest on _____ and _____.

7. Adult women friends _____; adult men friends _____.

8. Women most often fill the role of _____, a role which includes responsibility for maintaining family and friendship relationships.

(Check your answers to Practice Test #3 on p. 308.)

THE ROLE OF WORKER

Choosing an Occupation (pp. 396-398)

Objective 14.14: List the influences that affect a young person's choice of job or career.

43. List the factors that influence a young person's choice of job or career.

44. Give examples of how families influence a young person's choice of job or career in each of the following areas by completing the table:

Area of Influence	Examples
Education	
Value System	
Moral Beliefs	

45.   Describe the stereotypical differences between "women's jobs" and "men's jobs."

46.   Describe each of the six personality types (according to John Holland), and identify the work preferences of each.

Type	Description of Personality	Work Preferences
Realistic		
Investigative		
Artistic		
Social		
Enterprising		
Conventional		

Jobs over Time (pp. 398-399)

Objective 14.15: Trace the issues in keeping jobs over time.

47.   List the reasons that job satisfaction is at its lowest in early adulthood, and that it rises steadily until retirement.

48.   What are the variables that contribute to job satisfaction in young adults?

49.   What are the workplace variables that influence job satisfaction?

50.   Define career ladder (p. 398).

51.   Describe three generalizations about the developmental progression of work careers in early adulthood.

52.   List and describe the series of stages of work sequence proposed by Donald Super.

Sex Differences in Work Patterns (pp. 400-402)

Objective 14.16: Discuss the sex differences in work patterns.

53.   What are the most striking differences between women's work experiences and men's work experiences in early adulthood? What repercussions does this pattern have for women's work roles?

54.   List the reasons that women feel more role conflict among their roles as a worker, a parent, and a spouse, than men feel.

The Real World: Strategies for Coping with Conflict between Work and Family Life (p. 402)

Objective 14.17: List strategies for coping with conflict between work and family life.

55.   List strategies for coping with the conflict between work and family life.

AFTER YOU READ . . . PRACTICE TEST #4
THE ROLE OF THE WORKER

Indicate whether each of the following statements is true or false.

_____ 1.   Satisfying work seems to be an important ingredient in mental health and life satisfaction of men but not for women.

_____ 2.   Typically, young people tend to choose occupations at the same general social class level as those of their parents.

_____ 3.   Highly intelligent workers are more likely to advance, even if they enter the job market at a lower level than those who are less intelligent.

_____ 4.   Stereotypically male jobs are concentrated in service occupations and are typically lower in status and lower-paid.

_____ 5.   John Holland's hypothesis is that each of us tends to choose, and be most successful at, an occupation that matches our personality.

_____ 6.   Young adults engaged in careers for which they prepared in high school or college have higher levels of satisfaction.

_____ 7.   Most work advancement occurs early in a career path, after which a plateau is reached.

_____ 8.   According to Donald Super, the first stage of work sequence is the establishment stage.

_____ 9.   Women who follow the mommy track in their careers typically earn less and are less likely to be promoted than women who work continuously.

_____ 10.   Working women have less power in their marriages or partnerships than do non-working women.

(Check your answers to Practice Test #4 on p. 308.)

AFTER YOU READ . . . CRITICAL REFLECTION EXERCISES

Relationships in Early Adulthood

Utilizing the information in the text, provide detailed responses to the following questions:

1.   If the divorce rate is higher in the United States than in most other industrialized countries, what might cause this? Discuss at least three factors that may contribute to cultural differences in the divorce rate.

2.   Discuss the importance of the following quote, "to develop in a healthy fashion in young adulthood, one must risk what is so difficult to acquire in adolescence."

3.   If you are married, name and discuss three things you can do to maximize the success of your marriage. If you are not currently married, name and discuss three things that you can do with a potential partner prior to getting married to increase the likelihood that an eventual marriage will succeed.

Parenting an Adolescent

You are the parent of a fourteen-year-old. Based on the information in the text, discuss at least three things that you could do to enhance the likelihood that your adolescent will make a smooth and successful transition into young adulthood.

AFTER YOU READ . . . COMPREHENSIVE PRACTICE TEST
MULTIPLE CHOICE QUESTIONS

1. **For Erikson, the central crisis of early adulthood is _____.**
    a. industry versus inferiority
    b. identity versus role confusion
    c. intimacy versus isolation
    d. integrity versus despair

2. **The ability to fuse your identity with someone else's without fear that you are going to lose something yourself, is the definition of _____.**
    a. selflessness
    b. intimacy
    c. generativity
    d. role confusion

3. **All the roles an individual occupies, all his or her relationships, and the conflicts and balance that exist among them is called _____.**
    a. a life structure
    b. intimacy
    c. homogamy
    d. a kin-keepe

4. **The theory that contrasts men's and women's differing amounts of investment in bearing children is called _____.**
    a. mate-switching
    b. the parental investment theory
    c. assortative mating
    d. social role theory

5. **On average, what are women concerned with in a potential mate?**
    a. economic prospects
    b. education level
    c. physical attractiveness
    d. personality similarity

6. **Sternberg suggests that love has the following three key components:**
    a. intimacy, passion, and commitment
    b. sincerity, consistency, and convenience
    c. significance, maintenance, and playfulness
    d. lust, compatibility, and persistence

7. **Which of the following groups generally experience an improvement in their economic status after a divorce?**
    a. men
    b. women
    c. both men and women
    d. neither men nor women

8. **Cohabiting couples differ more often than married couples in each of the following ways EXCEPT:**
    a. religious beliefs
    b. educational levels
    c. socio-economic status
    d. age

9. **Which of the following statements about homosexual relationships is TRUE?**
    a. Homosexual couples report being less satisfied than heterosexual couples.
    b. Homosexual couples tend to be more monogamous than heterosexual couples.
    c. Homosexual couples are more egalitarian than heterosexual couples.
    d. Homosexual couples tend to experience more physical abuse than heterosexual couples.

10. **What is postpartum depression?**
    a. depression that starts with the realization of an unwanted pregnancy
    b. a transient depressed mood following all pregnancies
    c. a depression following pregnancy that lasts for several weeks
    d. an unusual depression that is more common in young mothers

11. **Why might the birth of a child affect marital satisfaction?**
    a. The child makes all of the effort seem so worthwhile.
    b. Spouses feel that their efforts are not being recognized.
    c. Both spouses gain so much satisfaction from the new parent role.
    d. The role of parent and the role of spouse are somewhat incompatible.

12. **According to John Holland, which of the following personality types tends to choose a career such as nursing or education?**
    a. social
    b. conventional
    c. artistic
    d. enterprising

13. **Which of the following statements about job satisfaction is TRUE?**
    a. It stays high for men until retirement.
    b. It is lowest in early adulthood.
    c. It is highest in young adulthood.
    d. It stays high for women until retirement.

14. **Which of the following accurately describes family roles?**
    a. Men feel more conflict between the roles of spouse, worker, and parent than women.
    b. Work and family roles tend to be sequential for women.
    c. Work and family roles tend to be simultaneous for men.
    d. Women view themselves as mother and wives all day.

15. **Recasting or reframing a situation in a way that identifies the positive elements is called _____.**
    a. conflict management
    b. depression
    c. homogamy
    d. cognitive restructuring

TRUE-FALSE QUESTIONS

Indicate whether each of the following statements is true or false.

_____ 1. Successful resolution of the intimacy versus isolation stage depends on a good resolution of the identity versus role confusion crisis.

_____ 2. Cross-cultural studies conducted over a period of several decades suggest that men prefer physically attractive, younger women, whereas women look for men whose socio-economic status is higher than their own, who offer earning potential and stability.

_____ 3. After a couple has been married for eight years, the probability that they will divorce increases significantly.

_____ 4. Close friends are likely to play a more prominent role in the social networks of singles than among married couples or cohabitants.

_____ 5. Childless married women are much more likely to have full-time continuous careers.

_____ 6. Most research shows men to be less satisfied with their friendships than women are.

_____ 7. Stereotypically male jobs are more varied, more technical, and higher in both status and income than stereotypically female jobs.

_____ 8. In most careers, workers tend to move from step to step through a series of milestones that make up a career ladder.

ESSAY QUESTIONS

1. Select the theory of social and personality development (Erikson's Psychosocial Theory, Levinson's Life Structures, Parental Investment Theory, or Social Role Theory) that you believe most accurately reflects development in young adulthood. Support your answer.

2. Discuss Sternberg's theory of romantic love. Explain why Sternberg emphasized the importance of the presence of all three elements (intimacy, passion, and commitment) in consummate love.

3. Select the personality type from John Holland's list (Table 14.1) that most closely resembles your personality type. Compare your chosen career to the personality and work preferences.

(Check your answers to the Comprehensive Practice Test on p. 308.)

WHEN YOU HAVE FINISHED . . . PUZZLE IT OUT

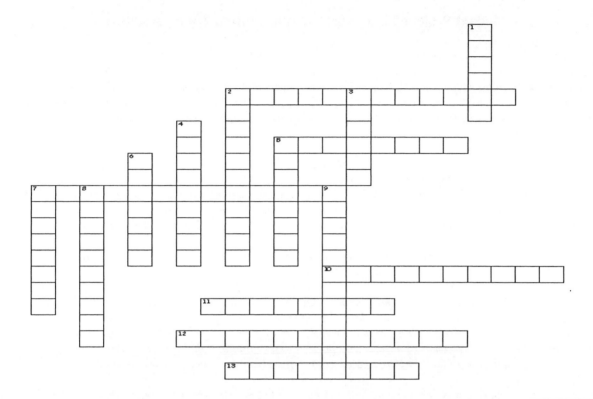

Across

2. Personality type that prefers structured activities and subordinate roles
5. Couples who are called "conflict minimizers"
7. Personality type that is oriented toward thinking, organizing, and planning
10. Depression experienced by some new mothers
11. Couples who squabble a lot, disagree, and don't listen to each other when they argue
12. Theory that explains behavior by focusing on survival value
13. Also known as assortative mating

Down

1. Personality type that is people-oriented, sociable, and needs attention
2. Third phase in Levinson's life structure
3. First phase in Levinson's life structure
4. Personality type that is aggressive, masculine, and physically strong
5. Personality type that is asocial and prefers unstructured, highly individual activity
6. Includes a feeling of intense longing for union with the other person, including sexual union
7. The capacity to engage in a supportive, affectionate relationships without losing one's own identity
8. Couples who have disagreements which rarely escalate
9. Personality type that his highly verbal and dominating

Created by Puzzlemaker at DiscoverySchool.com

(Check your answers on p. 308.)

WHEN YOU HAVE FINISHED . . . INVESTIGATIVE PROJECT

Student Project 25: Social Networks among Young Adults

For this project, based on the work of Antonucci and Akiyama (1987), collect some data from young adults. You should locate at least four adults, one each in the following age ranges: 20-24, 25-29, 30-34, and 35-40. It would be simpler if they were all the same gender, but that may not be practical. If you can, find eight willing subjects; try for one woman and one man in each group. (If all the students in your class complete this project, each with a minimum of four subjects, you could end up with quite a large sample, allowing you to look at sex differences and age trends.)

Procedure

You will need to obtain the appropriate informed consent from each subject, following the procedure as specified by your instructor. For each subject prepare an 8½" x 11" sheet of paper on which you have drawn a bull's-eye. In the center should be a very small circle (about the size of a dime) labeled "you." Around this circle draw three more concentric circles, spaced equally apart. This will give you three areas, each further from the center "you."

Tell your subjects that you are interested in knowing something about the people who are important in his (her) life. Present the sheet with the concentric circles on it and say:

> *The three circles should be thought of as including people who are important in your life right now, but to whom you are not equally close. The innermost circle (point to the circle immediately next to "you") includes people to whom you feel so close that it is hard to imagine life without them. Please put the names of anyone who fits that description into this innermost circle, along with some indication of how they are related to you—friend, parent, spouse, or whomever.*

When the subject has entered names in the innermost circle, point to the next circle and say:

> *Please put in this circle the names of people to whom you may not feel quite that close but who are still very important to you, and indicate your relationship to each one.*

Finally, point to the outermost circle and say:

> *Finally, put here the names of the people you haven't already mentioned but, who are close enough and important enough in your life that they should be placed in your personal network. As usual, indicate how you are related to each one.*

In addition, you will need to ask each subject a set of questions to amplify your analysis. Write the answers on the back of the subject's concentric circle sheet:

> *Are you married?*

> *How old are you?*

> *How many years of education have you completed?*

Also note the gender of the subject on the back of the sheet. Your subject's name should NOT appear anywhere on the sheet.

Analysis and Report

For each circle, count the total number of names, the number of males and females listed, and the relationship listed (family member, friend, spouse). Is there any noticeable difference in these characteristics as a function of age, gender, or education among your subjects?

Some other questions you might consider:
- Do all married subjects put their spouse in the center circle?
- How many put either or both parents in the center circle?
- Is there any married subject who put both the spouse and one or both parents in the center circle? If so, what does this say about the issue of the relative strength of a person's attachment to partner and parent?
- Is there a friend in the center circle, or do friends only begin to be listed in the second circle? Does this vary as a function of marital status? That is, do unmarried adults put more friends in the center circle?

Consider all these results in light of what is said in the text about networks and relationships in early life. What else might you want to know about your subjects to help you interpret their answers?

Reference

Antonucci, T. C., & Akiyama, H. (1987). Social networks in adult life and a preliminary examination of the convoy model. *Journal of Gerontology, 42,* 519-527.

CHAPTER 14 ANSWER KEY

Practice Test #1 Theories of Social and Personality Development

1. k   2. f   3. d   4. a   5. i   6. c   7. h   8. j

Practice Test #2 Intimate Relationships

1. d   2. b   3. b   4. c   5. a   6. c   7. d   8. b

Practice Test #3 Parenthood and Other Relationships

1.   men; women
2.   depression
3.   positive
4.   decline
5.   proximity
6.   mutual openness; personal disclosure
7.   talk to one another; do things together
8.   kin-keeper

Practice Test #4 The Role of Worker

1. F   2. T   3. T   4. F   5. T   6. T   7. T   8. F   9. T   10. F

Comprehensive Practice Test

Multiple Choice Questions

1. c   2. b   3. a   4. b   5. a   6. a   7. a   8. d   9. c   10. c
11. d   12. a   13. b   14. d   15. d

True-False Questions

1. T   2. T   3. F   4. T   5. T   6. T   7. T   8. T

Essay Questions

1. ▪ Answers should accurately describe the basics of the theory and provide evidence in its support.

2. ▪ Intimacy: Includes feelings of closeness and connectedness.
   ▪ Passion: Includes a feeling of intense longing or union with the other person , including sexual union.
   ▪ Commitment: To a particular other, often over a long period of time.
   ▪ Consummate love requires all three to fill a partner's needs.

3. ▪ Answers will vary; they should reflect the basics of Holland's theory.

Puzzle It Out

Across
2. Conventional
5. Avoidant
7. Investigative
10. Postpartum
11. Volatile
12. Evolutionary
13. Homogamy

Down
1. Social
2. Cumulative
3. Novice
4. Realistic
5. Artistic
6. Passion
7. Intimacy
8. Validating
9. Enterprising

CHAPTER 15

PHYSICAL AND COGNITIVE DEVELOPMENT IN MIDDLE ADULTHOOD

BEFORE YOU READ . . . CHAPTER SUMMARY

In middle adulthood, the period from 40 to 60, the story of human development in the physical and cognitive domains becomes more an account of differences than a description of universals. This happens because there are so many factors—behavioral choices, poor health, and so on—that determine the developmental pathway that an individual adult follows.

Physical Changes

- In most individuals, the brain is somewhat smaller at the end of middle adulthood than at the beginning of the period. Some declines in brain function are evident. However, middle-aged adults use a variety of strategies to compensate for these declines and, as a result, often outperform younger adults on practical tasks such as driving.
- Both males and females experience changes in reproductive hormones, the climacteric, in these years. In women, reproductive capacity declines slightly and then ceases altogether at menopause. In men, the process is more gradual, and most continue to be capable of fathering children into late adulthood.
- At about age 30, bone mass begins to decline. The process is accelerated in women at menopause. Lifestyle choices, such as diet and exercise, influence bone loss in both men and women.
- Both visual and auditory acuity decline in most middle-aged adults. Men experience greater hearing losses than women do.

Health and Wellness

- The rate of illness and death increase dramatically by the end of the middle adult years. Heart disease and cancer are the leading causes of death among middle-aged adults.
- Cardiovascular disease results from the build-up of a fatty substance in the arteries. Smoking, high blood pressure, high cholesterol, obesity, and a high-fat diet increase the likelihood that a middle-aged adult will suffer from cardiovascular disease. Men are more likely than women to have this disease.
- Some studies suggest that high-fat diets increase the risk of cancer. Smoking, obesity, and an inactive lifestyle may also contribute to this disease.
- On average, women live longer than men, but they are more likely suffer from chronic conditions such as arthritis.
- Ethnicity and socioeconomic class are linked to health in middle adulthood. African Americans, Native Americans, and Hispanic Americans experience higher rates of cardiovascular disease, cancer, and diabetes than members of other groups. Poor adults of all ethnic groups are more likely to suffer from chronic illnesses and have higher rates of death in middle age than peers who are better off economically.
- In general, the mental health of middle-aged adults is good. However, some disorders, such as alcoholism, may go undiagnosed until the middle adulthood years when their effects begin to interact with those of primary aging.

Cognitive Functioning

- Denney's model of aging hypothesizes that exercising physical and cognitive abilities slows down the rate of decline in the middle and later adulthood years. Such exercise may also improve the level of functioning according to this model.
- Research suggests that variations in health are associated with variations in cognitive functioning in middle-aged and older adults. Physical exercise clearly affects health and may also be related to cognitive functioning.
- Vocabulary continues to grow in middle adulthood. Some memory skills decline, but middle-aged adults maintain high levels of functioning in areas of expertise.
- In adults having challenging professions, creative productivity appears to be at its peak in middle adulthood.

AS YOU READ . . . LEARNING OBJECTIVES

After completing Chapter 15, you should be able to:
15.1 Summarize the research on the brain and nervous system in middle adulthood.
15.2 Describe the changes in the reproductive system in middle age.
15.3 Summarize the pros and cons of hormone replacement therapy.
15.4 Describe the change in the skeletal system in middle adulthood.
15.5 Identify the changes in vision and hearing in middle adulthood.
15.6 Describe the health trends at mid-life.
15.7 Summarize the risks of coronary heart disease in middle-aged adults.
15.8 Discuss the risk factors involved in cancer in middle adulthood.
15.9 Describe the relationship between gender and health in middle adulthood.
15.10 Identify the differences of socioeconomic class and ethnicity in health in middle age.
15.11 Discuss the issues involved in Internet addiction.
15.12 Summarize the issues surrounding mental health during the mid-life years.
15.13 Explain Nancy Denney's model of physical and cognitive aging.
15.14 Describe the relationship between health and cognitive functioning.
15.15 Describe the changes in memory and cognition in middle adulthood.
15.16 Discuss creative productivity at mid-life.
15.17 Summarize the research on maintaining the creative "edge" in mid-life and beyond.

AS YOU READ . . . TERM IDENTIFICATION

Alcoholism (p. 421)
Atherosclerosis (p. 413)
Cardiovascular disease (CVD) (p. 413)
Climacteric (p. 407)
Episodic memories (p. 426)
Hypertension (p. 419)
Menopause (p. 408)
Osteoporosis (p. 411)

Perimenopausal phase (p. 408)
Postmenopausal phase (p. 408)
Premenopausal phase (p. 408)
Presbycusis (p. 413)
Presbyopia (p. 412)
Semantic memories (p. 426)
Type A personality pattern (p. 415)

AS YOU READ . . . GUIDED STUDY QUESTIONS

PHYSICAL CHANGES

The Brain and Nervous System (pp. 406-407)

Objective 15.1: Summarize the research on the brain and nervous system in middle adulthood.

1.   Why is there so little information about the normal, undamaged brains of middle-aged adults?

2.   Describe the known information about the brains of middle-aged adults.

3.   Give examples of how cognitive tasks activate a larger area of brain tissue in middle-aged adults than they do in younger adults.

4.   Give examples of how the brains of middle-aged and younger adults respond differently to sensory stimuli.

The Reproductive System (pp. 407-409)

Objective 15.2: Describe the changes in the reproductive system in middle age.

5.   Define the following terms:
     a.   climacteric (p. 407)

     b.   menopause (p. 408)

     c.   premenopausal phase (p. 408)

     d.   perimenopausal phase (p. 408)

     e.   postmenopausal phase (p. 408)

6.   Describe the male climacteric, including the causal factor.

7.   How is the production of testosterone implicated in the incidence of erectile dysfunction?

8.   List the hormones involved in menopause.

9.   Describe the phases of menopause by completing the following table:

Phase	Description
Premenopausal Phase	
Perimenopausal Phase	

Phase	Description
Postmenopausal Phase	

10.   Describe the results of research on the psychological effects of menopause.

11.   How does menopause affect the sexual activity of middle-aged adults?

No Easy Answers: The Pros and Cons of Hormone Replacement Therapy (pp. 410-411)

Objective 15.3: Summarize the pros and cons of hormone replacement therapy.
12.   List the negative symptoms of menopause.

13.   Briefly trace the history of hormone replacement therapy.

The Skeletal System (pp. 411-412)

Objective 15.4: Describe the change in the skeletal system in middle adulthood.
14.   Define osteoporosis (p. 411), including how it is linked to the levels of estrogen and progesterone.

15.   Aside from taking replacement hormones, list the strategies to prevent osteoporosis.

Vision and Hearing (pp. 412-413)

Objective 15.5: Identify the changes in vision and hearing in middle adulthood.
16.   Define the following terms:
        a.   presbyopia (p. 412)

        b.   presbycusis (p. 413)

AFTER YOU READ . . . PRACTICE TEST #1
PHYSICAL CHANGES

Match the letter of the term in the right column with its description in the left column.

_____ 1. Drug therapy to treat the symptoms of menopause.

_____ 2. Loss of bone mass with age resulting in more brittle and porous bones.

_____ 3. The phase of menopause during which estrogen and progesterone levels are erratic, menstrual cycles may be very irregular, and women begin to experience symptoms such as hot flashes.

_____ 4. Normal loss of hearing with aging, especially high-pitched tones.

_____ 5. The term used to describe the adult period during which reproductive capacity of men and women declines or is lost.

_____ 6. The inability to achieve or maintain an erection.

_____ 7. The last phase of menopause; a woman has had no menstrual periods for a year or more.

_____ 8. The cessation of monthly menstrual cycles in middle-aged women.

a. Climacteric
b. Erectile dysfunction
c. Hormone replacement therapy
d. Menopause
e. Osteoporosis
f. Perimenopausal
g. Postmenopausal
h. Premenopausal
i. Presbycusis
j. Presbyopia

(Check your answers to Practice Test #1 on p. 326.)

HEALTH AND WELLNESS

Health Trends at Mid-Life (p. 413)

Objective 15.6: Describe the health trends at mid-life.

17. Give examples of how the health of middle-aged adults differs from younger adults.

18. What are the two leading causes of death in middle age?

Cardiovascular Disease (pp. 413-416)

Objective 15.7: Summarize the risks of coronary heart disease in middle-aged adults.

19. Define the following terms:
   a. cardiovascular disease (CVD) (p. 413)

   b. atherosclerosis (p. 413)

   c. type A personality pattern (p. 415)

20.   Describe the risk factors of heart disease by completing the following table:

Risk	Description of Risk for Heart Disease
Alcohol	
Blood Pressure	
Cholesterol	
Diet	
Heredity	
Inactivity	
Smoking	
Weight	

21.   State the two important points to be made about CVD.

22.   Explain how type A personality pattern may contribute to heart disease.

Cancer (pp. 416-418)

Objective 15.8: Discuss the risk factors involved in cancer in middle adulthood.

23.   Describe the risk factors of cancer by completing the following table:

Risk	Description of Risk for Cancer
Alcohol	
Blood Pressure	
Cholesterol	

Risk	Description of Risk for Cancer
Diet	
Heredity	
Inactivity	
Smoking	
Weight	

24. Summarize the current research on the relationship between diet and cancer.

25. List the infectious agents that are known to cause cancer.

Gender and Health (pp. 418-419)

Objective 15.9: Describe the relationship between gender and health in middle adulthood.

26. State the paradox involving the life expectancy of women and men.

27. Give examples of the sex differences in potentially fatal diseases such as cardiovascular disease and non-fatal diseases such as arthritis.

Socioeconomic Class, Race, and Health (pp. 419-420)

Objective 15.10: Identify the differences of socioeconomic class and ethnicity in health in middle age.

28. How is social class a significant predictor of variations in health in middle age?

29. List the three diseases that have been the focus of studies of racial differences in health.

30. Describe the racial differences in cardiovascular disease, diabetes, and cancer.

Disease	Racial Differences
Cardiovascular Disease (CVD)	
Diabetes	
Cancer	

31.   Define hypertension (p. 419).

Development in the Information Age: Is the Internet Addictive? (p. 421)

Objective 15.11: Discuss the issues involved in Internet addiction.

32.   What is Internet addictive disorder, IAD?

33.   List the criteria for diagnosis of IAD.

34.   What are the arguments of mental health professions who oppose the idea of Internet addiction?

Mental Health (pp. 421-422)

Objective 15.12: Summarize the issues surrounding mental health during the mid-life years.

35.   Compare the mental health problems of middle-aged adults to young adults.

36.   Define alcoholism (p. 421), and describe the evidence for a genetic basis for the disease.

37.   Among alcoholics who survive to middle age, how do the natural declines associated with primary aging interact with the effects of long-term heavy drinking?

AFTER YOU READ . . . PRACTICE TEST #2
HEALTH AND WELLNESS

1.   **The single variable that most affects the quality of life in middle and late adulthood is _____.**
       a.   employment
       b.   income
       c.   health
       d.   an intimate partnership

2.   **Which of the following statements about health trends at mid-life is TRUE?**
       a.   Most middle-aged adults are happy with their bodies.
       b.   Many middle-aged adults experience annoying aches and pains.
       c.   The number of truly healthy adults increases in mid-life.
       d.   Life expectancy has declined over the last few decades.

3.   **The key problem in cardiovascular disease is in the _____.**
       a.   lungs
       b.   arteries
       c.   intestines
       d.   bones

4.   **Which of the following statements about risk factors for heart disease is TRUE?**
       a.   The great majority of Americans have at least one of these risk factors.
       b.   The only consistent controllable cause is smoking.
       c.   Men are at a higher risk because they strain their hearts more than women.
       d.   The risk factors are completely controllable with the right effort.

5. **Which of the following statements about gender and health is TRUE?**
   a.   Women are more likely to die before men.
   b.   Women are less likely than men to get regular check ups.
   c.   Women are more likely than men to die from cardiovascular disease.
   d.   Women are more likely than men to suffer from nonfatal chronic ailments such as arthritis.

6. **Which of the following statements about ethnic differences in health in middle adulthood is TRUE?**
   a.   Mexican Americans have higher rates of heart disease than whites.
   b.   Mexican Americans have lower rates of cancer than whites.
   c.   African Americans have higher rates of cancer, but lower rates of heart disease, than whites.
   d.   Native Americans have lower rates of cardiovascular disease then whites.

7. **Each of the following statements about diabetes is TRUE EXCEPT:**
   a.   Men and women have equal rates of the disease.
   b.   It is estimated that there is at least one undiagnosed case of diabetes for every two individuals who have been diagnosed.
   c.   Diabetes can lead to severe complications such as cardiovascular disease, kidney failure, and blindness.
   d.   Diabetes itself kills more adults in the United States than cancer or heart disease.

8. **Each of the following statements about alcoholism is TRUE EXCEPT:**
   a.   Long-term use of alcohol causes damage to the digestive system.
   b.   Long-term use of alcohol causes losses in muscle strength.
   c.   Long-term use of alcohol causes a delay in the course of the phases of menopause.
   d.   Long-term use of alcohol is associated with a reduced likelihood of death from cancer.

(Check your answers to Practice Test #2 on p. 326.)

COGNITIVE FUNCTIONING

A Model of Physical and Cognitive Aging (pp. 422-423)

Objective 15.13: Explain Nancy Denney's model of physical and cognitive aging.

38.   Explain Nancy Denney's model of physical and cognitive changes in adulthood.

39.   Define and give examples of exercise as Nancy Denney uses it in her model.

Health and Cognitive Functioning (pp. 423-425)

Objective 15.14: Describe the relationship between health and cognitive functioning.

40.   How does Nancy Denney's model help illuminate the links between primary aging and cognitive functioning?

41.   Describe the longitudinal study of physical activity of Harvard alumni.

42.   What is the connection between physical exercise and cognitive abilities in middle-adulthood?

Changes in Memory and Cognition (pp. 425-427)

Objective 15.15: Describe the changes in memory and cognition in middle adulthood.

43.　　Why do researchers often infer the memory performance of middle-aged adults?

44.　　How might increases in the subjective experience of forgetfulness be an aid to metamemory?

45.　　Compare visual memory and memory for auditory stimuli in middle age.

46.　　Define the following terms:
　　　　a.　　episodic memory (p. 426)

　　　　b.　　semantic memory (p. 426)

47　　　How do semantic memories and episodic memories differ in young adults and middle-aged adults?

48.　　Give examples of how flashbulb memories demonstrate that age has no effect on episodic memories.

49.　　How does the dictum "use it or lose it" hold true for cognitive abilities? Give examples.

50.　　Give examples of how expertise in a particular field helps to compensate for age-related deficits in cognitive functioning.

51.　　How do middle-aged adults compare with younger adults in their ability to acquire new knowledge?

52.　　Describe Labouvie-Vief's view of memory change with age.

53.　　What is schematic processing, and describe how it is involved in solving everyday problems?

Creativity (pp. 428-429)

Objective 15.16: Discuss creative productivity at mid-life.

54.　　Describe Simonton's research on the lifetime creativity and productivity of notable scientists from the 19th century and earlier. Compare the results to the lifetime creative output of modern-day scientists.

55.　　Give examples of Streufert's research on how age is related to creativity or professional effectiveness.

The Real World: Maintaining the Creative "Edge" in Mid-Life and Beyond (p. 429)

Objective 15.17: Summarize the research on maintaining the creative "edge" in mid-life and beyond.

56.　　List the two conclusions from the research on maintaining creativity and productivity in the middle and late adult years.

AFTER YOU READ . . . PRACTICE TEST #3
COGNITIVE FUNCTIONING

Indicate whether each of the following statements is true or false.

_____ 1. Nancy Denny proposed that on nearly any measure of physical or cognitive functioning, age-related changes follow a typical curve.

_____ 2. Most fluid abilities are at least moderately exercised, whereas many cystallized abilities are relatively unexercised.

_____ 3. Many of the same characteristics that are linked to increased or decreased risk of heart disease and cancer are also linked to the rate of change of the maintenance of intellectual skill in the middle years.

_____ 4. Physical exercise during middle-age is positively correlated with scores on tests of intellectual functioning.

_____ 5. Physical exercise seems to have no effect on maintaining cognitive abilities in the middle adult years.

_____ 6. The subjective experience of forgetfulness clearly increases with age.

_____ 7. Both memory for visual and auditory stimuli seem to remain stable throughout adulthood.

_____ 8. Adults who engage in intellectually challenging activities show fewer losses in cognitive skills than those who do not.

_____ 9. Adults use schematic processing that is qualitatively different from those used earlier in life.

_____ 10. The ability to apply creative thinking to complex problems may be at its peak in the middle adult years.

(Check your answers to Practice Test #3 on p. 326.)

AFTER YOU READ . . . CRITICAL REFLECTION EXERCISE

Mid-Life Development

Utilizing information from the text, provide complete answers to the following questions:

1. What is the type A personality pattern? Suggest three things that an individual could do to minimize the likelihood of Type A characteristics influencing his or her health.

2. Do you believe in the concept of a "midlife crisis"? Why or why not?

3. Discuss how identity development in the early phases of development may be related to life satisfaction in middle adulthood.

AFTER YOU READ . . . COMPREHENSIVE PRACTICE TEST
MULTIPLE CHOICE QUESTIONS

1. **Which of the following statements is TRUE about the brain at mid-life?**
   a. There is no difference in the distribution of electrical activity in the brains of alcoholics and non-alcoholics.
   b. Cognitive tasks activate a larger area of brain tissue in middle-aged adults than they do in younger adults.
   c. In middle age, more new synapses are formed than are lost.
   d. Synaptic density continues to increase across adulthood.

2. **What reproductive event in middle adulthood is included in the term climacteric?**
   a. a gradual loss of interest in sexual activity
   b. a steady increase in the number of miscarriages
   c. the occurrence of menopause in women
   d. decreased incidence of impotence in men

3. **What seems to be the cause of the decrease in viable sperm in men across middle adulthood?**
   a. less sexual activity which results in decreased sperm production
   b. increased exposure to teratogens from the environment
   c. there is no drop in viable sperm production
   d. gradual decline in testosterone levels beginning in early adulthood

4. **What do we know about the incidence of osteoporosis in middle adulthood?**
   a. It only occurs in women.
   b. The process for women is accelerated by menopause.
   c. The process for men is linked to impotence.
   d. It is unavoidable.

5. **Presbyopia is _____.**
   a. a process by which muscle mass is lost
   b. the thickening of the lens that causes the eye muscles to have difficulty changing the shape of the lens for focusing
   c. the hardening of the arteries accompanied by a slight, but steady, decline in blood pressure during middle adulthood
   d. a sharp decline in taste sensitivity

6. **Health-wise, how do young adults and middle-aged adults compare?**
   a. Young adults have more acute diseases.
   b. Middle-aged adults have more acute diseases.
   c. Young adults have more chronic diseases.
   d. There are no real differences.

7. **What is atherosclerosis?**
   a. hardening of the arteries due to age
   b. clogging of the arteries with fibrous or fatty tissue
   c. a neuromuscular disorder often diagnosed in middle adulthood
   d. a normal part of aging that can be slowed but not avoided

8.   **In industrialized countries, what is the second leading cause of death in middle age and old age?**
        a.   cardiovascular disease
        b.   pulmonary disorders
        c.   cancer
        d.   accidents

9.   **Which of the following statements is TRUE concerning gender and health?**
        a.   Men are more likely to live longer than women.
        b.   Women have fewer diseases and disabilities than men.
        c.   Men live longer once they contract a disease than women.
        d.   Women live longer, but they have more diseases and disabilities than men.

10.   **What is hypertension?**
        a.   cardiovascular disease
        b.   high blood pressure
        c.   low blood sugar
        d.   elevated cardiac rate

11.   **Which of the following statements about diabetes is TRUE?**
        a.   At least three undiagnosed cases of diabetes exist for every individual who has been diagnosed with it.
        b.   More men than women have diabetes.
        c.   Minority adults who have been diagnosed with diabetes are more likely than their white counterparts to develop complications.
        d.   Diabetes itself frequently kills people.

12.   **Which of the following statements describes Nancy Denney's model of physical and cognitive aging?**
        a.   Denney uses the word exercise to refer to physical exercise.
        b.   Unexercised abilities generally have a lower peak of performance; exercised abilities generally have a higher peak.
        c.   Only crystallized intelligence is affected by exercise, not fluid intelligence.
        d.   Skills that are not exercised by age 30 can never be improved.

13.   **Which of the following statements accurately reflects the results of the longitudinal study of the physical activity of Harvard alumni?**
        a.   The more exercise a man reported in his 30s, 40s, and 50s, the lower his mortality risk over the next 25 years.
        b.   Physical activity and cognitive functioning are not related.
        c.   Physical activity and cognitive functioning are negatively correlated.
        d.   Cardiovascular disease is linked to the presence of lead in drinking water.

14.   **At about what age might we expect to see a decline in performance on more complex memory tasks, such as remembering lists of words and passages of text?**
        a.   at about age 35
        b.   not until age 45
        c.   around age 55
        d.   at about age 65

15.   **What happens to creativity and productivity as we age?**
        a.   It peaks around age 65, and then declines gradually.
        b.   It peaks at different ages for women and men.
        c.   It peaks around age 40.
        d.   Creativity is so individual that consistent results have not been found.

TRUE-FALSE QUESTIONS

Indicate whether each of the following statements is true or false.

_____ 1. The brains of middle-aged and younger adults respond differently to sensory stimuli.

_____ 2. During the perimenopausal phase, estrogen levels begin to fluctuate and decline producing irregular menstrual periods in many women.

_____ 3. The more high-risk health behaviors or characteristics you have, the higher your risk of heart disease.

_____ 4. There is little doubt that several types of cancers are caused by infectious agents.

_____ 5. The main cause for cross-racial variations in cancer incidence and death rates is family history of cancer.

_____ 6. Denney's model takes into consideration the wide degree of variation from one individual to the next in the pattern of skill maintenance or decline.

_____ 7. Physical exercise seems to help maintain cognitive abilities in the middle adult years, very likely because it helps to maintain cardiovascular fitness.

_____ 8. Age has no effect on our ability to recall flashbulb memories.

ESSAY QUESTIONS

1. Using Table 15.2 as a reference, design a plan to reduce your health risks for heart disease and cancer.

2. How would you encourage a middle-aged adult relative to "use it or lose it" to maintain her or his cognitive abilities in middle age?

3. Discuss the relationship between creativity and productivity in middle adulthood.

(Check your answers to the Comprehensive Practice Test on p. 326.)

WHEN YOU HAVE FINISHED . . . PUZZLE IT OUT

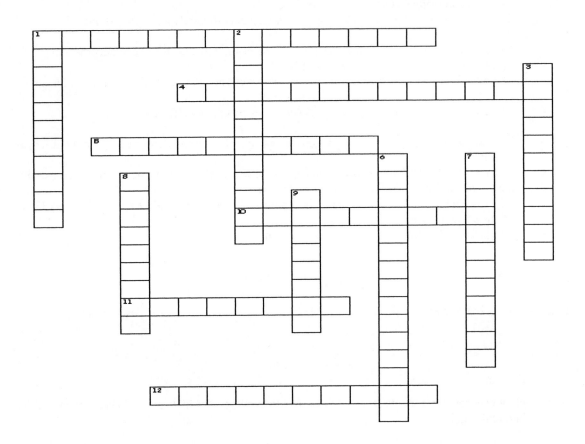

Across

1. Phase during which menstrual cycles may be very irregular and women experience hot flashes
4. Phase during which estrogen levels fall somewhat and menstrual periods are less regular
5. Physical and psychological dependence on alcohol
10. The inability to achieve or maintain an erection; also called erectile dysfunction
11. Memories of general knowledge
12. Normal loss of visual acuity with aging

Down

1. Normal loss of hearing with aging
2. Loss of bone mass with age resulting in more brittle and porous bones
3. The adult period during which reproductive capacity declines or is lost
6. Narrowing of the arteries caused by deposits of plaque
7. Elevated blood pressure
8. The cessation of monthly menstrual cycles in middle-aged women
9. Memories of personal events

Created by Puzzlemaker at DiscoverySchool.com

Check your answers on p. 326.)

WHEN YOU HAVE FINISHED . . . AT-HOME PROJECT

Student Project 26: Assessing Your Own Diet

Since both dietary fat and fiber intake are increasingly implicated as potentially casual factors in cancer, heart disease, or both, it may be useful and informative for you to analyze your own diet.

For five days, write down everything you eat. Do not change your normal eating pattern just to make yourself look good and feel less guilty. If you normally eat Twinkies, go ahead and eat them, but write it down—and keep the wrapper so that you can do a food analysis later.

You will also need some source of detailed information about the total calories, fat content, and fiber content of food. Some of this is now listed on most packaged foods, but for non-packaged foods, you'll need other sources. Your public library may have appropriate sources; some cookbooks offer good lists. (In that category, an excellent resource is a book called *Laurel's Kitchen*, which lists a great deal of information about many kinds of foods. But since it is a vegetarian cookbook, it will not give you information about meat, fish, or poultry.) Other possible sources would be the American Cancer Society, or the County Extension office in your area, which may have pamphlets or brochures.

For your food list for each of the five days, calculate the following:
- total calories
- total grams of fat
- percentage of total calories that is fat. Each gram of fat is nine calories. so simply multiply the total fat grams by nine, then divide that amount by the total calories to give the percent of calories that is fat
- number of grams of fiber

Average these figures over the five days, and then compare the averages with the recommendations from leading public health groups:
- You should be getting no more than 30% of your total calories from fat.
- You should have a minimum of 20 and a maximum of 35 grams of fiber per day. Some experts recommend levels of fat considerably lower than 30%, but 30 is the number that is presently recommended by both the American Heart Association and the American Cancer Society.

How does your diet measure up to these standards? If you do not meet either or both of them, what changes would you need to make in your diet to reach these goals? If your fat levels are too high, can you identify the foods in your normal diet that are raising the percentages? You may be surprised.

CHAPTER 15 ANSWER KEY

Practice Test #1 Physical Changes

1. c   2. e   3. f   4. i   5. a   6. b   7. g   8. d

Practice Test #2 Health and Wellness

1. c   2. b   3. b   4. a   5. d   6. a   7. b   8. d

Practice Test #3 Cognitive Functioning

1. T   2. F   3. T   4. T   5. F   6. T   7. F   8. T   9. T   10. T

Comprehensive Practice Test

Multiple Choice Questions

1. b   2. c   3. d   4. b   5. b   6. a   7. b   8. c   9. d   10. b
11. c   12. b   13. a   14. c   15. c

True-False Questions

1. T   2. F   3. T   4. T   5. F   6. F   7. T   8. T

Essay Questions

1.   ▪ Answers will vary, but could include changes in diet, increase in exercise, reduction of alcohol intake or quitting smoking.

2.   ▪ Most adults maintain or even gain skill on any task that they practice often or that is based on specific learning, Engaging in intellectually challenging activities reduces the likelihood of loss of cognitive skills. Answers will vary, but should include reference to engaging in intellectually challenging activities.

3.   ▪ In every scientific discipline represented, the thinkers produced their best work at about age 40, on average. Researchers proposed that the reason people tend to do their best work at about 40 is not that the mind works better at that age, but that productivity is at its highest at that time. Chance alone suggests that the best work will come during the time when the most work is being done.

Puzzle It Out

Across
1. Perimenopausal
4. Premenopausal
5. Alcoholism
10. Impotence
11. Semantic
12. Presbyopia

Down
1. Presbycusis
2. Osteoporosis
3. Climacteric
6. Atherosclerosis
7. Hypertension
8. Menopause
9. Episodic

CHAPTER 16

SOCIAL AND PERSONALITY DEVELOPMENT IN MIDDLE ADULTHOOD

BEFORE YOU READ . . . CHAPTER SUMMARY

In Western culture, middle-aged adults are viewed as highly competent and capable of assuming important family and occupational roles. Consequently, in most families, the middle-aged cohort provides some degree of both material and emotional support for both younger and older family members. Still, most middle-aged adults feel much less constricted by social roles than in earlier periods, and, for most, these roles shift considerably between the ages of 40 and 60.

Theories of Social and Personality Development

- For Erikson, the primary task of middle adulthood is the development of generativity through mentoring younger individuals.
- There is little empirical support for the popular notion of a "mid-life" crisis.
- Sociologists have proposed that the role changes of middle ages occur in a stage-life pattern. However, research suggests that such stage models don't fully explain middle adulthood development.

Changes in Relationships and Personality

- Marital conflicts decline in middle age leading to higher levels of relationship satisfaction.
- Middle-aged adults are "sandwiched" between younger and older cohorts. They provide assistance and advice both up and down the generational chain.
- When adult children leave home, most middle-aged adults experience a reduction in the role demands that accompany parenthood. As a result, the "emptying the nest" is usually a positive experience.
- The revolving door is the pattern in which adult children who have been living independently return to live in their parents' homes.
- Most adults become grandparents sometime in the middle adult years. For most, the role is a very rewarding one.
- A small proportion of middle-aged adults become primary caregivers for their elderly parents. Many report feeling burdened and depressed by the experience. Women are more likely to become primary caretakers for elders than are men.
- The number of friendships an individual adult has declines in middle age, perhaps narrowing the social network to include only those friends to whom an adult feels particularly close.
- The Big Five personality traits are stable across middle adulthood. However, some middle-aged adults exhibit "mellowing" of negative traits such as neuroticism.

Mid-Life Career Issues

- Job satisfaction peaks in middle age, however work takes on a less important role in an adult's overall sense of well-being during these years.
- Most middle-aged adults continue to be highly productive in their careers.
- Anxiety and depression sometimes accompany both involuntary and voluntary mid-life career changes.

- Preparation for retirement includes financial planning as well as a decline in the number of hours a middle-aged adult works each week.

AS YOU READ . . . LEARNING OBJECTIVES

After completing Chapter 16, you should be able to:

16.1   Describe the key points in Erikson's theory relevant to middle adulthood.
16.2   Examine the evidence of the possible existence of a mid-life crisis.
16.3   Summarize the effects of the overall changes in roles in middle adulthood.
16.4   Trace the pattern of partnerships in middle adulthood.
16.5   Summarize the research on the relationships of middle-aged adults with their children and their parents.
16.6   Describe the results of the empty nest.
16.7   Describe the relationship between parents and their adult children who live with them.
16.8   Describe the impact of grandparenting on middle-aged adults.
16.9   Summarize the issues involved in mother-in-law relationships.
16.10   Describe the issues involved in caring for aging parents during middle adulthood.
16.11   Summarize the evidence of who cares for aging parents.
16.12   Describe the friendships of adults in middle adulthood.
16.13   Identify the areas of continuity and of change in personality in middle adulthood.
16.14   Describe the satisfaction with work of men and women in middle adulthood.
16.15   Identify the processes in optimizing job performance in middle adulthood.
16.16   Describe the effects of unemployment on middle-aged adults.
16.17   Describe the preparations for retirement made by middle-aged adults.

AS YOU READ . . . TERM IDENTIFICATION

Caregiver burden (p. 444)
Companionate relationships (p. 440)
Flexible goal adjustment (p. 447)
Generativity (p. 433)
Generativity versus stagnation stage (p. 433)

Involved relationships (p. 441)
Remote relationships (p. 440)
Role conflict (p. 435)
Role Strain (p. 435)
Tenacious goal pursuit (p. 446)

AS YOU READ . . . GUIDED STUDY QUESTIONS

THEORIES OF SOCIAL AND PERSONALITY DEVELOPMENT

Erikson's Generativity versus Stagnation Stage (pp. 433-434)

Objective 16.1: Describe the key points in Erikson's theory relevant to middle adulthood.

1.   Define the following terms:
      a.   generativity versus stagnation stage (p. 433)

      b.   generativity (p. 433)

2.   Give examples of ways that generativity can be expressed, in addition to bearing and rearing one's own children.

3.   Describe Erikson's view of those who do not express generativity.

Mid-Life Crisis: Fact or Fiction? (p. 434)

Objective 16.2: Examine the evidence of the possible existence of a mid-life crisis.

4. According to Levinson, what difficult tasks must a person confront at mid-life?

5. Give examples of how dealing with the tasks at mid-life can create a crisis.

6. State the evidence to discount the existence of a mid-life crisis.

Role Transitions (pp. 434-436)

Objective 16.3: Summarize the effects of the overall changes in roles in middle adulthood.

7. Define the following terms:
    a.   role conflict (p. 435)

    b.   role strain (p. 435)

8. Give examples of statuses in a social system.

9. List two aspects of the concept of a role that are important for an understanding of development.

10. Describe Evelyn Duvall's stages of the family life cycle by completing the following table:

Stage	Description
1	
2	
3	
4	
5	
6	
7	
8	

11. List two major flaws of Duvall's theory.

12. What are life course markers?

13. Give examples of life course markers in middle adulthood.

AFTER YOU READ . . . PRACTICE TEST #1
THEORIES OF SOCIAL AND PERSONALITY DEVELOPMENT

Indicate whether each of the following statements is true or false.

_____ 1. According to Erikson, middle-aged adults' developmental task is to acquire a sense of generativity.

_____ 2. According to Erikson, middle-aged adults who fail to develop generativity often suffer from a "pervading sense of stagnation and personal impoverishment as if they were their own one and only child."

_____ 3. According to Levinson, each person must confront a constellation of difficult tasks at mid-life: accepting one's own mortality, recognizing new physical limitations and health risks, and adapting to major changes in most roles.

_____ 4. Status is the content of a social position—the behaviors and characteristics expected of a person filling that position. It is a kind of job description.

_____ 5. Each of us must occupy multiple roles at the same time, and this inevitably produces frictions of various kinds.

_____ 6. A person experiences role conflict when her own qualities or skills do not measure up to the demands of some role.

_____ 7. The concept of roles can help explain changes in adult life, because certain roles shift predictably with age.

_____ 8. A criticism of Evelyn Duvall's model is that in modern industrialized societies, a great many people don't move through the sequence of roles in the listed order.

(Check your answers to Practice Test #1 on p. 343.)

CHANGES IN RELATIONSHIPS AND PARTNERSHIPS

Partnerships (pp. 436-437)

Objective 16.4: Trace the pattern of partnerships in middle adulthood.

14. Why do marital stability and marital satisfaction, on average, increase in middle adulthood?

15. What is skilled diplomacy?

16. Describe how skilled diplomacy is helpful in solving problems in a partnership.

17. Why might divorce be less traumatic for middle-aged women than for younger women?

Children and Parents (pp. 437-439)

Objective 16.5: Summarize the research on the relationships of middle-aged adults with their children and their parents.

18. What is meant by mid-life squeeze and the sandwich generation? Give examples of how they affect middle-aged adults.

19. Describe the results of Hagestad's research on attempts to influence other generations in the family.

20.   How do men and women differ in the patterns of family conflict?

Emptying the Nest (p. 439)

Objective 16.6: Describe the results of the empty nest.

21.   What is meant by the term "empty nest?"

22.   Describe the folklore in Western cultures about the empty nest, and the evidence to support or dismiss it.

The Revolving Door (pp. 439-440)

Objective 16.7: Describe the relationship between parents and their adult children who live with them.

23.   Describe the possible conflicts between parents and their adult children living at home.

Grandparenting (pp. 440-442)

Objective 16.8: Describe the impact of grandparenting on middle-aged adults.

24.   Define the following terms:
        a.   remote relationships (p. 440)

        b.   companionate relationships (p. 440)

        c.   involved relationships (p. 441)

25.   Describe the ethnic and gender differences in the styles of grandparenting in the United States.

The Real World: Me, a Mother-in-Law? (p. 441)

Objective 16.9: Summarize the issues involved in mother-in-law relationships.

26.   Why is the role of mother-in-law perceived negatively? Give examples of how the stereotype may be somewhat accurate in some societies.

27.   List five recommendations to help middle-aged women adjust to the mother-in-law role and to forestall conflict.

Caring for Aging Parents (pp. 442-445)

Objective 16.10: Describe the issues involved in caring for aging parents during middle adulthood.

28.   What percentage of middle-aged adults are providing some kind of regular care for an older parents at any given time? How do we need to consider that percentage carefully?

29.   How might the role of caregiver of future cohorts of elderly be different than for the current cohort?

30.   Define caregiver burden, and give examples of the toll it might take on a middle-aged adult.

31.   Why are parents symbolically important to middle-aged adults?

No Easy Answers: Who Cares for Aging Parents? (p. 443)

Objective 16.11: Summarize the evidence of who cares for aging parents.

32.   Within a group of siblings, which are most likely to take on the task of caregiver of an aging parent? How does the gender of the frail elder affect who becomes the caregiver?

33.   Describe how daughters and sons typically are involved in the caregiver role.

Friends (p. 445)

Objective 16.12: Describe the friendships of adults in middle adulthood.

34.   What does research suggest about the total number of friendships of middle-aged adults? What does research suggest about the quality of the friendships of middle-aged adults?

Continuity and Change in Personality (pp. 445-447)

Objective 16.13: Identify the areas of continuity and of change in personality in middle adulthood.

35.   Describe the difference between the evidence for continuity of personality across adulthood and the perception of most people.

36.   State the evidence of real change in personality in adulthood.

37.   What are the cohort differences in continuity and stability?

38.   Define the following terms:
        a.   tenacious goal pursuit (p. 446)

        b.   flexible goal pursuit (p. 447)

AFTER YOU READ . . . PRACTICE TEST #2
CHANGES IN RELATIONSHIPS AND PERSONALITY

1.   **Each of the following is a reason for improvements in marital satisfaction EXCEPT:**
        a.   conflicts over child-rearing decline
        b.   the number of non-shared friends increases
        c.   increased sense of control
        d.   relationship stability is maintained through skilled diplomacy

2.   **Divorce in middle age is typically _____.**
  a.   less traumatic for middle-aged women than for younger women
  b.   more traumatic for middle-aged women than for younger women
  c.   more traumatic for middle-aged men than women
  d.   not traumatic for middle-aged adults

3.   **Middle-aged adults are sometimes called the _____.**
  a.   sandwich generation
  b.   companionate generation
  c.   friendship generation
  d.   remote generation

4.   **What do we know about multigenerational family conflicts?**
  a.   They are predominantly about parenting choices.
  b.   They are always about money.
  c.   The type of conflict differs based on the gender of the family members.
  d.   Multigenerational family conflict is rare.

5.   **Middle-aged women who are in the labor force are much more likely to experience the empty nest as _____ than women whose sense of self-identity has been heavily focused on the role of mother.**
  a.   negative
  b.   unsatisfying
  c.   uncomfortable
  d.   positive

6.   **Middle-aged adults are likely to feel extra strain, even a sense of failure, if children do not leave home by the time they are about _____.**
  a.   18
  b.   20
  c.   25
  d.   30

7.   **The least common type of grandparenting in the United States is _____.**
  a.   involved relationships
  b.   remote relationships
  c.   friendship relationships
  d.   companionate relationships

8.   **Which of the following statements about caring for an aging parent is TRUE?**
  a.   As life expectancy continues to rise, the likelihood of caring for an aging parent will decrease.
  b.   The role of caregiver for an aging parent is a common one in mid-life, but it is not a standard experience.
  c.   Future cohorts are likely to be less healthy than today's older adults.
  d.   Future cohorts are likely to be less financially secure than today's older adults.

9.   **Each of the following statements about friendship in middle adulthood is TRUE EXCEPT:**
  a.   The total number of friendships is lower than in young adulthood.
  b.   Mid-life friendships are as intimate and close as those at earlier stages.
  c.   Friendship depends less on frequent contact than on a sense the friends are there to provide support as needed.
  d.   The number of friendships increases throughout adulthood.

10.   **A behavior pattern in which middle-aged adults adjust goals in order to enhance the likelihood of success is called _____.**
    a.   determined goal accomplishment
    b.   tenacious goal pursuit
    c.   flexible goal adjustment
    d.   skilled diplomacy

(Check your answers to Practice Test #2 on p. 343.)

MID-LIFE CAREER ISSUES

Work Satisfaction (pp. 447-448)

Objective 16.14: Describe the satisfaction with work of men and women in middle adulthood.

39.   List the two paradoxes that characterize work in mid-life.

40.   What happens to men's work satisfaction in middle age?

41.   Give examples of how the patterns of work satisfaction among women may be more complex than are those of men.

42.   Distinguish between the differences in coping styles of men and women at work.

43.   List some reasons why both men and women in mid-life have a greater sense of control over their work lives than younger adults do.

Job Performance (pp. 448-449)

Objective 16.15: Identify the processes in optimizing job performance in middle adulthood.

44.   Give examples of occupations in which physical strength or speedy reaction time is a factor in job performance.

45.   Describe the three sub-processes of selective optimization with compensation.

Sub-process	Description
Selection	
Optimization	
Compensation	

46.   What is the relationship between increasing age and the use of selection, optimization, and compensation?

Unemployment and Career Transitions (pp. 449-451)

Objective 16.16: Describe the effects of unemployment on middle-aged adults.

47.   Why might career transitions be more difficult in middle age than earlier in adulthood?

48.   Describe involuntary career changers.

49.   Describe the direct and the indirect links between job loss and emotional or physical distress.

50.   How might the stages of men's work lives increase the negative effects of unemployment?

51.   Give examples of why unemployment is considerably more common among blacks than among whites in the United States and most European countries.

52.   Which of the Big Five personality dimensions contribute to mental health during involuntary career transitions?

53.   What suggestions do career counselors offer to assist a person who is an involuntary career changer?

54.   Describe voluntary career changers.

55.   How do voluntary career changers differ from involuntary career changers? How are they similar?

Differences	*Similarities*

Preparing for Retirement (pp. 451-452)

Objective 16.17: Describe the preparations for retirement made by middle-aged adults.

56.   Give examples of the gradual reduction in workload in mid-life.

57.   Describe several ways that the Baby Boom cohort's retirement plans may differ dramatically from their parents' plans.

AFTER YOU READ . . . PRACTICE TEST #3
MID-LIFE CAREER ISSUES

Fill in the blanks with the best answers.

1.   Work in mid-life is characterized by two paradoxes: First, work satisfaction is at its peak in these years despite the fact that _____. Second, the quality of work performance remains high, despite _____.

2.   Men's work satisfaction increases in middle-age because _____.

3.   When women returned to full-time work in middle adulthood, the most likely reasons were _____ and _____, not the final departure of children.

4.   Both men and women in mid-life have a greater sense of _____ over their work lives than younger adults do.

5.   In most occupations that demand high levels of _____, performance remains at essentially the same level throughout middle adulthood.

6.   According to Paul and Margaret Baltes, the three sub-processes involved in maintaining high job performance are _____, _____, and _____.

7.   Employers give middle-aged applicants higher rating on variables such as _____, but they tend to think that younger applicants will be able to _____ more rapidly.

8.   Involuntary career changers are people who are in transition because of _____ reasons.

9.   The Big Five personality dimensions, especially _____ and _____, contribute to mental health during involuntary career transitions across all racial and ethnic groups.

10.   Voluntary career changers have a better sense of _____ over their situation than do people whose job changes are forced on them.

(Check your answers to Practice Test #3 on p. 343.)

AFTER YOU READ ... CRITICAL REFLECTION EXERCISES

Mid-Life Transitions

Utilizing information from the text, provide complete responses to the following issues. Whenever possible, cite specific information from the readings to support your responses.

1. What are three major life transitions that may be experienced during middle adulthood? Be sure to discuss the positive and negative effects of these life transitions. What advice would you give someone about how he or she can respond successfully to these life transitions?

Generativity versus Stagnation

2. Discuss the concepts of generativity versus stagnation. What effects might divorce have on these life crises?

3. How would you define mentoring? What kind of a program could you develop to utilize the knowledge and experience of those in late middle adulthood? Be sure that the program you develop utilizes Erikson's concepts of generativity versus stagnation and integrity versus despair. Why would you design the program in these ways?

AFTER YOU READ . . . COMPREHENSIVE PRACTICE TEST
MULTIPLE CHOICE QUESTIONS

1.   **Which of the following individuals is exhibiting generativity? The person who _____.**
     a.   believes that having children is important for one's identity
     b.   is doing volunteer work training youth
     c.   has come to terms with what she has done with her life
     d.   feels that his life has had little meaning

2.   **Which of the following statements about mid-life crisis is TRUE?**
     a.   There is little evidence that the stresses in mid-life are more likely to overwhelm an adult's coping resources at this age than at any other.
     b.   The scores on the mid-life crisis scale are significantly higher at age 45 than at any other age.
     c.   There is a dramatic increase in divorce, depression, and alcoholism in men during mid-life.
     d.   Serious mid-life crises occur in 50 percent of middle-aged men.

3.   **Any situation in which two or more roles are at least partially incompatible is called _____.**
     a.   role status
     b.   role strain
     c.   role conflict
     d.   role incompatibility

4.   **During mid-life _____.**
     a.   marital satisfaction tends to increase
     b.   depression begins to increase gradually
     c.   role overload begins to set in
     d.   self-esteem increases but boredom also sets in

5.   **Middle-aged adults are sometimes referred to as the sandwich generation because _____.**
     a.   financial burdens of retirement begin to push in on these persons
     b.   these individuals are squeezed for help from both children and their own parents
     c.   time begins to seem like it is passing faster than ever before
     d.   the changes in role status cause these persons to feel less needed

6.   **The empty nest _____.**
     a.   is simply the time at which the grown children leave the home
     b.   is a time of stress because the children have moved and roles have changed
     c.   is a very stressful time for women, but not for men
     d.   involves the loss of role identity because of retirement

7.   **Which of the following statements about the revolving door is TRUE?**
     a.   Stress decreases for parents and their adult children when they share a home.
     b.   Few parents are satisfied with their arrangements with their live-in adult children.
     c.   Few parents with adult resident children manage to work out a good system for handling potential stresses.
     d.   Some parents enjoy social support from their resident children.

8.   **Which type of grandparenting is the most common in the United States?**
     a.   remote relationships
     b.   companionate relationships
     c.   involved relationships
     d.   friendship relationships

9. **What effect does caring for an ill elderly parent have on the middle-aged adult?**
    a.   It tends to increase some aspects of depression and to lower marital satisfaction.
    b.   It tends to give the individual a sense of direction and purpose.
    c.   It creates a sense of conflict and hostility.
    d.   It creates a jaded sense of futility about the future.

10. **What happens to friendships in middle adulthood?**
    a.   They become more numerous, but less satisfying.
    b.   They become more same-sexed again, just like in childhood.
    c.   The total number remains the same, but the degree of intimacy is lessened.
    d.   The total number of friendships is lower.

11. **Which of the following statements is TRUE about the continuity and change of personality?**
    a.   Masculinity and femininity are correlated with self-esteem in adults of all ages.
    b.   Neuroticism is fairly consistent across age.
    c.   Personality consistently changes with age.
    d.   Traits are gained across adulthood, but traits are not lost.

12. **Job satisfaction is _____.**
    a.   only minimally linked to self-esteem
    b.   typically at its peak in middle adulthood
    c.   at a plateau in young adulthood, and decreases after that
    d.   closely related to marital satisfaction in middle adulthood

13. **What is optimization?**
    a.   pragmatic strategies for overcoming specific obstacles
    b.   increases in job skills as a function of age
    c.   deliberate practice of crucial abilities
    d.   seeking jobs that most closely match our abilities

14. **Voluntary career changers _____.**
    a.   are people who are in transition because of external reasons
    b.   leave one career to pursue another for a variety of internal reasons
    c.   are young adults in the trial stage of employment
    d.   are older adults who retire

15. **Which of the following is a difference between Baby Boomers and their parents?**
    a.   Baby Boomers expect to die in their mid-70s or later; their parents expect to die long after age 80.
    b.   Baby Boomers saved for their retirement funds; their parents borrowed for their retirement investments.
    c.   Baby Boomers put their nest eggs into the stock market; their parents put their funds for retirement in very safe investments.
    d.   Baby Boomers expect to retire in their mid-60s; their parents expect to retire before age 60.

TRUE-FALSE QUESTIONS

Indicate whether each of the following statements is true or false.

_____ 1. Expressions of generativity appear to be normal middle-aged experiences that are relatively independent of ethnicity and economic factors.

_____ 2. Transitions that are highly predictable and widely shared in any given culture or cohort are called life course markers.

_____ 3. Skilled diplomacy is practiced more often by husbands than by wives, but it appears to be an effective technique for marital problem-solving no matter which spouse uses it.

_____ 4. When women are asked specifically about positive and negative transitions in their lives, those who list the departure of the last child are more likely to describe the event as positive rather than negative.

_____ 5. Among all ethnic groups, the role of grandfather is likely to be both broader and more intimate than that of grandmother.

_____ 6. A shift to full-time employment once the nest is empty is a very common pattern for women in current cohorts.

_____ 7. In the great majority of occupations, job performance remains high throughout middle adulthood.

_____ 8. The indirect effects of job loss include changes in family relationships and loss of self-esteem.

ESSAY QUESTIONS

1. Discuss the issues involved in achieving generativity rather than stagnation in middle adulthood.

2. Describe how caring for aging parents impacts overall life satisfaction.

3. Discuss the indirect and direct relationship between job loss and emotional or physical distress.

(Check your answers to the Comprehensive Practice Test on p. 343.)

WHEN YOU HAVE FINISHED . . . PUZZLE IT OUT

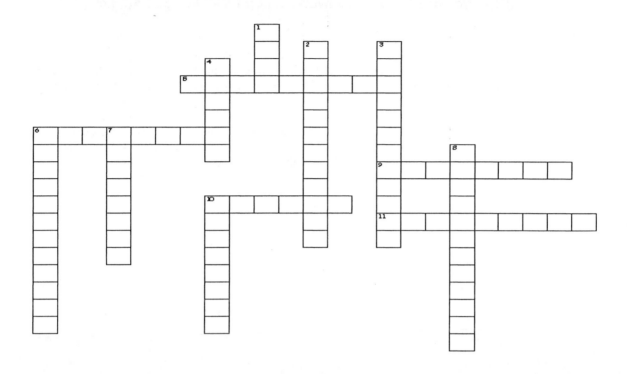

Across

5. Workers narrow their range of activities
6. Situation in which two or more roles are at least partially incompatible
9. Relationship in which grandparents are directly involved in everyday care of grandchildren
10. Experienced when a person's own qualities or skills do not measure up to the demands of some role
11. A behavior pattern in which middle-aged adults remain committed to goals that are difficult

Down

1. The content of a social position—the behaviors and characteristics expected of a person filling that position.
2. Workers deliberately "exercise" crucial abilities
3. A sense that one is making a valuable contribution to society
4. Relationship in which grandparents do not see their grandchildren often
6. Workers adopt pragmatic strategies for overcoming specific obstacles
7. A behavior pattern in which middle-aged adults adjust goals to enhance the likelihood of success
8. Relationship in which grandparents have frequent contact and warm interactions with grandchildren
10. Interlocking positions in a social system

Created by Puzzlemaker at DiscoverySchool.com

(Check your answers on p. 344.)

WHEN YOU HAVE FINISHED . . . RESEARCH PROJECT

Student Project 27: Social Networks among Middle-Aged Adults

It would be extremely interesting to repeat Project 16, except this time with middle-aged subjects. You should locate at least six adults between the ages of 40 and 65. They could be all men, all women, or three of each, and should cover the age range as much as possible. Obtain the appropriate informed consent from each, and follow the identical procedure as for Student Project 16. If a group of students in your class all complete this project, you will have a fascinating cross-sectional study.

If you have completed both Student Projects 16 and 17, compare the responses of the two age groups. Do your middle-aged subjects include fewer people in their three circles? Do they list fewer friends? Are their friends more likely to be in the first or second circle, rather than in the outermost circle? Any differences you can detect?

CHAPTER 16 ANSWER KEY

Practice Test #1 Theories of Social and Personality Development
1. T   2. T   3. T   4. F   5. T   6. F   7. T   8. T

Practice Test #2 Changes in Relationships and Personality
1. b   2. a   3. a   4. c   5. d   6. c   7. a   8. b   9. d   10. c

Practice Test #3 Mid-Life Career Issues
1.   most adults receive few work promotions in middle age; declines in some cognitive pr physical skills
2.   the issue of work is less central to their lives
3.   divorce; widowhood
4.   control
5.   cognitive skills
6.   selection, optimization; compensation
7.   dependability; acquire new skills
8.   external
9.   neuroticism; openness to experience
10.   control

Comprehensive Practice Test
Multiple Choice Questions
1. b   2. b   3. c   4. a   5. b   6. a   7. d   8. b   9. a   10. d
11. b   12. b   13. c   14. b   15. c

True-False Questions
1. T   2. T   3. F   4. T   5. F   6. F   7. T   8. T

Essay Questions
1.   ▪ Acquiring generativity involves an interest in establishing and guiding the next generation. It is expressed not only in bearing or rearing one's own children, but through teaching, serving as mentor, or taking on leadership roles in various civic, religious, or charitable organizations.
     ▪ The optimum expression of generativity requires turning outward from a preoccupation with self.
     ▪ Expressions of generativity appear to be normal middle-aged experiences that are relatively independent of ethnicity and economic factors.

2.   ▪ Most adult children give more assistance to their parents than they did before, but also continue to see them regularly for ceremonial and celebratory occasions and to feel affection as well as filial responsibility.
     ▪ Within a group of siblings, the one most likely to take on the task of caregiving is the one who has no children still at home, is not working, not married, and lives closest to the aging parent. It is most often a daughter or a daughter-in-law.
     ▪ Caregiver are more depressed and have lower marital satisfaction. Those who care for frail elders are more often ill themselves or have some reduced efficiency of immune system functioning.

3.   ▪ Direct: The financial strain of job loss contributes to heightened levels of anxiety and depression.
     ▪ Indirect: Include changes in family relationships and loss of self-esteem; marital relationships deteriorate rapidly after one or the other spouse has been laid off; the number of hostile or negative interactions increases, and the number of warm and supportive interactions declines; separation and divorce become much more common.

Puzzle It Out

Across

5. Selection
6. Conflict
9. Involved
10. Strain
11. Tenacious

Down

1. Role
2. Optimization
3. Generativity
4. Remote
6. Compensation
7. Flexible
8. Companionate
10. Statuses

POLICY QUESTION IV

WHAT TYPE OF COUPLES SHOULD BE SANCTIONED BY SOCIETY?

Learning Objective: Summarize the issues about the types of couples sanctioned by society (pp. 455-456).

1.   How did the sexual revolution of the 1960s and 1970s affect society's view of marriage?

2.   Distinguish between a registered domestic partnership and a civil union.

3.   State the case of the right-to-marry movement.

4.   State the case against the right-to-marry movement.

5.   Policies about the legal status of couples are different in every state. What are the relevant policies in your area? Student research could include answering the following questions:

    a.   How have policymakers in your area responded to the same-sex marriage movement? (go to http://www.stateline.org and http://www.gay-civil-unions.com to find out.) How much support does the movement have in your states' legislature and among the citizens of your state?

    b.   What do your classmates and friends think about the idea of covenant marriage?

    c.   Find our whether your city and/or state has a domestic partnership law. If so, does the law guarantee employer benefits such as health insurance coverage to domestic partners?

    d.   Interview a marriage therapist. What does this professional think about the effects of legal status on partners' commitment to one another, the quality of their relationship, and their development as individuals?

CHAPTER 17

PHYSICAL AND COGNITIVE DEVELOPMENT IN LATE ADULTHOOD

BEFORE YOU READ . . . CHAPTER SUMMARY

Most older adults experience some degree of physical and cognitive declines. Thus, the experience of aging often involves learning to offset weaknesses, such as increasing forgetfulness, with strengths, such as practicality and inventiveness.

Variability in Late Adulthood

- The elderly are often classified as young-old (60-75), old-old (75-85), and oldest-old (85+). The oldest-old are the fastest-growing group of elderly. There are significant individual differences in aging among all three groups.
- Heredity, overall health, current and prior health habits (especially exercise) contribute to variability among the elderly. Regularly used skills decline more slowly than those that are used less frequently.

Physical Changes

- Neurons are less dense in the elderly than in younger adults, resulting in slower reaction times to a variety of stimuli.
- Changes in vision and hearing affect the lives of most elderly adults. The senses of smell and touch become less sensitive in the later years.
- Aging theorists suggest that there may be genetic limits on the human lifespan. Further, the cumulative effects of cell malfunctions may be responsible for primary aging.
- Behavior changes that result from physical changes include general slowing, changing patterns of eating and sleeping, and an increased number of falls. Most older adults continue to be sexually active, although the frequency of sexual activity decreases in late adulthood.

Mental Health

- Dementia becomes steadily more common in the late adult years. The most common type of dementia is Alzheimer's disease. Its causes are not yet known.
- Mild forms of depression rise somewhat in the later years, but serious clinical depression is rare. African-American elders are less likely to be depressed than peers in other groups.

Cognitive Changes

- Cognitive changes result from the general slowing of the nervous system and perhaps from a loss of short-term memory capacity.
- Wisdom and creativity may be important aspects of cognitive functioning in old age.

AS YOU READ ... LEARNING OBJECTIVES

After completing Chapter 17, you should be able to:

17.1   Identify the characteristics of the elderly population.
17.2   Summarize the issues involved in the coming demographic crisis.
17.3   Describe the research findings on longevity.
17.4   Summarize the changes in the brain in late adulthood.
17.5   Identify the changes in the senses of the elderly.
17.6   Describe the theories of biological aging.
17.7   Describe the behavioral effects of physical changes on the elderly.
17.8   Summarize the research on the likelihood of institutionalization of older adults.
17.9   Identify the symptoms and causes of Alzheimer's disease and other dementias.
17.10   Summarize the research on mild cognitive impairment and Alzheimer's disease.
17.11   Summarize the information about computers and dementia.
17.12   Describe the research on depression in late adulthood.
17.13   Describe the changes in memory in late adulthood.
17.14   Summarize the research on wisdom and creativity in late adulthood.

AS YOU READ ... TERM IDENTIFICATION

Activities of daily living (ADLs) (p. 462)
Alzheimer's disease (p. 472)
Cross-linking (p. 469)
Dementia (p. 472)
Frail elderly (p. 458)
Free radicals (p. 469)
Geriatric dysthymia (p. 476)
Gerontology (p. 458)
Hayflick limit (p. 464)
Instrumental activities of daily living (IADLs) (p. 462)

Multi-infarct dementia (p. 475)
Programmed senescence theory (p. 468)
Satiety (p. 471)
Senescence (p. 468)
Synaptic plasticity (p. 466)
Telomere (p. 464)
Terminal drop hypothesis (p. 469)
Tinnitus (p. 467)
Wisdom (p. 482)

AS YOU READ ... GUIDED STUDY QUESTIONS

VARIABILITY IN LATE ADULTHOOD

Characteristics of the Elderly Population (pp. 458-463)

Objective 17.1: Identify the characteristics of the elderly population.

1.   Define gerontology (p. 458).

2.   Give examples of how life expectancy increases as adults get older.

3.   Define frail elder (p. 458).

4. Distinguish among each of the following sub groups of elders by completing the following table:

Subgroup	Ages	Description
Young Old		
Old Old		
Oldest Old		

5. Trace the growth of the number of centenarians in the United States, from the beginning of the 20th century to the middle of the 21st century.

6. State the findings of the New England Centenarian Study.

7. How do the majority of older adults regard their health? How does the health of older adults compare to that of younger adults?

8. Describe the cognitive functioning of the elderly.

9. How are sex hormones related to variations in cognitive performance?

10. Summarize the animal research by neurophysiologists on mental exercise.

11. What is a disability?

12. Define the following terms:
    a. activities of daily living (ADLs) (p. 462)

    b. instrumental activities of daily living (IADLs) (p. 462)

13. List the two physical problems or diseases that are most likely to contribute to some functional disability in late adulthood.

14. Summarize the racial and ethnic differences in late adulthood.

No Easy Answers: The Coming Demographic Crisis (p. 459)

Objective 17.2: Summarize the issues involved in the coming demographic crisis.

15. Why will there be a worldwide demographic crisis in the near future?

16. What are the two options with respect to the pension plans in the United States? State the pros and cons of each.

Longevity (pp. 463-465)

Objective 17.3: Describe the research findings on longevity.

17.   List the three major factors that interact to impact longevity.

18.   What seems to be the maximum lifespan for humans?

19.   Define the following terms:
a.   Hayflick limit (p. 464)

b.   telomeres (p. 464)

20.   What is the Hayflick limit for humans?

21.   What evidence exists to support the idea that longevity is inherited?

22.   Why is physical exercise said to be the most crucial health habit?

23.   How is physical exercise related to cognitive functioning in late adulthood?

AFTER YOU READ . . . PRACTICE TEST #1
VARIATIONS IN LATE ADULTHOOD

Match the letter of the term in the right column with its description in the left column.

_____ 1.	The theoretical proposal that each species is subject to a genetically programmed time limit after which cells no longer have any capacity to replicate themselves accurately.	a. Activities of daily living (ADLs)
_____ 2.	A person in his or her 80s.	b. Baby Boomers
_____ 3.	Self-help tasks such as bathing, dressing, and using the toilet.	c. Centenarian
		d. Frail elderly
_____ 4.	Elders aged 60-75.	e. Gerontology
		f. Hayflick limit
_____ 5.	String of repetitive DNA at the tip of each chromosome in the body that appears to serve as a kind of timekeeping mechanism.	g. Instrumental activities of daily living (IADLs)
_____ 6.	The scientific study of aging.	h. Octogenarian
		i. Oldest old
_____ 7.	Older adults whose physical and/or mental impairments are so extensive that they cannot care for themselves.	j. Old old
_____ 8.	Cohort in the United States who were born in the years from 1946 until the early 1960s.	k. Telomere
		l. Young old

(Check your answers to Practice Test #1 on p. 367.)

PHYSICAL CHANGES

The Brain and Nervous System (pp. 465-466)

Objective 17.4: Summarize the changes in the brain in late adulthood

24.   List the four main changes in the brain during the adult years.

25.   How does education relate to dendritic density?

26.   How does dendritic loss affect synaptic speed?

27.   Define synaptic plasticity (p. 466), and describe how it is related to dendritic loss.

The Senses and Other Body Systems (pp. 466-468)

Objective 17.5: Identify the changes in the senses of the elderly.

28.   List three problems with vision in late adulthood, in addition to presbyopia.

29.   State the gender difference in auditory problems of the elderly. How is the difference related to the work environment?

30.   Define tinnitus (p. 467).

31.   Describe the components of hearing difficulties in late adulthood by completing the following table:

Component	Description
Loss of ability to hear high-frequency sounds	
Difficulties with word discrimination	
Problems hearing under noisy conditions	
Tinnitus	

32.   Describe the changes in the sense of taste associated with aging.

33.   How does the sense of smell change in old age?

34.   What sex difference accompanies the change in the sense of smell? What is the environmental component that accompanies it?

35.   What changes in the sense of touch can occur in old age?

Theories of Biological Aging (pp. 468-470)

Objective 17.6: Describe the theories of biological aging.

36. Define the following terms:
    a. senescence (p. 468)

    b. programmed senescence theory (p. 468)

    c. cross-linking (p. 469)

    d. free radicals (p. 469)

    e. terminal drop hypothesis (p. 469)

37. How does each of the following theories explain biological aging?

Theory	Explanation of Biological Aging
Programmed Senescence	
Repair of Genetic Material	
Cross-Linking	
Free Radicals	
Terminal Drop	

Behavioral Effects of Physical Changes (pp. 470-472)

Objective 17.7: Describe the behavioral effects of physical changes on the elderly.

38. What is the biggest single behavioral effect of age-related physical changes?

39. List several factors that explain the general slowing down in late adulthood, and explain how general slowing down affects functioning in late adulthood.

40. Describe the changes in sleeping patterns in late adulthood, and how it affects functioning.

41.   Define satiety (p.)471, and explain how it is involved in functioning in late adulthood.

42.   How do each of the following affect functioning in late adulthood?

Factor	Affect
Stamina	
Dexterity	
Balance	

43.   How is sexual activity affected by the cumulative physical changes of aging?

The Real World: Institutionalization among the Elderly (p. 473)

Objective 17.8: Summarize the research on the likelihood of institutionalization of older adults.

44.   How does involuntary placement in a nursing home affect rapid decline and death?

AFTER YOU READ . . . PRACTICE TEST #2
PHYSICAL CHANGES

1.   **Each of the following is a major brain change during the adult years EXCEPT:**
       a.   a change in dendritic density
       b.   increase in brain weight
       c.   slower synaptic speed
       d.   loss of gray matter

2.   **The redundancy in the nervous system that ensures that it is always possible for a nerve impulse to move from cell to cell is called _____.**
       a.   brain weight
       b.   dendritic density
       c.   pruning
       d.   synaptic plasticity

3.   **Which of the following tends to happen to vision as we age?**
       a.   increased blood flow to the eyes resulting in blurred peripheral vision
       b.   an expanded field of vision, though with less lens focus
       c.   an enlarged blind spot
       d.   an increase in the density of the optic nerve

4.	**From which of the following would a man be more likely to suffer than a woman in late adulthood?**
	a.	auditory problems
	b.	cataracts
	c.	Alzheimer's disease
	d.	depression

5.	**Each of the following is a component of hearing difficulties in the elderly EXCEPT:**
	a.	hearing under noisy conditions
	b.	difficulties with word discriminations
	c.	the ability to hear high-frequency sounds
	d.	the ability to hear low-frequency sounds

6.	**Which of the following appears to be TRUE about the sense of taste?**
	a.	Older adults prefer salty foods because of a decline in taste discrimination.
	b.	The ability to taste the four basic flavors does not decline over the years.
	c.	Taste receptors are never replaced once they are lost.
	d.	The sense of taste declines or increases depending on life experiences.

7.	**_____ occurs when undesirable chemical bonds from between proteins or fats.**
	a.	The formation of free radicals
	b.	The production of antioxidants
	c.	Cross-linking
	d.	Senescence

8.	**_____ inhibit the formation of free radicals or promote chemical processes that help the body defend against them.**
	a.	Antioxidants
	b.	Collagens
	c.	Senescence
	d.	Satiety

9.	**The hypothesis that mental and physical functioning decline drastically only in the few years immediately preceding death is called the _____.**
	a.	repair of genetic material hypothesis
	b.	terminal drop hypotheses
	c.	programmed senescence hypothesis
	d.	satiety hypothesis

10.	**Older adults _____.**
	a.	become "night people" instead of "morning people"
	b.	wake up less frequently than younger adults, but they don't sleep as deeply
	c.	take more naps because they need more sleep than younger adults
	d.	show decreases in rapid eye movement (REM) sleep

(Check your answers to Practice Test #2 on p. 367.)

MENTAL HEALTH

Alzheimer's Disease and Other Dementias (pp. 472-475)

Objective 17.9: Identify the symptoms and causes of Alzheimer's disease and other dementias.

45. Define the following terms:
    a.   dementias (p. 472)

    b.   Alzheimer's disease (p. 472)

46. Trace the symptoms of Alzheimer's as the disease progresses.

47. How is Alzheimer's disease definitively diagnosed?

48. What are neurofibrilary tangles?

49. Describe the most common gene implicated in Alzheimer's disease.

50. Define multi-infarct dementia (p. 475). How is it different from Alzheimer's disease?

51. List other causes of dementia.

52. What is the incidence of Alzheimer's disease in the United States?

Research Report: Mild Cognitive Impairment and Alzheimer's Disease (p. 474)

Objective 17.10: Summarize the research on mild cognitive impairment and Alzheimer's disease.

53. Distinguish between mild cognitive impairment (MCI) and age-associated cognitive decline (AACD).

Development in the Information Age: Computers and Dementias (p. 476)

Objective 17.11: Summarize the information about computers and dementia.

54. List several ways that computers are used in the treatment of various neurological disorders affecting the elderly.

Depression (pp. 475-479)

Objective 17.12: Describe the research on depression in late adulthood.

55. Define geriatric dysthymia (p. 476), and distinguish it from a depressed mood and from full-fledged clinical depression.

56.   How can each of the following influence the diagnosis of depression in the elderly?

Factors	Influence
Ageism	
Confusion and memory loss	
Standard questionnaires used to assess depression	

57.   Describe the risk factors for depression.

58.   What factors impact the ethnic differences in depression? What cultural differences may impact the low incidence of depression among African-Americans?

59.   List the factors that predict suicide at all ages.

60.   Describe the therapies for depression for older adults. Why is the appropriate use of antidepressant medications among the elderly critical?

61.   Give examples of how each of the following can help prevent depression in older adults by completing the following table:

Factor	Example
Improving health	
Social involvement	
Support of spiritual needs	

AFTER YOU READ . . . PRACTICE TEST #3
MENTAL HEALTH

Indicate whether each of the following statements is true or false.

_____ 1. Dementia is the leading cause of institutionalization of the elderly in the United States.

_____ 2. The early stages of Alzheimer's disease usually become evident very rapidly.

_____ 3. At autopsy, the brains of Alzheimer's victims are far more likely to contain extensive neurofibrilary tangles than the brains of individuals with other kinds of dementia.

_____ 4. Dementia can be caused by depression, cardiovascular disease, and alcohol abuse.

_____ 5. Geriatric dysthymia typically progresses to clinical depression.

_____ 6. The risk factors for depression and dysthymia among the elderly include inadequate social support, inadequate income, and emotional loss.

(Check your answers to Practice Test #3 on p. 367.)

COGNITIVE CHANGES

Memory (pp. 480-482)

Objective 17.13: Describe the changes in memory in late adulthood.

62. What are the rules that apply to memory processes among both older and younger adults?

63. How is short-term memory affected in late adulthood?

64. How can strategy learning improve memory?

65. Compare retrospective memory tasks with prospective memory tasks in older adults.

66. Describe how everyday memory is impacted in late adulthood.

67. What is source memory?

68. Summarize Timothy Salthouse's research on the slower reaction times in older adults.

Wisdom and Creativity (pp. 482-483)

Objective 17.14: Summarize the research on wisdom and creativity in late adulthood.

69. Define wisdom (p. 482).

70. Describe Paul Baltes' research measuring wisdom, including the criteria that are central to wisdom.

71.   Describe Gene Cohen's four-stage theory of mid- to late-life creativity by completing the following table:

Age	Stage	Description
50s		
60s		
70s		
80s		

AFTER YOU READ . . . PRACTICE TEST #4
COGNITIVE CHANGES

Fill in the blanks with the best answers.

1.   The same basic rules apply to memory processes among both older and younger adults: recognition is easier than _____, tasks that require speed are _____, and metamemory skills are _____.

2.   Older adults typically perform more poorly than younger adults on tasks involving _____ (recalling something in the past); older adults' performance on _____ (those that require individuals to remember to do something on the future) depends on the type of task involved.

3.   Remembering where they heard something is an example of _____.

4.   Virtually all experts agree with Salthouse that loss of _____ is a key aspect of the process of memory decline.

5.   _____ reflects understanding of "universal truths" or basic laws or patterns.

6.   Baltes's five criteria of wisdom are _____, _____, _____, _____, and _____.

7.   The speed of accessing _____ remain constant across adulthood, unlike speed of information processing in other domains.

8.   Cohen's four stages are _____, _____, _____, and _____.

(Check your answers to Practice Test #4 on p. 367.)

AFTER YOU READ . . . CRITICAL REFLECTION EXERCISE

Longevity

Utilizing information from the text, provide complete responses to the following issues. Whenever possible, cite specific information from the readings to support your responses.

1.   Name and discuss three things that you do that you think will INCREASE your chances of living a longer life. Why do you do these things? (i.e., Were they taught to you by your parents? Did you learn them on your own?) How, specifically, do you think they will affect your longevity?

2.   Name and discuss three things that you do that you think will DECREASE your chances of living a longer life. Why do you do these things?(or where did these things come from - like genetics?) How, specifically, do you think they will affect your longevity?

3.   What four pieces of advice would you give a person on how to slow the effects of aging? What are these effects and what specific things can be done to slow them?

4.   Imagine that you are being hired by a Senior Citizen Living Community to develop an activity program for the adults. Describe two activities that you would develop and explain why you would develop them the way you have. What specific goals do you have for each of these activities? How would you explain these goals to the individuals living in the community?

AFTER YOU READ . . . COMPREHENSIVE PRACTICE TEST
MULTIPLE-CHOICE QUESTIONS

1. **The scientific study of aging is called _____.**
   a. senescence
   b. the Hayflick limit
   c. life expectancy
   d. gerontology

2. **Which of the following is consistent with the Hayflick limit?**
   a. the maximum number of times a cell can divide before degenerating
   b. understanding that human beings have a set maximum age limit
   c. life expectancy is limited more by environment than by genetics
   d. cognitive changes lead to physical changes which lead to death

3. **Which of the following appears to be TRUE about physical exercise?**
   a. it is more important in young adulthood than any other age
   b. it may be more important in older adulthood than other ages
   c. even with moderate exercising, genetics influences overall health more
   d. men benefit more from physical exercise than women

4. **What happens to dendritic density with aging?**
   a. it continues to thicken
   b. more redundant neural pathways are added
   c. it begins to thin as dendrites are lost and not replaced
   d. the loss of density is equally distributed throughout the brain

5. **An example of synaptic plasticity is _____.**
   a. expansion of dendritic tangling that leads to disorders such as Alzheimer's disease
   b. the elimination of redundant neural pathways
   c. the brain's ability to recall information memorized years ago
   d. the brain's ability to find the shortest routes between two neurons

6. **What is tinnitus?**
   a. a tendon problem associated with overexertion
   b. a recurring nasal problem that results in snoring
   c. a persistent ringing in the ears
   d. a gradual decline in taste sensitivity as a result of smoking

7. **The gradual deterioration of body systems that happen as organisms age is called _____.**
   a. life expectancy
   b. cross-linking
   c. terminal drop
   d. senescence

8. **What is a free radical?**
   a. an outspoken political deviant
   b. a derivative of beta carotene
   c. a molecule or atom that possesses an unpaired electron
   d. a toxin or carcinogen that floats in the body causing damage

9. **Which of the following statements about automobile accidents is TRUE?**
    a. Older adults have more accidents than younger drivers because they drive too fast.
    b. Older adults have fewer accidents than any other age group.
    c. Older adults have more accidents than younger drivers, but they are usually not fatal.
    d. Older adults have more accidents per mile than younger drivers, but fewer total accidents.

10. **What is the definition of dementia?**
    a. a sudden loss of memory
    b. a distortion of place or time
    c. any global deterioration of intellectual functions
    d. senility-induced paranoia

11. **Dementia caused by a series of small strokes is called _____.**
    a. Alzheimer's disease
    b. multi-infarct dementia
    c. Parkinson's disease
    d. presenile disease

12. **Chronic depressed mood in older adults is called _____.**
    a. geriatric dysthymia
    b. insomnia
    c. grumpiness
    d. schizophrenia

13. **Which of the following group of elders has the highest rate of suicide completion in the United States?**
    a. African-American men
    b. Asian-American men
    c. white-American men
    d. Hispanic-American men

14. **Older adults _____.**
    a. do as well as younger adults on recall tasks.
    b. tend to have faster reaction time than younger adults on new tasks.
    c. do as well on recognition tasks as younger adults.
    d. consistently perform better than younger adults on multiple-choice tests.

15. **Each of the following is one of Paul Baltes's criteria of wisdom EXCEPT:**
    a. understanding relevance of context
    b. semantic knowledge
    c. factual knowledge
    d. procedural knowledge

TRUE-FALSE QUESTIONS

Indicate whether each of the following statements is true or false.

_____ 1.   Life expectancy decreases as adults get older.

_____ 2.   A telomere is a string of repetitive DNA at the tip of each chromosome that appears to serve as a kind of timekeeping mechanism.

_____ 3.   The sense of smell clearly deteriorates in old age.

_____ 4.   The terminal drop hypothesis states that mental and physical functioning decline drastically in the ten years preceding death.

_____ 5.   The most common gene implicated in Alzheimer's disease is on chromosome 21.

_____ 6.   Depression may be mistaken for dementia because it can cause confusion and memory loss.

_____ 7.   Task-specific knowledge seems to make a difference in the everyday memory among the elderly.

_____ 8.   Baltes's research on wisdom found that intelligence and professional experience, rather than age, are correlated with responses to the dilemma task.

ESSAY QUESTIONS

1.   Discuss the finding that older adults who continue to challenge themselves with complex mental activities can delay, or even reverse, the normal decline in brain mass that is part of primary aging.

2.   Discuss the factors involved in the general slowing down in late adulthood.

3.   Does wisdom more likely to be found in middle-aged and older adults? Defend your answer with examples.

(Check your answers to the Comprehensive Practice Test on p. 367.)

WHEN YOU HAVE FINISHED . . . PUZZLE IT OUT

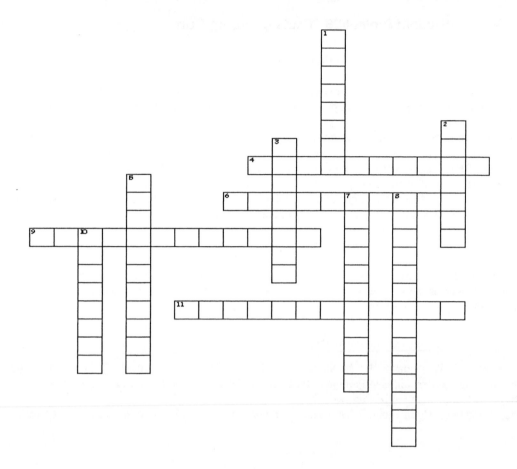

Across

4. A limitation in an individual's ability to perform certain roles and tasks
6. The gradual deterioration of body systems that happen as organisms age
9. Foods that inhibit the formation of free radicals
11. A person in his or her 80s

Down

1. Neurological disorders involving problems with memory and thinking that affect an individual's emotional, social, and physical functioning
2. The feeling of fullness that follows a meal
3. Persistent ringing in the ears
5. The scientific study of aging
7. A person over 100 years of age
8. Tangles found in the brains of individuals with Alzheimer's disease
10. String of DNA at the tip of each chromosome that serves as a kind of timekeeping mechanism

Created by Puzzlemaker at DiscoverySchool.com

(Check your answers on p. 367.)

WHEN YOU HAVE FINISHED . . . RESEARCH PROJECT

Student Project 28: Facts on Aging Quiz

Procedure

For this project locate at least six adults, of any age below 65. Each of your subjects must, naturally, provide written permission for participation in this project, following procedures specified by your instructor.

Tell each subject that you are interested in knowing how much people of different ages know about aging and the aged in United States. Ask each one to answer the 25 items, the Facts On Aging Quiz. (If your subject wishes to know the correct answers afterward, the scoring is easy: alternating pairs are true or false. 1 & 2 are true, 3 & 4 are false, 5 & 6 are true, etc., and item 25 is true. Item 21 was true in 1981, when this was originally written; it was not true in 1992 when it was revised.) After each subject has completed the items, mark on the back of each sheet the subject's gender and age. Do NOT put the subject's name anywhere on the sheet.

Analysis and Report

Determine the average number of correct answers for your subjects. Were there differences in knowledge as a function of either age or gender of the subjects? Also analyze each item: Were there more incorrect answers to some items than others? Does it seem important to correct some of the misconceptions?

References

Duerson, M. C., Thomas, J. W., Chang, J., & Stevens, C. B. (1992). Medical students' knowledge and misconceptions about aging: Responses to Palmore's facts on aging quizzes. *The Gerontologist*, *32*, 171-4.
Palmore, E. B. (1981). The fact on aging quiz: Part two. *The Gerontologist*, *21*, 431-7.
Palmore, E. B. (1992). Knowledge about aging: What we know and need to know. *The Gerontologist*, *32,* 149-150.

Facts on Aging Quiz

Indicate whether each of the following is true or false.

_____   1.   A person's height tends to decline in old age.

_____   2.   More older persons (over 65) have chronic illnesses that limit their activity than do younger persons.

_____   3.   Older persons have more acute (short-term) illnesses than persons under 65.

_____   4.   Older persons have more injuries in the home than do persons under 65.

_____   5.   Older workers have less absenteeism than do younger workers.

_____   6.   The life expectancy of blacks at age 65 is about the same as whites.

_____   7.   The life expectancy of men at age 65 is about the same as women.

_____   8.   Medicare pays over half of the medical expenses for the aged.

_____   9.   Social Security benefits automatically increase with inflation.

_____   10.   Supplementary Security Income guarantees a minimum income for needy aged.

_____   11.   The aged do not get their proportionate share (about 11%) of the nation's income.

_____   12   The aged have higher rates of criminal victimization than persons under 65.

_____   13.   The aged are more fearful of crime than are persons under 65.

_____   14.   The aged are the most law abiding of all adult groups according to official statistics.

_____   15.   There are two widows for each widower among the aged.

_____   16.   More of the aged vote than any other age group.

_____   17.   There are proportionately more older persons in public office than in the total population.

_____   18.   The proportion of blacks among the aged is growing.

_____   19.   Participation in voluntary organizations (churches and clubs) tends to decline among the healthy aged.

_____   20.   The majority of aged live alone.

_____   21.   About 3% more of the aged have incomes below the official poverty level than does the rest of the population.

_____   22.   The rate of poverty among aged blacks is about 3 times as high as among aged whites.

_____   23.   Older persons who reduce their activity tend to be happier than those who remain active.

_____   24.   When the last child leaves the home, the majority of parents have serious problems adjusting to their "empty nest."

_____   25.   The proportion of widowed persons is decreasing among the aged.

WHEN YOU HAVE FINISHED . . . RESEARCH PROJECT

Student Project 29: Definitions of Wisdom

For this project, you will need to locate two adults in each of the three broad age ranges of adulthood defined in the text: early adulthood, middle adulthood, and late adulthood.

Procedure

After obtaining suitable informed consent, following whatever procedure your instructor specifies, ask each subject the following four basic questions, with suitable probes:

1. What is your definition of wisdom? (If the individual gives you a very brief answer, or one you do not understand, probe by asking him or her to tell you more about it. If that still doesn't elicit anything useful, ask "How would a wise person behave that would be different from the way a non-wise person would act?")

2. Do you know people who are wise, according to your definition? How old are they? What gender? (Ask the subject to describe the wise individual(s), and say how they display their wisdom.)

3. Do you think that wisdom is something that only comes with old age, or can a young person or a middle-aged person be wise?

4. How do you think a person gets to be wise?

Analysis and Report

Compare the answers given by your six subjects in whatever way makes sense to you. Are there common themes in their definitions of wisdom, or in their ideas about origins of wisdom? What are the ages and genders of those named as wise?

If a number of students in your class complete this project, you can combine data, which will give you a cross-sectional comparison.

CHAPTER 17 ANSWER KEY

Practice Test #1 Variability in Late Adulthood

1. f   2. h   3. a   4. l   5. k   6. e   7. d   8. b

Practice Test #2 Physical Changes

1. b   2. d   3. c   4. a   5. d   6. b   7. c   8. a   9. b   10. d

Practice Test #3 Mental Health

1. T   2. F   3. T   4. T   5. F   6. T

Practice Test #4 Cognitive Changes

1.   recall; more difficult; important to memory functions
2.   retrospective memory; prospective memory tasks
3.   source memory
4.   speed
5.   Wisdom
6.   factual knowledge, procedural knowledge, understanding relevance of context, understanding relevance of values, recognition that it is impossible to know in advance how any decision will ultimately affect one's life
7.   wisdom-related knowledge
8.   reevaluation phase, liberation phase, summing-up phase, encore phase

Comprehensive Practice Test

Multiple Choice Questions

1. d   2. a   3. b   4. c   5. d   6. c   7. d   8. c   9. d   10. c
11. b   12. a   13. c   14. c   15. b

True-False Questions

1. F   2. T   3. T   4. F   5. F   6. T   7. T   8. T

Essay Questions

1.   ▪   Answers should include notion of "use it or lose it" as well as self-selection, social class, education, and physical health.

2.   ▪   Answers should include dendritic loss, arthritic changes in the joints, loss of elasticity in the muscles, changes in vision and hearing.

3.   ▪   Answers will vary, but should include a definition of wisdom and examples to support the answer.

Puzzle It Out

Across
4. Disability
6. Senescence
9. Antioxidants
11. Octogenarian

Down
1. Dementia
2. Satiety
3. Tinnitus
5. Gerontology
7. Centenarian
8. Neurofibrilary
10. Telomere

CHAPTER 18

SOCIAL AND PERSONALITY DEVELOPMENT IN LATE ADULTHOOD

BEFORE YOU READ . . . CHAPTER SUMMARY

Maintaining a sense of personal uniqueness can be especially challenging for older adults, who are often stereotyped by others as sick, disabled, or incompetent. Moreover, changes in social roles and relationships are just as important as the physical changes of late adulthood. Thus, late adulthood is perhaps the most socially and personally challenging period of life.

Theories of Social and Personality Development

- Erikson's ego integrity stage has been influential in studies of social and personality functioning in older adults; however, research does not support his view that ego integrity is essential to mental health in old age.
- Most older adults are not disengaged from the social world and seem to benefit from social involvement as much as those who are younger.

Individual Differences

- The successful aging paradigm emphasizes the degree of control individuals have over how they experience the aging process. Critics claim that emphasis on successful aging causes disabled elders to appear to be incompetent.
- Religious coping, defined both in social and psychological terms, appears to be important to health and well-being in late adulthood.

Social Relationships

- Many of the social roles evident at younger ages are discarded in late adulthood. Occupying a smaller number of social roles may provide elders with more opportunities for the expression of individuality.
- Most unmarried elders live alone, and the majority prefer this living arrangement.
- Older adults who are married exhibit high levels of relationship satisfaction. Many elderly spouses are primary caretakers for a spouse who is ill or disabled. The positive effects of marriage seem to be greater for men than for women, as is true at younger ages.
- Most older adults see their adult children regularly and enjoy satisfying relationships with them. Sibling relationships may be more positive than at younger ages.
- Contact with friends appears to be an important component of life satisfaction among the elderly.
- Women have larger social networks than men. Across ethnicities, African Americans have larger networks than members of other groups.

Career Issues in Late Life

- In most Western developed countries, adults retire in their early 60s. The timing of retirement is affected by an individual's health, economic circumstances, family responsibilities, and job satisfaction.
- Most of the elderly have adequate incomes, despite declines at retirement. Women and minorities are more likely to be poor in old age.

- Retirement is not stressful for most elders so long as the decision to retire is a voluntary one.
- Some elders choose not to retire and continue to be productive in their occupations. Research suggests that older adults can learn new job skills just as well as younger adults, although they do so at a slower pace.

AS YOU READ . . . LEARNING OBJECTIVES

After completing Chapter 18, you should be able to:

18.1   Describe Erikson's view of integrity.
18.2   Distinguish among other theories of late-life psychosocial functioning.
18.3   Identify the individual differences that impact successful aging.
18.4   Summarize the research on the use of religious coping in late adulthood.
18.5   Summarize the effects of the changes in roles in late adulthood.
18.6   Trace the pattern of the living arrangements of older adults.
18.7   Summarize the issues involved in deciding on nursing home care.
18.8   Describe partner relationships in late adulthood.
18.9   Summarize the research on elder abuse.
18.10   Describe the family relationships in late adulthood.
18.11   Assess the importance of friends in late adulthood.
18.12   Identify the gender and racial differences in social networks.
18.13   Identify the changes involved in the timing of retirement.
18.14   Examine the influences on a person's decision to retire.
18.15   Assess the effects of retirement.
18.16   Summarize the research on adults who choose not to retire.
18.17   Summarize the research on training older adults in the technological workplace.

AS YOU READ . . . TERM IDENTIFICATION

Aging in place (p. 495)
Activity theory (p. 488)
Amenity move (p. 508)
Compensatory (kinship) migration (p. 508)
Disengagement theory (p. 488)
Ego integrity (p. 487)
Ego integrity versus despair stage (p. 487)

Filial piety (p. 497)
Institutional migration (p. 508)
Religious coping (p. 492)
Reminiscence (p. 487)
Successful aging (p. 489)
Volunteerism (p.)491

AS YOU READ . . . GUIDED STUDY QUESTIONS

THEORIES OF SOCIAL AND PERSONALITY DEVELOPMENT

Erikson's Stage of Ego Integrity versus Despair (p. 487)

Objective 18.1: Describe Erikson's view of integrity.

1.   Define the following terms:
      a.   ego integrity versus despair stage (p. 487)

      b.   ego integrity (p. 487)

2.   Give examples of the behavior of an elder who has achieved ego integrity.

3.   Define reminiscence (p. 487), and describe how reminiscence is a healthy part of achieving ego integrity.

Other Theories of Late-Life Psychosocial functioning (pp. 487-488)

Objective 18.2: Distinguish among other theories of late-life psychosocial functioning.

4.   How does the Selective Optimization with Compensation theory relate to the elderly?

5.   Define the following terms, so as to distinguish between them:
        a.   activity theory (p. 488)

        b.   disengagement theory (p. 488)

6.   List the three aspects of the disengagement theory. Discuss the controversy involved with the third aspect.

AFTER YOU READ . . . PRACTICE TEST #1
THEORIES OF SOCIAL AND PERSONALITY DEVELOPMENT

Indicate whether each of the following statements is true or false.

_____ 1.   Ego integrity is the sense that one has lived a useful life.

_____ 2.   Adults become less reflective and somewhat less philosophical in orientation as they move through the late adulthood years.

_____ 3.   Young adults reminisce more often than middle-aged or older adults.

_____ 4.   According to the Baltes, as adults get older, they maintain high levels of performance by focusing on their weaknesses.

_____ 5.   More social involvement in late adulthood is linked to better outcomes, even among elders who suffer from disabilities.

_____ 6.   For most elders, some level of social involvement is both a sign—and probably a cause—of higher morale and lower levels of depression and other psychiatric symptoms.

(Check your answers to Practice Test #1 on p. 387.)

INDIVIDUAL DIFFERENCES

The Successful Aging Paradigm (pp. 490-492)

Objective 18.3: Identify the individual differences that impact successful aging.

7.   Define successful aging (p. 489).

8.   List and describe the five components of successful aging. Give examples of each.

Component	Description	Example

9.   What is the difference between a paradigm and a theory?

10.   List the factors that predict health and physical functioning across the lifespan.

11.   Give examples of aspects to staying healthy and able that most people never face until old age.

12.   How is cognitive functioning linked to education?

13.   Define and give examples of cognitive adventurousness.

14.   Give examples of why older adults giving support (not just receiving it) is important to successful aging.

15.   Define volunteerism (p. 491), and explain why it is beneficial to older adults.

16.   What is life satisfaction, and how it is related to a sense of control over one's life?

17.   Why is a person's perception of her own situation more important than objective measures of life satisfaction?

18.   List the criticisms of the successful aging paradigm.

Religious Coping (pp. 492-494)

Objective 18.4: Summarize the research on the use of religious coping in late adulthood.

19.   Define religious coping (p. 492).

20.   List the benefits of religious coping found among African Americans.

21.   What are the sex differences in religious coping?

22.   Give an example of the positive benefit of religious coping.

23.   List the benefits of attendance at religious services to the elderly.

24.   Describe the alternative explanations of religious coping.

AFTER YOU READ . . . PRACTICE TEST #2
INDIVIDUAL DIFFERENCES

Fill in the blank with the best answers.

1.   In recent years, one of the dominant themes in gerontology literature has been the concept of
        _____.

2.   The idea of successful aging is part of the overall trend in gerontology toward viewing old age in terms of
        _____ rather than _____.

3.   Life-long health habits contribute to successful aging, but _____
        _____also matter.

4.   In addition to education, the complexity of the _____ older adults are willing
        to take on influences their cognitive functioning.

5.   _____ is a willingness to learn new things, and is a component of successful
        aging.

6.   Social support contributes to successful aging because it provides opportunities for older adults to
        _____.

7.   _____, performing unpaid work for altruistic reasons, has been linked to successful
        aging.

8.   _____, or a sense of personal well-being, is also an important component
        of sucessful aging.

9.   What is critical to life satisfaction in almost all cases is an individual's _____ of her
        situation, which seems to be more important than objective measures.

10.   Psychologists use the term _____ to refer to the tendency to turn to religious beliefs and
        institutions in times of stress or trouble.

(Check your answers to Practice Test #2 on p. 387.)

SOCIAL RELATIONSHIPS

Social Roles (pp. 494-495)

Objective 18.5: Summarize the effects of the changes in roles in late adulthood.

25.   Describe the role changes in old age. How are some of them the result of ageism?

26.   Give examples of how the roles of the elderly contain far fewer duties or expectations.

27.   What is meant by license for eccentricity?

Living Arrangements (pp. 495-499)

Objective 18.6: Trace the pattern of the living arrangements of older adults.

28.   Define aging in place (p. 495).

29.   List and describe factors that influence an older adult's decision to live with an adult child.

Factor	*Description*

30.   List and describe four residential options for older adults.

Option	*Description*

31.   Define filial piety (p. 497), and give an example.

No Easy Answer: Deciding on Nursing Home Care (p. 498)

Objective 18.7: Summarize the issues involved in deciding on nursing home care.

32.   Give examples of the costs involved in nursing home care,

Partnership (pp. 499-501)

Objective 18.8: Describe partner relationships in late adulthood.

33.   Describe marital satisfaction in the late adult years.

34.   List the advantages of being married in late adulthood.

The Real World: Elder Abuse (p. 500)

Objective 18.9: Summarize the research on elder abuse.

35.   List the characteristics of a likely victim of abuse.

Family Relationships (pp. 502-503)

Objective 18.10: Describe the family relationships in late adulthood.

36.   Describe the contacts older adults have with adult children.

37.   Identify the effects of older adults' relationships with adult children.

38.   Describe the changes in the relationships of older adults with their grandchildren and with their siblings.

Friendships (pp. 502-503)

Objective 18.11: Assess the importance of friends in late adulthood.

39.   Why are friends important to older adults?

40.   What impact do friends have on the lives of the elderly?

Gender and Racial Differences in Social Networks (p. 503)

Objective 18.12: Identify the gender and racial differences in social networks.

41.   Compare the social networks of women and men in late adulthood.

42.   What is meant by the term "fictive kin"?

43.   Describe the racial differences in social networks of older adults.

AFTER YOU READ ... PRACTICE TEST #3
SOCIAL RELATIONSHIPS

1.   **What is a license of eccentricity?**
        a.   a loosening of role expectations that allows older adults to express their individuality.
        b.   a tendency in the United States to assume that all older adults are senile
        c.   the loss of driving privileges due to poorer vision and memory
        d.   the loss of ability to make strong cognitive associations

2.   **Making modifications to a non-institutional living environment to accommodate an older adult's needs is called _____.**
        a.   a continuing-care retirement community
        b.   an independent living community
        c.   an assisted living facility
        d.   aging in place

3. **Each of the following is a factor influencing an older adult's decision to live with an adult child EXCEPT:**
    a.   ethnicity
    b.   health
    c.   characteristics of the elder
    d.   income

4. **An apartment complex or housing development in which all the residents are over a certain age, typically 55 or 60, is called _____.**
    a.   an assisted living facility
    b.   an independent living community
    c.   a continuing-care retirement community
    d.   a skilled nursing facility

5. **Which of the following types of residential options provides the most flexibility and social continuity?**
    a.   a continuing-care retirement community
    b.   an assisted living facility
    c.   a skilled nursing facility
    d.   an independent living community

6. **Which of the following words best applies to long-term marriages in late adulthood?**
    a.   passionate
    b.   committed
    c.   intense
    d.   romantic

7. **Which of the following statements about elders' contact with adult children is TRUE?**
    a.   Most elders see their children out of a sense of obligation or duty.
    b.   Most older adults see their children as rarely as once a month or less.
    c.   Most older adults describe their relationship with their adult children in positive terms.
    d.   Most elders receive very little aid from their adult children.

8. **Each of the following statements about elders' friendships is TRUE EXCEPT:**
    a.   Friendships gain importance in their lives as elders age.
    b.   Contact with friends has a significant impact on overall life satisfaction.
    c.   Friends can provide the same sense of generational solidarity that siblings may provide.
    d.   The number of friendships increases dramatically after age 65.

(Check your answers to Practice Test # 3 on p. 387.)

CAREER ISSUES IN LATE LIFE

Timing of Retirement (p. 504)

Objective 18.13: Identify the changes involved in the timing of retirement.

44.   Describe the transition from work to retirement.

45.   Summarize how the age of retirement has changed in the United States in the last few decades.

Reasons for Retirement (pp. 504-505)

Objective 18.14: Examine the influences on a person's decision to retire.

46.   List six reasons for retirement, and describe how each may impact the decision to retire. Complete the following table:

Reason	Description

Effects of Retirement (pp. 506-509)

Objective 18.15: Assess the effects of retirement.

47.   How is income affected by retirement?

48.   Identify the factors that influence the poverty rates among the elderly.

49.   How does retirement affect the health and overall life satisfaction of older adults?

50.   What is the best predictor of life satisfaction in late adulthood?

51.   List the three types of moves that older adults make. Define each, and describe the elders who are likely to make that move. Complete the following table:

Type of Move	Definition	Likely Characteristics of the Elder
Amenity Move		
Compensatory (Kinship) Move		
Institutional Migration		

Choosing Not to Retire (pp. 509-510)

Objective 18.16: Summarize the research on adults who choose not to retire.

52.   List the two types of people who are likely to choose to continue working past the typical retirement age.

53.   Describe the two categories of men who are most likely not to retire.

54.   List the factors that predict learning success in older and younger adults.

55.   How are supervisors likely to rate older adults with respect to job functioning?

Development in the Information Age: Older Adults
in the Technological Workplace (p. 510)

Objective 18.17: Summarize the research on training older adults in the technological workplace.

56.   Compare the productivity of older workers with that of younger employees.

57.   Give examples of how technology training may be different for the young old and the old old.

AFTER YOU READ . . . PRACTICE TEST #4
CAREER ISSUES IN LATE LIFE

Indicate whether each of the following statements is true or false.

_____ 1.   The normal age of retirement is 65.

_____ 2.   Poor health lowers the average age of retirement by one to three years.

_____ 3.   Persons who are still supporting minor children retire earlier than do those in the post-parental stage.

_____ 4.   In general, working-class adults retire earlier than do middle-class and upper-class adults, often as a result of ill health and social norms.

_____ 5.   Extensive pre-retirement planning seems to be more important to men than women.

_____ 6.   Overall, retirement seem to have positive effects on the lives of older adults.

_____ 7.   Over the past several decades, poverty rates among the elderly have increased substantially.

_____ 8.   Those who respond least well to retirement are those who had the least control over the decision.

_____ 9.   Amenity moves usually occur early, kinship or compensatory migration is likely to occur in middle to late old age, and institutional migration clearly occurs late in life.

_____ 10.   Supervisors typically give older adults higher ratings than younger adults.

(Check your answers to Practice Test #4 on p. 387.)

AFTER YOU READ . . . CRITICAL REFLECTION EXERCISE

Elderly Adults

Utilizing information from the text, provide complete responses to the following issues. Whenever possible, cite specific information from the readings to support your responses.

1.   Think about where your life has gone.
    - Discuss three things that you think will lead to feelings of integrity for you as you age. Why will these lead to feelings of integrity? Is there anything you would do to change these things? If so, how?
    - Discuss three things that you think might interfere with your developing feelings of integrity as you age. Why will these interfere with developing feelings of integrity? Is there anything you would do to change these things? If so, how?

2.   Imagine that you have a six-year-old child. She is asking you questions about why Grandma cannot do the things that other adults can do. How would you answer her questions? Suggest at least three things you would tell her.

3.   You are working as a nurse and are approached by a family member of one of your patients. This person's father has just been diagnosed with Alzheimer's but he does not know anything about the disease. Describe the suspected brain changes that may lead to Alzheimer's. What advice would you give this person about what effect these cognitive deficits will have on his father? What advice would you give this man on what can be done to help the family adjust to these cognitive changes?

AFTER YOU READ . . . COMPREHENSIVE PRACTICE TEST
MULTIPLE-CHOICE QUESTIONS

1. **Reflecting on past experiences is called _____.**
   a. senility
   b. senescence
   c. reminiscence
   d. a waste of time

2. **Each of the following is part of the disengagement theory EXCEPT:**
   a. shrinkage of life space
   b. grandiose reminiscence
   c. increased individuality
   d. acceptance of old age changes

3. **Each of the following is one of the three components of successful aging EXCEPT:**
   a. retention of cognitive abilities
   b. good physical health
   c. continuing engagement in social and productive activities
   d. financial independence

4. **Psychologists use the term _____ to refer to the tendency to turn to religious beliefs and institutions in times of stress or trouble.**
   a. faith-based aid
   b. divine power
   c. religious coping
   d. religious involvement

5. **Which of the following statements about social roles is TRUE?**
   a. An older person's belief about his own competence does not impact his decisions about role transitions.
   b. Elderly adults are very unlikely to hold ageist stereotypes.
   c. Negative stereotypes of appearance are more often applied to men than to women.
   d. The older people look, the more negatively others stereotype them.

6. **The idea that children have a duty to care for their aging parents is known as _____.**
   a. aging in place
   b. filial piety
   c. assisted living
   d. an amenity move

7. **Marital satisfaction in late adulthood _____.**
   a. increases for elder women, but decreases for elder men
   b. tends to drop as health becomes problematic
   c. is higher than when children were still at home
   d. drops initially, but then plateaus

8. **Each of the following statements about family relationships is TRUE EXCEPT:**
    a. Most elders rarely see their adult children.
    b. Family relationships represent an important component of most elders' overall life satisfaction.
    c. Three-quarters of elders live within an hour's travel of at least one on their children.
    d. Most of the time, when older adults need help that cannot be provided by a spouse, it is provided by other family members, principally children.

9. **Contact with friends in older adulthood _____.**
    a. can decrease life satisfaction as the elders mourn the "good old days"
    b. can actually increase depression because these adults watch each other's health deteriorate
    c. is less important than contact with family in influencing life satisfaction
    d. has a positive impact on self-esteem and overall life satisfaction

10 **Each of the following statements about gender differences in social networks is TRUE EXCEPT:**
    a. Men's social networks are just as important to them and provide them with the same kinds of emotional support as women's networks do.
    b. Older men's networks tend to be smaller than those of older women.
    c. Older women's networks tend to be larger than those of older men.
    d. Women and men in late adulthood appear to form different kinds of social networks, with men's friendships involving less disclosure and less intimacy than women's.

11. **Which of the following phrases accurately portrays the transition from work to retirement?**
    a. Most elders demonstrate a remarkable capacity for adaptation.
    b. It is the beginning of the long downward slide into death.
    c. Women make this transition with much less difficulty than men.
    d. The age of the retiree impacts how positive the transition is.

12. **What is happening to the retirement age of individuals?**
    a. The age is declining in most countries.
    b. The age is increasing slowly in most countries.
    c. The age is dropping slowly in the United States, but increasing slowly in others.
    d. The age is dropping rapidly for men, but increasing slowly for women in the United States.

13. **What is the most significant factor determining when a woman will retire?**
    a. her health
    b. when her husband retires
    c. the characteristics of the job
    d. the lucrativeness of the retirement package

14. **What effect does retirement have on health?**
    a. It has a strong positive effect.
    b. It has a slight negative effect on blood pressure and heart rate.
    c. It has no negative effects on health.
    d. It depends on gender and physical condition at the time of retirement.

15. **Which of the following persons is most likely to continue working past the typical retirement age?**
    a. a man who is highly educated and healthy
    b. a woman who is highly educated and healthy
    c. a man who is in poor health
    d. a woman with a limited education and poor retirement benefits

TRUE-FALSE QUESTIONS

Indicate whether each of the following statements is true or false.

_____ 1.   To achieve ego integrity, the elder must come to terms with who she is and has been, how her life has been lived, the choices that she made, the opportunities gained and lost.

_____ 2.   The perspective typically referred to as disengagement theory, argues that the psychologically and physically healthiest response to old age is to maintain the greatest possible activity and involvement in the greatest possible number of roles.

_____ 3.   Volunteerism, performing unpaid work for altruistic reasons, has been linked to successful aging.

_____ 4.   Men make more use of religious coping than women.

_____ 5.   Older adults are actually more likely than younger adults to be prejudiced against their elderly peers.

_____ 6.   In late adulthood, contact between grandchildren and grandparents declines as the grandchildren become adults themselves.

_____ 7.   Persons who like their work and are highly committed to it, retire earlier than do those who are less gratified by their work.

_____ 8.   What predicts life satisfaction in late adulthood is not whether a person has retired but whether he was satisfied with life in earlier adulthood.

ESSAY QUESTIONS

1.   According to Erikson, what must a person do throughout adulthood to increase the likelihood that she or he is in the ego integrity rather than despair in late adulthood?

2.   Discuss the five components of success aging, and give examples of each.

3.   Discuss the advantages that married older adults have over unmarried elders.

(Check your answers to the Comprehensive Practice Test on pp. 387-388.)

WHEN YOU HAVE FINISHED . . . PUZZLE IT OUT

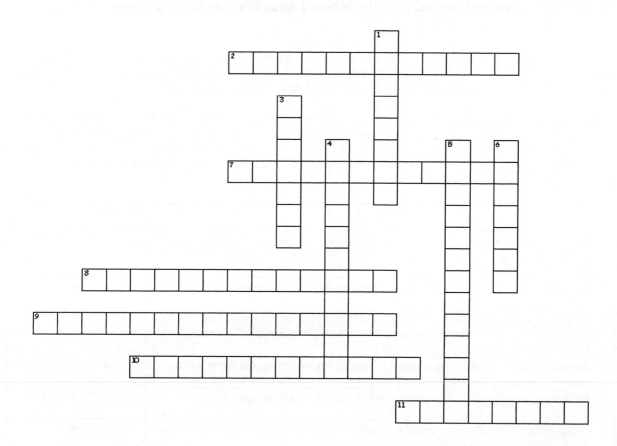

Across
2. Reflecting on past experiences
7. Performing unpaid work for altruistic reasons
8. Migration of older adults to a nursing home
9. Cognitive willingness to learn new things
10. Migration of older adults to a location near family and friends
11. Theory that it is normal and healthy for older adults to try to remain active

Down
1. Living facility for older adults who need help with one or two ADLs
3. Nursing facility for older adults who require help with three or four ADLs
4. Living community in which all residents are over a certain age
5. Theory that it is normal and healthy for older adults to scale down their social lives
6. Move in late life away from kin to a location that has some desirable feature

Created by Puzzlemaker at DiscoverySchool.com

(Check your answers on p. 388.)

WHEN YOU HAVE FINISHED ... INVESTIGATIVE PROJECT

Student Project 30: Visiting and Assessing a Nursing Home

Procedure

In this visit imagine that you are looking for a suitable nursing home for your aged parent, and you are evaluating several such institutions. You should spend at least an hour in each institution, preferably at a meal time or activity time. You will also want to obtain brochures or other literature available about each institution.

During your visit, take notes if you wish and chat with those you may fall into conversation with (although you should not harass the staff). At the end of your visit, rate the nursing home on each of the following 10 scales, where 5 always indicates "optimum" or "ideal" and a rating of 1 always means "unacceptable." If you find you simply do not have the information you need for any scale, you may choose NA (not available), but try not to do that.

Rating Scales	Circle One Number
1. *Achievement fostering*: To what extent does the environment provide opportunities for and encouragement to residents to engage in goal-directed activities, or reward them for doing so?	1 2 3 4 5 NA
2. *Individualism*: To what extent are individuals encouraged to express individuality, and are treated as unique?	1 2 3 4 5 NA
3. *Dependency fostering*: To what extent are residents "coddled" in ways that discourage or prevent development of self-sufficiency or autonomy? (A rating of 5 in this case means that this was not done.)	1 2 3 4 5 NA
4. *Warmth*: Did the staff express warmth toward the residents, and did the residents express it toward each other?	1 2 3 4 5 NA
5. *Affiliation fostering*: To what extent is social interaction encouraged, or is occurring naturally in the environment?	1 2 3 4 5 NA
6. *Recognition*: To what extent does the institution recognize, respond to, and reward the activities and accomplishments of the residents?	1 2 3 4 5 NA
7. *Stimulation*: How much variety of sights, sounds, and activities is there?	1 2 3 4 5 NA
8. *Physical attractiveness*: How aesthetically appealing is the physical setting?	1 2 3 4 5 NA
9. *Cue richness*: How clear and varied are the cues for orientation, such as signs, distinctive colors, odors, textures, sounds, and clutter?	1 2 3 4 5 NA
10. *Health care adequacy*: Is the institution equipped and well-staffed to provide physical exams, physical therapy, and nursing care?	1 2 3 4 5 NA

Analysis and Report

In preparing your report, think about how confident you feel that you could make a decision about each individual nursing home based on your brief visit. What additional information would you need or like to have to do a better job of evaluating this or any other nursing home? Are there other items you would add to the checklist? Do some of the items seem more important than others? Why? If you really were making such a choice for your parent, would you use a checklist like this, or do you think you would use some other process? Consider, also, whether your own attitudes and biases about nursing home care have been altered or strengthened by this visit. Were you impressed or depressed, if either? By what?

CHAPTER 18 ANSWER KEY

Practice Test #1 Theories of Social and Personality Development
1. T   2. F   3. T   4. F   5. T   6. T

Practice Test #2 Individual Differences
1. successful aging
2. variability; universal decline
3. individuals' responses to the health crisis of old age
4. cognitive challenges
5. Cognitive adventurousness
6. give support as well as receive it
7. Volunteerism
8. Life satisfaction
9. perception
10. religious coping

Practice Test #3 Social Relationships
1. a   2. d   3. c   4. b   5. a   6. b   7. c   8. d

Practice Test #4 Career Issues in Late Life
1. F   2. T   3. F   4. T   5. T   6. T   7. F   8. T   9. T   10. T

Comprehensive Practice Test
Multiple Choice Questions
1. c   2. b   3. d   4. c   5. d   6. b   7. c   8. a   9. d   10. b
11. a   12. a   13. b   14. c   15. a

True-False Questions
1. T   2. F   3. T   4. F   5. T   6. T   7. F   8. T

Essay Questions
1. - Achieve Identity rather than Role Confusion
    - Achieve Intimacy rather than Isolation
    - Achieve Generativity rather than Stagnation

2. - Good physical health: Factors such as diet, exercise, avoidance of tobacco, etc. predict health and physical functioning across the lifespan.
    - Retaining cognitive abilities: The degree to which elders maintain cognitive abilities seems to be linked to education—those who are best educated show the least cognitive decline. Additionally, the complexity of cognitive challenges older adults are willing to take on also influences their cognitive functioning.
    - Social engagement: Social connectedness and participation in productive activities are clearly important to successful aging, but social support does not mean dependence on other. Helping other contributes to one's own health and sense of well-being.
    - Productivity: Contributing to a social network, such as volunteering, may be one important way of remaining productive. Some older adults remain productive by venturing into new pursuits, such as learning new hobby.
    - Life satisfaction: A sense of personal well-being is an important component of successful aging. Factors include a sense of control, the individual's perception of her or his situation, and social comparisons.

3.   ▪   Higher life satisfaction
      ▪   Better health
      ▪   Lower rates of institutionalization

Puzzle It Out

Across

2. Reminiscence
7. Volunteerism
8. Institutional
9. Adventurousness
10. Compensatory
11. Activity

Down

1. Assisted
3. Skilled
4. Independent
5. Disengagement
6. Amenity

POLICY QUESTION V

HOW SHOULD STEM CELL RESEARCH BE FUNDED AND REGULATED?

Learning Objective: Summarize the issues about how stem cell research should be funded and regulated (pp. 512-513).

1.   What are stem cells, and why are they important to researchers and policymakers?

2.   Distinguish among the following types of stem cells:

Type	Source	Potential Use
Totipotent		
Pluripotent		
Multipotent		

3.   List the reasons why stem cell research is controversial.

4.   What are the obstacles to using stem cells to cure diseases?

5.   Summarize the policies about stem cell research of the United States and other industrialized nations?

	United States	Other Industrialized Nations
Emphasis		
Regulation		
Priority		

6.   Which approach do you think is best? Finding the answers to these questions may help you decide.
   a.   How do organizations for (e.g., the American Medical Association) and against (e.g., U.S. Conference of Catholic Bishops) embryonic stem cell research explain and support their positions?

   b.   What do the Democratic Party and Republican Party platforms say about the issue? (go to http://www.democrats.org/pdfs/2004platform.pdf and http://www.gopconvention.com/platform/2004platform.pdf to find out.)

   c.   How do scientists grow stem cells in the laboratory?

   d.   What are the top five diseases that scientists currently believe are most likely to be helped through stem cell research?

   e.   Other than the treatment of diseases, what implications might there be for stem cell research?

CHAPTER 19

DEATH, DYING, AND BEREAVEMENT

BEFORE YOU READ . . . CHAPTER SUMMARY

For most people, death happens in late adulthood. However, many younger individuals contract fatal diseases or may die in accidents. Thus, like most developmental events, the timing and mode of a particular individual's death affect its meaning and its effects on others.

The Experience of Death
- Medical personnel distinguish between clinical death, brain death, and social death.
- In the industrialized world, death most often occurs in hospitals. For the terminally ill, hospice workers and facilities provide an alternative form of care.

The Meaning of Death across the Lifespan
- By age six or seven, most children understand that death is permanent. Teens sometimes have distorted ideas about death, especially their own mortality.
- Many young adults see themselves as invulnerable to death. For middle-aged adults, the death of a loved one, often a parent, signals a change in social roles.
- Among the middle-aged, fear of death is common. Older adults fear death less, especially those who are very religious.
- Preparation for death may include practical activities such as writing a will. Many dying adults also prepare by sharing life experiences with younger family members. Some dying adults exhibit dramatic changes in cognitive and personality functioning just prior to death, a phenomenon often called terminal drop.

The Process of Dying
- Kübler-Ross's five stages of dying (denial, anger, bargaining, depression, and acceptance) have been widely studied. Research suggests that not all dying individuals go through these stages.
- Critics of Kübler-Ross suggest that her stages may be culture-specific and that the process of adjusting to impending death does not occur in stages.
- Attitudes appear to affect a terminally ill individual's longevity. Those who have a "fighting spirit" survive longer than do peers who are resigned to the inevitability of death.

The Experience of Grieving
- Funerals and other rituals redefine the roles of the bereaved, bring families together, and give meaning to the lives of both the deceased and the bereaved.
- Grief responses depend on the age and mode of death of the deceased as well as characteristics of the bereaved.
- Losing a spouse appears to bring about the most intense grief response. The health of widows and widowers declines in the first year following spousal loss. The effects appear to be greater among widowers than widows.

Theoretical Perspectives on Grieving
- Psychoanalytic theory emphasizes the traumatic nature of grief and the defense mechanisms that often accompany the experience.

- Attachment theories suggest that grieving involves a series of stages across which the bereaved adjust to life without the deceased.
- Alternative approaches emphasize the individual nature of grieving, claiming that the experience is poorly explained by general theories.

AS YOU READ . . . LEARNING OBJECTIVES

After completing Chapter 19, you should be able to:

19.1   Define the three aspects of death.
19.2   Compare death in hospitals with death in hospices.
19.3   Describe children's and adolescents' understanding of death.
19.4   Describe the meaning of death for adults.
19.5   Discuss the issues involving fear of death.
19.6   Describe people's preparations for death.
19.7   Summarize the research on dying persons saying goodbye to their family and friends.
19.8   List Kübler-Ross's stages of dying.
19.9   Summarize the criticisms and alternative views of Kübler-Ross's research.
19.10   Discuss the issues impacting the responses to impending death.
19.11   Identify some of the psychological functions of death rituals.
19.12   Discuss the issues involved in the process of grieving.
19.13   Summarize the issues surrounding "copycat" suicide.
19.14   Discuss the issues surrounding widowhood.
19.15   Explain the issues involved when an infant dies.
19.16   Describe how Freud's psychoanalytical theory explains grieving.
19.17   Describe how Bowlby's attachment theory explains grieving.
19.18   Summarize the alternative perspectives on grieving.

AS YOU READ . . . TERM IDENTIFICATION

Brain death (p. 516)	Hospice care (p. 516)	Social death (p. 516)
Clinical death (p. 516)	Palliative care (p. 517)	Thanatology (p. 527)
Grieving (p. 530)	Pathological grief (p. 535)	Unique invulnerability (p. 520)

AS YOU READ . . . GUIDED STUDY QUESTIONS

THE EXPERIENCE OF DEATH

Death Itself (p. 516)

Objective 19.1: Define the three aspects of death.

1.   Define the following terms:
        a.   clinical death (p. 516)

        b.   brain death (p. 516)

        c.   social death (p. 516)

Where Death Occurs (pp. 516-518)

Objective 19.2: Compare death in hospitals with death in hospices.

2.   In the United States, where do the great majority of adults die?

3.   Define the following terms:
       a.   hospice care (p. 516)

       b.   palliative care (p. 517)

4.   List and describe the five aspects of the philosophy of the hospice care movement.

Aspect	Description

5.   List and describe the three general types of hospice care.

Type	Description

AFTER YOU READ . . . PRACTICE TEST #1
THE EXPERIENCE OF DEATH

Match the letter of the term in the right column with its description in the left column.

_____ 1.	A form of care for the terminally ill that focuses on relieving patients' pain rather than curing their diseases.	a. Brain death
_____ 2.	A period during which vital signs are absent but resuscitation is still possible.	b. Clinical death
_____ 3.	Hospice program where a small number of patients in the last stages of a terminal disease are cared for in a homelike setting.	c. Home-based
_____ 4.	The point at which family members and medical personnel treat the deceased person as a corpse.	d. Hospital-based
_____ 5.	Hospice program in which one family caregiver provides constant care for the dying person with the support and assistance of specially trained staff who visit regularly.	e. Palliative care

a. Brain death
b. Clinical death
c. Home-based
d. Hospital-based
e. Palliative care
f. Social death
g. Special hospice center

(Check your answers to Practice Test #1 on p. 409.)

THE MEANING OF DEATH ACROSS THE LIFESPAN

Children's and Adolescents' Understanding of Death (pp. 519-520)

Objective 19.3: Describe children's and adolescents' understanding of death.

6. Compare the understanding of death for each of the following age groups.

Age Group	Understanding of Death
Preschool-Aged Children	
School-Aged Children	

7. How do unrealistic beliefs about personal death contribute to adolescent suicide?

The Meaning of Death for Adults (pp. 520-521)

Objective 19.4: Describe the meaning of death for adults.

8. Define unique invulnerability (p. 520), and give examples of how it influences young adults.

9. Explain how the deaths of relatively young celebrities provide insight into young adults' ideas about death.

10. How does death change the roles and relationships within a family?

11.   Give examples of how the prospect of death shapes one's view of time.

12.   What is the most pervasive meaning of death for adults of all ages?

13.   How does the potential loss that is feared or dreaded the most change with age?

Age Group	Greatest Fear or Dread
Young Adults	
Older Adults	

Fear of Death (pp. 521-523)

Objective 19.5: Discuss the issues involving fear of death.

14.   Give examples to explain why middle-aged adults are the most fearful of death.

15.   The elderly think and talk more about death than do other age groups. How does this help them overcome their fear and anxiety of death?

16.   How do religious beliefs affect a person's fear of death?

17.   How are feelings about death linked to one's sense of personal worth?

Preparation for Death (pp. 523-525)

Objective 19.6: Describe people's preparations for death.

18.   Describe how people prepare for death at a practical level.

19.   Describe the psychological changes associated with terminal drop.

No Easy Answers: Saying Goodbye (p. 524)

Objective 19.7: Summarize the research on dying persons saying goodbye to their family and friends.

20.   Why is it important for dying persons to say goodbye to family and friends?

AFTER YOU READ . . . PRACTICE TEST #2
THE MEANING OF DEATH ACROSS THE LIFESPAN

Fill in the blanks with the best answers.

1. Preschool children typically believe that _____,
    that _____, and that at least some people
    _____.

2. By the time they start school, most children seem to understand both the _____ and the
    _____ of death.

3. Like those of children, adolescents' ideas about death are affected by their _____.

4. Young adults have a sense of _____, a belief that bad things, including death,
    happen to others but not to themselves.

5. In middle and late adulthood, a death changes the _____ and _____
    of everyone else in a family.

6. At an individual level in middle and late adulthood, most people exhibit a shift in thinking about time,
    thinking less about "_____" and being more aware of "_____."

7. Although you might think that those closest to death would fear it the most, research suggests that
    _____ are most fearful of death.

8. Religious beliefs may moderate fears of death because religious people tend to view death as _____
    _____.

9. Adults who have _____, who have
    _____, and who have
    _____ are able to face death with
    greater equanimity.

10. According to most people, in addition to purchasing life insurance and making a will, such preparations
    should include directives regarding end-of-life care, often called a _____.

(Check your answers to Practice Test #2 on p. 409.)

THE PROCESS OF DYING

Kübler-Ross's Stages of Dying (pp. 525-526)

Objective 19.8: List Kübler-Ross's stages of dying.

21.   List, in order, the five stages of grief proposed by Kübler-Ross, and give examples of each. Complete the following table:

Stage	*Example*

Criticisms and Alternative Views (pp. 526-528)

Objective 19.9: Summarize the criticisms and alternative views of Kübler-Ross's research.

22.   Summarize the methodological problems of Kübler-Ross's research.

23.   Give examples of how Kübler-Ross's research may not incorporate culture-specific behaviors.

24.   Of the five stages in Kübler-Ross's model, which one seems to be common among Western patients?

25.   Define thanatology (p. 527).

26.   List the themes involved in the dying process that were suggested by Shneidman.

27.   List the four tasks for the dying person that were suggested by Corr.

Responses to Impending Death (pp. 528-530)

Objective 19.10: Discuss the issues impacting the responses to impending death.

28.   List and describe the five types of responses to impending death, according to Greer.

Type	Description

29.   What were the findings of Greer's research about the relationship between the patient's survival rate and the five groups of responses to impending death?

30.   List two cautions that relate to Greer's findings.

31.   How does social support relate to an individual's response to imminent death?

AFTER YOU READ . . . PRACTICE TEST #3
THE PROCESS OF DYING

Indicate whether each of the following statements is true or false.

_____ 1.   Kübler-Ross's model predicts that most people who are confronted with a terminal diagnosis react with some form of denial.

_____ 2.   The anger a dying person expresses seems to be a response not only to the diagnosis itself but also to the sense of loss of control and helplessness that many patients feel in impersonal medial settings.

_____ 3.   Cross-cultural studies suggest that cultures vary very little in what they believe to be a "good death."

_____ 4.   Of the five stages of Kübler-Ross's model, only anger seems to be common among Western patients.

_____ 5.   According to Charles Corr, coping with dying is like coping with any other problem or dilemma: you need to take care of certain specific tasks.

_____ 6.   According to Greer's research results, psychological responses contribute to disease progress.

_____ 7.   Terminally ill patients with positive and supportive relationships describe lower levels of pain and less depression during their final months of illness.

(Check your answers to Practice Test #3 on p. 409.)

THE EXPERIENCE OF GRIEVING

Psychosocial Functions of Death Rituals (pp. 530-531)

Objective 19.11: Identify some of the psychological functions of death rituals.

32.   Define grieving (p. 530).

33.   Give examples of how each of the following psychological functions that funerals, wakes, and other death rituals serve in helping family members cope with grief:

Function	Example
Specific set of roles to play	
Bring family members together	
Understand the meaning of death	
Transcendent meaning to death	

The Process of Grieving (pp. 531-533)

Objective 19.12: Discuss the issues involved in the process of grieving.

34   How do each of the following age groups express their feelings of grief?

Age Group	Expression of Grief
Children	
Adolescents	

35.   Give examples of how the mode of death impacts the grief process.

Mode of Death	Example of Impact
Death of a spouse after a period of illness	
Death that has an intrinsic meaning	
Sudden and violent death	
Death in a natural disaster	
Death in a "politically motivated" mass murder	
Death by suicide	

Development in the Information Age: "Copycat" Suicides (p. 532)

Objective 19.13: Summarize the issues surrounding "copycat" suicide.

36.   What is meant by the term "copycat" suicide? Give examples of how fictional or journalistic accounts of suicide can influence an individual.

Widowhood (pp. 533-536)

Objective 19.14: Discuss the issues surrounding widowhood.

37.   Describe the long-term and short-term effects on the immune system of the experience of widowhood.

38.   List several factors that contribute to the variability of how long the effects of bereavement last.

39.   Define pathological grief (p. 535), and explain why some psychologists believe it should be thought of as a separate disorder from depression.

40.   Give examples to explain why the death of a spouse appears to be a more negative experience for men than for women.

41.   How can support groups help a person manage their grief?

The Real World: When an Infant Dies (p. 534)

Objective 19.15: Explain the issues involved when an infant dies.

42.   How might the grief of parents be different when an older child dies than when an infant dies?

43.   List the guidelines that can be useful to family members or friends in supporting parents who have lost an infant.

AFTER YOU READ . . . PRACTICE TEST #4
THE EXPERIENCE OF GRIEVING

Indicate whether each of the following statements is true or false.

_____ 1.   In virtually every culture, the immediate response to a death is some kind of funeral ritual.

_____ 2.   Funerals, wakes, and other death rituals help family members and friends manage their grief by giving them a specific set of roles to play.

_____ 3.   Death rituals typically weaken family ties.

_____ 4.   Teenagers may be more likely than adults to experience grief responses to the deaths of celebrities or to idealize peers' suicides.

_____ 5.   In general, family and close friends of someone who commits suicide experience feelings of rejection and anger.

_____ 6.   The experience of widowhood appears to have both immediate and longer-term effects on the immune system.

_____ 7.   Older adults who enter widowhood with a history of depression are less likely to experience depression after the death of their spouse.

_____ 8.   Many aspects of grief are culturally determined.

_____ 9.   Depression and suicidal thoughts are more common among widows than in widowers.

_____ 10.   In the long run, illness and depression among bereaved workers who return to their jobs too soon may be more costly to employers than providing additional time off.

(Check your answers to Practice Test #4 on p. 409.)

THEORETICAL PERSPECTIVES ON GRIEVING

Freud's Psychoanalytic Theory (pp. 536-537)

Objective 19.16: Describe how Freud's psychoanalytical theory explains grieving.

44.   Explain why Freud believed that defense mechanisms were only temporary devices for dealing with negative emotions.

45.   Give examples of how each of the following defense mechanisms could be used in grief therapy.

Defense Mechanism	Example
Sublimation	
Identification	

Bowlby's Attachment Theory (pp. 537-538)

Objective 19.17: Describe how Bowlby's attachment theory explains grieving.

46.   According to John Bowlby, how is attachment to the loved one related to the experience of grief?

47.   List and describe Bowlby's and Sanders's stages of grief by completing the following table:

Stage	Bowlby's Label	Sanders's Label	Description
1			
2			
3			
4			

Alternative Perspective (pp. 538-540)

Objective 19.18: Summarize the alternative perspectives on grieving.

48. List two reasons that revisionist views of grieving give a rather different picture from that of either Freud or of the attachment theorists.

49. Describe a compromise model that predicts the likely trajectory of the key themes in the grieving process.

50. List two ways in which Wortman and Silver dispute the traditional view of grieving expressed in Freud's and Bowlby's theories.

51. Describe the following patterns of grieving by completing the following table:

Pattern	Description
Normal	
Chronic	
Delayed	
Absent	

52. Summarize the results of Wortman's and Silver's research.

53. Explain how the loss of a loved one can also lead to growth.

AFTER YOU READ . . . PRACTICE TEST #5
THEORETICAL PERSPECTIVES ON GRIEVING

Indicate whether each of the following statements is true or false.

_____ 1. From the psychoanalytic perspective, the death of a loved one is an emotional trauma.

_____ 2. Psychoanalytically based grief therapy for children often emphasizes the use of regression and displacement to cope with grief.

_____ 3. According to Bowlby, the stronger the attachment between a mourner and a lost loved one, the deeper and more prolonged the grief response.

_____ 4. According to Catherine Sanders, the first stage of grief is characterized by depression and despair.

_____ 5. A compromise model suggests that each of the key themes in the grieving process may have a likely trajectory.

_____ 6. According to Wortman and Silver, high levels of distress are neither an inevitable nor a necessary aspect of the grieving process.

(Check your answers to Practice Test #5 on p. 409.)

AFTER YOU READ . . . CRITICAL REFLECTION EXERCISES

Death of a Loved One

Utilizing information from the text, provide complete answers to the following questions:

1.   What do you think would be the best way to describe a grandparent's death to a four- year-old? Why would you describe it this way?

2.   How does our society appear to approach the reality of death? Do you agree with this approach? Why or why not?

3.   Why is mourning an important part of the grieving process? Briefly discuss at least three reasons that it is important.

Imminent Death

Imagine that you have just discovered that you have four months to live. Consider how you would address each of the following issues knowing that the four months will be pain free and you will not be debilitated.

1.   Describe what you think your initial reactions might be. Why do you think you would react this way?

2.   What are the five things you would do with your remaining time? Why did you pick each of these?

3.   Using Erikson's theory of human development as a model, write a eulogy of your life. What would you most like people to remember about you and the life that you have lived?

AFTER YOU READ . . . COMPREHENSIVE PRACTICE TEST
MULTIPLE-CHOICE QUESTIONS

1. **Which of the following accurately describes clinical death?**
   a. The person can still breathe, but she is in a vegetative state.
   b. There is no evident brain functioning.
   c. The heart can still beat.
   d. There is no activity in the brain.

2. **In comparing hospital care to hospice care, _____.**
   a. no major differences in length of survival, or reports of pain were found
   b. it was discovered that hospital care was rated as significantly more satisfying by the dying patients
   c. hospital care was associated with increased length of survival of chronic patients
   d. significant differences in perceptions of quality of care were found

3. **When will a child most likely first be able to understand the permanence of death?**
   a. age 2
   b. age 4
   c. age 6
   d. age 10

4. **The belief that bad things, including death, only happen to others is called _____.**
   a. unique invulnerability
   b. a flashback
   c. denial
   d. sublimation

5. **Older adults _____**
   a. look forward to death
   b. fear death significantly
   c. fear the process of dying more than death itself
   d. do not contemplate death

6. **Which of the following is one of the ways a person prepares for death at a practical level?**
   a. inventing a personal fable
   b. becoming a nicer person
   c. reminiscences
   d. making out a will

7. **Which stage, according to Kübler-Ross, is a necessary preparation for the final stage?**
   a. denial
   b. bargaining
   c. depression
   d. acceptance

8. **What is the study of dying called?**
   a. bereavement
   b. euthanasia
   c. thanatology
   d. life transition analysis

9. **Which of the following individuals fit Greer's label of stoic acceptance in response to a diagnosis of terminal cancer?**
   a.   A person who is devoid of hope.
   b.   A person who denies the diagnosis.
   c.   A person who responds with anxiety.
   d.   A person who ignores the diagnosis.

10. **Each of the following is a psychological function of death rituals EXCEPT:**
    a.   bringing family members together
    b.   helping the survivors understand the meaning of death itself
    c.   showing others how much the survivors loved the person who died
    d.   giving some transcendent meaning to death

11. **Which of the following modes of death would be most likely to cause intense grief responses?**
    a.   a soldier who died heroically in the line of duty
    b.   a spouse whose death brought an end to his long-term suffering
    c.   an elderly person who died of natural causes
    d.   a person who died a sudden and violent death

12. **Symptoms of depression brought on by death of a loved one are called _____.**
    a.   philosophical grief
    b.   psychosomatic grief
    c.   psychological grief
    d.   pathological grief

13. **A defense mechanism in which children are encouraged to express their feelings through art is called _____.**
    a.   identification
    b.   sublimation
    c.   denial
    d.   creativity

14. **Which of the following is the correct order of Bowlby's stages of grief?**
    a.   numbness, yearning, disorganization and despair, reorganization
    b.   yearning, awareness, healing/renewal, numbness
    c.   shock, awareness disorganization and despair, yearning
    d.   healing/renewal, reorganization, conservation/withdrawal, shock

15. **Revisionist theories of grieving suggest that _____.**
    a.   grieving occurs in a series of distinct stages
    b.   grieving and mourning are actually the same thing
    c.   grieving displays significant gender-differences
    d.   there may be common themes in grieving, but there are no set patterns

TRUE-FALSE QUESTIONS

Indicate whether each of the following statements is true or false.

_____ 1. Brain death occurs when the deceased person is treated like a corpse by others.

_____ 2. The most pervasive meaning of death for adults of all ages is loss.

_____ 3. Feelings about death are linked to one's sense of personal worth or competence.

_____ 4. According to Kübler-Ross, in order to reach the anger stage of grief, the dying person must grieve for all that will be lost with death.

_____ 5. According to Greer's research, persons with a fighting spirit act overwhelmed by the diagnosis and see themselves as dying or gravely ill and as devoid of hope.

_____ 6. Grieving is the emotional response to a death, and it may take months or years to complete.

_____ 7. Although the behavioral aspects of adolescents' grief responses vary little from those of adults, teens may be more likely to experience prolonged grief than children or adults.

_____ 8. According to Wortman and Silver, the normal pattern of grief is one in which the person feels no notable level of distress either immediately or at any later time.

ESSAY QUESTIONS

1. Discuss the pros and cons of hospice care for someone with a terminal illness.

2. According to Piaget, children in the preoperational stage are egocentric, which may limit their ability to reason. Give examples of how egocentrism may be related to children's lack of understanding of death.

3. Give examples of how unique invulnerability may influence teenagers' understanding of death.

(Check your answers to the Comprehensive Practice Test on p. 409.)

WHEN YOU HAVE FINISHED . . . PUZZLE IT OUT

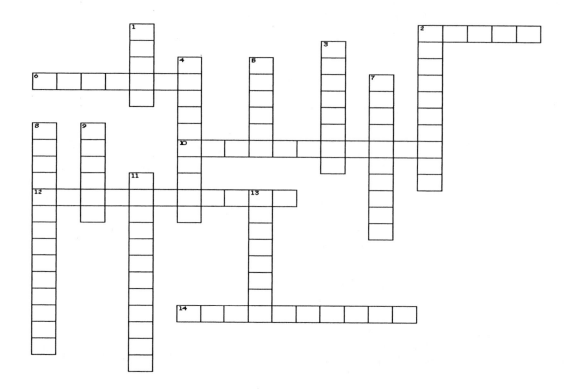

Across

2. Stage two in Kübler-Ross's model
6. Care for the dying that emphasizes individual and family control of the process
10. Defense mechanism used to help children express their feelings through art
12. The scientific study of death and dying
14. Stage three in Kübler-Ross's model

Down

1. Aspect of death when resuscitation is no longer possible
2. Stage five in Kübler-Ross's model
3. Aspect of death that refers to the period during which vital signs are absent, but resuscitation is still possible
4. Stage four in Kübler-Ross's model
5. Aspect of death when the person is treated like a corpse by others

7. Care that emphasizes controlling pain and maximizing comfort
8. Defense mechanism used to help children manage grief by watching popular films depicting grief
9. Stage one in Kübler-Ross's model
11. Grief with symptoms of depression brought on by death of a loved one
13. The emotional response to a death

Created by Puzzlemaker at DiscoverySchool.com

Check your answers on p. 410.)

CHAPTER 19 ANSWER KEY

Practice Test #1 The Experience of Death

1. e   2. b   3. g   4. f   5. c

Practice Test #2 The meaning of Death Across the Lifespan

1.   death can be reversed; dead people can still feel or breathe; can avoid death
2.   permanence; universality
3.   personal experiences
4.   unique invulnerability
5.   roles; relationships
6.   time since birth; time till death
7.   middle-aged adults
8.   a transition from one form of life to another, from physical life to some kind of immortality
9.   successfully completed the major tasks of adult life; adequately fulfilled the demands of the roles they occupied; developed inwardly
10.   living will

Practice Test #3 The Process of Dying

1. T   2. T   3. F   4. F   5. T   6. T   7. T

Practice Test #4 The Experience of Grieving

1. T   2. T   3. F   4. T   5. T   6. T   7. F   8. T   9. F   10. T

Practice Test #5 Theoretical Perspectives on Grieving

1. T   2. F   3. T   4. F   5. T   6. T

Comprehensive Practice Test

Multiple Choice Questions

1. b   2. a   3. c   4. a   5. c   6. d   7. b   8. c   9. d   10. c
11. d   12. d   13. b   14. a   15. d

True-False Questions

1. F   2. T   3. T   4. F   5. F   6. T   7. T   8. F

Essay Questions

1.
   - Pro: Provides preparation for death; includes the family in the patient's care; control over care is in the hands of the patient and the family; medical care is palliative rather than curative; economic costs are reduced; includes grief support for caregivers.
   - Con: No effort to prolong life; possible sense of burden on caregivers; some care may be too complex to be handled; hospital staff may be better able to provide pain relief.

2.
   - Answers will vary, but should include an understanding of egocentrism and that children believe death can be reversed, that dead people can still feel or breathe, and that some people can avoid death.

3.
   - Answers will vary, but should include an understanding of unique invulnerability (a belief that bad things, including death, happen to others but not to themselves).

Puzzle It Out

Across

2. Anger
6. Hospice
10. Sublimation
12. Thanatology
14. Bargaining

Down

1. Brain
2. Acceptance
3. Clinical
4. Depression
5. Social
7. Palliative
8. Identification
9. Denial
11. Pathological
13. Grieving

POLICY QUESTION VI

DO PEOPLE HAVE A RIGHT TO DIE?

Learning Objective: Discuss the pros and cons of the issues involved in euthanasia (pp. 542-543).

1. Define the following terms:
    a. euthanasia, or mercy killing
    b. passive euthanasia
    c. active euthanasia, or assisted suicide
    d. living will

2. Why are living wills not always followed? What legislation has been passed to ensure compliance with living wills?

3. Describe the assisted suicide law in the Netherlands.

4. List three arguments against assisted suicide, and give examples of each.

5. List reasons that most oncologist oppose assisted suicide.

6. Why is there a waiting period between a request for assisted suicide and the fulfillment of the request?

7. What arguments do proponents of assisted suicide legislation present?

8. What are the relevant policies addressing living wills and assisted suicide in your state? Student research could include answering the following questions:
    a. Find out from a local medical society whether hospitals and physicians in your area generally honor living wills. Does your state require medical personnel to ask all hospitalized people whether they have a living will?

    b. The medical society should also be able to tell you whether your state allows family members to authorize health professionals to terminate aspects of care such as tube feeding in cases where a terminally ill or seriously injured individual can't speak for himself.

    c. Has anyone in your state ever been prosecuted for helping a dying person hasten death? If so, what were the circumstances and outcome of the case(s)?

    d. Are there efforts underway in your state to legalize assisted suicide? If so, what do opinion polls suggest about voter support for such laws?

NOTES